D0881159

EDWARDIANS

EDWARDIANS

London Life and Letters, 1901–1914

JOHN PATERSON

Ivan R. Dee
CHICAGO 1996

Title page and part-title ornaments are taken from designs that appeared in *The Studio* magazine (London, 1894–1920).

Photographs: Brown Brothers

Library of Congress Cataloging-in-Publication Data:
Paterson, John 1923–
Edwardians : London life and letters, 1901–1914 / John Paterson.
p. cm
Includes bibliographical references and index.
ISBN 1-56663-101-7 (alk. paper)
1. London (England)—Social life and customs—20th century—
Sources. 2. London (England)—Intellectual life—20th century—
Sources. 3. Great Britain—History—Edward VII, 1901–1910—
Sources. I. Title.
DA684.P293 1996
942.1082'3—dc20 95–45742

For Susanna Sarah, my dear companion

Contents

EDWARDIANS

Prologue

Henry James was disconsolate. On the eve of September 22, 1901, he had left the Reform Club, his London retreat, and had witnessed at once on a billboard the terrible tidings, "DEATH OF THE QUEEN." Not many days later, he'd watch from the balcony of a wealthy friend the great solemn funeral procession of the perished Victoria. Her coffin would be resting, tiny, pathetic, on a large moving gun carriage and, following behind it, bejeweled and bemedaled, the plumed princes of Europe and empire and the hooves of the cavalry and the slow, ceremonial steps of the soldiers and sailors. The drums would be muffled and the bells would be tolling and, lining the streets in the hundreds of thousands, the grief-stricken people in funereal black would be troubled, uneasy. James himself would be troubled, uneasy. For what must become of them now, great London, the nation, the empire? The queen, "that pathetic old monarchical figure," had stood, James said, "for the dignity of things," had thrown herself "into the scales of general decency." But Edward, her son, now Edward VII, who was fat and near sixty and known in some circles as "Edward the Caresser" and was even now "carrying on" with Mrs. George Keppel, the sister-in-law of Lord Albemarle, would be certain to make "for vulgarity and frivolity." He would make, alas, for much worse. "The brave old woman's beneficent duration" had served, said James, for oneness, for unity, had "held things magnificently—beneficently—together. . . ." But now he was full of gloomy forebodings. Victoria's death would "let loose," he feared, "incalculable forces for possible ill." "It's a new era," he declared in distress, "—and we don't know what it is."

Well, James would know soon enough what it was, this new era. Just five years later, in 1906, the Liberal party would win the general election in an astonishing reversal that no one at all had foreseen or expected, least of all the proud Tories who had governed the country for some twenty years but would now have to witness the certain destruction of all they held dear. For had the new party in power not threatened a socialist coup? Had it not threatened to pass into law such

3

horrors as old-age pensions and national insurance and taxes on land, on their own Tory land? Would it not threaten indeed to alter the form of the government itself and reduce or even abolish the powers of the old House of Lords? Just as bad, would it not go so far as to force on the nation a law that would make Ireland free and abandon poor Ulster, poor Protestant Ulster, to a Catholic fate? Why, by this time an enraged Tory party would consider the most desperate measures, would conspire to rebel, commit treason, foment civil war.

But by this time something near civil war was already general all over England. It wasn't just that the workers were restive, were joining the unions, and in 1900 were forming their own Labour party and in 1906 would send to Westminster, along with the Liberals, their own representatives. It was that by 1910 and the death of King Edward, neither unions nor parties sufficed. Exploited by masters who refused them fair wages, shorter hours, better working conditions, the workers would take to the streets and the strikes, would battle the police and the soldiers, and would sometimes call themselves socialists or anarchists or syndicalists. Nor was it the workers alone who threatened the peace. So too did the women who, led by the Pankhursts, mother and daughters, would insist on the vote and the power they were sure would come with it. After 1906 when they established in London their Women's Social and Political Union, their conduct would be moderate enough, with marches and demonstrations and sometimes the heckling and disrupting of political meetings. But even before 1910 and the death of the king, there were signs of more militant action with the stoning of candidates and the smashing of windows, the arrests and the jail terms and the hunger striking. After 1910 and the death of the king the movement would grow in volume and violence with burnings and bombings and, yes, the wanton destruction of property.

The new civil disorder was social in fact no less than political. As long as the grand old queen reposed on her throne, the rule of respect and restraint would prevail in the land. The working classes would honor their betters, would know their place in the great divine order of things. But even before the fateful death something had happened to change all this. It was education, free elementary school education, and for the very first time in the history of England a working-class people capable of reading and thinking and questioning their place in the social design. Of course they wanted more pay, less hours, decent working conditions. But they also wanted to live and be happy, to read and to learn and to make something new of themselves and their time on the earth. It was, however, the young men and women of middle-class standing who led the brave fight against the old social order and its rules and restrictions. Why should they follow the modes and manners of their parents and grandparents? Why should young women wear formal dress and attend formal dinners and exchange formal speech with formal young men and become in due time their formal young wives? For the war against social decorum was fought even more by the women than by the men. Of course they wanted the vote, the young women of England. Of course they wanted political equality with the men. But they also wanted to live and be free, to think and create and find their own selves and live their own lives. Indeed, it was more than social freedom they wanted, the more daring among them. It was sexual freedom as well. Marriage, for example. Why must they enter the marriage market? Why suffer its social and moral indignities? Why surrender their freedom to a marital code that was made more for men than for women? The men for that matter were inclined to agree. It was after all a defunct institution, this thing they called marriage. A betrayal of the freedom that the men as well as the women held dear. Indeed there were those who'd go further, much further. Not enough that the laws governing heterosexual love be rescinded. They'd demand that the laws governing homosexual love be rescinded as well.

But after Victoria's death what wouldn't be open to doubt and to change? For more than a century the theatre of London had had no honest existence. Condemned by the censorship to exclude from its picture all signs of real life or ideas, condemned, furthermore, to the heart-stopping melodrama cherished by grocers and clerks or to the drawing-room comedies cherished by mindless milords and their ladies, the theatre in London had no status at all. But just three years after the death of the queen the scene would be changed. Inspired by Shaw and his protégé, young Granville Barker, the stage would be open again to the life of the mind and the action of wit. Ezra Pound and his peers would soon be complaining that poetry in England was dead, had lost touch with the age and in fact had surrendered its function as history, real history, to the muse of the novel. For what after all was the poetry of the day but watered-down Wordsworth and Keats or, in the case of the poets of the nineties, weak imitations of Charles Baudelaire and the Frenchmen? And indeed, at the turn of the century, was the novel itself more alive, more inventive? If it wasn't producing second-rate Dickens and Scott, it was producing cheap gaudy tales of heroic adventure and baleful romance for the edification of the uninformed masses. Pound, as it happened, was unable to create a new poetry in Edwardian London and by 1920 he'd leave it forever. But the fate of the novel was quite something else. Between 1901 and 1914, between the death of the queen and the outbreak of war, a new life, a new spirit, would enter fiction in London. James and Conrad, Bennett and Wells, Forster and Galsworthy would be at the top of their form, and young writers like Lawrence and Ford and Mansfield and Richardson would be reaching for theirs. The Jameses and Conrads and Fords would be calling in fact for a new kind of novel. No more the old English novel so large and so loose and so carelessly made. They'd opt for the novel of Flaubert and France, more serious, more compact, more carefully crafted. "As well a well-wrought urn becomes/ The greatest ashes, as half-acre tombs." London, it's true, was no Paris. No Gauguins, Picassos, Matisses haunted its attics. London was poetry, was novels. It didn't much care for painters and painting. But in 1910 Roger Fry, the eminent art critic, forced London to "care." He brought from Paris the odd-looking canvases of a new school of art, a school he called postimpressionist, and hung them for thousands to fear and despise. For were they not dangerous, these new ways of seeing, these new modes of expression? Were they not rejections of the *ancien régime*, its old social forms and formalities, its old ways of living and being? James had been right. "The wild waters," as he said, "are upon us now."

And what indeed would become of it now, James's great London, the seat of his fame, the source of his pleasure and pride? Art and letters were booming, yes, but the cries in the street, the shouting, the clamor! Was it the end of something or the beginning? Only time would tell and the "march of events" and the terrible war that James himself could never imagine and now scarcely believed. "Falling towers/ Jerusalem Athens Alexandria/ Vienna London."

PART ONE
London Denied

"Ah, London, you too then are impossible?"

Of course there were natives among them, genuine Londoners. Roger Fry, the father of modern painting in England, came out of Highgate and Edward Garnett, the godfather of modern fiction in England, came out of Regent's Park and Ford Madox Hueffer (who would later call himself Ford Madox Ford) was raised just two doors away from the Garnett family at No. 1 St. Edmund's Terrace. As for the tribes of the Chestertons, Stephens, and Stracheys, they were Kensington-born and Kensington-bred, Gilbert and Cecil on Campden Hill, Vanessa and Virginia and their brothers at 22 Hyde Park Gate, and Lytton and James and their sisters at 69 Lancaster Gate. This isn't to mention those who came from the less poshy precincts of town, Leonard Woolf and Dorothy Richardson from Putney, Edward Thomas the poet and Granville Barker the playwright from Lambeth, H. G. Wells from Bromley and J. Middleton Murry, the critic and editor, from Camberwell. There were even unreformed cockneys among them and not only Wells but F. S. Flint, the Francophile poet, who emanated from Lambeth and Sidney Webb, the Fabian Socialist, who was born on Cranbourne Street not far from the Charing Cross Road.

With respect to the rest of them, though, they were, the distinguished Edwardians, quite strangers to London: visitants from the southwest like Thomas Hardy and Sir Edmund Gosse or down from the midlands like Arnold Bennett and D. H. Lawrence or from the northern ridings like T. E. Hulme, the poet-philosopher, and young Gilbert Cannan, the playwright and novelist; visitants from Scotland like J. M. Barrie and William Archer or from Ireland like W. B. Yeats and G. B. Shaw or from Wales or its environs like the painter Augustus John and the poets Ernest Rhys and Arthur Symons and W. H. Davies. Indeed, to London they came, it would seem, from just about every quarter, Rudyard Kipling from India and Katherine Mansfield from New Zealand, Joseph Conrad from Poland and the sculptor Henri Gaudier from France, W. H. Hudson from the exotic South Americas

9

and from the barren North Americas Henry James and Jacob Epstein, Ezra Pound and the poet H.D. as Ezra would designate Miss Hilda Doolittle of Philadelphia.

Nor did they always come to stay. "They came like swallows and like swallows went." Some, to be sure, not far away—the Woolfs, Leonard and Virginia, repairing to Richmond, the Garnetts, Edward and Constance, to Limpsfield, but others would venture still farther afield in quest of some quaint little village, some dreamy old town, in Surrey or Sussex or Kent, like Wells in Sandgate or Kipling in Burwash, like James in Rye or Conrad near Hythe or Hueffer in Aldington and Winchelsea. Was it in fact enough in those days to be a Londoner merely? It was to the credit of the good Thomas Hardy that he had "the air of a man who, whatever else he might be, was certainly no Londoner," and it was to the credit of Edward Thomas that he had, though Lambeth-born, the "aspect of an open-air countryman, not at all that of a Londoner." London might well assume, in the novels of Galsworthy, "an air that might be called Galsworthian," but for all that, it was "as a Devon man first and a Londoner afterward" that the good man endeared himself to his friends and admirers.

They may well have been right. Maybe it wasn't possible to love the London of Edward VII. For Ernest Rhys it was a place of "dust and smoke," for the poet Richard Aldington "a medley of fog, mud, an endless rumble, the violent ammonia smell of horses at Victoria, the stifling coal smoke of the underground." Would he ever return to it, Richard Le Gallienne was asked after his defection to New York City? "No," said that poet, "old London smells like a stable." And then there was the sheer heartbreaking immensity of it all, the sheer human and social complexity. The mighty metropolis assimilated everything and everyone; but nothing and no one assimilated it. Not young Bert Lawrence who, fresh from his Nottingham nursery, was hurt to the quick by "the unintelligibility of the vast city." Not Henry James who, retired in distress to his rural Rye, was now disinclined to reenter, he said, the "bewildering Babylon." Not, not certainly, Joseph Conrad who had left behind him a wilderness of waters and jungle and wasn't about to adventure now, he confessed, the "vast and unexplored wilderness" of London.

"Enthusiastic pedestrians"

And if London had been less bewildering than it was, less Babylonian, would it still have won over the souls of its ghostly inhabitants? Not very likely. A hundred years of Wordsworth, a hundred years of unrelenting nature worship, had all but excluded the town from the range of English affections. So no longing for London in the bosom of young Rupert Brooke, the beautiful poet of Cambridge and Grantchester, who preferred to go "dancing and leaping through the New Forest . . . singing to the birds, tumbling about in the flowers, bathing in the rivers, and, in general, behaving naturally." As for the poor London sparrows themselves, they were only too eager to leave the dust and grime of the city behind them, Lawrence, the young Croydon schoolteacher, taking the train to Purley, at the time still a village, for regular rambles over the great North Downs, and old Hudson the naturalist, his urban spirits in tatters, going for "a six hours' ramble on the windy downs," and Wells and the painter Will Rothenstein regaling their Hampstead guests with grand Sunday breakfasts before boarding the tram or the train for some rural spot outside city limits. "In the huge world which roars hard by/ Be others happy if they can!/ But in my helpless cradle I/ Was breathed on by the rural Pan."

Joseph Conrad, it's true, had little respect for this rural Pan. Like Marlow in *Chance*, he could "walk a ship's deck a whole foggy night through" and still show no interest at all in tramping and rambling "on solid, rural earth," and in fact he'd ridicule poor Mr. Fyne, the novel's "enthusiastic pedestrian," who is the author of the *Tramp's Itinerary* and a recognized authority on the footpaths of England and the father of an extraordinary daughter who will "wander away for miles if not restrained." But then why wouldn't Conrad make fun of this cult of the country? He was, after all, no born-and-bred Englishman. E. M. Forster, on the other hand, was, and so was H. G. Wells, and by 1910, the year of the one's *Howards End* and the other's *The History of Mr. Polly*, even London's poor cockney clerks and her grocers' and drapers' assistants were exploring the countryside and discovering the charms of "its deer parks and downland, its castles and stately houses, its hamlets and old churches. . . ." They didn't, of course, belong to the land, these poor counterjumpers. Ramble and tramp as they might, they had no standing, no footing, in it. Since paid summer vacations were not yet the thing, "they were doomed to toil behind counters . . . ," Wells sadly observed, "for the better part of their lives." Nevertheless, for a moment at least, it was, this revered English countryside, the romance of their lives. Leonard Bast, Forster's sad London clerk in *Howards End*, is a bit disappointing. Inspired to leave the city behind him and wander abroad in the country, he gets hopelessly lost in the dark and when he returns the next morning can't help but be bookish and boring about it, reciting the names of his literary heroes—Thoreau, Jefferies, E. V. Lucas, the author of *The Open Road*—with their tiresome talk of the "love of the earth." But Forster who was himself an unrestrained rambler would forgive the poor fellow his failure, for "within his cramped little mind dwelt something," he said, "that was greater than Jefferies's books—the spirit that led Jefferies to write them. . . ."

"I am partial to fisher-folk"

So, one of the most sophisticated cities on the face of the earth would have a special place in its heart for the primitive. When Edward Thomas discovered W. H. Davies in a cheap London lodging house, he may have discovered a bona fide poet, but it couldn't have hurt that he'd also discovered a bona fide tramp. Not a summer tramp like Brooke nor a Sunday tramp like Wells and Will Rothenstein but a full-time, full-blooded tramp and, as such, "a short, dark man with eyes like stewed prunes, coarse skin and a wooden leg," very much in demand at literary "evenings" and "at homes." The poor man was indeed just a little bit rattled. These London hostesses, these Lady Ritchies and Lady Churchills, what did they mean by their invitations? Did they not have designs on his body? But no, they did not. The only tramp-poet in town, and the author to boot of *The Autobiography of a Super-Tramp* with an introduction by Mr. George Bernard Shaw,

Davies was simply the catch of the season, "the observed of all ob-
servers." "He went along country roads . . . and looked at fresh new
things, and felt as happy and irresponsible as a boy with an unexpected half-holiday." The tramp-poet wandering the pathways of England and gathering fresh flowers of thought for "his quiet little lyrics"?
Not at all. It's the hero of Wells's *Mr. Polly* in a state of revolt. An unhappy husband and shopkeeper, he has burned down his house and
burned down his shop and, taken for dead, has risen from the ashes
and wandered away as "a leisurely and dusty tramp. . . ."

It was with gypsies as with tramps. The Gypsy Lore Society had
lately been founded and, joined by the lords and ladies of London, the
poets and professors were flocking to study the Romany life. So when
London discovered the young Augustus John, it may have discovered a
real painter but it couldn't have hurt that it had also discovered a
gypsy, if only a part-time one. Deeply dejected by the city's Cimmerian
gloom, by the meanness of its people and streets, its commerce and
Christianity, John had come under the Borrovian spell and had studied
the tribes and their camps and their stories and songs. "Nothing so fills
me with the love of life," he would say in his grandiose way, "as the
medieval—*antique*—life of camps; it seems to shame the specious per-
manence of cities, and tents will outlast pyramids." So, all operatic in
red beard and slouch hat and gold earring, he would travel the byways
of England in caravans sky blue or canary yellow with his dogs and
mistress and children. Of course there were difficulties. There were
these squires and farmers who were not at all willing to welcome a
mysterious stranger who was long-haired and bearded and six feet
tall and was asking to camp for the night in their fields. And then
there was this horse, "a huge, ungainly, half-trained animal," which
slipped one day in the mud and lay there kicking and struggling while
the artist stood by, magisterial, indifferent, smoking a cigarette. And
then there was Arthur, his groom, a difficult fellow, who refused to
leave Cambridge, their port of call, and had in a violent battle to be
brought to his senses. And then . . . well, there was this portrait to
paint and Liverpool to get to and so, black eye and all, John boarded a
train and left all behind him—sky blue caravan and battered groom,
women and dogs and children—with imperious instructions " 'to
come on steadily' or not at all."

The gypsy life was not, to be sure, for everyone. It wasn't for Lady
Ottoline Morrell, the wife of Philip Morrell, the Liberal M.P. Invited by

John to join him at Grantchester, she set off gaily enough in her very best muslins and feathers but, alas, soon returned, her gaiety and feathers quite, quite down. "I was given a crust of bread and some fruit for dinner, and I returned to London, chilled and damp and appreciative of my home and Philip." Nor was it quite, this gypsy life, for the chic little Gräfin Von Arnim-Schlagentin, the famous author of *Elizabeth and her German Garden*, or for young E. M. Forster who had served her once, in her Pomeranian *schloss*, as her daughters' tutor and was summoned now to join her at Ashford with her family and friends and her two jolly caravans and the two great carthorses hired to convey them. The trip would not be a total disaster. The Gräfin would gather material for a novel, *The Caravanners*, recording the joys of the simple life and Morgan Forster, who was zealous to seek out the great god Pan, would later recall it as "the happiest spell since Greece," and it *was* rather fun, he thought at the time, this sleeping in barns and pushing the van up the hill whilst the Gräfin tossed them biscuits and fruit from out of the window. But he didn't much care for putting up tents and the cooking of stews and neither, it seemed, did the lady herself. "Tired and rather low," he set down in his tablet. "Tents to be put up and there sat the [Gräfin] reading Jane Austen." And then there was the weather, the abominable weather. "It was inclined to rain," Morgan noted one day. "It did rain," he noted the next. By the time they reached Aylesford it was all too much and all was abandoned, the camps and tents and horses and caravans. Toad, the irrepressible hero of Kenneth Grahame's *The Wind in the Willows*, is delighted with his gypsy caravan, with its canary-colored cart and bright red wheels, with its pots and kettles and pans and, hanging beneath it, its baskets and nose-bags. "There's real life for you . . . ," he cries out to his friends. "The open road, the dusty highway, the heath, the hedgerows, the rolling downs!" But the details, alas, the dreadful details! The fire to be lit in the dreary dawn and last night's cups and plates to be scrubbed and the wearisome trudge to the nearest village for milk and eggs and Toad no longer in raptures about "the simplicity of the primitive life." Toad indeed will defect to the enemy, to the automobile and the twentieth century and "I've done with carts for ever," he'll say. Not Augustus John, however. Pipe in mouth and reins in hand and looking, with his women and children, like the "magnificent patriarch of a Nomad tribe," he'd push grimly forward into the past.

But no matter. London found his gypsy glamour irresistible. The cut of his hair made him look "like a Renaissance prince" and his hands, said Lady Ottoline, "were more beautiful than any man's hands I have ever seen" and then his eyes, his "mysterious pale grey-green" eyes, they seemed to expand, she said, "like a sea-anemone." This isn't to mention the grand manner: the terrible rages and the even more terrible silences and the look, the famous or infamous look, intense and "rather méfiant," and then, inevitably, "Will you sit to me?" Lady Ott was doubtless entranced by this *homme fatal*, but so, it would seem, were they all. In the presence of a John painting, Rupert Brooke found himself "sick & faint with passion" and, estranged as he was from his own strait-laced family, fell half in love with the painter's gypsy ménage and "O," he would cry in distress, "for ten minutes with the John family!" Roger Fry was quite overcome by *The Smiling Woman*, John's portrait of Dorelia, his main model and mistress. "The vitality of this gypsy Gioconda," the distinguished art critic was writing ecstatically, "is fierce, disquieting, emphatic." Well, a Gioconda she may well have been but a gypsy one not. "Dorelia" was, in point of fact, one Dorothy McNeill, an exquisitely beautiful but perfectly urban young woman who had come out of Camberwell and worked as a secretary on Basinghall Street and, after falling for John, had willingly shared his gypsy passion and life. And indeed there were skeptics and scoffers enough. Lady Gregory was plainly displeased. She had commissioned Augustus to do etchings and oils of her protégé Yeats and what after weeks had the fellow made of the poet? He had made him look like a gypsy, a wretched gypsy, like "a sheer tinker," as Yeats would put it himself, "drunken, unpleasant and disreputable." It was too much for Percy Wyndham Lewis, who in Paris had been John's devoted disciple but now disavowed his "boring Borrovian cult of the Gitane." It was all too romantic, Percy decided, all too hothouse and *fin de siècle*.

"Thou, Nature, art my goddess . . ."

It was with the naturalists, with the nature-lovers, as with the tramps and the gypsies. Poor souls whose tragic plight it was to be immured in cities, they were everywhere honored and mourned. Edward Thomas and W. H. Hudson, for example. Everybody felt sorry for Edward Thomas and W. H. Hudson. In Thomas's case there were certainly grounds. Married as a penniless undergraduate and a father only six months later, he had come down from Oxford and had soon to rehearse the miseries of Grub Street: the overwork, the underpay, the fatigue, the fatigue, and then of course the self-contempt and melancholy, the opium and suicidal wish. In addition to some twelve hundred reviews, he was responsible for as many as sixty "nature" books with titles like *Beautiful Wales, In Pursuit of Spring, The Heart of England.* "I am sorry to hear that Thomas has broken down again," Hudson would write at a time when his unhappy friend was at work on no less than six different volumes at once. "Why will he work so incessantly and so furiously?" But under the circumstances why would he not? He had by this time a growing family, wife Helen and the three little ones they named Merfyn and Bronwen and Myfanwy, and an annual income of but three hundred pounds to support them. To be sure, there was much to be thankful for. There was Nature, English Nature, to be thankful for. The hovel in Steep, the tweeds and clay pipe, the pure vegetarian diet and the solemn prose-poems that sometimes recalled a wan Walter Pater (". . . so grand the silence, the nightingale dares not sing; only now and then its voice leaps forth—like a sigh from the breast of silence"), at others a pathetic Thoreau ("as I was pausing to count the first white clusters of nuts or to remind myself that here was the first pale-blue flower of succory, I knew that I took up eternity with both hands . . .").

Nevertheless, there was something heartbroken about it, this retreat to Nature, something less like pride than like defeat, less like life than like death. Ashamed of himself and his sadness and poverty,

16

Thomas would rail at the children, at Merfyn and Bronwen and Myfanwy, would rage at his wife who had once studied Ruskin and Morris
and wore "Liberty dresses" with their simple lines and colored embroi-
dery. "Tired! Tired is not what I am. I'm sick of the whole of life—of
myself chiefly, of you and the children. You must hate and despise me
but you can't hate me as much as I hate the whole business, and as I
despise myself for not putting an end to it." Once he did walk into the
woods with a rusty revolver in hand, but he soon changed his mind
and returned to the fold and "Weep no more, woeful shepherds, weep
no more,/ For Lycidas, your sorrow, is not dead. . . ."

London was nonetheless moved by the man and his melancholy,
by his look of grieving Hamlet, of suffering Jesus. He had, it was said,
"a beautiful sensitive face." The Gethsemane of this world had given "a
cast of melancholy to his fine chiseled features." Ah, "what a beautifully
sculptured melancholy face was his." London was moved above all by
the man and his legend, by the English simplicity of his home and his
habit and habits. There was the humble farmhouse itself, "all very rustic and cottagey," with its whitewashed walls and black oak beams and
its mugs and pottery, the one half reserved for his writing den, the
other for his hives and his honeybees, added to which was the humble
fare, the porridge and homemade bread and jam for breakfast and for
supper the bowls of brown bread and milk and the nuts and Dutch
cheese and hot buttered scones, or, in the city itself, at Eustace Miles's
famous health-food restaurant on William IV Street, the simple luncheon of nut cutlets dipped in breadcrumbs and eggs and the por-
tions of buttered spinach and parsnips sprinkled with plasmon
powder. This isn't to mention the good man himself with his strong
boots and fawn Harris tweeds and the knapsack "that carried all that
he needed" and, "lighting a clay pipe (for he never smoked by any
other means), he would sit in the wide inglenook." With Diggory
Venn, no doubt, and Christian Cantle.

Thomas, to be fair, didn't always deceive himself. One of his genial nature books he put down as "pseudo-genial . . . Borrow and Jefferies sans testicles & guts." And he did know the real thing when he
saw it: the *Personae* of Pound, for example, who didn't share, he recognized, "the current melancholy or resignation or unwillingness to
live. . . ." Still, there *was* something self-conscious about his melancholy, his self-deprecation. He was a victim all right, but he wasn't an
unwilling victim. "What Thomas lacked," said the novelist Norman

Douglas, who had a little touch of bestiality about him, "was a little touch of bestiality. . . ." So, the war, when it came, would not be for him a disaster. Wasn't it what in his heart he had longed for? For him as for Egbert in Lawrence's "England, my England" the consummation devoutly to be wished? On April 9, 1917, in the Battle of Arras, a German shell brought it to pass. It wasn't, they said, his country he died for. It was the country, the long lanes of England, its fields and flowers and farms.

> Marsh-marigolds or "bubble" in blossom with the dull-flowered lilac butterbur.
> Ash-sprays out to greet the earliest sedge-warbler.
> Coots laying in piled nests of drenched water-weeds and jointed "mare's tail."
> Young dipper abroad at Coate Reservoir.
> Cuckoo-flowers in the damp meadows.

Bird-haunted, village-haunting Hudson had the same profound effect on London. His splendid books—*Birds in London, Afoot in England, A Shepherd's Life,* for example—touched the soul of the city where it lived, in its feeling for nature. But for all that, they didn't sell and so, like Thomas, Hudson was always short of funds. He early married a woman some fifteen or so years his senior and so much shorter than his own six feet that she didn't come up to his elbow. A concert singer with, it was said, a distinguished career ahead of her, she had "wilfully refused to sing a note after Hudson married her" or maybe, as more reliable memories than Hueffer's recalled it, had simply and tragically lost her voice. They were reduced at any rate to living on the meager proceeds of the dreariest boardinghouse in dreariest Bayswater, which establishment—"Tower House," it was called—the untuned singer had inherited heavily mortgaged and the second floor of which the couple themselves occupied, composing what some considered the most dismal domestic quarters in London. "Poor Hudson, so fastidious as a writer, lived with the most forbidding furniture, the commonest pictures and china, the ugliest lace curtains and antimacassars." Even as it was he could hardly call it home. Emily was in the habit of moving from flat to flat as they fell vacant so that "poor Hudson"—he was never called anything but "poor Hudson"—was treated like a portable piece of property and indeed she couldn't have made his life a joy forever. "Mrs. Hudson did not appear," said Conrad's wife Jessie, "until I was on the point of leaving" when "she kept up a string of complaints as to her husband's shortcomings." "While talking to him," the novelist Violet Hunt would report, "I was always conscious of this witch of German legend, this Rapunzel, sitting there in her tower, her short legs propped up on a huge footstool, claiming the constant society of her distinguished husband." Hudson was not for a fact in any great hurry to announce her existence. He had known the painter Will Rothenstein for some time before he mentioned her at all. "Married!" Mrs. Rothenstein exclaimed, "and you never told us. How long have you been married?" "As long as I can remember." Which rueful reply affected Rothenstein as "the gloomiest verdict on married life" he had ever heard. Hudson in any case hated great London and longed for the country. Leaving his Bayswater lodgings behind him and passing through "the most lugubrious streets the world could imagine" with his tiny wife at his elbow "incessantly telling him that he was going the wrong way," he would reach nearby Paddington Station and there, happy shepherd, entrain for greener fields, for pastures new.

Of course the London he left behind him loved him dearly. It loved the magic of his sudden disappearances into the pastoral deeps of Hampshire and Cornwall and Devonshire, the mystery of the strange communion he kept with the rocks and birds and animals he so sedulously studied. He was, said his London friends, "a lonely man, with something of the animal about him." His head seemed to them "as if chiseled by the wind, as rocks are," and even to Norman Douglas, that skeptical man, he seemed "an old Hawk on its perch, observant and silent." Indeed, "not altogether human." As for Hueffer, who had known the country life and its rigors and should have known better, it was, this Hudson story, the stuff of romance. "And there," Hueffer would write, carried away by a wayward emotion, "that great tall man would sit by the shepherd's table, drinking the terribly strong tea . . . and eating the fleed-cake and the poached rabbits. . . . And then . . . would arise, brushing the beams of the cottage ceiling with his hair, and stroll down the broad valley." Did Hudson deserve these ridiculous encomiums? Only too well. Their image of him was his image of himself. "My object in life is to look after birds." "I am a red man . . . a wild man of the woods." "I dislike all books—excepting purely informative ones like Kelly's Directory & the Almanac."

There may in fact have been in the man just a touch of the hypocrite. Not all, it seemed, was pure romance. He may have crossed his bridges all right en route to his rooks and his rocks, but he took good care not to burn them behind him. So the man who never lost in London the sense of his exile and took "no interest in the doings of [its] innumerable multitude" didn't fail to attend Edward Garnett's Tuesday luncheons at the Mont Blanc and Hueffer's famous suppers in his Holland Street flat. He may have detested the British upper classes who were only interested in golfing and motoring and not at all in the proper care of trees and birds; but he wasn't therefore prevented from prizing their company. "Were not Cunninghame Graham, Sir Edward Grey and the Ranee of Sarawak, his chosen friends?" Society-loving shepherd! It was even possible that he lacked simple kindness. The man who worshiped the God in Nature wasn't likely to care for the sorry citizens of godless London. "If I were a beastly bird," his friend Conrad once said, "Hudson would take more interest in me than he does." He was jesting of course. He didn't really mean it. But it was true, quite true, what he said. Garnett who loved and published his work liked to tease him a little. You should be writing novels and making characters, he told him, instead of wasting your time on adders and warblers. But Hudson wasn't amused. "I am a naturalist," he shouted back angrily. "I care nothing about people." So when war with Germany was imminent, he made clear enough what a century of nature-worship had come to express: a peevish disgust with the human world and the modern world in particular. "I thank the gods," said the man who loved birds, "*we* are going to have a touch of war, the only remedy for the present disease." And when that "touch" of war providentially came and with it the "remedy" and millions died in mud and tears, it pleased him to think that of "the rottenness which comes of everlasting peace the blood that is being shed will purge us." Hudson had big bony hands and a small grizzled head and a twisted aquiline nose. "His coat, made of rough tweed, had tails with pockets in them and a waistcoat and trousers to match. He always wore a shirt with a stand-up starched white collar and starched linen cuffs, and he wore black lace-up boots."

Not every Londoner, it's true, was stuck on Nature. Hadn't Oscar Wilde and his monstrous crew already insulted a God-fearing nation by exalting the town and bemocking the country? The mighty Atlantic had been, he had said after the crossing to America, "a disappointment," and as for stupendous Niagara, it must have been, he considered, "one of the earliest, if not the keenest, disappointments in

American married life." Oscar was dead now and all but forgotten but his spirit still lived. It still lived in the being of young Lytton Strachey who for all that he hated multitudinous London and was all for weekends in cottages and long happy rambles and "choirs of birds, blossoms and butterflies" was never at heart an ardent Wordsworthian. "We're surrounded," he was likely to cry in dismay, "by deserts of green vagueness [and] multitudes of imbecile mountains." "A lake now—there is nothing more beautiful than a lake," announces the vicar in Leonard Woolf's novel *The Wise Virgins*, but Leonard's young modern hero won't have it. "Most lakes—all, I expect—are repulsive," he says. This may have been Bloomsbury talking, frivolous Bloomsbury, but not only Bloomsbury. The penniless Conrad who, after marrying Jessie, had little choice but to live in the country, was less than elated. "A perfectly idyllic but also no doubt a hateful kind of existence," he sourly predicted. "No outdoors for him," his friend Jacob Epstein reported. "The sea captain hated out of doors, and never put his nose into it." No outdoors for G. B. Shaw, either. "I am at present groveling among the thistles and bees on the brink of a sandpit," he was writing from Surrey. "Nothing," he said, "could have been less successful with me than the country air" and he referred with contempt to "the restless demagnetized atmosphere of this pretentiously rural place." They might just as well, these Stracheys and Shaws, have come out of the stories of "Saki," the nom de plume of the irreverent Hector Munro. "The country is looking very green," says one of his characters, "but, after all, that's what it's there for."

"Everything in the garden's lovely"

By this time, however, Nature had all but become for the English a patriotic emotion, a national longing. England was Nature and Nature was England, and to love the one was to love the other. So everyone would have to have his own little cottage in Kent or in Sussex, some "charming and quite idyllic little farm," where no farming was done but where it was possible, on the easiest terms, to renew one's link with the land. Like Shaw's friends the Salts, Henry and Kate, who were holding their own in a laborer's cottage in Surrey where the visiting giant would play Wagner on their big grand piano or sing pianoforte duets with the missus herself. Like Gilbert Chesterton, the Gargantuan journalist, who, with his wife Frances who hated Fleet Street and its roisterous life, hoped to retire "to an oak-timbered cottage on a wold or a weald" but settled instead, and much sooner perhaps than he liked, in Beaconsfield not far away. Like the actress Ellen Terry who, after a performance at the Lyceum, would flee in her pony trap out of the city and onto the land to witness the sun coming up near Winchelsea and would soon purchase Smallhythe, an old Tudor farmhouse, with open hearth and dipping floors and low beamed ceilings. Like, above all, the Georgian poets, that tweedy little band of unredeemed lovers of nature who took, as young Richard Aldington would describe it, "a little trip for a little weekend to a little cottage where they wrote a little poem on a little theme."

One day in September 1911, Edward Marsh, who was Winston Churchill's secretary and a monocled patron of letters, would have to lunch in his Gray's Inn apartments a few of these bolder new spirits, like Rupert Brooke and Wilfred Gibson, Harold Monro and John Drinkwater. They were on the verge, he was saying, of a brave new era in poetry. They were studying simplicity, simplicity of theme and of thought, of form and of language, were studying country people and country matters, bees and flowers and birds and such things. Why not give the new poets a shove? Why not publish every two years the best of their work, Masefield and Davies and Lawrence and Lascelles Abercrombie to name but a few. Tennyson and Swinburne were dead after all, and 'twas time for the poets to get down, down to earth, from their high philosophic and poetical horses, and Wilde and Dowson and their decadent lot were thankfully dead and 'twas time to abandon their bordellos and boudoirs and strike once again for the old open air and the old open road. So Marsh consented to serve as their editor, to be the "policeman of poetry," as Lawrence would call him, and in 1912 and the following years he would push through the presses the five little volumes he named *Georgian Poetry*. They were, it turned out, an instant success. The first volume in 1912 sold fifteen thousand copies. Never before had poetry in England been so much the rage and it seemed for a time that it never would end. But end it did, as it had to. Childlike simplicity was all very well, but a "simpering simplicity"?

A little seed best fits a little soil,
A little trade best fits a little toil:
As my small jar best fits my little oil.

This was their song. They sang this song. "Before verse can be made human again," the Irishman Synge had been telling them, "it must learn to be brutal." But this? Brutal? The Georgians had moved, no mistake, from Alfred Lawn Tennyson but they hadn't moved forward at all. They had only moved backward—backward to Wordsworth. Nevertheless, it was all rather nice while it lasted. The poets, for a change, made some money and they rather enjoyed the rough cider and the picturesque farms and the walks and the talks on the old rural byways of England. Lascelles Abercrombie was bewitched by the country experience but not more bewitched than his wonderful wife. "I had," she said, "a permanent gypsy tent under the Seven Sisters, as the elms at the end of the garden were called and sometimes I would have an iron pot over the fire with a duck and green peas stewing in it, and Lascelles and John Drinkwater and Wilfred Gibson would sit around and read their latest poems to each other, as I lay on a stoop of hay and listened and watched the stars wander through the elms and thought I really had found the why and wherefore of life."

It wasn't entirely a sentiment of course, this cult of the cottage. For impoverished poets and painters it was more like the grimmest necessity. Lucky as writers to earn five pounds a week, poor creatures like Davies and Thomas and Lawrence and Murry would flee to the country where, with the rural depression and the falling prices and the flight of the folk from village and farm, it was all so cheap, so mercifully cheap. You could rent a cottage for five shillings a week and actually purchase the charming old thing—"mine be a cot"—for as little as twenty-three pounds. It wasn't, it's true, all cakes and brown ale. Thomas's farmhouse near The Weald was sparingly furnished with scrubbed pine table and rush-bottomed chairs and Davies's small cottage nearby on Egg Pie Lane had naught but a table and chair, a pail full of water, and a stout wooden packing case. Hueffer and Elsie, his teenage bride, were prepared to delight in their idyllic cottage near Hythe but there were, they discovered, some grave disadvantages. No system of drainage, for one thing, and no drinking water that wasn't a good mile away, and as for their boots, their mud-caked boots, they had to be lowered into a well with a cord and afterward dried in front of a fire. Indeed, it was worse. The picturesque lanes of old England inevitably led to dank little hovels where one made do with a paraffin lamp and a muddy path to the privy outdoors and, in the cruel light of dawn, a cold bath under the pump in the frostbitten garden. There were, to be sure, rural fanatics who adored the discomfort; but Katherine Mansfield who had come from New Zealand to live in great London and be a great writer was not to be one of them. At the cottage in Cholesbury she was sharing with Middleton Murry, by this time her mate, she shed tears of rage and despair. She just couldn't cope with that badly blocked sink. "It is a very grey day . . . ," she'd sadly report, "and a loud roaring noise in the trees." "It is very cold here," she'd write from Rose Tree Cottage, another location. "It is winter and the sky from my window looks like ashes." Rose Acre Cottage. Berryfield Cottage. Yewtree Cottage. What pretty names! Alas, they were sinks of disease and distress. The roof of her cottage in Buckinghamshire leaked so badly that Katherine contracted arthritis and rheumatism. The Thomases' Ivy Cottage was sufficiently pretty, but Bronwen fell seriously ill and after her Helen and what could they do but abandon the place? There were, indeed, more forms of misfortune than one. When Arthur Symons, the poet of the nineties, bought a seventeenth-century cottage in Kent, he was soon disillusioned. He found he'd inherited repairs that quickly amounted to four hundred pounds and in 1906, to defray the expenses, was arising at four in the morning to work on some thirty-six articles and reviews as well as on three or four books. Lytton Strachey had much better luck. Country cottages were good, he said, for his health and his work. There were, even so, discouraging moments. At the Green Farm, near Bury St. Edmunds, the rural retreat of the Desmond MacCarthys, the garden was somewhat decayed and the fires were always going out and at another, more luxurious cottage in Sussex, there was, Lytton found, just one little problem: "Most of the ceilings [came] down to . . . our shoulders, and we [had] to creep about on all fours."

And in point of fact it wasn't always appreciated, this pastoral life. Not, at any rate, by young Ezra Pound. With Hueffer and Violet Hunt, Hueffer's lover, he passed a week in a cottage in Buckinghamshire that had once belonged to John Milton, but Ezra cared not a jot for John Milton and the place, anyway, was a "beastly dark low-ceilinged hole" and a week in the country was, he decided, "about five days too much." The rustic experience wasn't appreciated, certainly, by W. H. Davies's uncle. When this grungy old shepherd came down from his mountains in Wales and walked all the way to the cottage in Kent to share in his nephew's fame and good fortune, he was sore disappointed. There, look you, was his nephew, the poet, stripped to the waist and washing his only shirt in the yard. He cursed him in Welsh and promptly returned to his mountains and sheep and the simple life he quite thoroughly hated.

"O Lord! I suppose you're going to become one with the earth . . ."

But it wasn't just Nature that called them. It was also the Land and the sacred life of the land. For something dreadful had happened and was happening. For centuries now the rich had grown richer and the poor had grown poorer. Dispossessed first by the powerful landowners, then by the powerful mill owners, the folk by the hundreds of thousands had been leaving their farms for the cities at home, for the strange habitations abroad. But now there were panic and longing. It was time to come back, back to the land which was the simple life, which was the past, which was England, our England. "I am the land of their fathers./ In me the virtue stays./ I will bring back my children,/ After certain days." So, no more imperializing, the pundits were saying, no more colonizing abroad. "We must colonize the countryside," they were saying. After getting rich on *King Solomon's Mines*, H. Rider Haggard would pass for a country gentleman in Norfolk and produce noble works like *Rural England* and *The Poor and the Land*, and back from barbaric America, Rudyard Kipling would "rediscover" the "wonderful land" England was, "my favorite foreign country," and would establish himself on the thirty-three acres of "Bateman's" at Burwash (pronounced "Burridge") in Sussex, a fine old house with

paneled walls, beamed ceilings, and old oak staircases. As for Maurice
Hewlett, the prolific producer of historical novels, he would, on the
profits, return to his England from Italy and acquire a romantic old
nunnery in Wiltshire with a millrace and everything, where he'd medi-
tate *The Song of the Plow,* his epic in verse on the English farm worker,
his *Hodgiad,* as he'd name it, "a noble project" which didn't, however,
"come off." It was in art as in life, the hero of Conan Doyle's *The
Hound of the Baskervilles* returning from the colonies to restore to its
greatness old Baskerville Hall and the hero of Hugh Walpole's *The
Wooden Horse* "rediscovering," after twenty years in New Zealand, his
ancestral acres and the Duchy of Cornwall and its folktales and folk-
ways and the heroines of Forster's *Howards End* "rediscovering" in
Mrs. Wilcox's charming old place in the country, England itself, the
real England. Even the musicians, the Vaughan Williamses, Gustav
Holsts, Percy Graingers, were implicated, producing exercises in pastoral nostalgia and resolved in the process to recover that ancient folk
music to whose disappearance the poor folk themselves, now displaced
and discouraged, were entirely indifferent.

There were those, to be sure, for whom it all seemed, this return
to the land, more like the end of something than the beginning. Conrad's Marlow can refer with nostalgia to the English soil he has left far
away, to "the spirit that dwells . . . in its fields, in its waters and its
trees—a mute friend, judge, and inspirer." But what's possible for English Marlow isn't possible for Polish Conrad, and it's clear that for him
as for Jim, who has had to endure the modern experience, its cruel
complication, its dark ambiguity, there can be no return to the land
and its ancient simplicities, to "the little church on a hill" and "the rec-
tory [which] gleamed with a warm tint in the midst of grass-plots,
flower-beds, and fir-trees. . . ." It was finished, too, the charm of old
England, for the bitter young Lawrence, the hero of whose *Aaron's Rod,*
after the bold landscapes of Lombardy—"all exposed, exposed to the
sweep of plain, to the high strong sky, and to human gaze"—will decline to return to England's green pastures and "the cozy ambushed
English life." It was certainly finished for Norman Douglas whose
bishop in *South Wind* had long sighed in Africa for the "drowsy verdant opulence" of home, for "the smell of hay, the flowery lanes, the
rooks cawing among slumberous elms . . ."; but after "the tingling realism" of Capri can't bear the thought of the place: "Rather parochial,
rather dun . . . subdued light above—crepuscular emotions on earth."

No Lawrence, no Douglas, Henry James must have felt to the full the appeal of old England, its charm, its ancestral beauty; but he surprisingly didn't. "One has the sense," he would groan as the squire of Lamb House, "of being 'looked to' from so many 'humble' quarters that one feels . . . quite like a country gentleman, with his 'people' and his church-monuments."

As for Wells, he may have longed for the country life like the hungry street urchin he was, but not in the Tory sense of a Kipling or Hewlett. Ernest Ponderevo, his huckster "hero" in *Tono-Bungay*, may be all for it, this romance of the land, for "Merrymakings. Lads and lasses dancing on the village green. Harvest home. Fairings. Yule Log—all the rest of it." But no Ponderevo himself, Wells isn't wholly converted. "You see," he'll say with his vicar, "all the brisker girls go into service in or near London. The life of excitement attracts them. . . . And generally— freedom from restraint. So that there might be a little difficulty perhaps to find a May Queen here. . . ." Wells's friend Arnold Bennett did purchase at Hockcliffe in Bedfordshire a dullish old place called Trinity Hall Farm with its grounds and its outbuildings, thus amusing his coarse city friends who dubbed him the Heir of Hockcliffe, and some time later Arnold would move into "Comarques" at Thorps-le-soken in Essex, a Queen Anne house with pale red brick and a large, charming garden where, he wryly predicted, "our deaths will one day cause a sensation in the village which we shall dominate." These were hardly, however, the sentiments of a true believer, of a Haggard or Hewlett, and Arnold was for a fact, on this as on other subjects, just a little bit crass. He wasn't much interested in farming and he certainly wasn't much interested in his spiritual reform or redemption. What he *was* interested in was a Dalmatian and a dog cart and the chance to cut a dash for himself as a country author and gentleman. But by this time even the most passionate Back-to-the-Landers would be having their doubts. After India, after America, after South Africa, Kipling would find the English village and its squires and its vicars as deadly and dull as would a James or a Wells. Was the voice of the tommy returned from South Africa not the voice of his own discontent?

> 'Ow can I ever take on
> With awful old England again,
> An' 'ouses both sides of the street,
> An' 'edges two sides of the lane,

An' the parson an' gentry between,
An' touchin' my 'at when we meet—
Me that 'ave been what I've been?
Me that 'ave watched 'arf a world . . .
An' I'm rollin' 'is lawns for the Squire. Me!

It wouldn't be long, in any event, before the land would lose much of
its market value and the gentry abandon their declining estates. By the
end of the war even H. Rider Haggard would have to sell out. He
could increase his income considerably, he found, by divesting himself
of the land that he'd cherished and investing the cash in more practical projects.

Of Chickens and Bees

But it wasn't just the Tory gentlemen who had urged
them back to the land. So too had the socialists. It was time, William
Morris had said with Edward Carpenter and other founding fathers of
"The Fellowship of The New Life," it was time to get back to nature, to
renew one's link with the land and the life of the land. The world was
a nightmare, an industrial nightmare. What to do? Change the world,
to be sure, but first change the self, the individual soul, and what better way than by exposure to nature? Back to nature? Nay, it was more.
It was back to the farm and communal existence and manual labor:
the tilling of the soil, the spinning and weaving, the bricklaying, pot-
ting, and basket-making. So in sandals and corduroys and loose-
collared shirts the youth of the nation would go forth in the thousands
to be full-time rustics, not part-time ones. They would be producers,
"Small Producers"; would be agriculturists, "romantic agriculturists."
Instructed by Morris and Carpenter "and other Cockneys," they'd cul-
tivate some little farm in Kent or in Surrey, working the fields, spreading the compost, staying up with the pigs. Ford Madox Hueffer for
instance. In the prime of his youth he would occupy, with his young
wife Elsie, "a real old farm" near Romney Marsh, "very jolly and all the

rest of it with oak beams and a number of other advantages in ceiling and floor," and a few years later would join at Limpsfield a gaggle of socialist rustics who, with Edward and Constance Garnett for gurus, were dwelling in rough stone cottages and dressing "more or less medievally" in homemade boots and queer homespun clothes, and drinking the "mead out of cups made of bullock's horns," and discoursing at length on "Gas and Water Socialism." Here Elsie would assume the beads and rope belts and rich loose-hanging garments that Morris himself had designed and Hueffer, ashplant stick in hand, a Morris man all the way, would affect the smock and gaiters and hobnailed boots of the peasant. "Yaws . . . yaws . . . Rye is the largest of our crops . . . but we export it all to Prussia and Poland."

Chickens, it seems, were the rage. Chickens and bees. Chickens and bees were easier, weren't they, and cleaner and much more aesthetic? "I've always hated London. Perhaps I shall try a poultry farm and bees." Thus Marion, the witless young wife in Wells's *Tono-Bungay*. "They are wonderfully beautiful in troops on green fields. . . . I shall sit all day long upon the terrace, watching them and the pattern they weave on the field. . . ." Thus the witty Camilla in Leonard Woolf's novel. Forster, a disciple of Carpenter, may have thought better of the rural endeavor than the Wellses and Woolfs. Mr. Wilcox, his hardheaded businessman, rejects the whole thing ("Small holdings, back to the land—ah! philanthropic bunkum"); but he's no match at all for Forster's Miss Schlegel and "In these English farms, if anywhere," she intones in Arnoldian wise, "one might see life steadily and see it whole." And indeed by the end of the novel her vision prevails and with sister Helen and poor Mr. Wilcox, now sadly dismantled, unmanned, she's back on the farm, dear Howards End, and "The field's cut . . . !" Helen cries out in a rapture. "We've seen to the very end, and it'll be such a crop of hay as never!" Even for Maugham, that incurable skeptic, hay was the way to see life steadily and see it whole. For some six hundred pages the poor crippled hero of *Of Human Bondage* must witness the horrors of life in the city, the hunger and poverty, the suffering and death. It's life, cruel life, no exit, no hope, the end of the world. But stay. Bloodied and bowed and all but extinguished, the hero is saved in the end. He simply leaves London to go picking hops, to watch sunsets and dawns, to win the love of a pure country girl, "a Saxon goddess" with, all about her, the scent of the hay and the savor of hops.

The tone of the movement was in fact just a trifle high-minded. The wife of one London stockbroker acquired "a quiet little cottage" where she hoped "to keep herself by keeping fowls," but the kitchen was, it turned out, "an *idealized* farm kitchen" where no cooking was done and where household glass and crockery were all mixed up with aesthetic pots and pans. When four vegetarians in sandals took over a nice little place at Witley in Surrey, they were taken aback. "The Fowl House"? Was it possible, really, to live in a cottage with a name like "The Fowl House"? They hastily changed it to "Godspeace." Arnold Bennett would later move into the place for a while but, wonderful man, would have no spiritual designs upon it. "Last night I dreamed that I wore sandals," he would jot in his journal, "and was ashamed." Young Lawrence, it's true, had "a ripping time" at The Cearne, as the Garnetts would call their bucolic abode at Limpsfield near Edenbridge. But though the house was only thirteen years old, it looked, "exactly, exactly," said Lawrence, astounded, "like the 15th century: brick floored hall, bare wood staircase, deep ingle nook with a great log fire. . . . You would be moved to artistic rhapsodies, I think."

It wasn't in any case a total success, this "grassy path to socialism." An acquaintance of Shaw's started in Surrey a cooperative farm, but for all that he used the latest scientific equipment, he could only grow radishes. And then there was Hueffer who turned out to be, his gaiters and corduroys notwithstanding, a smaller producer than Morris intended. He was known to keep a vegetable garden and perhaps a few ducks, and when Wells would cycle from Sandgate to the cottage at Aldington it was to "drink of the mead which [Hueffer] brewed according to the best medieval recipes." But this was as far as it went. For a cockney like Wells it was out of the question. Not for him and his kind the feeding of hogs and the trimming of hedges. In *Tono-Bungay,* he'll have Mr. Ramboat and his ineffectual family abandon the city for a farm in the country but, alas, not for long. "They got very muddy and dull; Mr. Ramboat killed a cow by improper feeding, and that disheartened them all. A twelvemonth saw the enterprise in difficulties . . . and then they returned to London." Slim, elegant, silk-bearded, Carpenter himself, to be fair, did give it a try. On a smallholding at Millthorpe near Sheffield, he took to a little market-gardening with the help of a young working couple and later of Merrill, his companion. There he consumed the simple vegetarian meals he was zealous to advocate, the "vast vegetable pie," for example, with "satellite platters" of oatcakes and fruit, and there also he wore the homemade woolens he was zealous to advocate, the sandals and shirts and the loose-fitting jackets and trousers. But somehow or other the experiment didn't come off. It barely produced enough vegetables to supply his companions, and all it produced for public consumption were the sandals that Carpenter made or taught Merrill to make.

And well, truth to tell, not everyone found the wisdom of Morris and Carpenter medicinal. The time would come when Hueffer would exchange for the gaiters and smock of the peasant the top hat and frock coat of the London gentleman. Grown older and wiser, he was in fact rather cutting on the subject of Morris and his school and his gospel, angrily mocking in his novel *The Simple Life Limited* the Limpsfield Garnetts and their socialist crew. "A singularly unhealthy frame of mind," he would call it, wasting the lives of a host of young men who "took small holdings, lost their haycrops, saw their chickens die." As for Shaw and his good friends the Webbs, Sidney and Beatrice, they had never thought much of Morris and Carpenter and their grassy path. What? The world was not to be saved until and unless the individual was saved? Good god, what nonsense! Wait for every individual to discover himself and the world would never be served, and how for that matter could the individual be saved if the world about him was lost? So Sidney and Beatrice and Shaw had long ago broken with Carpenter's high-minded New Lifers, joining with Pease and with Bland and their Fabian Society and splitting the socialist movement into halves, "one to sit among the dandelions, the other to organize the docks." On the subject of the well-sandaled sage of Millthorpe, Shaw could in fact be scathing enough, calling him "The Noble Savage" and referring to him as "that ultra-civilized impostor."

No, there was no going back to the fields and the farms. Hadn't old Hardy, that lover of woodlands and heaths, already thrown in the sponge? No woodlands or heaths in *Jude the Obscure*, his last and bitterest novel. Only the towns and the railroad stations and the iron rails that link one terrible town to another. O how she would love to go back, would sad Sue Bridehead! After she and her lover spend the night in a poor shepherd's cottage and share a supper of boiled bacon and greens, "I rather like this," Sue says. But Jude won't have it. "An urban miss is what you are," he tells her severely. And if she wasn't an urban miss, what then? Was there anything left to go back to? Only a withered old hamlet and a population too aged and discouraged to matter. The shepherd's old mother hasn't a tooth in her head and he hasn't the money to roof his poor cottage. Hardy of course had regretted the rural decline, but H. G. Wells hadn't. "One hears," he would write, "a frightful lot of nonsense about the Rural Exodus and the degeneration wrought by town life. . . ." But wasn't the townsman "more courageous, more imaginative and cleaner," he'd ask, "than his agricultural cousin?" Sherlock Holmes and his maker would surely have thought so. "It is my belief . . . ," he'd tell Watson, "that the lowest and vilest alleys of London do not present a more dreadful record of sin than does the smiling and beautiful countryside."

PART TWO

London Deliver'd

"London, the bloody world!"

There was this story Hueffer would tell. "Where do you come from?" a young cockney was asked by a recruiting sergeant in Canada. "London," he answered. "London what?" roared the sergeant. "London, Ontario? London, N.Y.? London, Mass.?" "London, the bloody world!" the young cockney roared back. And indeed, when all was said and done and the tramps and gypsies and simple-lifers had all had their day, great bloody London remained irrefutable. Whatever it was not, there was no denying the particular thing, the immense and stupendous thing, that it was. It was still after all the palpitating heart of the universe. It still sent men and money, ships and goods, to every quarter of the globe. It was still the huge habitation of a multitude of human creatures variously engaged in the works and ways of an empire that ruled one-fifth of the earth. Who could resist it? The vast and multitudinous thereness of it? Not Frank Harris who declared it "the queen city of the world," nor Henry James who called it "the great beating heart of the thick of things"; not Arnold Bennett who rejoiced in "the roar of London, majestic, imperial, super-Roman," nor H. G. Wells for whom it was—"giant London"—the "great rainswept heart of the modern world." The town's very hugeness was a value, its confusion, its complication. It might be too much for Pan-seeking Forster who called it "intelligent without purpose and excitable without love," or for earth-loving Lawrence who thought it "the end of the world" and felt in its streets "like one of the damned," or for poor homesick Yeats who, recalling on Fleet Street the obscure little island where he once longed to live like Thoreau and be happy, was moved to compose "The Lake Isle of Innisfree." It was even too much at times for an incurable Londoner like Wells who, finding that it rather resisted, with its mud and its muddle, his Utopian formulas, called it "a witless old giantess of a town, too slack and stupid to keep herself clean." But it wasn't too much for Ford Madox Hueffer who had been to Innisfree and back and in any case cared not a whit for utopian visions like Wells's. Purposeless, was it? Inexplicable? Precisely, and just for this reason it was surely "good business to be born in London." As the new age itself, as the great modern world alive and fully incarnate, London taught you the very first lesson that you had as a modern artist to learn, "that you are merely an atom amongst vastnesses. . . ."

"Annus mirabilis"

There was first of all the politics of the place. It was 1906 and a general election and a new excitement were shaking the country. After nearly two decades of Conservative rule, some four hundred Liberals were en route to Westminster to storm the bastions of power and wealth. Pledged to wage against squalor and poverty "implacable war," they were coming to town with brave new proposals for old-age pensions and health insurance and other help for the weak and the weary: eight-hour days, workers' compensation, labor-exchanges for job-seeking workers, free school meals for hungry children, and free school medical services. They were also thinking of disallowing the teaching in school of religious doctrines and eventually perhaps of a measure of independence for poor old Ireland. Even young Churchill, born a true Tory, now a good Liberal, was preaching the gospel. "We want to draw a line," he was boldly announcing, "below which we will not allow persons to live and labor." Nor was this all, this Liberal accession. The same election that was seating their members was also seating some fifty-three new creatures called Labour men, the avant-garde of a political party but lately created in 1900. For Edwardian workers were not to be as their fathers had been. The first beneficiaries of the national system of free education established in 1870, they were now voting Labour in the hundreds of thousands where their unlettered dads, lucky to vote at all, had gratefully voted Tory and sometimes Liberal. So the jubilation this year was nearly unbounded. The New Jerusalem was surely at hand.

The court, it's quite true, was alarmed. "The old idea that the House of Commons was an assemblage of 'gentlemen' has quite passed away," Lord Knollys, King Edward's aide and adviser, would sadly observe. Churchill would do, the troubled monarch supposed. The man was a gentleman. But David Lloyd George, who came from the world of Welsh farmers and cobblers, seemed scarcely to fit, in the royal mind, the part of a cabinet minister. Banish religion from the schools? What in the name, His Majesty cried in a rage, was the government coming to? "Do they wish," he said, "to copy the French!" As for the Tories, their numbers sadly reduced to a paltry 157, they were hurt and dismayed. Not since 1832 had they suffered so damned a defeat. And that Liberal program, was it not socialism, pure and unvarnished? Old-age pensions? Five shillings a week for those over seventy? Good heavens, what would the workers do with their wages, their six shillings a day? Would they not squander them all in lurid debauches? More perhaps to the point, who was to pay for them, these detestable pensions? Would it not be them themselves, the respectable people, the people in power? But all over the country the young and advanced were in ecstasies. For them it would be, this Liberal smash, the best and most exhilarating thing that would ever happen to them. "Bliss was it in that dawn to be alive,/ But to be young was very heaven!"

Among them were even some who thought themselves radicals and socialists, and why would they not? Never before had the gap between the rich and the poor been more tragic, more terrible. While the king and his wealthier subjects devoured prodigious amounts, sometimes fish, flesh, and fowl at one sitting, one-third of the world's greatest and most prosperous city was being starved to death or nearly to death by the other two-thirds. In the filth and the dirt under the fish barrows, they'd be groping for the heads and tails of fishes to boil for their children, and under the Waterloo Bridge, to ward off the night and the cold and the rain, they'd be lying with their heads to the wall and their feet on the pavement, and, in the meantime, the children, pale, undernourished, and verminous, would be going to school in a stupor of hunger and falling asleep at their desks, and "Louisa," a depressed D. H. Lawrence would be asking his girlfriend, "do any of your youngsters limp to school . . . because they are crippled with broken boots . . . ? Have you seen [them] gathered to free breakfasts at your school—half a pint of milk and a lump of bread . . . ?" When the novelist Gissing was called into Lambeth to identify the corpse of poor Mary Ann, once his wife, once a lively young woman with dark glossy hair, he just couldn't recognize her. Wasted by time and starvation her body had mummified. Under the circumstances, did political parties suffice after all? Wasn't it needful to install a new system of government, more humane, more efficient? Wasn't it needful in fact to socialize things, to collectivize the national wisdom and will?

The Fabian Society certainly thought so. From their office in the cellar of Clement's Inn, Shaw and the Webbs had been working for some twenty-five years for a saner and juster order of things. All good people, good middle-class people ("gruesomely respectable," May Morris had called them), their faith was not in the inevitability of Marxian revolution but in "the inevitability of gradualness," not in the romance of a proletarian apocalypse but in the sober good works of a professional elite that assembled facts and statistics and turned out tracts and reports ("Municipal Trading," "Municipal Banking," and so forth) and thus armed and enlightened, labored to "permeate," as they called it, slowly perhaps but nonetheless surely, the existing political forces and forms. By this time in fact they were the most sophisticated and successful of all the city's socialist groups. They consorted and consulted with ministers and party members, with civil servants and union heads, and in general with people in power. Why bother with parties and votes? Why bother converting the country? Convert the cabinets. Convert the county councils and the committees. Hueffer, who wasn't at all sympathetic, called the Fabian Society "a Socialist Tammany Hall," but Edgar Jepson, the novelist and journalist, considered it "the only repository of statesmanship the country had enjoyed for generations."

It was, to be sure, by design no doubt, a little exclusive. A London club wasn't harder to enter. A single blackball was enough to rule out the eagerest candidate. It limited itself to seven hundred souls and of these no more than one hundred were active. The meetings were sparsely attended. Sometimes by as few as twenty or so. It was also withal just a touch complacent. Was she not frightened, Bertrand Russell would ask Mrs. Beatrice Webb, to address as she must the great public figures and meetings? Not at all, the lady'd reply. She would simply say to herself, "You're the cleverest member of one of the cleverest families in the cleverest class of the cleverest nation in the world, why should you be frightened?" But were they not temporizers, these Fabian people? Compromisers only too eager to defer the revolution that as good English burghers they couldn't help fearing? But this wasn't the case. Their socialist goal was specific and radical. It was "not," said Beatrice, "a vague and sentimental desire to 'ameliorate the condition of the masses,' but a definite economic form . . . the communal or state ownership of Capital and Land." As for their doctrine of "gradualness," it expressed less an ignoble counsel of caution than a generous counsel of action. The radical changes they fought for they expected today or tomorrow, not in some distant future.

But now it was 1906 and surely, with the Liberal awakening and the aroused expectations of a new dispensation of things, it was time to revise the prudential old Fabian doctrines. The omens were certainly good. They had just recruited a young popular writer. Short and slight with small hands and feet and "a thin little voice," H. G. Wells didn't make an impression at once. But he had keen blue eyes and a natural charm and a witty intelligence, and had recently revealed, in his *Anticipations* and his *Modern Utopia*, a cast of mind agreeably congenial with theirs. Did he not disdain as they did the whole wretched business of parties and politics? Did he not speak of a new order of Samurai, of a ruling elite of planners and experts? Had he not called for a purely sober and scientific approach to all the grave problems that afflicted the poor human creature? Revolution? A violent class war? Not a bit. A reasoned readjustment of the current class system was all he was thinking of. He was hardly a Marxist at all for that matter. He was a modern Voltaire, an Enlightenment man. In any event, he was off to a ripping good start. He delivered a paper entitled "The Question of Scientific Administrative Areas in Relation to Municipal Undertakings." Perfect. What could have been more soundly and solemnly Fabian?

But all was not well. Not for little H. G. the policy of permeation. Not for him the inevitability of gradualism. No Quintus Fabius Maximus, he wanted apocalypse and he wanted it now. Indeed he wanted, he told his friend Hueffer, to turn the Society "inside out and then throw it into the dustbin." So, in the very month of the great Liberal triumph, he gave the Society not some tedious talk on "municipal gas and water" but "This Misery of Boots," a lively attack on the nation itself, its fatal commitment to unbounded free enterprise, and just a month later "The Faults of the Fabian," a lively attack on the Society itself, its middle-class snobbery, its drawing-room manner, and its levity, its Shavian levity, that reduced its meetings to a "giggling excitement" and the "high business of socialism" to "an idiotic middle-class joke." He attacked above all its resistance to change, to the spirit of reconstruction that was everywhere rising. The Fabian Society, was it? It was all too Fabian. It should change its name to the "British Socialist Society"; should expand its executive, broaden its membership; should abandon the old path of permeation and join with other socialist groups to compose a socialist party. Eventually he might even ask them to alter that most sacred of all institutions, the middle-class marriage, might ask them to take up with him the daring position that women be endowed as mothers not by their husbands but by the state.

The Old Gang, as the founding fathers were called, wasn't wildly enthusiastic. Why bother to form a new party at all? Why not continue to permeate, like influenza or rabies, the parties already in power? It had always worked in the past. As for the business of Endowed Motherhood, free love, really. . . . Someone referred to "This Misery of Wells, by H. G. Boots." All things considered, another suggested, "All's Well That Ends Wells." But they weren't altogether against him. They *did* understand that they needed a change. "An Opposition," Shaw had already stated, "is needed to balance the old gang." He was even ready to consider a Fabian party in Parliament. Anything at all, he had said, "to make Fabianism interesting again." So he and his consorts would allow Wells his reform committee, his little committee of friends and admirers. But the man was never the soul of diplomacy. "You must study people's corns when you go clog dancing," Shaw had helpfully warned him, but Wells, impetuous man!—a collectivist who wouldn't join a collective and contemptuous of Shaw and his middle-class friends— just wouldn't listen. Not enough that the members support his reforms. They must also condemn and expel and humiliate the Old Guard who had *made* the Society and long made it work. It was all too much, even for his fondest supporters. They had wanted a change all right, but on these outrageous terms? And then how serious was he after all, how responsible, really? Did he know what he wanted? Did he have an alternative plan? Or was he merely a man with a grievance? It wasn't quite clear. So it turned out no contest that day in December 1906 when Wells appeared on the stage of the Essex Hall with his bag of reforms. A lively thinker but a wretched speaker and a worse tactician, he was no match at all for a man like Shaw with his wit and red beard and his grand platform manner. Though the vote was close, Wells was soundly defeated.

Nevertheless, it was all great fun while it lasted. Blood and Fire. Another Salvation Army. No empty meeting halls now. In that single year, that *annus mirabilis,* the Fabian membership leaped from its sedate seven hundred to a lively two thousand, Arnold Bennett among them and Edgar Jepson and Granville Barker and solely to vote for their good friend Wells's reforms, Ford Madox Hueffer and, much to the distress of Constance Garnett who was a good Fabian, her mischievous husband Edward who wasn't. Wells even won for a time the wives of the Old Gang, "Edith Nesbit," the wife of the bold Hubert Bland, the Society's founder, and Maud, the wife of Pember Reeves, the socialist representative for New Zealand. Even Beatrice Webb who, as Fabian first lady, had never been for the ballot at all, was inspired by Wells to join up with the suffragists. As for the young, they were simply enchanted. They were forming Fabian branches in Oxford and Cambridge. They were all for Wells, for "the wee, fantastic, Wells," as Rupert Brooke, an early convert, was fondly describing him, though one morning at breakfast he had had to endure from Cambridge friends like the Stracheys, Lytton and James, a vicious attack on his political taste. So too for Wells were the children of the Old Gang, the glorious girls of the Blands and the Reeveses and the Oliviers, Rosamund and Amber and Brynhild and Margery. They formed their own Fabian group. They called it the Fabian Nursery. This isn't to mention young London admirers like Richard Aldington and Eric Gill the sculptor and Harold Monro who would later be publishing *Georgian Poetry* but in 1907 was starting a press called the Samurai Press in honor of Wells and his samurai notion; and just down from Leeds, A. R. Orage, the youthful Theosopher and Platonist, who thought "no end," he wrote Wells, "of your ideas." Wells was their hero, their prophet, the Mohammed who would lead them "in a holy war/ Against the infamous grown-ups" and "the horrible nurses/ Itching to boil their children."

And indeed, soon after the great Wells debacle, Orage would be founding the city's first socialist weekly. He would pay Mr. Shaw an important visit. Would Mr. Shaw care, for the sake of the cause, to invest in the *New Age,* a Liberal-Radical weekly now on the verge of collapse? He would and he did, in the amount of five hundred pounds. Orage, to be sure, wasn't Shaw's sort of socialist or even Wells's. Not for him a world of engineers and bureaucrats. He was a romantic socialist, a visionary one. Not for him, either, an audience of self-satisfied Fabians. He hoped for a wider and more various one. But Shaw didn't mind. For the Society's sake and good name he wanted, under its vigilant eye, a forum for all kinds of socialists. So Orage moved into the two crowded rooms near Chancery Lane that would serve for its office, and, after changing its subtitle from "A Democratic Review" to "An Independent Review of Politics, Literature and Art," would make the *New Age,* with his editorial flair and his personal charm and his eclectic intelligence, one of the livelier journalistic events of the time. Of course he would publish the old Fabian stalwarts, the Blands and the Webbs, but he'd also publish the rebels, the Wellses and Bennetts. Of course he would print the usual pages on politics and economics but he'd also print the less usual pages on letters and art. He was good at inspiring discussion and controversy. He didn't care for terms like "essay" and "article." What he wanted was talk, "causerie." So in the very first year of the journal's existence he was promoting a debate on the issue that still was convulsing the Fabians, printing Wells in support of a socialist party and Cecil Chesterton in opposition to one, and the next year was orchestrating the great Chesterbelloc affair, printing Bennett on why he was a socialist and Hilaire Belloc and G. K. Chesterton on why they were not and Shaw making sport of them both as the pantomime elephant he called "Chesterbelloc." The *New Age* didn't make money. It sold for only a penny a number. But it was an instant success and by the end of 1907 was selling five thousand copies a week and by the end of 1908 twenty thousand. All things considered, the socialist cause was alive and well in London, England.

The socialist cause? Every radical cause, it seemed, was alive and well in London, England. At the time there was even at large in the city a pestilence of anarchists, poor souls maddened by sickness and poverty or by the sickness and poverty of their suffering brethren, and thinking by killing a king or a prince or one of their toadies to abolish the infamy and create a new world. Drawn by London's kindness to strangers, they had come from the continent like a virtual plague, Prince Peter Kropotkin among them and Felix Volkhovsky, the notorious nihilist, and Sergius Stepniak, the assassin of the head of the tsarist security police, and all of them hotly pursued, it was widely believed, by secret agents of the Russian and European governments. Conrad wasn't wholly unsympathetic. He preferred them to socialists. The socialists would collaborate with society which, like everything else created by man, was evil, but these good "dynamiters" wanted nothing less than its total destruction. Conrad was scandalized nevertheless. Didn't they work to exterminate all he held dear? Order and grace, duty and discipline? London as it was was anarchic enough. What could even anarchy do to dismantle it more? But Liberal London wasn't at all scandalized. Not even after 1894 when a person or persons unknown attempted to bomb the Greenwich Observatory. The Royal Geographic Society would have Prince Kropotkin to dinner and the Teachers' Guild invite him to one of their meetings and a London journal describe him as "England's most distinguished refugee." This isn't to mention the Garnetts, Edward and Constance, who would keep open house in their Chelsea apartment for "the anarchist prince" and other émigré friends, and whose Limpsfield retreat would come to be known as "Dostoevsky's corner." As O'Leary told Yeats, who knew Stepniak well, "no gentleman [could] be a socialist," though "he might," he would add with a thoughtful look, "be an anarchist." As for the young they were naturally beguiled. Dorothy Richardson, who had come to town to work in a doctor's office for one pound a week, considered them harmless enough and a great addition to the color and charm of the city, and the Rossetti children were allowed by their mother, an indulgent sort, to operate in the basement of her London home an anarchist press called the *Torch* and it was all but impossible, Hueffer remembered, to walk before that respectable house without running "the gauntlet of innumerable gimlets," of English detectives and French police spies and Russian *agents provocateurs*. The father, William Michael Rossetti, was perhaps understandably annoyed. He was after all an important official, secretary to the Inland Revenues no less. But what could he do? The house, it appeared, belonged to his wife. After her death he wasted no time. He descended into the bowels of the basement and ordered them out, the press and the *Torch* and the anarchist friends.

No wonder this London would react like a mob on the Seine to the case of Francisco Ferrer, the Spanish freethinker who had devoted his life to establishing secular schools and now in 1909 was under arrest for fomenting, it was charged, an anticlerical rising in Barcelona. Under Orage, the *New Age* didn't involve itself in specific political causes, but Ferrer's it considered a passionate exception. It sent the foreign secretary, Sir Edward Grey, a public telegram demanding the government's intervention. There was even an unconfirmed rumor that certain staffers, Orage included, were planning to kidnap the Spanish ambassador and were only prevented by a cabinet minister's secret assurance that the government was working to save the reformer. Whatever the case, it didn't or couldn't, and the unhappy man was summarily shot. All over Europe there were riots and bold remonstrations and "Feuilletons were wildly sold in the streets," Lady Ottoline Morrell was reporting from Paris. But London itself wasn't less turbulent. Catholic Belloc did his best to defend the Spanish authorities but Conrad's friend Cunninghame Graham and other Radical leaders were making passionate speeches on Trafalgar Square and ten thousand souls were singing "The Red Flag" and "The Marseillaise" and setting out for the Spanish embassy with Cunninghame Graham out front in a hired taxicab, and soon in the mud before Whitehall the police were engaged in a battle and in front of the embassy were charging on horseback. "The *New Age* to Sir Edward Grey," read the bitter telegram Orage now printed. "*New Age* holds you responsible as accessory to Ferrer's murder." Morgan Forster felt just a twinge of remorse. All that year he had amused himself "by finding apologies for the Papacy," he confessed. "The execution of Ferrer may remind me what this leads to."

"Go and rouse London"

But the men weren't the only ones troubling the streets of the city. The same great year that brought in the Liberals and Labourites also brought in the Women's Social and Political Union which, just three seasons before, Mrs. Emmeline Pankhurst and her daughters, Christabel and Sylvia, had started in Manchester. In January 1906 Mrs. Pankhurst had placed in the hands of Miss Annie Kenney two pound notes. "Go," she had said in her fine contralto voice. "Go and rouse London." And rouse it she had. For Edwardian women were not to be as their mothers had been. It wasn't for them to submit to mindless marriages and serve their husbands as slaves or as ornaments or, failing that, to creep in the houses of the "great" as poor companions and helpless governesses or, failing that too, to languish at home at the mercy of burly Victorian fathers. There were options now. They could be teachers, it seems. In 1870 when the Education Act had been passed, there had been in all of England but 14,000 of them, two-thirds of them men. By 1900 there would be 100,000 and three-quarters of them would be women. And this wasn't all. The modern business office had by this time come into existence and with it a sudden demand for clerks and for secretaries and for the single women to "man" the positions. She doesn't want to get married, says the heroine of Bennett's *Hilda Lessways*, but what else can she do? Well, there *is* something else, it would seem. Pitman's shorthand. "It'll be the Open Sesame to everything," she's told. Nor would this be the only Open Sesame for eager young women like Hilda. So would the machine they were calling the typewriter. The tyrannical husband in Barrie's one-acter *The Twelve-Pound Look* is badly shaken. He has just discovered why his first wife had long ago left him. Not for another man, as he'd thought all these years, but for, of all things, a typewriter! She could make it alone, she'd decided, "if I first proved my mettle by earning twelve pounds; and as soon as I had earned it I left you," she informs him, pressing her hand on her typewriter, Barrie lovingly tells us, "as lovingly as many a woman has pressed a rose."

But in truth neither Barrie's contraption nor Sir Isaac Pitman's conception were the Open Sesames promised. Bennett's poor Hilda had only exchanged one servitude for another: for a tyrannical husband a tyrannical boss. And Ann Veronica, the lovely and lively young heroine of the H. G. Wells novel of that name? Quitting the home of her wretched Victorian father, she bravely sets off for London and life, but can only serve, it turns out, as a typist at tenpence per one thousand words or as receptionist or shopgirl at one pound a week. She returns as she must in defeat to her father and home. But then the business of teaching wouldn't prove to be very much better, as the heroine of Lawrence's *The Rainbow* would sadly discover. For new life and liberty, Ursula Brangwen, like Ann Veronica, will leave father and family behind her and enter the world as a teacher, but will find the exchange no blessing at all. For a bullying father a bullying headmaster, for the sordid and meaningless life of the home the sordid and meaningless life of the classroom. As for the social rewards, there just weren't any. The valiant Sophia of Bennett's *The Old Wives' Tale* would go for a teacher but her parents won't have it. Teaching was strictly for orphans and widows and spinsters and other unfortunates. A teacher, was she? The beautiful Gudrun in Lawrence's *Women in Love*? Gerald, her wealthy admirer, rather wishes she wasn't. "I don't think teachers as a rule are my equal," he says. And they weren't in fact. They were recruited, these new hordes of teachers, from the lower-class ranks, Lawrence and Wells and Orage, for example, and, for another, Miss Florence Emily Dugdale, the second wife of old Thomas Hardy, who had trained as a teacher but exhausted by large and unruly classes and ashamed of her social subservience to the vicar and the wife of the vicar, had turned her attention to typing. Hardy was in fact just a little uneasy. When she brought down to Max Gate her London typewriter, she was not, he insisted, "what is called a 'typist.' " Oh she did do some typing for him on the side, but only, he said, "as a fancy." No, London was not yet the New Jerusalem. For the eager young women who came there with hope in their hearts, it was still the same Old Jerusalem.

So the Pankhursts and Miss Annie Kenney would find legions of ladies at once wistful and wrathful and in either case willing to fight the new Liberal government that denied them the franchise and the power that went with it. They'd march in the streets by the thousands and fill the Queens Hall every Monday and heckle the Liberal candidates in the by-elections. They'd meet in Caxton Hall for "Women's Parliaments" and send deputations to the Commons just a few blocks away and be charged on the pavements of Parliament Square by policemen on horseback, by the "London Cossacks" as one newspaper called them. They'd even rush the cordons of police and be carried away to Holloway Prison to languish for weeks and sometimes for months in the mean little cells.

Sunday, June 21, 1908, and a mighty concourse of people. Thirty special trains bring women from every corner of the country. Seven great processions, each consisting of seven thousand marchers in purple and white and green, move under their banners, their 770 banners, toward Hyde Park and the twenty platforms newly assembled for the occasion. The bugles sound and from the platforms the speakers begin their addresses. Many hours later, at the end of the day, the bugles sound again, the addresses cease, and a resolution calling for the immediate passage of a bill for women carries unanimously. The bugles sound again and half a million people cry out in one voice, "Votes for Women!" "Votes for Women!" "Votes for Women!" Was Prime Minister Asquith impressed by this great gathering of people, the greatest, it was said, in Hyde Park's history? Apparently not. He declined to take action. At the end of the month Mrs. Pankhurst called for a deputation and a demonstration, but the PM refused to receive it and that very night on the square, in a struggle that lasted till midnight, the women were dispersed by charges of police and twenty-nine were arrested. Poor Mrs. Pankhurst, it wasn't the rules that she minded at Holloway or even the food. Terribly claustrophobic, it was the confinement. In one desperate moment she piled every single thing in her cell on the top of her bed and, though inclined to obesity, managed to reach to the small pane of glass at the top. "I cried, my dear. I cried to know that life was going on out there."

"O brave new world . . ."

But the action in London wasn't only political. It was social, too. For centuries they had been, the poor people of England, no better than peasants, than serfs, uncouth, unlettered, uncared for. Rebecca West—the brilliant young journalist who had assumed the name of Ibsen's freethinking heroine—was indeed in a state. She had never been taught, she protested, that there once "was a green and happy England in which the common laboring man was neither starved nor landless," had never been taught "that this class was betrayed into poverty. . . ." But already something had happened around her, something quite unprecedented—not only the Reform Bill of 1867 which gave working people the vote but the Education Act of 1870 and for their children a national system of free public schooling and by the end of the century a vast new audience able and eager to read for the very first time. Not enough now the old vicar's sermons on Sunday. Now at last they could see them and read them, the wonderful words, in the papers, the weeklies, the journals, the books that were flooding the country to answer their need. The newspapers, for instance. In Edwardian London there would be not five, not fifty, but a hundred and more of them. Alfred Harmsworth's *Times* would be read of course by the respectable people, but the *Daily Mail* he had started in 1896 was meant, at a halfpenny, to be read by the new lettered masses, as were Beaverbrook's *Daily Express* and illustrated dailies like the *Graphic* and *Sketch* and, for weekend consumption, the Sunday newspapers. This isn't to mention the journals. Not just the venerable monthlies like

Blackwood's, the *Strand*, and the *Pall Mall* and solid old weeklies like the *Athenaeum*, the *Spectator*, and the *Saturday Review* which were dear to conservative clubmen and clerics. But, under Orage, the lively *New Age* with its daring ideas and its popular prose which was read not alone by colonial governors and high civil servants but, as Hueffer reported, by "board school-teachers, shop assistants, servants, artisans, and members of the poor generally." Or under Hueffer himself the *English Review* with its "fine blue cover and handsome black type" and its nearly two hundred pages of masters and masterpieces, among them the poems of Hardy and Swinburne and the stories of Tolstoy and James. On Christmas Eve 1908 young Lawrence arrived at a farm called Haggs Farm to share a copy of Hueffer's first number with his fiancée, Jessica Chambers. How excited they were, how enraptured, this shy miner's son, this plain farmer's daughter! It was, after all, in the remoteness of Nottingham, a very real "link with the world of literature." And at half a crown, what a bargain it was, what a godsend!

As for the books, the hundreds of thousands of books, it would be for them, for the clerks and the servants and the poor people generally, that the four hundred publishing houses of Edwardian London would produce them and produce them so cheaply. "All that is greatest in literature," Arnold Bennett assured them, "could be bought for fourpence-halfpenny a volume." It was possible, he'd tell them, to assemble an adequate library for as little as twenty-eight pounds and a penny. The cheap reprint edition was, to be sure, a Victorian invention but, carelessly edited, crudely printed, it wasn't to flourish till after the turn of the century when Grant Richards produced his World's Classics series and John Buchan produced for the publisher Nelson the Sixpenny Classics and the Sevenpenny Library, and, most famous of all and most influential, Ernest Rhys produced for the publisher Dent his *Everyman's Library*. It was of course Democratic, *Everyman's* was. There was the title itself which dropped from Heaven, the editor recalled, "like a good lyric," and the Noble Intention which was, as they said, "to foster a taste for books among the proletariat," and, best of all, the price, the Democratic Shilling as it was called by the publisher, who remembered the days when the books he so longed for he couldn't afford. It was certainly Prodigious! Plutarch in three volumes, Livy in six, Hakluyt in eight, Grote's *History of Greece* in twelve. *Everyman's* was planning to issue, in batches of fifty, no less than a thousand Best Books! They'd be Elegant too, in a *fin de siècle* way. The spines with their gilt-trellis roses and the title pages with their still thicker tangle of foliage and the allegorical end-papers with their heavily draped handmaiden suggesting Good Deeds. Indeed, were they not, these solemn productions, just a little intimidating? "Precious life blood of a master spirit"; "The Sages of old live again in us"; "This is fairy-gold, boy, and 'twill prove so": after such mottoes, such dire admonitions, flower-embroidered of course, who could enter these volumes without fear and trembling and a sense of unworthiness? Just the same, they were generous men, John Dent, Ernest Rhys, and did generous things. "O brave new world/ That hath such people in't."

Was there ever a time, for that matter, when books were more loved and revered, when literature itself was more honored and treasured? By the end of the century a new set of publishers—not John Dent alone but Methuen, Heinemann, Unwin, John Lane, and Elkin Mathews among others—had brought to the business a new vision and vigor, a new dedication. For "to say," said Lawrence's Jessie, "that we read the books gives no adequate idea of what really happened. It was the entering into possession of a new world, a widening and enlargement of life." So too for Wells who'd refer to "the quickening sunshine of literature," to its wonderful power to awaken the souls of the poor working people, and "Literature," he'd declare in a rapture of hope, "the clearing of minds, the release of minds, the food and guidance of minds, is the way." Morgan Forster, it's true, had his doubts. Those children of the abyss, their brains "filled with the husks of books, culture—horrible," did they not make a mockery, really, of letters and learning? "I care a good deal about improving myself by means of Literature and Art . . . when you came in I was reading Ruskin's *Stones of Venice*. I don't say this to boast. . . ." Thus says the absurd Leonard Bast in *Howards End*. He's destined, however, to perish—Forster will see to it—under an avalanche of the World's Finest Books. So much, evidently, for Wells and his sunshine of literature and for Dent and for Rhys and their Books for the People!

But socialist Shaw, though he couldn't help mocking them too, was delighted in the Basts and their new opportunities. "Oh, don't think, because I'm only a clerk," says Gunner to Tarleton in the play *Misalliance*, "that I'm not one of the intellectuals. I'm a reading man, a thinking man." Mr. Tarleton, the play's principal character, is in fact very much of his time: a rich manufacturer of men's underwear, he has the self-made man's obsession with books ("Read your Darwin, my

boy"; "Read Browning"; "Read Chesterton") and his passion for en-
dowing free public libraries all over the land. As for the Bennetts and
Wellses they knew well enough what they meant, these bold new developments, for the meek and discouraged. "If I'd had money...," Mr.
Haim says in Bennett's *The Roll Call*, "I should have improved myself.
Reading, I mean. Study. Literature.... But what could I do?" Infatu-
ated with a lovely young upper-class girl, the hero of Wells's *The
Wheels of Chance* looks into a mirror and sees he's unfit and "I'm
nothing," he cries in his pain. "I know nothing." But the hero of *Love
and Mr. Lewisham* will have much better luck. By dint of his "bookish
intentions" he'll be able to make his "desperate get-away from the shop
and the street." Indeed, Wells was moved by the plight of his clerks and
assistants and their hunger for knowledge and freedom. Had they not
been his own, their plight and their hunger? Had his mother, the worst
kind of snob, the lower-class snob, the ex-lady's maid at Uppark, not
stood in the way of her son's education as outside his station in life
and, like Dickens's mother who had sent her son to a blacking factory,
stupidly sent him to serve as a draper's assistant? So he'd delight in his
poor counterjumpers and their joyous discoveries of wonderful people
like the Italian "Bocashieu" and the French fellow "Rabooloose." Lady
Horner's son Edward, who had just finished reading *The White Peacock,* the unknown Lawrence's first published novel, was frankly in-
credulous. Could mere peasants talk as they did in this novel? Could
they possibly have knowledge of art or of music? But then Edward, it
seems, wasn't in touch with the times. Back in the nineties the parents
of Lawrence's Jessie had read to each other in the *Nottingham
Guardian* the weekly installments of Hardy's *Tess,* and now in the fields
near their farm young Lawrence and their daughter would be reading
The Prisoner of Zenda and *Lorna Doone,* "Hiawatha" and "Evangeline"
and "Launcelote and Elaine." Of course it was troubling too, this dan-
gerously new exposure to things. Should Jessie read Maupassant?
Should she read *Wuthering Heights*? Lawrence was pained. Unhappy
books that they were, would they not bruise her soul, her innocent
faith in life and the world? Be that as it may, Ford Madox Hueffer was
impressed. When he visited Lawrence's Nottingham home, the author's
young friends were descanting at ease in the kitchen or living room on
Nietzsche and Wagner, on Flaubert and Marx. He'd report his findings
to Wells. "Didn't you know?" Wells would exclaim. "English public education is the best in the world." The story, alas, is apocryphal. If Huef-

fer ever visited Lawrence in Eastwood, there's no evidence of it, not a scrap. But his fantasy wasn't too far from the fact. Out of the new educational system there had sprung and was springing a new race of Englishmen, literate, aspiring, and hungry for life and experience.

Of Bicycles and Motor Cars

"Nothing enlarges the mind like Travel and Books," Wells's Kipps is informed, and indeed it became in Edwardian London, for his clerks and his grocers' assistants, almost as easy to travel as read. Throughout human history it had been the lot of the poor to be born and to suffer and die in one wretched village, sometimes in one wretched hovel, and to see and to know nothing else. But now in the eighties and nineties something amazing was happening, something quite unprecedented. The range of life and experience was suddenly broadening. What with railways and railway excursions it was possible, it seemed, to consider not just Brighton or Blackpool but Devon or Cornwall and even Dieppe and the continent. For a man of the north like Arnold Bennett, London's great railway terminals, its Paddingtons, King's Crosses, Waterloos, were gateways to freedom, exits out of the dreary, the woebegone provinces. But for Forster and the heroine of *Howards End* they were exits not into but out of the dreary, the woebegone city, were gateways to Nature, "to the glorious and the unknown." "In Paddington," as Forster's Miss Schlegel would tell it, "all Cornwall is latent . . . Scotland is through the pylons of Euston; Wessex behind the poised chaos of Waterloo."

But the paid holiday was still for the masses a thing of the future and the railway train an upper- and upper-middle-class pleasure. Not so the bicycle. Transformed by the low wheel and the pneumatic tire, by the tubular frame and light alloys generally, the modern bicycle had entered the scene and with it a new and remarkable freedom for all. Before, if one wanted to go anywhere, one must have a horse and a carriage or a gig or a trap or otherwise belong to the gentry. But now with the bicycle, the blessed bicycle, that in 1901 had cost as much as nine pounds but by 1909 would cost as little as four, the meanest clerk, the most wretched of butcher boys, could go where he wanted and with ease and élan, and if he wasn't tramping and rambling all over the countryside now, he was cycling all over it. Freedom? Independence? Ah, it was more. To ride this machine was to assert one's manhood, one's pride in one's life. It was to convert flab into muscle, self-doubt into self-admiration. It was to leave one's village or suburb behind and enrich one's contacts with people and places, with lovers and friends. John Galsworthy was in fact overwhelmed. The bicycle was responsible, he could claim, "for more movement in manners and morals than anything since Charles II." Wells, the best spokesman the poor and the young ever had, was ecstatic of course for their sake and in novels like *Kipps* and *Mr. Polly* and especially *The Wheels of Chance*, his prose celebration of bicyclehood, he'd rejoice in their new power and pleasure, in their freedom to see and experience what the lost generations of their fathers and forefathers could not have imagined: England itself and its picturesque villages and hearty old inns, its grassy downs and its heathery moorlands and its strange trees and rivers and animals. Mr. Hoopdriver, the poor draper's assistant in *The Wheels of Chance*, is beside himself with delight. He has just seen a weasel, "the first weasel he had ever seen in his cockney life." More important, he has met and befriended for the very first time in his cockney life an enchanting young lady far above him in culture and class. Of course he can't have her, this admirable creature, but at least he discovers a different reality, a reality that but for the accident of his meager upbringing might well have been his to enjoy. Even so, it was democratic all right, this bold new contraption. Used and enjoyed by people of so many classes and callings, by "judges and stockbrokers and actresses, and, in fact, all the best people," the bicycle would be certain to have, Wells's Hoopdriver believes, a leveling effect. As the clergyman tells him "with a broad smile" on his face, "we are all cyclists nowadays."

It was certainly true of the artists and writers and intellectuals generally. They were all cyclists now. Arnold Bennett took trips not only inside London but also outside it to Ipswich and Halifax, and Leonard Woolf and his brother thought nothing at all of pedaling from Putney to Edinburgh, and when the Webbs came down from London to Sandgate to enlist H. G. Wells in their Fabian enterprise, it was on their bicycles, and even the Hudsons would take to the wondrous invention, the old man's machine being of solid construction with its big frame and great double bars. As for the Hardys, Thomas and Emma Lavinia, they'd ride in tandem through Puddletown (formerly Piddletown) and look neither to right nor to left for fear of having to witness the coarse plebeian faces of his numerous kinsmen. This odd couple rode all over Dorset in fact, Hardy in knickerbockers, Emma Lavinia in the kind of green outfit recommended by Mrs. Amelia Jenks Bloomer. Even James, though by this time inclining to stoutness, could be seen in peaked cap and knickerbockers cycling as many as twenty-two miles between luncheon and teatime "with my irrepressible Scot." Of course there were repercussions: fractures, bruises, and concussions. Bennett dislocated an elbow and had to be put under chloroform and operated on. Emma Hardy, who was accident prone, was for some time disabled by a badly bruised ankle and Hardy himself, between Bath and Bristol, fell off his bicycle, his fine Rover "Cob," and was "rubbed down," he said, "by a kindly coal-heaver with one of his sacks." But the unluckiest cyclist of all had to be Shaw. On his way down a hill, a stone lodged itself in the mudguard and locked the wheel dead "and a Homeric spill followed." Hurtling down another steep hill on his way home from Hertfordshire, he missed a woman who got in his way but not without veering and toppling and hitting the road with his face. After passing the National Gallery and approaching the foot of the Haymarket at a fairly good pace, he'd run into a horse-driven van and gone down "in a forest of horse's legs, van wheels and whirling bicycle machinery." But what matter, the danger, the damage? For Shaw and his contemporaries at the turn of the century it meant, the exciting new bicycle, the multiplication of life and experience.

What the bicycle was to lower-class people the motor car was to the middle and upper. For if by 1900 we were all cyclists now, by 1910 we were all motorists now and not least of all the poets and novelists. Kipling, for example, who as early as 1897 was driving a six-horsepower touring car at a rate of fifteen miles per hour and was later exploring the country in a steam motor car and whose Lanchester, "Amelia," after stalling in front of James's Lamb House, would speed the twenty-eight miles between Rye and Rottingdean in one hour and twenty-five minutes. Poor Mrs. Hardy was distraught. As the wife of a world-class writer she naturally desired the prestige of a car and chauffeur but the frugal old man wouldn't have it. She would get her revenge. On occasional Sundays she would have the gardener push her to church in a Bath chair. Mary Barrie, the young actress-wife of another world-class writer, was a little bit luckier. J.M.B. didn't himself care a jot for these infernal machines but for her pretty sake he'd acquire as early as 1901 a steam car with a chauffeur named Alfred attached to it and later a Lanchester with a chauffeur named Frederick attached to it and later a Fiat with a chauffeur named Alphonse attached to it. As for the Shaws, they had no choice but to employ a full-time chauffeur. Their first motor car, a twenty-eight- to thirty-horsepower De Dietrich, Charlotte crashed on the very first day and their gardener Higgs was never, it seemed, quite at home at the wheel and Shaw himself, though enthusiastic, was "shockingly careless" and not to be trusted.

Even the indigent Conrad found it hard to resist it. After publishing *Chance*, his first and only best-seller, he'd purchase a secondhand two-seater Cadillac, "a worthy and painstaking one-cylinder puffer," and later a large four-seater Humber, which he found rather useful for picking up guests at the station, though Jessie was in fact a more competent driver than the author who was nervous and reckless and tended to end up in ditches. Was anyone ever more wedded to his home and his study than James, more resentful of the surprise visit, the unexpected intrusion? Nevertheless, when his friend Edith Wharton descended from Paris in her "chariot of fire," as he called her open-top Panhard, he just couldn't say no and soon they'd be off for two or three days on the road, the Master reposing at ease and in goggles, and, "as jubilant as a child," witnessing scenes move and vanish before him as they did in the cinema. Indeed he was happy to learn that Conrad himself had acquired one and "I hear with fond awe," he would coyly address him, "of your possession of a (I won't say life-saving, but literally life-making) miraculous car. . . ." For the motor car was, James was quick to perceive, "a huge extension of life, of experience and consciousness."

Not of course for everyone. Evil little boys would run alongside it and jeer and their troglodyte parents who called it a "stink pot" would pelt it with stones. It wasn't in fact until 1896 that a law was repealed that restricted its speed in the towns to a mere two miles per hour and required a man with a red flag of warning to walk in front of it. So in Marie Corelli's *The Devil's Motor* Satan makes his appearance on earth in "the stench and muffled roar of a huge Car," and in Galsworthy's *Fraternity* a City businessman and his A.1 Damyer are blamed for "the reek of petrol" that darkens the road, and in Forster's *Howards End* the philistine Wilcoxes are aptly defined by their vulgar attachment to a "throbbing, stinking car." H. G. Wells was excited. The new locomotive would make Englishmen think, would it not? But his friend Fordie Hueffer was less optimistic. Nothing, he said, would make Englishmen think. Some twenty years later, it's true, he would alter his story. It would be Mr. Kipling, not Mr. Wells, who was of the opinion that the automobile would make Englishmen think and Mr. James, not Mr. Hueffer, who'd reply that, his splendid machine having just broken down in front of Lamb House, it was more likely "to make Mr. Kipling think." But no matter. It was the day of the motor car, no doubt about that, and its freedom and power. King Edward himself was by this time a passionate automobilist and by 1902 had accumulated a fleet of a rich claret color and soon would be driving from Pall Mall to Windsor Castle in just sixty minutes and racing the Brighton Road at a speed of some sixty miles per hour. He could never abide another car racing before him. *Lèse-majesté.* He'd order his chauffeur instanter to pursue and speed by it.

Active Verbs

Things were not all, to be sure, for the best. At the turn of the century a new plague of despair, of Darwinian darkness, had swept across middle-class Europe and hardly an intellect wasn't affected. Shaw refused to accept it, "the universe as a senseless chapter of cruel accidents." But "there was no meaning in life," said Somerset Maugham, "and man by living served no end," and Bertrand Russell saw it all plainly enough, "the darkness of a godless universe," and we were "all exiles," he said, "on an inhospitable shore," and Conrad who called it "the eternal Error" saw it all as a mindless knitting machine that "ought to embroider" but just went on knitting and knitting and "it has knitted," he'd go on to say, "time, space, pain, death, corruption, despair, and all the illusions,—and nothing matters."

Nonetheless it was 1901 and the mood of the nineties, despondent, despairing, was passing away and a lively new spirit, more hopeful, more energetic, was taking its place. Old Queen Victoria was dead now and gone and the time had come, surely, to abandon the old social corsets and codes. "Live all you can," cries the middle-aged hero of James's *Ambassadors*; "it's a mistake not to." "No Jump about the place, no Life," fumes the ebullient "hero" of Wells's *Tono-Bungay*. "Live!" he cries fiercely. For life itself was fast becoming a subject, an issue. They were forming little societies to improve it. They were meeting in drawing rooms to discuss it. Was there life after death? Good heavens, that wasn't the question. The question was, was there life before death? Hats, for example. Top hats, bowler hats, all kinds of hats. Was it really necessary, as custom dictated, to cover one's head with a hat? Leonard Bast, Forster's unlucky clerk, forgets, as he walks down Regent Street, to wear a hat on his head and for this sin of omission is stared at and glared at. But a new and hatless day was already dawning. Already emancipated people like Thomas and Lawrence and Aldington were boldly appearing in town with nothing at all to cover the hair on their heads, and the heroine of Wells's *Ann Veronica* would be going to socialist meetings with friends of the hatless persuasion, and "plenty of cranks," a reformed Lawrence would later be sourly observing, "went out nowadays without hats, in the rain." Cafés, cabarets, restaurants! How droll! How enchanting! It was the way things were managed in Paris these days, but it wasn't the way they were managed in London where restaurants were scarce and the café and cabaret didn't exist and in all the vast spaces of London, so dark and so wet and forbidding, where on earth could young lovers rencounter or young friends converse or young people simply be young? But now came a development, a new social development. The Aerated Bread Company had lately established in London a new chain of teashops, ABC teashops, where, for the price of two cups of tea and an order of buns, the young could meet to exchange their ideas or even perhaps their mutual affection.

One day in 1910 Frida Strindberg, the estranged second wife of the great Swedish dramatist, came to Chelsea in search of young Wyndham Lewis, her lover, but not finding him there instead passed the night in the bed of his friend, the agreeable Augustus John. It turned out to be a serious mistake. A woman of strong sexual passions which she'd put to the service, she boldly decided, of men of great genius, she haunted Augustus for two nightmare years, uncannily anticipating his every move, greeting him warmly wherever he chanced to appear, threatening him with physical harm should he dare to think well of another or, still more alarmingly, threatening to take her own life. She disappeared from the scene in due time but would soon reappear bringing with her from Paris one of London's first cabarets, the Cave of the Golden Calf. Located in a basement off Regent Street, its center-piece, a golden calf, was fashioned by young Eric Gill and its walls were frescoed, "hideously," by Lewis and company and its columns adorned by Epstein himself with the heads of hawks, cats, and camels, and here, all in furs, her face chalk white, Madame Strindberg who was, as she said, "in kneedt of money" and had "tagen upp brosditdooshun in thiss bardigular forum," would superintend the night's entertain-ments, the amateur theatrics and the young couples dancing the bunny hug and the turkey trot and here avant-garde poets like Pound were glad to be seen in the company of literary swells like Fordie Hueffer and Violet Hunt, and here Rebecca West who, while still in her teens, was already famous as a handsome and fearless young feminist-journalist, would see Katherine Mansfield looking very pretty in a Chinese costume and playing the role of *commère* at a show, and Madame Strindberg herself would one night send one of her guests from her table with the expostulation that she'd sleep with him, yes, but talk to him, never, for "one must," as she put it, "draw a line *some-where*." Pound liked to think that hers was the only nightclub in town to open its doors to "impoverished artists," but two years later, on the eve of the war, John would establish on Greek Street his own cabaret club, the Crabtree, for the delectation of the artists and ac-tresses who came for the live boxing matches that were staged on the premises.

For it wasn't just middle-class men who were pushing the fron-tiers of living. It was also their daughters and even their wives. They wanted to vote, no mistake about that, but even more than to vote they wanted to live, to live and enjoy and be free of all the old moral restraints. Not for naught after all had Ibsen's Nora left her home and her husband behind her. Nor for naught were Nora's descendants, the children of Barker and Shaw, of Bennett and Wells, asserting them-selves in the new British novels and plays. Whether they got the vote or they didn't, they wanted, these eager and angry young women, like Hy-patia in Shaw's *Misalliance*, "to make a fight for living." Like the hero-ine of Wells's *Wheels of Chance*, they wanted "to live a Free Life" and "be [their] own mistress" and "take [their own] place in the world." Good? Bad? Good Lord, what did she care about good and bad? cries the Shavian heroine: "I want to be an active verb." Poor Gwen in Leonard Woolf's novel will try to be such a verb and will fail, but not before she's read Ibsen and thought of herself as another Hilda and "Oh, it all seems to me so foolish—so foolish! Not to be able to grasp at your own happiness—at your own life!" Even Miss Susan Grosvenor, a pretty patrician who was hardly emancipated and would marry the straitlaced John Buchan, would be less than content with her lot. "I want to do something better," as her cousin would say, "than rush up and down Oxford Street looking for beastly bits of tulle."

The bicycle was in fact as important for the New Woman as for the New Man. It may represent for the hero of Wells's *Wheels of Chance* an escape from his lower-class prison and a license to travel at will, but it also represents for the charming young heroine an escape from her middle-class prison and a license to travel about in the world on her own. In skirts? In layers of Victorian skirts that went down to the ankles? "Not bloody likely," as Shaw's Eliza Doolittle would have put it. Bicycle chains being the nasty things they were, a radical change in women's apparel would surely be necessary. Shorter and fewer skirts would be necessary or no skirts at all but knickers instead or the loose-fitting trousers invented for the occasion by Mrs. Bloomer herself. So Annie Horniman who later described herself as "a middle-class, suburban, dissenting spinster," who in 1894 had subsidized Shaw's *Arms and the Man* and would later subsidize Yeats's Irish national theatre, had announced her independence of her rich Quaker family by donning the bloomers and ascending a bicycle. The results were alarming enough. First ankles began to appear and then legs, sometimes up to the knees, but so was born the new woman, "the splendid girl," who was everywhere mounting her bicycle and sailing away to college or work. She and her sisters whirled about in the dense London traffic with such reckless abandon that surely, said Hardy, they risked life and limb; but "oh, nao," he was told by a morose bus conductor; "their sex pertects them. We dares not drive over them, wotever they do; & they do jist wot they likes." In *Love and Mr. Lewisham* Wells had mocked the new woman and her daring new slogan: "What a beautiful phrase that is—to live one's own life!" he had one of his characters scornfully say. But his feelings were mixed. Her slogan was after all his own slogan too. He was himself in the vanguard of those who would live their own lives, who were ready, like workers and women, to take their lives seriously.

Young Bloomsbury may have been skeptical. Life? Good heavens! "I can't believe people think about Life," Lytton Strachey declares. "There's nothing in it." Skeptical too is the "Vanessa" in Leonard Woolf's novel. "He fusses about life with a big L," she complains of the hero who was doubtless Leonard himself. It was nevertheless the Edwardian thing, this passion for life with a big L. It was, for that matter, the Bloomsbury thing. It had started in 1904. Led by Vanessa herself, their tall, stately, duskily beautiful sister, the children of Sir Leslie Stephen, the lately deceased Victorian sage, had walked quickly and quietly out of the nineteenth century. Abandoning Kensington which was a good address for Bloomsbury which was not, the gloomy old mansion at 22 Hyde Park Gate for the braver and brighter apartments at 46 Gordon Square, they were all hope and excitement. No more the Morris wallpaper and the red plush furniture and the rich heavy carpets and drapes and the knickknacks and mats and antimacassars. Their floors would be bare and their walls off-white and their windows, their large, spacious windows, would be hung with blue or white curtains. Why bother with table napkins? Why tea at nine, why not coffee after dinner? Why, for that matter, all social conventions, the search for a husband, the grotesque marriage markets? They wanted, these Bloomsbury girls, a new social agenda. They wanted to paint, they wanted to write, they wanted to be active verbs.

Not, perhaps, at the start. When Leonard Woolf went off that year for Ceylon, their Thursday "evenings" were still rather male, still sedately Victorian. Lytton Strachey was still called Strachey in the sturdy but stuffy Victorian fashion and Maynard Keynes was still called Keynes and when the young ladies were seen at all, it was to take their hands shyly and address them as Miss Stephen or Miss Strachey. But when Leonard returned in 1911 all had changed, had utterly changed. Strachey was now Lytton and Keynes was now Maynard and the ladies were very much there and were greeted with kisses and called Marjorie and Vanessa and Virginia. It was possible, it seemed, for men to treat women as people very much like themselves. It was possible, it seemed, to greet one's friends with their Christian names like the character in Bennett's *The Roll Call* ("I say, what's your Christian name? I hate surnames, don't you?") or, for that matter, like the character in *Women in Love* who plays Lady Ott (" 'How do you do, Gudrun?' sang Hermione, using the Christian name in the fashionable manner"). It was even possible for young men to enter a drawing room without the hat, stick, and gloves that made the handling of teacups and saucers a positive nightmare. Not for them, certainly, for Sir Leslie's daughters, the formal manner and dress of their father's old friends. Vanessa despised the dinners and dances and the fans and the corsets and the long buttoned gloves reaching up to the armpits and, on her part, sister Virginia despised "pouring tea and talking like a lady," despised the chaperone and the cream and the sugar and the passing of buns to blushing young men and the small talk the small talk. Now they were free to discourse till all hours of the night and on serious topics—politics, painting, philosophy—scarcely becoming young ladies of fashion and family and on terms of equality with solemn young men in loose-collared shirts and corduroy trousers who smoked uncouth pipes and languished in basket-chairs and could be silent, it seemed, for minutes, nay hours, at a time.

Lady Ott who was trying to break loose from her family of blue-blooded Philistines was all curiosity. Who, she wanted to know, were these wonderful people who sat round a fire in the darkness and said nothing at all except, on occasion, something terribly witty or clever? Why, these Bloomsbury people, they were her kind of people, exactly. But poor dead Sir Leslie's old friends and companions were a little disheartened. "Deplorable, deplorable!" Henry James would declare. "How could Vanessa and Virginia have picked up such friends?" Bad enough that the glorious Vanessa should have wed in a registrar's office—"What a nuptial 'solemnity'!" But to marry the "stoop-shouldered, long-haired, third-rate Clive Bell" and now to look "as if she had rolled in a duck pond": well, this was too bad. "Tell Virginia—tell her," he wailed, "how sorry I am that the inevitabilities of life should have made it seem possible even for a moment that I would allow any child of her father's to swim out of my ken." One Thursday evening, on the balcony of Lady Ott's Bedford Square place, he would importune the lady not, not on any account to descend below where the scruffy young poets and painters were milling about in their rough day-clothes. "Look at them, dear lady, over the banisters. But don't go down amongst them."

"... That dare not speak its name"

Luckily for James, there were abominations to come that he may by this time have known of but not without fear and reluctance. For those Bloomsbury changes wouldn't be social alone. They'd be sexual too. Not at first. When she joined Henry Lamb, John's dashing disciple, in a tea shop on the Kings Road, Vanessa, unchaperoned, was almost amused. How shocked, she was thinking, her friends and relations would be! And when she invited him to one of her Friday Club meetings, it was necessary to conceal his mistress behind one of the curtains. But then one summer evening in 1908 Lytton Strachey, tall and thin and cadaverous, entered the drawing room. He noticed a stain on Vanessa's white gown and pointed a long bony finger. "Semen?" he asked. There was astonishment first and then laughter and after that Bloomsbury was never the same. "Sex permeated our conversation," Virginia remembered. "The word bugger was never far from our lips. We discussed copulation with the same excitement and openness that we had discussed the nature of good." So, with a word, the old Victorian restraint and reserve fell in ruins. Lytton would be received by the Bells as they lay side by side in their bedroom and would soon be reciting to a delighted Vanessa his most indecent poems. Bad enough that she and Virginia should appear at a ball dressed as Gauguin girls, bare-shouldered, bare-legged, and drive from the hall the shocked elderly ladies. But at Oliver Strachey's fancy dress party, one guest would turn up as a eunuch, another as a pregnant whore, and at Adrian Stephen's, Vanessa would dance stripped to the waist and Marjorie Strachey cover herself with nothing of note but a miniature of the Prince Consort. Even Virginia, who was a touch more prudish, wasn't unliberated. When she paid Rupert Brooke a visit at Grantchester, she swam with him naked one moonlit night in Byron's pool. And when she moved into Brunswick Square it was to share a house with three unattached males, Maynard Keynes and Duncan Grant occupying the ground floor and Leonard Woolf the top. Her

61

stepbrother George was naturally scandalized but "it's quite alright, George," Vanessa assured him, "you see it's so near the Foundling Hospital."

Heterosexual freedom was still more openly preached than practiced in Bloomsbury. But the homosexual passion, that was something else again. Strachey who made no secret of his "amiable absurdity" was highly elated. He had taken to Duncan Grant, his young artist-cousin, and Duncan had more or less taken to him. To his good friend Keynes, Lytton wrote ecstatic letters, to Duncan he ridiculed Keynes and his loveless condition. But his laughter and joy, alas, were but brief. Cousin Duncan became almost instantly friend Maynard's lover. Lytton, whose shame and distress were nearly unbearable, went to Virginia. Would she marry him? he asked her. She would, she replied. He was aghast, however, almost at once, and so for that matter was she. The next day, by mutual agreement, they recanted their "vows." Vanessa was doubtless amused. She would have liked to have Lytton for a brother-in-law, she had thought at one time, but could never imagine it happening unless "he were to fall in love with [brother] Adrian—& even then Adrian would probably reject him." But Virginia who wasn't for nothing Sir Leslie's daughter wasn't amused. Buggery in Plato's Greece was one thing but buggery in Bloomsbury? Buggery at home on Fitzroy Square? "I suppose Duncan has seduced Adrian," she would write rather sadly. "I imagine a great orgy on the river tonight." How could she read, she wrote in distress to Clive, her virile russet-haired brother-in-law, "with Adrian and Duncan swarming on the floor, making it like the bottom of an alligators tank"? And indeed they were quite unashamed, the buggers of Bloomsbury. Generations of dons and schoolmasters had sentimentalized the homosexual affair. It reincarnated, they liked to think, an ancient male passion, the sacred relation of David and Jonathan, Socrates and Alcibiades, Harmodius and Aristogiton. But for the new generation of Stracheys and Keyneses, it was nonsense, sheer nonsense. Their objective was bed and their motive pure pleasure. They called it the Higher Sodomy. As for the women and the lovers of women they made no attempt, these new sodomites, to conceal their revulsion. Is a cow real or isn't it? In the very first chapter of Forster's *Longest Journey* Rickie and his undergraduate friends are busy debating the question, but enter Miss Agnes Pembroke, the abominable female, and at once they disperse in dismay and why indeed would they not? Uneducated, childbearing, long-suffering, the angel in the house was, all things considered, a bore, and her sister, the bluestockinged one, wasn't much better. Out of his window Keynes sees Rupert Brooke "taking her hand, sitting at her feet, gazing at her eyes." "Oh these womanizers," he writes Duncan Grant. "How on earth and what for can he do it." "The love that dare not speak its name"? Not, evidently, in Bloomsbury circles.

"Th' expense of spirit . . ."

Well, it wouldn't be long before the heterosexual life would be just as hectic as the homosexual one. Vanessa, it appeared, was hurt and exasperated. "I hope you'll see your whore soon," she was writing her husband who had already found him a mistress and would never in fact be without one. But this wasn't the problem. The problem was Clive was flirting with sister Virginia and Virginia with him. There were lovers' quarrels and lovers' scenes but they didn't turn out to be Clive's and Vanessa's. They were Clive's and Virginia's, Clive resenting the attention that Strachey was getting from Virginia and denying him access to Gordon Square and Virginia enjoying "the terrible ructions which have split our world." Clive didn't achieve the consummation he may devoutly have wished. You are the cuckoo that lays its eggs in other birds' nests, Virginia told him many years later. "My dear Virginia," he coolly replied, "you never would let me lay an egg in your nest." Just the same, something did change in those palmy days. It was marriage that changed. There was "nothing shocking," Virginia discovered, "in a man's having a mistress, or in a woman's being one."

It was April 1911 when Clive and Vanessa in the company of Roger Fry, at the time the leading lord of the arts in London, set off for Constantinople for a look at the famous mosaics. They were carried away by what they saw, Vanessa and Roger. They would paint thereafter, they said, as if they were doing mosaics. In the bright Turkish sunlight they were happy together, working and sketching. But their idyll wasn't to last. At Broussa in Anatolia, a day's journey from Constantinople and far from medical help, Vanessa miscarried, collapsed, fell gravely ill. The incompetent Clive couldn't cope, but Roger, who was skilled, energetic, omniscient, could. He took command on the spot, and doctored and nursed her to life. In fact he did more: he fell madly in love with his beautiful patient, as she did with him. But wait. On the eve of his Turkish adventure he had called on his friend, Lady Ott, and by the very next morning they were more than good friends and by the time he got back to London it was all over town. Poor Roger was sick with anxiety. He called on Lady Ott and denounced her and left her in tears. But Vanessa was not disaffected and their Anatolian passion was not discontinued and Roger could hardly believe his good luck when the glorious creature would look "round in delight at being so beautiful and at my feeling all of it so much."

Of course there were grave complications. Roger had a wife who was now in a home for the mentally ill and Vanessa had a husband with whom she continued to live and make love. And indeed it wouldn't be long before she'd long for the satyrlike Duncan, once Lytton's and Maynard's joint darling and now her own brother Adrian's and also young David Garnett's, the bisexual son of Edward and Constance. Would he mind it, Vanessa asked Bunny, as David was called, would he very much mind it if Duncan gave her a child? Not at all, he replied. Delighted, in fact. Needless to say, Roger Fry was in agony. Duncan has asked me to sit for him, Vanessa would taunt him. Would you care to paint me at the same time? Would that console you? Why, she'd bathe in the bathroom while Duncan was shaving and why would she not, she'd be telling her lover, for "he wanted to shave and I wanted to have my bath . . . and he didn't see why he should move and I didn't see why I should remain dirty. . . ." But it was all in the end very civilized. Vanessa and Duncan would be lovers for life and Clive would be as before the good-natured husband who felt for his rivals no unseemly resentment and was perfectly free to live and to love as he pleased, and as for Roger himself, he'd continue as their intimate friend and offer critiques of their work which they'd laugh at and in point of fact did Vanessa ever forsake him entirely, her one-time beloved? Many years later, at the time of his death, her daughter Angelica would hear a strange noise coming out of her bedroom. It didn't sound like her mother at all. It sounded more like a creature howling in anguish. H. G. Wells was thoroughly mystified. How could the odious Clive have fathered Vanessa's exquisite Angelica? The answer was that he hadn't. Angelica Bell was Duncan's daughter.

Just a month before Fry and the Bells had departed for Constantinople, Bertrand Russell, en route to Paris, had arrived at Bedford Square to spend the night with his friends the Morrells. Philip wasn't at home as it happened, but Lady Ottoline was. That night the philosopher unburdened himself. "There is always a tragedy in everyone's life," he told her sadly. His own, for example. He wasn't happy at all in his home. Nine years before, as he bicycled near Grantchester, he had discovered to his horror that he no longer cared for his wife who was all Quaker virtue and wore flannel nightgowns to bed. What to do? What else but destroy her affection. He told her his love was dead. He declined to share her bed. He treated her with disdain. Alys, poor soul, was in misery. She wept bitter tears. She was lonely. Occasionally she would come to him in her poor flannel gown and beg him to join her and sometimes he would but then only rarely and with scant satisfaction. Of course he regretted it. He wasn't a monster. "Oh the pity of it! How she was crushed and broken!" But not for nothing was he called "The Day of Judgment." Lady Ott had been apprehensive. Would she not bore the distinguished logician? But she didn't. *Au contraire.* To his surprise and delight she responded at once to his first shy advances. The next morning, like Fry a few weeks before, Russell left London the happiest of men.

For Lady Ott had had a very different life history. Not for her the flannel nightgown. Not for her nine years of barren self-denial. She had always loved men for their souls but since souls, it seemed, didn't come without bodies, she had had to love them for their bodies as well. The mysterious Dr. Axel Munthe, for one, who had declined, however, to marry the six-feet-tall evangelical maiden on the grounds that he had as it was "quite enough nerve cases among my patients." Herbert Asquith, the future prime minister of England, for another, who would rush up the stairs to the room at the top of the great family mansion near Buckingham Palace, though since he had a passion for poetry no less than for women, it was hard to say just what was his object. A kiss? An embrace? A discussion of "poetry, religion and the ways of life of Wordsworth, Tennyson and Browning"? Of course there was marriage, early in the century, to the awfully nice Philip Morrell ("I'm glad I'm not in your shoes," her brother Lord Charles had informed him. "I wouldn't undertake her for anything"); but this didn't slacken the flow of her lavish affections. At a Christmas party in 1907 in the London house of Ethel Sands, an American painter and art patroness, Augustus John was late. There was talk of his life and loves, of Dorelia, his marvelous mistress, of the tragic death in Paris of his young wife Ida. By the time he arrived, Lady Ott may well have been smitten already. "Would you sit to me?" he would ask her at table with a manly abruptness, and why would she not? The very next day she'd be off to his Fitzroy Street studio with Philip beside her and many a day thereafter with Philip no longer beside her. Augustus himself wasn't indifferent. A devotee of the arts in London, the lady was a power to be reckoned with, in addition to which there was the majesty of her person and presence, her towering height and her long pale face and her masses of dark red Venetian hair, the color of marmalade, as Russell remembered it, but darker, and her hats, her extravagant hats, one of which recalled, it was said, "a crimson tea-cozy trimmed with hedgehogs," and her long muslin veils and her dresses, bizarre and baroque, which could be Grecian one day and Cossack another and oriental another. For Gertrude Stein she was a "marvelous female version of Disraeli," for Osbert Sitwell "a rather oversize Infanta of Spain or Austria," and for Virginia Woolf a "Spanish Armada in full sail" which, many years later, was exactly how John would put her on canvas.

At the time, though, he must have been just a little dismayed by the monster of love he'd created, by the baronial nose and the prognathous jaw, by the rumble and drawl of her upper-class speech and the streams of her letters and presents and unannounced visits. 'Twas Dorelia he loved and only Dorelia, he pleaded, in loving whom he was true to the memory of his dear deceased wife. "You will not continue to suffer too much. You will have the fortitude of great hearts & unconquerable . . ." But he needn't have worried. His mistress Dorelia was as strong and shrewd as she was charming and beautiful. When she asked Lady Ott to help her look for a school for Gus's young boys, she stopped by at the Fitzroy Street studio where the bewitching young Lamb was then staying and "Won't you come in for a moment?" he would ask the great lady who was waiting outside in the taxi and indeed would she not? With his pale face and his golden hair and his strange goat eyes, the young man "seemed to come," she'd declare, "from a vision of Blake." Dorelia who had once been his mistress hadn't miscalculated, and "I burn to embrace you," Lamb was soon writing the lady, "& cover all your body with mine," and Lady Ott for her part would invite him to her cottage at Peppard near Henley-on-

Thames, converting the coach house into a studio and finding him lodgings in the Dog Inn nearby.

That year she had met Lytton Strachey whose reputation for scandal and wit quite alarmed her. Would he come to Peppard, she asked him nervously? Henry Lamb, a ravishing youth, would be there. Lytton accepted with joy. He worshiped noble names and noble dames but, more to the point, he worshiped the ravishing youth whom he'd met once before and allowed to elude him. Indeed, Ottoline wondered at first if he hadn't come to see Henry rather than her. She could hear them at night laughing and jesting together in the sitting room beneath her bedroom, and soon, she was noting, the lovesick Lytton was "wearing his hair very long, like Augustus John, and having his ears pierced and wearing ear-rings" and round his neck, instead of a tie, a "rich purple silk scarf." But there was, *mirabile dictu*, no division. Henry was, she was happy to find, incurably heterosexual and she and Lytton were soon tittling and tattling together like a pair of old dowager duchesses. Lytton was never quite sure which of the two he cared for the more, "Our Lady of Bedford Square" as he called her, or the delectable boy with the strange goat's eyes. Henry discovered them locked in a violent embrace and thought he saw blood on Lytton's pale lips. But it was quite all right. The lady was but doing her best to make Lytton bisexual.

In May 1911, however, all Lady Ottoline's roosters came home to roost. There was Henry Lamb fled in a fit of grief or rage to Paris, she joining him there in "that incredible little room where you, holy woman, lay . . . & received me." Then there was Roger Fry who had left for the East her lover and returned now her enemy and was entering her home to confront and disown her. And then last but not least there was Bertie Russell who knew nothing at all of Lamb or of Fry and had just returned from Paris to claim her. He had gone straight to Alys, who had raged and raged. She would divorce him. She would implicate his titled lover. But he had been adamant. After giving her niece a lesson in Locke, he had mounted his bicycle and ridden away to his new life and love, to Bloomsbury rooms and hotels and to Studlands in Dorset where Philip, "infuriatingly broadminded," would allow his wife and her lover three idyllic days together. Their passion was perhaps incomplete. She had, Bertie said, "a long thin face something like a horse." And she, she "could hardly bear," she confessed, "the lack of physical attraction." Nevertheless they were happy together. He adored her, he said, "with all the passion of a fierce nature long starved and lonely," and what, she cried on her part, was body compared to the soul? Indeed, she came out of her crisis that month in fairly good shape. She persuaded Russell that she was necessary to Lamb and Lamb that she was necessary to Russell and Philip that she was necessary to both. Her Russell affair would come to an end in 1916. "What a pity," he would tell her in parting, "your hair is going grey."

"Black beetles"

For some of course it was all too much, this Bloomsbury life. Walter Lamb, the amiable but diffident brother of the libidinous Henry, would like perhaps to marry her, he told Virginia, but . . . But what, she asked him? "You live in a hornets' nest," he said. Walter was, it may be, a little lacking in push but bolder spirits than his would be troubled by Bloomsbury's brazen new manners and morals. Rupert Brooke's, for example. He had fallen in love with Katherine Cox whose simple peasant good nature was such that "to be with her was like sitting in a green field of clover." But Katherine—Ka to her friends—had developed a crush on the ubiquitous Lamb and when she and Rupert joined their Bloomsbury mates for a weekend in Dorset, she persuaded Strachey, himself in pursuit of the glamorous youth, to invite him too. Rupert was naturally distraught. Neopaganism was all very well in its way but this was more than even the Prince of Pagans could bear. And when Ka refused to part with Lamb and his malevolent genius, the handsome young poet lost much of his charm and aplomb. He denounced not Strachey alone, whom he accused of pandering for Lamb, but all his old Bloomsbury friends and their gargoylish world, Lady Ottoline included and Duncan Grant and Virginia who had bathed with him naked in the good old neopagan days. He referred darkly to "the subtle degradation of the collective atmosphere of the people in those regions" and soon would be dining with James and the Duchess of Leeds and cruising on the Admiralty yacht with the Asquiths and Churchills and writing those famous war sonnets that were rather derisive on the subject of sick loves and empty hearts.

Rupert may well have been at the time, as his friends suspected, just a little deranged. But Bloomsbury affected young Lawrence in much the same way. One day in Cambridge he had called with Russell on Maynard Keynes. "It was," he said, "one of the crises in my life." Keynes had emerged from his darkened bedroom at noon and, as he stood in his pajamas blinking in the sunlight, "a knowledge passed into me, which has been like a little madness to me ever since." What was it, this knowledge, this knowledge that maddened? These Bloomsbury people—Keynes and Grant and their sodomite kind—were "beetles, black beetles." "I like men to be beasts—but insects—one insect mounted on another—oh God!" "You must leave these 'friends,' these beetles," he was telling young David Garnett. "Go away, David," he was saying, "and try to love a woman." By this time the Morrells had moved into Garsington, their exotic estate near Oxford, where the new sexual bliss would become orgiastic and Fry would listen all night "to doors opening and shutting in the long passage" and everyone making passionate love "from the pugs and the peacocks to Ott and the Prime Minister." Poor Lawrence was deeply distressed. It was, he thought, the end of the world. "All along the Bristol Channel the gorse was coming out," he was sadly reflecting, "but it will never be springtime in the world for us." Well, he may have been right to be horrified, terrified. He was himself, it appeared, a black beetle of sorts. His marriage to Frieda, his golden-haired, green-eyed Brunhild, was a touch overwhelming and soon he'd be courting a young Cornish farmer and "the nearest I've ever come to perfect love," he would later confess, "was with a young coal miner when I was about sixteen."

"The open sex war of 1900–1914"

But it wasn't of course just a Bloomsbury phenomenon, this free-and-easy homo- and heterosexuality. It was an Edwardian and post-Edwardian phenomenon. Live, live, cried the eager Edwardians. But to live, what was that but to love, and to love, what was that but to make love, somehow, anyhow? God was dead, was he not, and religion a shambles and what was there left to revere but the man and the woman and the relation between them? It was time for a new dispensation. After two thousand years of Christianity ("twenty centuries of stony sleep"), the war between spirit and flesh had all but disabled your middle-class Englishman. Like J. M. Barrie who had married a pretty young actress but was powerless to rise to the sexual occasion. Like little Max Beerbohm who'd marry his Florence and take her to Italy but couldn't promise to consummate their marital union, for "I like you better than any person in the world," as he told her. "But the other sort of caring is beyond me." Like young George Trevelyan, the budding historian, who, on the day of his wedding, left his poor anxious bride to languish alone in a room in the Lizard whilst he went on a vigorous forty-mile hike, "a somewhat curious beginning," Bertrand Russell believed, "for a honeymoon." Or, for that matter, like the great flabby Gilbert Chesterton who, on the night of *his* wedding, left his dearly beloved at the White Horse near Ipswich while he went for a walk in the country and managed inevitably to get himself lost, and forsooth when he plucked up his courage and found his way back and entered her bed with his large childish body, it was to have her cry out in anguish and shrink from his touch and drive him away full of guilt and remorse.

No wonder he cherished his childhood, those untroubled years before the demon of sex had invaded the nursery. For like Barrie's strange Peter Pan, that eternal child forever unsullied by sex and the world, he was one of those boys who just couldn't grow up, who made a point of being helplessly childlike, or childishly helpless, of finding himself in the wrong part of town or struggling into the wrong pair of trousers or having his Frances, his little wife/mother, put on his bowtie which he never did learn how to fasten, much less how to find, dear fellow, dear Dickensian fellow. Mr. Dick? Mr. Skimpole? ("O joy! that in our embers/ Is something that doth live. . . .") Robert Blatchford the socialist was frankly disgusted. While he had gone out in the rain to get a cab for his wife, Frances had gone out to get a cab for her husband. Frances was in fact just a little exasperated. Why, she would ask Gilbert, why did he find it impossible to get to a train on time? "My dear," he'd reply, "I couldn't earn our daily bread if I had to study timetables." "Fear not," he'd assure her after the death of her favorite sister. "I shall wash myself." Gilbert chuckled a lot and was jolly and liked jolly things like the Catholic church and medieval tapestries and old English taverns and pubs and of course old English peasants. But poor fretful Frances wasn't amused. She called him, acidly, the "Jolly Journalist." "Labour is blossoming or dancing where/ The body is not bruised to pleasure soul," as the poet would be putting it. But it wasn't blossoming or dancing for the likes of the Beerbohms, Trevelyans, and Chestertons.

Nor for the likes of the George Bernard Shaws. The Fabian giant wasn't a sexual incompetent. For years "a compulsive philanderer"—he had the head, Rebecca West said, of "a flirtatious Moses"—he had loved and been loved in his day by Annie Besant, by Edith Nesbit, by May and by Eleanor, the daughters, respectively, of Morris and Marx. It's even on record that he went to bed with his mother's good friend, the widowed Jenny Patterson who was fifteen years his senior, and, following her, with Florence Farr, the freethinking, free-loving beauty who was dearly beloved of many. But in spite of it all Shaw's heart wasn't in it. He was no more, it turned out, than a sheep in wolf's clothing. Ejaculation he came to detest as obscene and copulation itself, "the syringeing of women by men," as an act of aggression for which he felt bound to apologize. The *ménage à trois* wasn't, it's true, entirely unknown to him. Back in bohemian Dublin his ambitious mother and alcoholic father had been joined by a third, by one Vandeleur Lee, an inspired teacher of voice who became her Zvengali, her musical master. Doubtless preferring the role of the one to that of the other, Shaw would become for his married friends and associates—the Salts and the Blands among others—what Vandeleur Lee had been for his parents, *l'ami de la maison*. More likely to love than to make love, and enjoying the role of the "Sunday husband," he'd have all the pleasures of family and home without having to pay the sexual price. So when in the 1890s he came to renounce the habit of marriage, it wasn't alone that it reduced women to slavery. It was also on the grounds that it reduced men to slavery. Dionysiac Wells's quarrel with marriage was that it wasn't licentious enough. Apollonian Shaw's was that it was all too licentious, a man and a woman alone in one room for eight hours and not every month, not every week, but, God save the mark, every night. Not in vain the refugee from the Protestant chapel, Shaw was in fact sure that the life of the body must diminish the life of the mind and that had he succumbed to sexual indulgence, "a startling deterioration would have appeared in my writing before the end of a fortnight." Hence his decision to abandon the bed for the sake of his art. The last lines of *Candida*—"Let me go now. The night outside grows impatient"—were originally meant for the heroine, for marriage and sex in their fullness, but Shaw changed his mind and gave them to Marchbanks, the anemic young poet, and declared that the ecstasy of the body was as nothing compared with the ecstasy of artistic creation. "Do you know anyone who will buy for twopence a body for which I have no longer any use? I have made tolerable love with it in my time; but now I have found nobler instruments—the imagination of a poet, the heart of a child. . . ." Shaw would shrewdly call Chesterton the real Peter Pan of his time and for very good reason. He would himself be the child, be the bodiless boy who wouldn't grow up.

It was indeed with the women as with the men, this bruising the body to pleasure the soul. Virginia Stephen had no intention of marrying Leonard. "As I told you brutally the other day I feel no physical attraction in you." But then Leonard on his part felt no physical attraction in her. What moved him, he seemed to think, was "a curious excitement of the mind, rather than the body." Beatrice Webb had no intention of marrying Sidney. A tall dark-eyed beauty with sensuous mouth and flowing brown hair, how could she bear to suffer his body, "his tiny tadpole body"? But bear it she did, for what was bodily intercourse compared with the mental, "the act of *combined thinking*," as she herself phrased it, "in which the experience . . . of the two intellects became inextricably mingled"? So when poor Sidney sent her his photograph, she declined to look at it. "No dear . . . ," she told him. "It is too hideous . . . it is the head only that I am marrying." For all her pleasure in sex Lady Ottoline was no less than Beatrice a slave to the spirit. What a torment to her was that dry little body of Russell's! Yet what a pleasure was the power of his mind! At Peppard where they had tea in the forest and read Plato, Spinoza, and Shelley together, she was, she said, so inspired by "the pure fire of his soul" that "his unattractive body seemed to disappear, his spirit and mine united in one flame, the flame of his soul penetrated mine." But the strain, the unendurable strain! When she left his Bloomsbury hotel she dreaded looking up at the window and seeing the pale hungry face of her lover glaring down like a gargoyle's, and at last reaching home she would fling out her arms and dance round her room and "free! free!" she would cry in ecstatic relief.

Small wonder the author of *Women in Love* was distressed, and in his Hermione, his portrait of Ottoline, would denounce this addiction to soul. For was this not, said Lawrence, the English disease, the disease that had cankered the lives of Ruskin and a whole generation of middle-class Englishmen and was cankering now the lives of a new generation of Beerbohms and Chestertons? Not to mention, God help him, his own. "I'm in exactly the same predicament," he'd write after reading Barrie's *Sentimental Tommy*. For no less than Shaw he was anguished by sex, "Sex, which breaks up our integrity, our single inviolability, our deep silence,/ Tearing a cry from us." There must be a new dispensation, he said, a new dispensation that restored the communion of body and soul. In *Sons and Lovers* he'd attempted to exorcise the ghost of the spirit and the dread of the flesh. Now in his poems to Frieda and in novels like *The Rainbow* and *Women in Love* he'd attempt to celebrate marriage, not the *mariage blanc* of the Barries and Beerbohms but bodily marriage, real, unashamed. Lawrence, to be sure, was troubled, divided. Like the Shaws and the Chestertons he was never quite free to accept the new order of things, the summons of sex, the appeal of the body. Not so, however, were others like Hueffer, like Hulme. "The only thing really interesting and unfathomable was love," Hueffer would surprisingly say, "not the higher kind, but the lower kind." "If the mind is immortal, the body must be too," the philosopher Hulme would insist, "for they can't exist apart—so that sex shall endure." As for Norman Douglas, he would shortly announce the death and destruction of all the Victorians had thought written in stone. Sanctity? "I believe you have the making of a saint in you. Fight against it." Chastity? "Chastity is a dead donkey. . . . Who killed it? The experience of every sane man and woman on earth." Soul? "Get rid of it . . . you've perhaps got something better than a soul, after all." "What is that?" "A body."

The king, it's quite true, would not have approved. He was a bit of a stickler for form and fidelity. But, "a pleasant, affable sort of royalty," he wasn't about to be priggish about it. "It doesn't matter what you do," he would say, "so long as you don't frighten the horses." So he'd expel from the court the Duke and Duchess of Marlborough on the ground of their pending divorce and still consort with his Mrs. George Keppel and his other *amours*. Was it alone "the birds singing in Greek" that Virginia Woolf heard at the time of her breakdown and madness? Nay, it was also His Majesty among "the azaleas using the foulest possible language." As for the lords and ladies of the realm, their freedom from marital cant and convention was already legendary. At the London theatres it wasn't unusual to see the "wives and mistresses of the same men all mixed up and friendly together," and in the long weekend parties at their country estates it wasn't unusual for lovers to be thoughtfully placed in adjoining apartments. By reason of their high-minded interest in art and philosophy and because they would sit and discuss at some length their spiritual states, the beautiful people who gathered at Stanway, the great country house of Lord and Lady Elcho, were known as "the Souls." But the Countess of Warwick thought them "more pagan than soulful" and not without reason. Lady Mary was, from the very first days of her marriage, the lover of Balfour, the Tory commander, and her husband, Lord Hugo, a "card-playing and cynical aristocrat," was consoled by the company of a beautiful lady who had just left her husband. It was a very wise child, it was said of the Souls and their world, that knew its own father.

Henry James who was all for propriety and adored the estates of the rich and the titled may not himself have escaped the contagion. He deplored it of course. It saddened him. The accession of Edward VII, "an arch-vulgarian," was bound to reduce, he believed, the tone of the court and the country. In the meantime, however, he had suffered, poor man, an awful "vastation," had undergone a sea change of sorts, a sexual sea change. After a long life of fear and repression, he was fondly befriending Morton Fullerton, a Parisian journalist with a vivid and various sexual history, and falling in love—"first love"—with young Hendrik Anderson, an American sculptor he'd encountered in Italy, and soon he'd be shaving the beard which had made him look old and Victorian and consorting with ardent young men like Hugh

Walpole, the newly arrived London novelist, and Percy Lubbock who adored the man and his work, and Jocelyn Persse, the enchanting blond nephew of Lady Gregory, and was writing long letters in the language of sensual affection ("I lay my hands on you and draw you close to me"; "You touch and penetrate me to the quick . . ."; "Hold me in your heart, even as I hold you in my arms") and words were appearing, in point of fact, which had never appeared in his letters before, words like "penis" and "bottom." Bernard Shaw was astounded. In an access of tenderness, James, once the soul of discretion, had thrown his arms about him and kissed him on both cheeks. When James and John Buchan were invited to look into Lord Byron's letters, these "masses of ancient indecency" as Buchan would call them, it was Buchan who recoiled from them, not Henry James. "His only words for some special vileness," Buchan remembered, "were 'singular'—'most curious'—'nauseating, perhaps, but how quite inexpressibly significant.' " Little wonder he could sympathize with his friend Edith Wharton whose sexual life, like his own, had of late been aroused for the very first time. After a barren marriage of some twenty years, she'd surrendered herself first to James's friend Fullerton, "the priapean New Englander," and then perhaps to one Walter Berry, an old Paris hand and a friend of long standing, a "soul mate." When Edith and Berry came over to join him in London, it was James himself who arranged for their rooms at the Berkeley though it was, he nervously noted, "for her (not *them*)" that he did it. He had even had Edith and Morton to virginal Lamb House, "to dinner and for night," and "I don't pretend to understand or to imagine," he'd write her, his own Lambert Strether all over again. "And yet . . . I am still moved to say 'Don't *conclude!*' . . . Live it all through, every inch of it. . . ."

It was for freethinking Edwardians as for high-thinking ones. What was good for the lords was good for the commons. So Galsworthy, grey and subdued, lived more or less secretly with his married cousin and for some forty years Edward Garnett had a liaison with one Nellie Heath, he and Constance living together or apart as they pleased, and William Archer, the drama critic and translator of Ibsen and, it would seem, as solemn and dry as a stick or a Scot, would long have an interest in Elizabeth Robins, the blue-eyed, dark-haired Ibsenite actress. Even old Hardy, by 1910, an ancient of seventy, wasn't inactive. For several years he'd been covertly courting the thirty-year-old Florence Emily Dugdale whom he'd introduce to Lady Gregory as his "young cousin" and eventually make, with the death of the first, the second Mrs. Hardy. Conrad, it's true, wasn't this way inclined. Like Joyce he'd cherish the bourgeois marriage, the homemaking wife with no literary pretensions. In 1896, taking shelter in the National Gallery from a downpour of rain, he had made Jessie George an offer she couldn't refuse. "Look here, my dear, we had better get married and out of this. Look at the weather." Jessie who was slender and beautiful at the time and sixteen years younger than this strange refugee from the sea would take on weight with the years, Virginia Woolf calling her "a lump of a wife," Lady Ott "a good and reposeful mattress for this hypersensitive, nerve-racked man." But no matter. After twenty years abroad and afloat and at large in a world that he didn't love and that didn't love him, the sea-wanderer must have longed for the haven, the heaven, of a family and home. "Waving from window, spread of welcome,/ Kissing of wife under single sheet."

In the free-living, free-loving world of Edward VII, however, Conrad wasn't exemplary. Bland, Hubert Bland of Fabian fame, on the other hand, was. Grandly attired in frocked coat, stiff shirt, and high collar, and claiming a military background not to mention descent from the old Catholic gentry of Yorkshire, he was every inch the Victorian gentleman and was quick to denounce the sexual fads of the time and all deviations from the social proprieties. The young artists and socialists who came for the weekend to Well Hall, the rambling old house at Eltham he occupied with his wife, "Edith Nesbit"—she wrote children's stories and earned heaps of money—were rather impressed by this boisterous, broad-shouldered man who wore a fierce eyeglass and had "a voice like the scream of an eagle," and they quite adored Edith—they called her Madame—who was tall and dark and attractive and, very artistic, "a raffish Rossetti," wore a long trailing gown of peacock blue satin and Indian bangles from her wrist to her elbow and a long cigarette holder that she puffed on incessantly. Yet though all seemed a refuge of charm and content, the young men were sometimes perplexed. The romantic old house was filled, it appeared, with unattached females and blithe little children of mysterious origin. From behind closed doors there sometimes came sounds of anger and tears. And, truth to tell, all was not as it seemed. In addition to chain-smoking Edith who was already seven months pregnant when she married her Hubert, there was one Alice Hoatson whom, big with child, the generous Hubert had installed as their housekeeper on the grounds that, as virtuous socialists, they could hardly neglect an un-married mother and whose child, Rosamund, the good Edith was per-suaded to adopt as her own even before she discovered that Bland himself was the father. Later on, Miss Hoatson would even produce, this time with Edith's consent, a fine little son. H. G. Wells, no mean womanizer himself, was amused. As his Fabian associate cheerfully ex-plained, in the course of recounting his sexual adventures, why would he not give his all to the social and moral conventions? If they didn't exist in full force, where or wherefore the pleasure in flouting them? The charm of it all escaped Edith's biographer. The man, she protested, would never let women alone. But then why would he? Edgar Jepson responded. "Had they wished him to leave them alone . . . ," ran his logic, "they would surely have told him so." In the ten or more years of their friendship, he had never known Hubert "to have more than two, or perhaps three, at a time." Intolerable, was it? Not at all. Married or not, Hubert would go his way and Edith hers, "an arrangement," said Jepson, "not uncommon . . . among both the fashionable and the ad-vanced."

No need to frighten the horses of course. Nevertheless, there were those in Edwardian London who didn't mind frightening the beasts and even stampeding them. Havelock Ellis and Edward Carpenter, for example. Not for them the clandestine sexual vagaries of the king and the Souls, whose pleasure it was to fly in the face of all rule and re-straint. Ellis and Carpenter would change them, these rules and re-straints, would attack them in print and in public with the frankness and freedom that Bloomsbury attacked them at home and in private. This sexual passion wasn't, they said, a moral question at all, of right and wrong, of normality and abnormality. It was simply there, ir-refutably there. Why fear it, then, why repress it? Enjoy, enjoy. Of course there was marriage, the Christian middle-class marriage, but this was the problem. It was too cribbed and confining, too mean and exclusive. "Bigoted connubiality," G. B. Shaw called it. "*Égoisme à deux*," D. H. Lawrence would call it. The monogamous marriage had long been considered, said Havelock Ellis, the only legitimate form of the man-woman relation, but was it? Men and women were naturally polyerotic, he said. They were "able," he said, "to experience affection for more than one person." The pity of it, Edward Carpenter cried, and the tragedy too! All over England the great gaunt Victorian houses were haunted by poor maiden aunts, poor creatures condemned by the social conventions to withering loneliness, to sexual starvation. Why not release them, relieve them? Let there be marriages, Carpenter said, but let them be larger and more generous ones. Why not "intimacies with outsiders"? Why not "wide excursions of the pair from each other?" Why not "triune and other such relations"? Why not . . .

Why not indeed, said H. G. Wells who, calling our civilization "a sexual lunatic," was very much on their side. Not for him, either, the closet philanderings of the Blands or the solemn asides of the Garnetts and Galsworthys. He'd join what he'd call "the open sex war of 1900–1914," would openly practice what he'd preached in his *Anticipations* and *Modern Utopia*, freedom to love and let love, freedom from marriage's sexual restrictions. With new contraceptives available now, it was possible, surely, to treat sexual intercourse as a social diversion on a level with golfing or cards. So he'd reach this agreement with his gentle wife Jane. The marriage of course would continue but there'd be what in Paris they called the "passade," not, you understand, an enduring affair, but a lighthearted sexual digression that civilized people naturally indulged. True, they were none of them Jane's, these little passades. They were all H.G.'s, on the average some three or four conquests per annum. Dorothy Richardson, for example, Jane's old school companion, who briefly became, more or less willingly, his lover, and at roughly the same time, Violet Hunt, who was not to be lured into the tool shed he used for a study at Spade House but who didn't deny him herself in the lodging-house bedrooms of Soho and Pimlico. Later on would be Rebecca West who, though, at nineteen, twenty-six years younger than he, "demanded to be my lover," and the droll little Countess von Arnim, now Lady Russell, who had once caravaned in the rain with the young Morgan Forster and, later on still, Odette Keun who, asked condescendingly by Lady Grenfell what her interest in life chiefly was, candidly answered, in a thick foreign accent, "fucking."

What on earth did they see in the man? Short and slight and with small hands and feet, he was no Henry Lamb, no Rupert Brooke. But he had gusto and charm and "limpid blue eyes" and perhaps, as he chose to believe, there did come from his flesh the sweet odor of violets. Was it his mind, his humor, his energy she found most seductive in him? Maugham asked one of Wells's lovers. None of all three, she replied. His body, she said, smelled of honey. Whatever the cause, not even the daughters of his Fabian friends were safe from his sexual

charms. Hubert Bland was enraged. Bad enough that the cad had betrayed a confidence, had reported to Rosamund, his teenaged daughter,
brown-eyed and tender, the facts of her father's roosterish history. The
blighter would practice on the innocent creature the same dastardly
wiles of which he was master. Indeed, he'd rush off to Paddington Station, rescue the child from a fate worse than death, and deliver to her
ravening, would-be seducer a towering Victorian lecture. Why, the man
was a fox let loose in a hencoop and soon would seduce Amber Reeves
who was brilliant and beautiful and just out of Cambridge and at
twenty a whole generation his junior and "Give me a child!" she would
cry. By April 1909 she'd be pregnant and that fall would be fleeing to
France with the adulterous adult and on New Year's Eve, back in England again, would give birth, H.G. would announce, to "a ripping
child." Needless to say, there was consternation in London. Maud, her
mother, an ardent feminist who had fought at Wells's side at the
Fabian barricades, was sick with remorse and Pember, her father, was
denouncing "Wells and his paramour" and sitting in the big bow-
window of the Savile Club, where, pistol beside him, he was scanning
the street in either direction. Enter, too, Shaw and his Fabian friends
like a chorus of old maiden aunts. H.G. was a rotter, a scoundrel. He
must break with Amber or, failing that, must divorce poor Jane and
marry the girl. Wells wasn't ready to yield. ("Bacon-fed knaves, they
hate us youth.") He was ready, he said, to flee once again with Amber
and child to the Continent. ("What, ye knaves, young men must live!")
But Amber wasn't ready for the sake of one marriage to break up another and had discovered in any case that her middle-aged lover wasn't
quite the folk hero she'd imagined. He was but a half-time bohemian.
The other half was all very British, the scolding, tyrannical male who
was often impatient and would run over to Hampstead to join Jane
and his boys. Besides, Wells didn't want, after all, to be the bounder
from Bromley, to be banished from the Savile and the best London
houses. He liked playing the part of "the Goethe-like libertine," as Mrs.
Webb put it, but he couldn't help wanting to be in addition "the respectable family man and famous littérateur."

So, chastened a little, a little contrite, H.G. would capitulate. He'd
stop seeing Amber, he'd put her behind him. Of course he was also
chagrined and bewildered. The world had failed him, he must have
been thinking, but hadn't he somehow or other failed it? He had offered himself as the hope of the future, as the hope of the young, the

refused, the unhappy, but he hadn't been good enough. Alas, was this what in Paris they called a "passade"? This social confusion? This public disgrace? No need to mock the man and his failure, however. He *was* an adventurer, a bold buccaneer, but the world out there was immense and uncaring, and what could he do in the end but give way, return in defeat to Jane and the home and the smiles of the great? They were his purchase against the world, his only purchase. His stay against darkness, his only stay. In a gallery on Bond Street he caught sight of the young and beautiful Brynhild Olivier, she of the Fabian Nursery, and outcast and shy and ashamed, he hid behind one of the pictures. When she saw him and called out his name in her young clear voice, he took to his heels, but, wonderful girl that she was, she pursued and chastised him. "I won't let you cut me, Mr. Wells. So don't ever dare to try to do it again."

Now Augustus John, he was quite something else. No half-time bohemian like little H.G., what were the horses to him and his band of marauders? Not for him, certainly, the bourgeois marriage, "the dull home, the unspeakable fireside, the gruesome dinner table." Would she, he asked Ida, his handsome young wife, share his heart and his home with his mistress Dorelia, and Ida, marvelous creature, agreed. Two years later, to the mutual grief of husband and mistress, Ida would die in a Parisian hospital of childbed fever. In John's inner circle the *ménage à trois* was not for a fact the very last word. The *ménage à quatre* was always a distinct possibility. After Ida's death Dorelia would sleep with Henry Lamb and John with Euphemia, Henry's exquisite young bride, and there was an agreement, it seems, that they'd live and love and travel together, except that Euphemia demurred and was found one day with a loaded revolver and ready to shoot herself and/or Henry whom she soon decided, however, to abandon instead. No matter. Not many years later the irrepressible Lamb would propose to Lady Ottoline not a *ménage à trois* or a *ménage à quatre* but a *ménage à six* consisting of her and Philip and John and Dorelia and Helen Maitland, his own current mistress, with himself in the middle, one happy bee, flitting from one to the other. Homosexual Bloomsbury, it goes without saying, was downright disgusted. "That Lamb family sickens me," Duncan Grant was writing to Strachey, calling John and Dorelia "the devils and the others merely absurd." And "Oh John!" Lytton was writing him back. "Oh . . . what a 'warning'! as the Clergy say. When I think of him, I often feel that the only thing to do is to chuck up everything and make a dash for some such safe secluded office-stool as is pressed by dear Maynard's happy bottom."

In the meantime the young green-eyed Pound had already established a phallocratic renown not inferior to that of Augustus himself. In the drawing rooms of the time, they were reciting a poem called "Virgin's Prayer."

> Ezra Pound
> And Augustus John
> Bless the bed
> That I lie on.

Not in vain after all had he studied the troubadour poets of Provence ("Lovely thou art, to hold me close and kisst . . .") with their dreams of fair women unhappy in castles, Francescas, Isoldes, Contessas of Beziers. On the mantel of his flat in South Kensington stood the picture of a girl and beneath it, perpetually burning, a candle. Who was she, this adored, this adorable one? Bride Scratton, a young married woman he'd encountered at one of Yeats's Monday night meetings? Dorothy Shakespear, the daughter of Olivia Shakespear, "the most charming woman in London"? Hilda Doolittle of Philadelphia, tall, blond, and blue-eyed, and dreamy, and wistful, who'd become under his influence the notable poet H.D.? The mysterious identity, William Carlos Williams remembered, "he never revealed to me." To her or some other he wrote a love letter on a separate sheet of which he indited the words, "To build a dream over the world." Under the circumstances what was marriage, the boring middle-class marriage, to Ezra? It was love, illicit love, he would sing with his Guidos and Arnaut Daniels. "Ah me, the darn, the darn it comes toe sune!"

In 1901 in benighted America he had fallen in love with the striking Miss Doolittle and by 1905 had pledged her his troth and in 1910 would persuade her to join him in London. But by the time she arrived he was already courting Miss Shakespear and, as she'd soon learn from others, not from Ezra, was already engaged to the young English lady. What a dilemma for a shy, inexperienced Philadelphia girl, but Pound took it all in his stride. As a latter-day troubadour he was in no hurry to marry Miss Shakespear and in the Kensington studio of the novelist, May Sinclair, he'd be plying Miss Doolittle with kisses and offering to make her his mistress along Provençal lines. Small wonder the parents were wrathful and denied or deferred their consent. "Why,"

Professor Doolittle had long ago told him, "you're nothing but a nomad!" and as for poor Mrs. Shakespear who had made the mistake of exposing her daughter to this lawless American, she was nearly beside herself. "You *ought* to go away . . . ," she assailed him, "any man who wanted to marry her wd be put off by the fact of yr friendship (or whatever you call it). . . ." But they needn't have worried perhaps, the Doolittles, the Shakespears. As things turned out there were marriages enough to go round, Hilda marrying Richard Aldington, Ezra's young friend and disciple, to whom she had turned in her pain, and moving into a flat in Holland Park Chambers, and Ezra marrying Miss Shakespear just six months later and moving into rooms across from the Aldingtons and bursting into their quarters after dinner to recite them his poems. Sophie Brzeska who was Gaudier's common-law wife attacked Pound as much too "advanced" for a mere institution like marriage. But Pound was undaunted. He smiled. "Wife or mistress— it's the same thing," he said. "It's just a question of a few procedures for the sake of convenience."

T. E. Hulme must have cared even less for the middle-class marriage than Ezra. Himself a poet of sorts (he may have been the first British imagist) and an ardent philosopher (he may have been the first of the British Bergsonians), Tom Hulme was more thinker than writer and more talker than either and so in the Tour Eiffel or the Café Royal he'd hang out for hours with companions like Lewis and Epstein, discoursing on war, on the world, on Ezra's poems or the manifestos of Marinetti. He tended to dominate. An Edwardian Samuel Johnson, he had a strong and original mind and, standing over six feet tall and weighing some two hundred pounds and with the burly shoulders and legs of your average plowman, had a forcible way of making his points. Like, for example, seizing the arm of an opponent and threatening to throw him downstairs. Some found him a jovial giant and the enemy only of sham and pretension, and in this they may have been right. He made no effort to lose the nagging nasal dialect he'd brought down from North Staffordshire and could have been mistaken for a North Country farmer attending a fair or in town for the weekend. A nonsmoker and nondrinker, he was fond of sweets, of suet puddings and treacle. Nevertheless he did have a history of violence and the poet Frank Flint may not have been wrong in calling him "dangerous." He was remembered at Cambridge as "a big fellow with a genial open face" but he was also remembered for broken shop windows and cat-callings in theatres and was eventually sent down for "perpetual rows in his rooms" and for hitting a policeman during May Week. Youthful high jinks perhaps. Nevertheless, when he later took up the cudgels for a favorite poet or painter, he was only too likely to take up the cudgels. The knuckledusters he commissioned Gaudier to make him were, it was said, harmless things after all. Sex symbols perhaps. But knuckledusters are knuckledusters and are so very much what they are, that it's hard to mistake them for anything else. They consisted in any case with Tom Hulme the swashbuckler, the truculent streetfighter. He was accosted by a policeman for passing water in broad daylight in a Soho Square gutter. "Do you know," Hulme asked him haughtily, "you are addressing a member of the middle classes?" The constable apologized for his indiscretion and continued his rounds.

The mode of Hulme's lovemaking was no less aggressive. At his table in the Café Royal he'd look at his watch. "I've a pressing engagement in five minutes' time," he would tell his associates, before rising and striding away. Twenty minutes later he'd be back at the table still wiping the sweat from his brow. The emergency exit of the Piccadilly Circus Tube Station had to be, he'd announce, the most uncomfortable place in the world to copulate. Affectionate companionship he reserved for his friend Mrs. Kepplewhite, sexual satisfaction for the poor little skivvies of London, its servants and shopgirls. It gave them great pleasure, it pleased him to think, to connect with a man of his class and intelligence, and indeed it wasn't for nothing that Lewis would dub him "the didactic amorist." He was, by his own account, "a man of astounding sexual prowess" and, the Restoration rake *redivivus,* was always prepared to discuss in some detail the more philosophical aspects of sexual behavior. He had fair curly hair and a massive brow and quick blue eyes. His mouth, compared to his other features, was small. When he died in the war, "half the women in London," it was reliably reported, "went into mourning."

But then why would they not make the most of their sex, the creators of London, not only Tom Hulme but Wells himself and the Johns and the Pounds and the Lewises, Lawrences, Epsteins, and Gaudiers. If you couldn't make love, how could you make art? Was there not after all a vital connection between the sexual and the poetical powers? Eliot seemed to have thought so. Prufrock's failure as man and as artist is surely a function of a sexual failure. Ezra Pound most certainly thought so. The failure of Hugh Selwyn Mauberley as man and as artist is even more plainly a function of a sexual failure and indeed the decline and fall of the poetic impulse in England had something to do, Pound was sure, with the sexual blight that afflicted the land. "I can't express pain and abhorrence. Nor can I express reverence and joy. . . . I can only giggle!" Thus Max Beerbohm and thus in effect a whole generation of Barries and Chestertons, "Sakis" and Shaws. But for Pound and his peers who were out to renew the dead art of poetry in England, this just wouldn't do. Nothing would do but to "shake off the lethargy of this our time, and give/ For shadows—shapes of power,/ For dreams—men."

In the great sex war of 1900–1914, however, there wasn't a warrior like Master Frank Harris, the boisterous author and hero of *My Life and Loves*. Armed with a phallus he must have regarded as larger than life and a magical syringe guaranteed, he believed, to remove all chances of pregnancy, he was to the world of beds, chemises, and midnight suppers what the great Cecil Rhodes was to his. Imperial. Imperious. "I had got my fingers to her warm flesh between the stockings and the drawers and was wild with desire, soon mouth to mouth I touched her sex." "As I pushed back the clothes I found she had kept her chemise on. I lifted it up and pushed it round her neck to enjoy the sight of the most beautiful body I have ever seen. . . . The next moment I had touched her sex and soon I was at work. . . ." They were fabulous of course, his life and his loves, but fabulous, perhaps, in more ways than one. There were, it seemed, in his gorgeous accounts a touch or so of pure fable. Nevertheless they couldn't have been entirely fictitious. With his jet-black hair, basilisk eyes, and Bismarck mustache, his bejeweled hands and gold-headed cane and fur-lined overcoat, he did make an impression, combining, it was said, the look of a ruffian and the air of a stallion. Like Wells, moreover, he may have been pressing a point. Not for himself alone was he sowing his seed far and wide. It was for England he did it and the mothers and daughters of England. "I write of all these things quite frankly," he said, "because I believe that Puritanism is not only dead but deserved to die, and . . . that bodily pleasure . . . will be more and more sought after in the future." Love thy neighbor? Why not? It was the counsel of Christ as well as the counsel of Harris. Only connect, so to speak. "We are developing . . . ," as he put it, "the cult of the body at the same time that we are extending the new commandment given to us by the Christ." Not that the man was entirely ridiculous. His language may have been, on occasion, somewhat coarse and obstreperous. She has, he would roar of a lady he didn't approve, a cunt the size of a horse collar. But again it was for England's sake that he did it. Like the author of *Lady Chatterley's Lover,* he'd restore to the nation the robustious language it had had to suppress since the days of the Chaucers and Fieldings. Shaw was fair taken with Harris, with his "shiny hats and Café Royal lunches and Hooleyisms and all sorts of incongruities!" He called him "a male Hedda Gabler." But all Wells could remember was an "ugly dark face" and a "dwarfish ill-proportioned body" and a "lust-entangled vanity and greediness."

As things turned out, however, Harris was a model of social and sexual decorum by the side of some souls who were also inspired to make England safe for a new sexuality. Eric Gill, the young sculptor, for example. Quite taken by John and his sexual heroics, he acquired a wife and a mistress, wore a red beard and sandals, made statues so erotic that even Roger Fry was reluctant to place in his garden one of their kind, a pair of young lovers, for fear of offending his sister's philanthropical friends on their way to their meeting. An earlier carving later called "Ecstasy" was originally entitled, more alarmingly, "Fucking." Inspired by Chesterton's cult of peasants and villages, Eric would join up with Epstein to establish at Ditchling on the Sussex Downs an Edwardian "commune" of artists and artisans, "a sort of twentieth century Stonehenge," where he and his children could walk about naked and he and Epstein attempt enormous nude statues of Wells and, of all people, Shaw. John and his friends were less than persuaded, however. They called him the "precious cockney," "the naughty schoolmaster," the "artist of the Urinal." "He is much impressed by the importance of copulation," Augustus would say, "possibly because he has had so little to do with that subject in practice." But then Augustus may have miscalculated the young man's determined resolve to serve as a model for the national regeneration. For no one, it seems, was quite safe from Gill's physical embraces. Not his wife, not his mistress. Not his sisters and daughters. Not even—good heavens!—his dogs. As for Aleister Crowley who proclaimed himself the Wickedest Man in the World and was pledged to save "this god-awful country where one has to sleep with one's penis under one's pillow," the less said the better. Except that in the Rabelaisian abbey in Sicily he called Do What Thou Wilt, he'd involve his disciples and concubines in the most sordid sexual orgies, would employ in the making of the pills he called his Elixir of Life the most unmentionable sexual fluids.

But the men weren't the only ones eager to live and to love on their own sexual terms. So too were the women. The gifted Florence Farr, for example, who was slender and beautiful and wore huge hats and scarlet and purple scarves and had played Rebecca West in Ibsen's *Rosmersholm*. Early abandoned by her first and last husband, she called marriage "a pigsty" and determined thereafter to live quite without it, though not without sex. She "set no bounds," Shaw said, "to her relations with men whom she liked" and kept, he reported, "a sort of Leporello list of a dozen adventures." Ezra Pound was all admiration.

> Great minds have sought you—lacking someone else.
> You have been second always. Tragical?
> No. You preferred it to the usual thing:
> One dull man, dulling and uxurious . . .

But Yeats, who was doubtless one of the great minds referred to, may have been just a little put off by her infinite variety. For him at least, Olivia Shakespear, Dorothy's mother, was a godsend of sorts. His first kiss, it appeared, was "but a brother's kiss" and when, on their first railway journey together, she gave him "the long passionate kiss of love," he was "startled," he said, "and a little shocked." But then he moved into Woburn Buildings, Mrs. Shakespear helping him purchase the furniture, including, embarrassingly, the bed, and though the poet at first was too nervous to perform his part well, he was soon relieved of his troubled virginity. Many a woebegone man of the time owed something in fact of his sexual sanity to the good ministrations of such women as these. Violet Hunt, for example, whose favors to Hueffer were partly medicinal or Lady Ott whose favors to Strachey and Russell and Lamb among others she thought of as sexual therapy. Even in Nottingham, as Lawrence discovered, such magnanimities weren't impossible. Alice Dax or some married woman of generous instincts took him upstairs to her room where, as she put it, she "gave Bert sex." How else, she explained, could she help the poor fellow to finish the poem he had long and in vain been struggling with?

"Oh, darling, it's really women I love," says a woman in H.D.'s novel, *Bid Me to Live*. For they were not only free to love men as they pleased, some Edwardian women; they also felt free to love women. Vernon Lee, for example, who reproached H. G. Wells for his cavalier treatment of his Janes and his Ambers, or Veronica Lee-Jones, who attached herself to Dorothy Richardson at the same time that Dorothy was detaching herself from H.G. Like Katherine Mansfield, for another, who made her friend Ida Baker her slave and factotum and called her "a revolting hysterical ghoul" but was nevertheless devoted to her and "try and believe and keep on believing," she'd tell her, "that I do love you and want you for my wife." It was indeed for some, this Saphhic passion, an act of revolt against the intolerable regimen of men. Were Vita Sackville-West's lesbian interests exclusively sexual? Not at all, said her son. She was battling the convention, he was pleased to report, "that women should love only men, and men only women."

"Let yourself, on the contrary go—in all agreeable directions"

Freedom for heterosexuals? Why not freedom for homosexuals, for "misogynists," for "confirmed bachelors," as the Victorians were accustomed to call them. Carpenter had asked for a more generous conception of marriage, but he hadn't stopped there. In *Love's Coming of Age* (1896) and *The Intermediate Sex* (1908) he had called for a more generous conception of sexuality itself. Since the 1880s laws had been passed to control homosexual behavior, but how could they succeed? Uranian love, as they named it, was neither abnormal nor vicious, Carpenter said, but natural and human, "a distinct variety of the sexual passion." Pathological indeed! cried Havelock Ellis. It was no more pathological than albinism or color-blindness. Consider, said Carpenter, pre-"civilized" man, the Polynesians who permitted themselves "the most romantic male friendships," the Balonda and other African tribes who conducted betrothal rites between comrades, the heroes of ancient Greece whose ideal passion was the passion of fellowship "carried over into the regions of love." Consider, moreover, said Havelock Ellis, the ancient Assyrians and Egyptians who regarded homosexual love as more worthy of worship than the heterosexual kind. Why, in primitive times, were men not accustomed to copulate with just about everything that moved? "All creatures great and small"? In the vocabulary of the Salish of British Columbia, for whom animals were seen as no lower than humans, there was no such word, said Ellis, as "bestiality." What, then, was civilization, as Carpenter saw it, but "a temporary alienation from true life"?

Heterosexual love was necessary, it's true, for the reproduction of children and the advance of the species, but this wasn't, he said, its primary function. That, he said, was the fulfillment of the individual soul which sought the ultimate union of which physical union was "the allegory and expression." Homogenic attachments were not in any case incompatible with the reproductive ends of the race. They served to prepare the young male for marriage itself, to provide him with an innocent safety valve in the long barren years before marriage. But this was the least of Carpenter's proud vindications. Far from inferior to heterosexual love, homosexual love was, he insisted, superior to it. In Victorian England the sexes were polarized, the masculinity of the male, the femininity of the female; but the role of the intermediate sex as Carpenter named it was precisely to act as mediator, as "the interpreter of men and women to each other." In England the classes too were polarized. Didn't heterosexual marriage create and control the noxious class system that kept men apart from each other? But Eros, said Carpenter, was "a great leveler" and the fate of democracy might well depend on the Uranian sentiment, "on a sentiment which easily passes the bounds of class and caste." It might well depend on an entirely new ethic in fact, not the middle-class competition for women and property but a new sense of comradeship when "Love, the Beloved Republic" would rule in the land. The middle-class male, all will and aggression, had mastered the material world but, emotionally "ungrown" as he was, was "in matters of love" no more than "a child." More sensitive, more sympathetic, the intermediate sex would herald a new breed of men who would substitute "the bond of personal affection . . . for the monetary, legal and other external ties" which now governed mankind. In 1896 Carpenter came out of the closet. In the famous cottage at Millthorpe he set up house with George Merrill, a "working-class bloke from the slums," who, told that Our Lord Jesus

Christ, on his last night on earth, had slept at Gethsemane, had asked, in all innocence, "Who with?"

Carpenter was, to be sure, far ahead of his time, far ahead, at any event, of some good Edwardians who preferred to remain Uranians in hiding. Somerset Maugham, for example. Young and successful, his plays all the go, he would play the proper Edwardian, would don for the dinners and dances the top hat and tails of the dandy and would have his romantic affairs with the best of them. As a matter of fact he was eager to marry. Sue Jones, for one, the lascivious daughter of the famous playwright, who would disappoint him, however, with "if you want to go to bed with me, you may, but I won't marry you" and Syrie Wellcome, for another, who didn't disappoint him in this but would later divorce him. So, in the end, unhappy, reluctant, he would have his male chauffeurs and secretaries. Hugh Walpole wasn't deceived by the top hat Maugham wore with such rakish effect. "A definite pose of dandyism," he remarked, "in which the wearer obviously did not believe." Hugh had after all an eye for these things. He had developed a fondness for Turkish baths which satisfied his passion for cleanliness as well as his passion for strangers who might, who knows?, prove Ideal Companions. He too would be famous and wealthy and have his male secretaries, Harold Cheevers, for one, a burly Cornish constable with a wife and two sons. Poor Henry James, aging now and depressed, was enchanted with his little disciple, with his youth and ebullience and naive delight in London and letters. Hugh was his "belovedest little Hugh," his "darlingest Hugh," his "darling darling little Hugh!" But alas there were limits on what he could give and receive. He had offered himself, Hugh would later disclose, to the suffering Master but it was, after so many years of denial, just a little too late. "I can't, I can't, I can't," he had groaned, abject and miserable. "Have you seen Hugh lately? Is he well?" he would later ask as he left his publisher's office. Hugh was, it appeared, in the best of spirits. "I'm so glad," said the old man devoutly, adding a moment later, shyly and breathlessly, "Please don't tell him I asked."

Carpenter's cottage at Millthorpe was in the meanwhile a shrine of sorts for the distressed and discouraged. Young Lawrence may have gone to him once. Someone thought she remembered seeing him there. Whether or no, he was certainly under Carpenter's influence, made it perfectly clear that homosexual love had a place in his new scheme of things. His industrial magnates, his Criches and Chatterleys, are the types of Carpenter's "ungrown" men who are sexually infantile and powerless to love. But his homogenous heroes, his Birkins and Mellorses, are the types of Carpenter's "grown" men, who being men and women at once, belong to the future and "the manly love which alone can create a new era of life." Lawrence would even endorse Carpenter's notion of homosexual love as a species of *rite de passage,* as an anticipation of heterosexual marriage. Gerald Crich didn't have to fail and die, he intimates in *Women in Love.* Had he "pledged himself with the man" he would have been "able to pledge himself with the woman." What for that matter was Lawrence's "Rananim" but a reincarnation of Carpenter's "Fellowship of the New Life"? Eager like Carpenter to plant the germ of a better and more beautiful human estate, Lawrence would try to establish a colony of like-minded spirits, Murry and Katherine Mansfield among them and Pound's Hilda Doolittle and, most unlikely of all, E. Morgan Forster who, Lawrence said, must take him a woman and "fight clear to his own basic, primal being." But a man is never a prophet in his own country and his "Rananim" didn't seem to please everyone. Not Hilda Doolittle who may have loved Lawrence but after her exposure to Pound and her marriage to Aldington couldn't have cared for Lawrence's man-centered credo, for "his blood-stream, his sex-fixations, his man-is-man, woman-is-woman." Nor Katherine Mansfield whose sexual experience was fairly inclusive but who could nonetheless never quite see it as the road to a Heaven on Earth, could *"never,"* she said, "see sex in trees, sex in the running brooks, sex in stones & sex in everything." It certainly didn't please Forster who wanted a sexual revolution all right but not quite the one that Lawrence was thinking of, who was fond of the prophet "who talks to Hilda [Doolittle] and sees birds . . . and wrote *The White Peacock,* he doesn't know why," but resented "the deaf impercipient fanatic who has nosed over his own little sexual round until he believes that there is no other path. . . ."

Forster, in any case, had already made the pilgrimage to the wizard of Millthorpe. "Oh do sit quiet," said the sage to the novelist who was nervous and fidgety. His companion Merrill, as was his wont on such social occasions, touched Forster gently "just above the buttocks." The sensation, said Forster, was rather unusual. "It seemed to go straight through the small of my back into my ideas, without involving my thoughts. If it really did this, it would . . . prove that at that precise moment I had conceived." Conceived? Good heavens, what was he

LONDON DELIVER'D 91

getting at? Some mystical sense of the real source of things? Not the mind but the body the source of creation? Or did he mean simply his release from artistic sterility? His decision to write in a state of high exaltation his homosexual novel, *Maurice*? It wasn't a very good novel and he didn't dare publish it until after the death of his mother, but Carpenter liked it and well he might. It rehearsed, it extolled the life he and Merrill were actually living. It was certainly full of his doctrines. Maurice loses Clive, his first lover, to a wife and a marriage but not in vain: "But for Maurice [Clive] would never have developed into a being worthy of Anne. His friend had helped him through three barren years. . . ." Not only that: for Forster as for Carpenter, Uranianism was a state of rebellion against the rotten class system and the bigoted connubiality that sustained it. Like Lady Chatterley and her gamekeeper-lover, Maurice and his gamekeeper-lover "must live outside class, without relations or money." But all would be well in the end. "England belonged to them . . . ," Forster exulted, "not the timorous millions who own stuffy little boxes, but never their own souls." The buggers of Bloomsbury couldn't help laughing. Sexual inversion the wave of the future? The condition of a classless society, a loving democracy? What nonsense it was! The homosexual passion, they said, needed no high-minded justification. It justified itself. Beyond Carpenter and his "yogified mysticism" there would issue from Strachey "a series of little squeaks" at the very notion of this high priest of masculine sex. Not for Lytton Carpenter's vision, his Uranian dream.

Nor for the coarse Norman Douglas. After his marriage was ended he made no secret of his sexual affections. They were all for boys, for fine little boys, whom he pursued with abandon all over Capri. At the end of 1910, at the Crystal Palace Fireworks Display, he became enamored with Eric, a twelve-and-a-half-year-old child of the back streets of Camden whom he took off to Italy and, on their return, made his constant companion. Not many years later he was arrested and charged at South Kensington Underground Station "for being a suspected person frequenting for an unlawful purpose." The place he had frequented was the Natural History Museum and the unlawful purpose for which he frequented it was the dereliction of a youth of sixteen. Conrad, who refused his bail, must have known of his friend's peccadilloes but Mrs. Conrad could not. All for grace and gentility, she was charmed by the elegant man who was often her guest. "His success with my sex was certain and assured," she would write with majestic aplomb.

Nevertheless. The eccentricities of Douglas notwithstanding and notwithstanding the muffled fears of the Maughams and Walpoles, the intermediate sex would hardly arouse by the time of the war the old Victorian shiver of horror. Not at any rate among the young and enlightened. When Forster had his friends reading *Maurice* in manuscript, there was boredom, perhaps, but astonishment, no. "Even in 1915," Bunny Garnett remembered, "it was out of date." Gaudier was "young enough," Epstein recalled, "to wish to startle people." He announced with emotion "that he was homosexual, expecting us to be horrified." But Jacob and his friends weren't about to be horrified. By this time it took more than this to horrify them. Sex had become for a fact, with the death of God and Victoria, the new evangel. The young undergraduates, Mrs. Webb was complaining, were more interested in sexual than in social reform. In 1907 Florence Farr was proposing in Orage's *New Age* that prostitution be made sacramental as it was in the East and in 1913, more practically perhaps, Doris Marsden was proposing in her *New Freewoman* that prostitutes form their own trade union. In 1907 again, in Orage's journal, Havelock Ellis was suggesting that the laws governing homosexual conduct be modified and two years after that a manifesto would circulate denouncing the laws that made homosexual coupling a crime. Amazing in fact, were they not, the Edwardians, the Georgians? They rushed to the brink of what would have seemed to their parents the most dangerous abysses, but they didn't shrink, they didn't draw back. They jumped. They leaped. The brave new hopes of Liberals and socialists, the rages of women for votes and of workers for wages, the struggles of thousands to achieve as creatures the life and fulfillment that had long been denied them: they'd feel for them, join them, fight for them all. Indeed, it was scarcely a secret, this exciting new ferment. We live, said Wells at the time, "in a period of adventurous and insurgent thought, in an intellectual spring unprecedented in the world's history." Pledged to construct "a new society," we were "living," Leonard Woolf would recall, "in the springtime of a conscious revolt against the . . . institutions, beliefs, and standards of our fathers and grandfathers." No doubt about it at all, the London of Edward VII was an exhilarating place, an exhilarating time to be alive and well in.

"Who killed the king?"

Maybe all too exhilarating. For the old Victorian establishment wasn't ready, it seemed, to give up the battle without a good fight. The Conservative party may have lost the election of 1906 but had it therefore lost the country? Not necessarily. It could always depend on the old House of Lords, its ancient ally, to veto those Liberal measures it couldn't abide. It could even think the unthinkable, could even think of vetoing a government budget. Of course it just wasn't done. It hadn't been done for two hundred years. But bitter new passions were entering the city, and if the party couldn't rule by the will of the people, it was ready to rule by the will of the Lords. So when in April 1909 David Lloyd George, chancellor of the exchequer, presented the People's Budget, a budget that would provide not only four dreadnoughts to cope with the new German power but pensions for old British workers and would pay for these pensions by taxing the rich and the great estates of the earls and the barons themselves, the Lords threatened to commit what amounted to suicide. They threatened to veto the budget. Prime Minister Asquith was furious. The power of the Lords, their absolute veto, would have to go. But Lloyd George, the demon Welshman, the silver-tongued demagogue, was delighted. Was it a class war they wanted? A class war he would give them. "Shall peers or people rule?" he would shout. "A fully-equipped Duke," he'd declaim, "costs as much to keep up as two dreadnoughts." One July evening, before a great crowd of cockneys in Limehouse, he vividly rehearsed the terrors of work in the mines, the groaning weight of the rock and shale, the creaking and cracking of the weak wooden props, the sinister gases that invaded the miles of dank, dark corridor and that could, in a fiery apocalypse, snuff out the lives of the poor, helpless men. "And yet," he went on, "when the Prime Minister and I knock at the door of these great landlords and say to them—'Here, you know these poor fellows who have been digging up royalties at the risk of their lives, some of them are old . . . [and] are broken, they can earn no more. Won't you give them something towards keeping them out of the workhouse? . . .' They say, 'You thieves!' And they turn their dogs on to us. . . ." The king was, it followed, upset. Was it for them, his own ministers, to ignite in the simple hearts of the poor a bitter contempt for their betters? Would they not incite the Lords to reject the detestable budget and would the Liberal government, in its turn, not abolish their power?

It was not of course to be believed that the Lords would bring down on their ancient grey heads the inevitable wrath and affliction. But on November 30 they rejected the budget and the king's worst fears were fulfilled: the dissolution of Parliament in December and in January a general election and, albeit a meager one, the Liberal victory expected, and in April the government proposal to limit the power of the Lords. What next? Would the lords not veto this Parliament Bill as they called it, and if they did would the king not flood their noble house, as he'd promised to do, with hordes of new peers of a Liberal persuasion? Already the home secretary, Winston Churchill ("a born cad"), was composing a list of strange new peers with names like G. P. Gooch and Sir Abe Bailey, not to mention J. M. Barrie and Thomas Hardy. The king, poor man, was worried to death. Invent new Lords? How crass, how unsacramental! Reduce or abolish the power of the Lords? The thin edge of the wedge. Reduce or abolish one hereditary power, why not another? The crown itself. *His* crown. "Zounds, will they not rob us?"

It was not a corruption the old man was called on to witness. Early in May he died. "You have killed the king, you have killed the king," they were shouting at Asquith and his cabinet members in the streets of the city. One day in July a nervous prime minister arose in the House to announce that in the event of a veto the new king would create whatever peers would be needed to assure the passage of the Parliament Bill. But he wasn't allowed to deliver his message or even to finish his opening sentence. From the opposition benches came shouts of "Who killed the king?" and "Traitor Traitor Traitor Traitor," and after forty-five minutes of hooting and howling the PM, "white with anger," had to fold up his speech and sit down, and for the very first time in its history the House was adjourned as "a disorderly assembly." But the day of judgment must and did come. Less than a month later the Lords met to decide whether or not they'd consent to their own destruction. It wasn't the usual meager and moribund assemblage of peers. Down from the remotest shires of the realm they had swarmed, the Die-hards, the Ditchers, the angry old noblemen who had vowed to "die in the last ditch" before they'd surrender. Was it true? Would the new king create, should they veto this bill, a host of parvenu peers? Would he act, as the twenty-seventh Earl of Crawford would put it, "to vulgarize our order"? But he would. It wasn't a bluff or a rumor. The king's assent to the deed was read to the stupefied Lords and, after the long, bitter silence that followed, the vote was taken. It was 131 to 114 against vetoing the Parliament Bill.

"Force majeure"

If all this wasn't enough, there was always the lively suffragette business. In vain had they marched in processions and distributed pamphlets and heckled speakers and disrupted their meetings. It was 1909 and they were ready now for more dangerous action. For Herbert Gladstone, who was not quite the man his father had been and was proving to be a hopeless home secretary, had blundered again. Argument wasn't enough, he had said to the House. To obtain the vote the women would have to use, like the men before them, *force majeure.* He'd been very explicit about it. "The time comes," he had said, "when political dynamics are far more important than political argument." He had meant of course to discourage the women, but Mrs. Pankhurst and her Christabel were, all things considered, encouraged. *Force majeure?* Political dynamics? Exactly. Just what *they* had been thinking. Mr. Asquith and his ministers were in trouble. With a general election impending, they'd be taking their case to the country. Well, then, the Pankhursts and their minions would be there in some force, *force majeure,* to meet them and greet them. While Lloyd George was wildly heckling the dukes and the barons in Limehouse, they would be there wildly heckling *him,* and when Asquith was addressing a rally in the great Bingley Hall in Birmingham, they would be pelting the roof with slates. It was quite disconcerting. It was even quite dangerous. Mr. Churchill stepped from a train at Bristol where he was scheduled to speak in the Colston Hall. His face went white and he raised an arm to defend himself. A young lady with a riding switch was before him and "Take that," she was crying, "in the name of the insulted women of England." On his way home one night, Augustine Birrell, who would soon be named, for no obvious reason, chief secretary for Ireland, was all of a sudden attacked by a gang of bacchantes, and after a struggle of some six or seven minutes, his trusty umbrella notwithstanding, he fell to the street, and but for the passing motorist who came to his rescue, all for sure would not have gone well with him. Was nothing safe any more? Was nothing sacred? Mr. Asquith and his home secretary were assaulted one day with fists and umbrellas on the ninth hole of a golf course where Harry, the indignant club official, was moved to inform them that whatever their quarrel with the prime minister, they could not and must not walk on the greens. On Lord Mayor's Day, Mr. Asquith was about to address a distinguished banquet in the Guild Hall. It was an annual occasion, genial, civilized. But then of a sudden came a shattering of glass and two voices shrieking "Votes for Women! Votes for Women!" It was not to be borne. The head and members of a British government couldn't appear on the London streets without a phalanx of police and detectives. They had to be smuggled like criminals, like hardened criminals, into and out of their homes and hotels.

There were arrests of course and prison terms. But this, it turned out, was the problem and not the solution. For the women had discovered a new and terrible tactic. No longer enough the bleak little cells of Holloway Prison. Nothing would serve now but hunger strikes and the moral and physical indignities of forced feeding with the iron machines for opening mouths and the rubber tubes to force down the food. There was the deplorable case of Lady Constance Lytton, the daughter of a viceroy of India and the granddaughter of a world-famous novelist. Lady Constance was arrested and jailed for casting a stone at a car that contained the person of Sir Walter Runciman but, after a brief hunger strike, was released for reasons that had nothing to do, Mr. Gladstone insisted, with her social position. Not many months later Jane Warton was impounded for playing a part in a protest rally and, after refusing hard labor, was placed in a punishment cell and force-fed. She wasn't released, but this wasn't the trouble. The trouble was, it wasn't Jane Warton at all. It was, under an assumed name, the recurrent Lady Constance. Poor Emily Davison had no upper-class title to protect her. Imprisoned eight times, she went on seven hunger strikes and suffered forty-nine forced feedings. Once she hurled herself five flights down the well of the prison. Too badly hurt to resist, she was forcibly fed.

There were those who lamented the government's action, but Winston Churchill wasn't among them. At Newbuildings, the country estate of the poet Sir Wilfred Scawen Blunt, the host and his guest Granville Barker, the actor-producer, expostulated with him, referring to torture and the Spanish Inquisition. But the statesman was not to be moved. Nor was the king who found the suffragettes' conduct "outrageous." When Gladstone relented and released thirty-seven hungerstrikers, His Majesty was mortified. He wanted "to know why the existing methods . . . for dealing with prisoners who refuse nourishment should not be adopted." But he was a popular monarch and spoke no doubt for his people. When, in those hot summer days on Parliament Square, the bobbies lost much of their vaunted composure, there were rogues in the side streets to give vent to their rage. When, at a by-election in Croydon, suffragettes in numbers turned up to heckle the candidates, Lawrence would record the reaction, "the vicious rush of one solid mass of men towards the car where the two women were alone, one standing crying scorn on the brutes, the other sitting with dark, sad eyes!" and, at another location, "a big splendid woman" with "great swinging ear-rings," who mounts her cart boldly to laugh at the mob and then ask them for respite, but in vain: "Their souls are lusted with cruelty."

After the January election and the death of the king, there would be a brief moratorium. But when the government declined as before to take action, the women resumed their offensive and on November 18—"Black Friday" they'd call it—while Mrs. Pankhurst and her elderly delegates waited in vain for Asquith to hear them, twenty-five squads of a dozen women each were waving their banners—"Asquith Has Vetoed Our Bill," "Women's Will Beats Asquith's Won't"—and struggling to reach the Parliament buildings. The thousand policemen were at first good-natured enough, but the women were pushing and pressing and the home secretary was no longer the diffident Gladstone but the combative Churchill and so as the hours went by, the brave banners were trampled and torn, and the women, battered and bruised, were repulsed. The next day the police were astonished. Mrs. Pankhurst and her people were invading Downing Street where Asquith had to be hustled into a taxi and Mr. Birrell, in the act of leaping for one, sprained his ankle. So no wonder the PM and his aides were on edge. Every bush was burning. Attacking on one front the Tories and Lords, the government was attacked from the rear by implacable women. It wasn't a question of there being too little life in the British metropolis. It was a question of there being only too much of it.

Of Poets and Politics

To all of this, to all that was passing in the squares and streets of the city, the actions and reactions, the "revolutions" and "counterrevolutions," who could be indifferent? Not, it would seem, its poets and painters, its playwrights and philosophers. In the great election of 1906 little James Barrie sat huddled and silent on a platform in Coventry while his good friend, the Liberal candidate, spoke himself hoarse, and Hilaire Belloc, the novelist and journalist, ran as a Liberal for South Salford near Manchester and defeated his opponent, a Tory brewer, by 852 votes, and in the January election of 1910, good socialists like the Shaws would be motoring into the fog of south Wales to campaign for Labour's Keir Hardie, and Arnold Bennett would be publishing a four-page pamphlet decrying the Lords whose only claim to be ruling the country, he said, was that "their ancestors were royal bastards" or had "bought their titles . . . from ancient kings." If he hadn't contracted a touch of food poisoning, young Rupert Brooke was telling his friends, he would gladly have worked for "some jolly Labour man" as he would in December that year when in twelve motor cars he would transport voters to the polls and rejoice that at last "we [were] going to get rid of the Lords."

Lodged, in that critical January, in Brighton's Royal York, Arnold Bennett, the celebrated author of *The Old Wives' Tale*, was making good progress on his next. At 9:45 a.m., Wednesday, January 5, he was writing the first words of his *Clayhanger*. By 1:30 he had written 1,000, by January 9 4,500, and by the end of the month 33,200. All the same, his spirit was troubled. "At this election time," he was thinking, "when all wealth and all snobbery is leagued together against the poor, I could spit in the face of arrogant and unmerciful Brighton, sporting its damned Tory colors." On Saturday night, January 14, he stood anxiously by in the wind and rain to witness on the *Daily News* lantern screen the early election returns, and they weren't encouraging. The country wasn't going Tory but neither was it going Liberal. "The fools won't vote right," Bennett complained, "and I lie awake at night thinking about their foolishness."

Well, no surprises here. Bennett was a Liberal and a radical one and Barrie had been born and bred a Liberal and Fabian Shaw was always as much a man of politics as a man of letters, as were others like Hilaire Belloc and Cunninghame Graham. But what of Maurice Hewlett, who always traveled first class and was an eager medievalist and wrote, Ezra Pound said, "RRRRomantik nuvls" and was, said Shaw, "a most proud & sensitive grandee, as you may imagine from his books"? He openly declared himself a socialist and that January at Leicester addressed a crowd of some five thousand souls and would later say, moved no doubt by the historic occasion, "I have had such gifts as I possess for thirty years or so and have only just begun to put them to the service of my brothers and neighbors." Even James for whom the city mansions and country houses were sacred places wasn't untouched by the latest developments. "The Election fight," he wrote, concluding a letter, "has revealed to me how ardent a Liberal lurks in the cold and clammy exterior of your/ HJ." He even "felt tempted," he wryly reported, "to call himself a rabid socialist."

To be sure, not every Edwardian man of letters was of the Liberal persuasion. In 1911 Scottish John Buchan ran as a Conservative candidate for the counties of Peebles and Selkirk, though, to be honest, he had friends on both sides and had trouble deciding which party to serve. But Imperialist Kipling, whose hatred of politics in general and of Liberals in particular was near pathological, had no trouble deciding whose side he was on. In his carefully considered opinion, you could no more "prevent a Liberal from lying" than prevent a small dog "from lifting up his leg against a lamp post." Before 1906 it was the idle, corrupt ruling classes who invited his scorn, but after 1906 it was workers and women and liberal reformers and "howling syndicalism." Still, Kipling, with his black top hat and his bristling eyebrows and his glare of a child-killing Dickensian deacon, was one thing, but H. G. Wells, surely, was quite something else. He was after all the Champion of the Poor and Oppressed, of the Young and Aspiring. Nonetheless he was now to pass over, it seemed, to the unclean side. The Liberal hero of his *New Machiavelli* defects to the Tories. "I am not so keen against the Lords," he declares. These Tory Backwoodsmen were nothing, it's true, like his wonderful Samurai. But declined though they were, they were still, he'd insist, "the class upon which we had hitherto relied . . . and an influence upon our collective judgments that no other class seemed prepared to exercise." Of course he despised in *Tono-Bungay* old Bladesover Castle and its Tory nobility and its ancient injustice, but he didn't admire what he feared would replace it. He didn't want power for the working class, for those he dismissed as "children of the abyss." "We must," he said, "have an aristocracy" one way or another.

Ford Madox Hueffer would have heard of all this with the liveliest interest. Once offended by Wells, Ford had predicted—"O, my prophetic soul"—that if he didn't end up in "the chains and straw of Bedlam," he was sure to end up in "a country-house with a Tory Seat attached to it." But then Fordie himself wouldn't have been very keen against the Lords. By this time he'd be, like his Christopher Tietjens, the most romantic of Tories. Oh, he'd socialized in his day with Morris's people and had Fabianized with the Garnetts and Wellses, but these, it appeared, had been passing fancies. What were the two greatest institutions invented by man? They were, he'd now boldly asseverate, His Britannic Majesty's army and the Roman Catholic church. As for his good friend Conrad, he would doubtless have shared these political sentiments. At one of her elegant Camden Hill dinners, Violet Hunt had declared that, all things considered, Marie Antoinette had deserved her demise. The air had turned blue. The teacups had rattled. I believe, the great man had declaimed from his end of the table, his fist coming down on the tea tray, I believe, he'd declaimed, in the Divine Right of Kings.

But his was no doubt a minority opinion. Generally speaking, the great republic of letters was well on the side of the people's party, "the party of progress." Even Bloomsbury. Forster himself wasn't up to electioneering. Too mild, too diffident. Besides, he wasn't convinced "that the artist must be a rebel." Just the same, he was in his way against the Lords and "their attempt to overturn the poor and the constitution." So too did Strachey, who loved lords and ladies all right but after the crisis of 1910 had discovered politics and a lively contempt for the governing classes. Lytton even thought for a moment, for an improbable moment, of entering politics himself, but then with his poor spindly body and his high piping voice . . . Stick to writing, Lady Ott told him. In any case bolder Bloomsbury spirits than his were at work that January. There was Bell, as vigorous as ever, extending himself for the radical cause and Keynes who was asking roaring crowds in Birmingham to vote for the Liberal, and in December, at Histon, was exhorting meetings which were all very male and exciting and was thinking that "life without a howling audience to address every evening will seem very dull." This isn't to mention Philip Morrell, the Liberal MP, who was working hard to retain his South Oxfordshire seat and his wife, Lady Ott, who stood tall by his side and Bertie Russell who had kindly offered to help them.

It wasn't something Russell was obliged to do. He had had half a mind to run as a Liberal himself, but he was an agnostic and made no secret of it and "the party of progress" saw fit to reject him. He certainly didn't think much of Morrell—nobody did—nor, at the time, did he think very much of the grand Lady Ott whose extravagant manner and dress and immoderate powders and scents disturbed his dry Quaker soul. No matter. He thought he should help the party anyway and since he couldn't support the candidate of his own Oxford constituency, was supporting Morrell and haranguing the crowds by night and canvassing for votes by day. It wasn't an easy assignment. "Do you think I'd vote for a scoundrel like that?" a retired colonel at Iffley had roared at him from his Tory grotto. "Get out of the house, or I'll put the dogs on you!" At some places Philip and his lady were booed at and stoned, and when Bertie first joined them at Watlington there were catcalls and whistles until "something in his passionate sincerity and intellectual force arrested them" and so, Lady Ott said, "intellectual integrity triumph[ed] over democratic disorder." In point of fact, though, she rather rejoiced in the democratic disorder. "I loved it," she'd say of it all. "I wanted to cry out to them, 'Go on! Shout at us! Throw things at us! I don't care.' " And she'd spread out her arms "in an ecstasy of martyrdom." Bertie was impressed. For all her airs and her graces and appalling perfumes, she was, he decided, "in earnest about public life." It was all, however, in vain. Weary and depressed, they returned to London. Philip had lost.

"Bunga, bunga!"

There were Bloomsberries, to be sure, who didn't take it too seriously, this political pother. Once at a dinner Vanessa asked the gentleman next to her whether or not he was interested in politics. It seemed he was. It was Asquith himself, the current PM. As for sister Virginia, she was bitterly skeptical of the man's world of parties and politics from which she was, as a woman, excluded. In the company of her Tory stepbrothers, she and Vanessa had joined the jubilant throng on Trafalgar Square to cheer for the great Liberal victory of 1906 and in 1910 she was persuaded to occupy a chair on a platform "next Portuguese Jews, whose sweat ran into powder, caked and blew off." Hers was no passionate commitment, however. One morning in February the emperor of Abyssinia and his modest retinue of three, richly attired in the costume of their country and accompanied by an interpreter and an official of the Foreign Office, boarded a train at Paddington Station for Weymouth Bay where the Home Fleet was then proudly standing. Notified by telegram of the imperial visit, the British navy rose to the occasion. A flag lieutenant was there at the station to salute the royal party and see it aboard the little steam launch which carried it then to the *HMS Dreadnought* itself. Greeted there by Admiral May and by Captain William Fisher, his flag commander, they were invited to tour the ship, led by an officer who graciously explained the guns and turrets and other wonders of this greatest and presumably most secret of all British warships. The bandmaster, unhappily, could find no copy of the national anthem of Abyssinia, but the anthem of Zanzibar was resoundingly played to everyone's satisfaction. The emperor declined the refreshments and a twenty-one-gun salute, but on the train home the waiters were instructed to wear, as protocol demanded, white kid gloves. All in all, the navy had done itself proud. Admiral May and Captain Fisher and the officers in their gold-laced uniforms had been kindness itself. The emperor and his aides were even feeling a little guilty about it. Guilty? Ah, that was the rub. There was no emperor, no suite, no interpreter, and no official of no Foreign

Office. The official, properly attired in top hat and tails, was Horace de Vere Cole, a notorious prankster, and the interpreter was Adrian Stephen in beard and bowler, and the emperor and his suite had been recruited from friends like Duncan Grant and Virginia Stephen, wearing turbans and caftans and other exotic regalia. "A rum lingo they speak," one of the officers had muttered that day on the *Dreadnought*. It was much rummer than he knew. A few words in Swahili patched together with garbled borrowings from Homer and Virgil. So much for the pomp and circumstance of the Tory establishment. So much, from Virginia's angle, for masculine conceit and stupidity. And since poor Captain Fisher was her cousin and Adrian's, so much too for their stuffy Victorian relations.

There were inevitably headlines and full-page photographs, outraged letters to editors and to Mr. McKenna, First Lord of the Admiralty, embarrassing questions from the floor of the House, like "Is it not a fact that certain pairs of white kid gloves . . ." One Sunday morning a bell was rung on Fitzroy Square and Virginia, just out of bed, heard a loud voice in the hall below. It was cousin Willy Fisher, the flag commander, with brother officers waiting outside in a taxi. Did they realize, he was shouting at Adrian, that in the streets of Weymouth little boys were running after Admiral May screaming "Bunga, bunga"? That in the officers' mess they were calling Virginia "a common woman of the town"? That Adrian and his confederates were impertinent and ought to be whipped through the streets? He demanded their names and addresses and Adrian, cowed and crestfallen, delivered them instantly. In Hampstead, Duncan Grant was sitting down to Sunday breakfast with his mother and father. The doorbell rang. A gentleman friend was waiting outside and wanted to talk. Duncan went down to the street in his bedroom slippers and, in an instant, was on the floor of a taxi at the feet of three naval officers with canes in their hands. "What on earth are we to do?" Mrs. Grant said who had seen from the window a son's slippered feet disappear in a taxi. "Someone's kidnapping Duncan." Major Grant smiled. "I expect it's his friends from the *Dreadnought*." "You'll see plenty of *Dreadnoughts* where you're going," said one of these friends on the way to the Heath, but once there, Duncan just stood like a lamb in his slippers and how could they cane him? So they gave him two ceremonial taps and released him. A few days later, Adrian and Duncan, a little contrite, turned up at the Admiralty to confer with the First Lord himself. They wanted, they said, to apologize, to get his officers off the embarrassing hook on which they had hung them. But Mr. McKenna laughed a weak hollow laugh. Admiral May and his men in trouble? For the foolish prank of a few foolish persons? Absurd to think so. Never do it again, he told them, and bustled them out of his office.

"Odors from the abyss"

Meanwhile, what of the workers, the millions of oil- or coal-stained workers? What of the strikers who in 1910 and thereafter were running amok in the streets and requiring the soldiers to shoot them down and everywhere threatening the peace and prosperity of their betters? Captain Conrad couldn't have been sympathetic. He wasn't for nothing of the *szlachta* of Poland, of its old landed gentry, and in the figure of Donkin, the malingering crewman in *The Nigger of the "Narcissus*," had already expressed his contempt for the radical worker. "They all knew him! He was the man that cannot steer, that cannot splice, that dodges the work on dark nights. . . . The pet of philanthropists and self-seeking landlubbers." And indeed on this subject some literary folk were inclined to be savage. "I'd batten them down. I'd make them work," Mrs. Julia Frankau the novelist was saying at the time of the great miners' strike. "They *should* work. I'd force them down." "Labor will come out of it," Kipling was hoping, "like a sort of singed Ishmael—with every man's hand against it," and he almost wished "that the strike would go on till the very name of 'miner' stank like 'suffragette.' " James was no Kipling, no Mrs. Frankau; but by this time he, even he, was a little put out by the ill-humored strikers. "The Government [was] proceeding very justly . . . ," he was saying, but Labor was "rising everywhere like a huge Bugaboo, and happy . . . the country that tackles him first and has it out with him to a practical issue. . . ." Leonard Woolf had thought that, like Hardy, the Master had joined the revolt of the young against their Victorian elders but no, he now sadly concluded, "he was never really upon our side in that revolt."

Bennett on the other hand was. His only regret was that the strikers had lost, that "the poor [had] *suffered* all over the country" while the rich had "merely been infinitesimally inconvenienced." "Workmen on strike are always in the right . . . ," he'd say with one of his characters. "They don't starve themselves for fun." "War on employers, get all you can out of them," he'd say with another, "for they will get all they can out of you." This would be also the thinking of the Chesterton brothers, Gilbert all for rough tactics in handling blacklegs and scabs and Cecil envying life in America where the "police shot down strikers but the strikers bombed the police." Gilbert could wax almost tearful in fact on the subject of the poor and downtrodden. Albeit the victims of a brutal economic and industrial system, they were still, don't you know, "the sanest, jolliest and most reliable part of the community." Rebecca West, young, bitter, sardonic, wasn't, however, persuaded. She abhorred the fat populist, "the condescension with which he slaps the working man on the back." As for Shaw and the strikers, what could he say that, as a good socialist, he hadn't said over and over again? Nationalize, of course. Nationalize. Take the mines and the factories out of the hands of the arrogant masters. In the meantime, however, a strike made no sense. It was "nothing," he said, "but the old eastern plan of starving on your enemy's doorstep until he surrenders." But what did Shaw count in the scale of the heroic endeavors of the great Tory anarchist? Cunninghame Graham had early supported the Scottish Labour party, but what good in the end were parties and unions? Only revolution, a bloody apocalypse, would suffice. Violent? The strikers? By God, they weren't near violent enough. "It needed a volcano of blood to break out," he would say, "before the British people would be really roused." Once, at a Caxton Hall meeting, he appeared on the platform looking, with his Vandyke beard and exquisite apparel, like Charles I. "I am not one of those," he gravely began, holding aloft a thin and well-manicured hand, "who tremble at the word—ASSASSINATION!" There was WILD APPLAUSE. For several minutes they wouldn't let him go on. He worked "with the under-dog," one bitter skeptic observed, "in order . . . to continue to feel aristocratic." This was doubtless unjust. Nevertheless, with friends like him and the Chesterton brothers, the poor proletariat hardly needed an enemy.

"... And the women gibbered with rage"

Now "the Woman Question," the question of the suffrage for women, that was something else again. No proletarian odors here, no "odors from the abyss" as Forster had called them. Christabel Pankhurst, an ardent royalist with a passionate hatred of Labor, made sure of that. Sister Sylvia, who cared for poor women workers and wanted to get them involved in the cause, Christabel expelled from the ranks. Her movement was to remain a middle- and upper-class one to the utter dismay of Rebecca West who felt it was fatal to split the emancipation of women from that of the men. To the utter dismay, for that matter, of Cecil Chesterton who denounced it as the work of a handful of higher-class women and mocked the whole movement as "Votes for Ladies." For some nonetheless it was all too advanced as it was. For the rebarbative Kipling, it goes without saying, but for Henry James too, who wasn't eager at all "for the *évènement* of a multitudinous and overwhelming female electorate" and was only eager, he said, with the German menace in mind, "for Dreadnoughts and Aeroplanes and people to man, not to woman, them!" Write for Miss Harriet Weaver's feminist organ, the *New Freewoman*? He'd just as soon not. Indeed, it bored him "to extinction," he had to confess, this whole woman question. "Strangely," he said, "it isn't interesting...." This rather surprised him, but then there you are. "I give it up."

In the meantime, Bennett was suggesting that "the most powerful argument for woman's suffrage [was] the fact that women want it" and Leonard Woolf was suggesting that "if they [didn't] want it, they ought to" and Russell was suggesting to his love, Lady Ott, that *she* certainly "ought to." Even the skeptical Strachey would enter the fray. He was apprehensive of course. "I believe the ladies will try to forbid prostitution," he said; "and will they stop there?" Nevertheless, at sister Pippa's behest, he joined the men's league for the promotion of female suffrage and marched with three thousand women in the first of the great demonstrations and in 1910 hoped to join the ladies in the visitors' gallery of the Commons where he'd "have," he expected, "to shriek and be torn to pieces." As for Hueffer, who had always to be in the thick of things, he was happy to be seen dancing with Christabel Pankhurst, "very obtrusively feminine, holding up her long train with a ribbon attached to her wrist in the Victorian method," and was telling Lawrence's Jessie that although he had two votes, he "had never voted once, and never would, until women also were able to vote." He would later recall that a distressed Lady Gregory had asked him to rescue the Abbey from the wrath of Miss Horniman who was so enraged by the appearance of the actress Sara Allgood at a suffragette rally that she threatened to cancel the Abbey's subsidy unless every member of the company apologized, a reminiscence more correct than Hueffer's reminiscences usually were: *except* that it was Yeats who was asked to apologize and that Lady Gregory was most unlikely to have come to Hueffer for help of any kind. No matter. He was sympathetic. Even Conrad was sympathetic. For all his patrician views and his Winnie-Verloc wife who couldn't have thought such things bore looking into, Conrad was in his way for the franchise. "It will please them," he said, "and certainly it won't hurt me."

Not, to be sure, a ringing endorsement. But then even the best-intentioned among them would hide in their hearts some secret and perhaps unmentionable doubt. Wells wanted freedom for women all right, but he didn't like women acting like men and hence wouldn't have them "badgering cabinet ministers or padlocking themselves to railings." Nor was James entirely against them, "the shrieking sisterhood," but he too didn't like seeing them acting like men and hence could admire Elizabeth Robins who had "hurled herself . . . into the Suffragette agitation, but not," he was happy to say, "in the obstreperous, police-prodding or umbrella-thumping way of [so] many others." Nor was Morgan Forster, who was nothing if not a good Liberal, against them, the dears. Of course they should have the vote, if they wanted it. But then . . . but then . . . there was this nasty hunger-striking and window-smashing business and what if the vote should do them no good? Morgan once went to hear Christabel speak. She was, he decided, "very able, very clever, and very unpleasant." Rupert Brooke, young and enlightened, must have been for them, the women, in principle. But in fact? "It was great fun," he said of a Fabian conference where the women's cause went down to defeat. "The Northern delegates were superb men. They lashed the women with unconquerable logic and gross words. There were most frightful scenes, and the women gibbered with rage...."

For some of course it wasn't possible to believe in the movement at all. If they couldn't believe in votes for men—and they frequently couldn't—how could they believe in votes for women? Somerset Maugham saw "no reason why women shouldn't vote if they care to but," he said in his already world-weary way, "I can't see why they want to. Voting is not interesting. I don't vote. I don't want to." Ezra Pound didn't vote, didn't want to. Democracy was a failure, wasn't it, and how on earth would a million more uninformed ballots make any difference? At a table in the old Café Royal, Sophie Brzeska was seething with anger. Since women, Ezra was saying to Gaudier, exercised on their husbands a subtle behind-the-scenes influence, what was the point of their voting at all? Even Shaw would assume the Ezraic position. A clever wife refuses the right to the vote, he would say, "knowing well that whilst the man is master, the man's mistress will rule."

But, on this as on other grave questions, Shaw was never uncomplicated. From the very beginning, before Christabel, before Mrs. Pankhurst, he was a passionate feminist and regarded their "participation in public affairs as a matter of course." He knew very well what the Victorian patriarchy had cost and was costing, and would do what he could to demolish that beautiful pedestal on which women had been carefully placed—and abandoned. "Unless," as he said, "Woman repudiates her womanliness, her duty to her husband, to her children, to society . . . to everyone but herself, she cannot emancipate herself." So he'd do his best for the suffragette cause: give money, denounce forced feeding, address public meetings. "Women should have a revolution—" he'd say in a rage, "they should shoot, kill, maim, destroy—until they are given the vote." Just the same, he was a feminist first and a suffragist second. He cared a great deal for Sylvia Pankhurst, for her "idiot-genius," but he didn't much care for her mother and sister and their royalist politics and in any case didn't doubt for a moment that votes for women were just as futile as votes for men and "What use is the vote?" he'd have his characters cry. "Men have the vote." "And men are slaves."

Wells was doubtless on Shaw's side in this matter. He was all, to be sure, for the women, for their social and political rights. He had worked to free them from all that would bind them to home and to husband, had dared to propose that the state, not their mates, endow them and free them as mothers. But Christabel and her myrmidons wouldn't have him. They wanted votes, not babies. They wanted political, not sexual, power. They didn't in fact want sex at all. Sex was just what bound them to men. The banners they carried didn't read "Votes for Women" alone. They read "Votes for Women and Chastity for Men." Christabel went even further. In her book *The Great Scourge* she charged that 75 percent of the males carried gonorrhea and 25 percent syphilis and that exposure to them meant the instant decay of the feminine flower. Wells was naturally appalled. He was all for women but for women who liked to like men, and some of Christabel's women quite obviously didn't. There was, he was sure, behind the movement itself, something vaguely unpleasant, a suspicion perhaps of sexual perversion. Conrad would think so too. In *Chance* Mrs. Fyne is more feministic than feminine and her relations with her girlish disciples seem implicitly lesbian. Young Lawrence would certainly think so. Clara Dawes, his suffragist female in *Sons and Lovers,* is at times just a little bit sinister and Winifred Inger, his feminist woman in *The Rainbow,* is presented in a chapter called "Shame" as sexually repellent. Even Forster, amazingly, had the same ill thoughts. He was all for homosexual freedom but not, it would seem, for its feminine variant. He "thought Sapphism disgusting," he said to Virginia Woolf. Women should not, he believed, be independent of men.

The women members of the London academy were less ambiguous about it—Ethel Smyth, the composer whose *March of the Women* for organ and cornet was played in 1911 at an Albert Hall rally; Doris Marsden who had hunger-struck and suffered forced feeding and was founding in 1911 the *New Freewoman,* "A Weekly Feminist Review"; Rebecca West who at eighteen was writing for the *New Freewoman* and with such slashing effect that she was widely admired as a "Shaw in skirts"; and, visiting now from America, Miss Harriet Monroe, who witnessed from the windows of the Lyceum Club ("a center for more or less militant suffragists") a great river of feminist saints flowing by on the road to the Albert Hall where Mrs. Pankhurst "and her eloquent daughter Christabel" were scheduled to speak. Violet Hunt had turned her house, South Lodge, into a meeting place for the women's committees and, gaily and gaudily dressed, would parade with other suffragette swells while her friend, Brigit Patmore, would sell *Votes for Women* on Kensington High Street and be scolded by an angry old gentleman for not taking care of her children. Indeed, Katherine

Mansfield was expelled from an omnibus for calling an antisuffragette woman a whore, and "a dear old lady in rustling black silk and widow's bonnet" brought down on the head of Rebecca West's sister her ancient umbrella and "Thank God," she would cry, "I am a womanly woman." Even Mrs. Webb was moved to link arms with her sisters. On May 19, 1909, at a testimonial dinner to herself and Sidney, she made her announcement. She was ready, she said, to break with the Old Gang, to "make a new start" as a suffragette of the militant sort.

As for the shy Virginia Stephen, she too was emboldened at last to stand up and stand out. No, she wouldn't write articles for the magazines nor would she compose a history of the franchise in New Zealand, but she would pass hours in a stuffy suffragette office "writing names like Cowgill on envelopes." She was, it's quite true, a trifle sardonic about it. "The office," she said, "with its ardent . . . young women, and brotherly clerks, [was] just like a Wells novel." But Virginia's misgivings weren't uncommon. Dorothy Richardson was all for the cause. She even agreed with her good friend Veronica, in her sordid cell in Holloway prison, that for some things a price would have to be paid. But she didn't believe for a moment, as Veronica did, that one had to *seek out* the price. And she didn't. For sure Lady Ottoline didn't. She listened to Russell patiently enough but was never persuaded, and after they pelted the prime minister with rotten eggs she'd have nothing whatever to do with them. Rebecca West who was young and impassioned was not to be deflected so easily and yet she, even she, had her doubts. When Christabel published her singular theories of men and marriage and venereal disease, she was appalled and embarrassed, and indeed, with Shaw and Wells less on Christabel's side than on Sylvia's, she lamented the movement's snobbish indifference to the cause of the poor working woman. Window-smashing for votes was all very well but striking for wages might be even better and equal wages for women, she went so far as to say, might be much better still. "Where," she cried, "are our women syndicalists?"

A Political Generation

But the cognoscenti of London didn't just labor at large for the workers and women. They wrote for them too, or of and about them. Was there a flaw in the system, a blight or a blemish, they didn't expose, or a solution, a plan or a program, they didn't propose? The strikes and the struggle between masters and workers? Galsworthy wrote *Strife*. The unequal courts and the harsh justice meted out to the poor? He wrote *The Silver Box*. The problem of poverty? Shaw wrote *Major Barbara*. Of prostitution and the rights of women? He wrote *Mrs. Warren's Profession*. Of the problems of marriage and poor women and wives? Pinero had written *The Second Mrs. Tanqueray* and Wilde *Lady Windermere's Fan* and now Shaw was writing, on a higher and more serious plane, *Man and Superman, Getting Married, Misalliance,* to which Barker would add *The Madras House*. And what of the Poor Laws of England? Mrs. Webb, who was on the royal commission to review and reform them, was beseeching the dramatists—Galsworthy and Masefield and Barker among them—to put her minority report on the stage. But she got no response. There were bigger fish to be netted. The character and conditions of the new proletariat in England, now awake and alert and still unrecorded? Wells would write his haberdashery novels, *Love and Mr. Lewisham, Kipps, Mr. Polly*. The effect of the sexual passions on poor men and women, a topic untouched and untouchable hitherto? He would write *Tono-Bungay, Ann Veronica, The New Machiavelli*. There were even those who would fasten not on this problem or that one but on the whole tangled problem of England herself, "the condition of England." For the nation was surely falling apart under the stress of the struggles between the rich and the poor, the male and the female, England and Ireland. Galsworthy had already published *The Island Pharisees* and Conrad *The Secret Agent* and Wells *Tono-Bungay* and Forster would be writing *Howards End* and Hueffer *The Good Soldier* and Shaw *Heartbreak House*. They were indeed a political generation, the Edwardians were, the most political perhaps since the generation of Dryden and Swift. The leading literary figures of the day, they weren't just literary figures. Like Kipling and Chesterton, Barker and Galsworthy and, eventually, Lewis and Pound, they were also political figures and, in the cases of Shaw and Wells, Belloc and Cunninghame Graham, they were practical, practicing ones.

It's even on record that one of them made something happen. On Monday, February 21, 1910, the curtains rose at the Duke of York's Theatre on Galsworthy's *Justice* to expose the cruelty of prison conditions and, more especially, the cruelty of solitary confinement. The play was at once a success. By the time the curtains came down that opening night the audience was wild with excitement and just wouldn't go home and "We want Galsworthy, we want Galsworthy," it was shouting. First the band left, then the lights were lowered, then the lights were put out and the house plunged in darkness, and still they refused to leave until Barker, the director, had himself to come out and tell them the author wasn't there and they were all very tired and would they please to depart? The play wasn't of course to the liking of everyone. The playwright was "the kind of man," one thoughtful observer complained, "who thinks that a few bylaws would solve the dark human problem." But London was otherwise carried away. "Good God," John Masefield exclaimed, "it is a revelation." "We all cried and couldn't speak to each other," declared Robert Morley who was there with two actresses. Mrs. Webb was quite overcome. It was her kind of play, exactly, she said, "great in its realistic form, great in its reserve and restraint, great in its quality of pity." As for Wells, he was all respect and contrition. "I've always opposed myself to your very austere method . . . ," he'd confess, "but since it leads you at last to the quite tremendous force of the play—well, I give in." Most impressive of all, the state itself would give in. When Ruggles-Brise saw the play, he was naturally, as head of the Prison Commission, alarmed. "His eyes were observed to start out of his head." But Winston Churchill, the new home secretary, was deeply moved and a few months later rose in the House with a modest proposal to reduce the length of solitary confinement.

The playwright was understandably pleased. As a liberal reformer and man of probity, why wouldn't he be? Wasn't it better to have saved many people from months of confinement, Gilbert Murray suggested, "than to have sent any number of overfed audiences into raptures!" But Galsworthy wasn't so sure. At a dinner arranged to introduce

Galsworthy to Churchill, Eddie Marsh asked him a question. Would he rather improve the prison system or be known a hundred years hence as a classic? To Marsh's surprise, the playwright decided he would very much like to be classic. He was not after all of the party of Barker and Shaw who would alter the world and make it safe for socialism. He was of the party that had gone to school to Flaubert and the French and adored Henry James and others like Conrad who thought that a work of art should have not one but twenty meanings so that no one could tell from the work itself just what, exactly, the author was or believed. Yet not even they were wholly immune to the current contagion of causes. James's *Wings of the Dove* asked serious questions about the state of the ruling classes in England and Hueffer's *Good Soldier* asked serious questions about their moral and sexual values. Conrad had already revealed, in his earlier fictions, the human disaster abroad, the disgrace of Western imperialism. Now ashore and witnessing the same social and political failures as other London men and women of letters, he'd reveal the human disaster at home. He wouldn't think much of the revolutionaries who had settled in Geneva or London, but neither would he think much of the established powers, whether English or Russian, and in *The Secret Agent* and *Under Western Eyes* would expose their coldness, their cruelty, their moral obliquity.

"Cowgill"

Though it would come up in Wells's *New Machiavelli*, the great constitutional fight between the Lords and the Liberals was perhaps too recent, too topical, for representation. But the plight of the poor and exploited was hardly neglected. It was, to be sure, by Henry James who "had no use," so Violet Hunt thought, "for the third class on his literary railway." But it wasn't neglected by Gissing and Galsworthy and it wasn't even neglected by Forster who had been close enough to the abyss to smell it and was somehow aware that beneath the "superstructures of wealth and art there wanders"—good heavens!—"an ill-fed boy" and who knew very well that his Tory Wilcoxes in *Howards*

End hadn't the answers and that, for all she was silly and hapless, his liberal heroine had. "Give them money," she says with Shavian directness. "Don't dole them out poetry-books and railway-tickets like babies." But Morgan wasn't for nothing a liberal. He would like to have liked his poor Leonard Bast, but the man had "the lilting step of the clerk" and swore "in a colorless sort of way" and even after his sentimental night-journey into the country is quite without dignity: "He put his hat on. It was too big; his head disappeared like a pudding into a basin. . . ."

But then this wasn't just Forster's failure. It was the failure of liberals in general who couldn't help fearing, detesting, as good middle-class people, the wretched creatures they were proposing to save. With what meticulous detail Gissing had painted the lives of his London slum-dwellers! Yes, but with what bitter loathing! "I hate low, uneducated people!" cries his hero in *Born in Exile.* "I hate them worse than the filthiest vermin!" As for Hugh Walpole, how could he possibly love them, these vermin? In his *Mr. Perrin and Mr. Traill,* West, "little West," has "that sallow, unhealthy complexion that two generations of ill-fed progenitors tend to produce" and exists to suggest, says his author, "what a Board School education and a pushing disposition can do for a man." Virginia Woolf did her best to be kind and in *Mrs. Dalloway* and *To the Lighthouse* would create her Septimus Smiths and her Tansleys, not to mention her poor Doris Kilmans, but given her feeling for "brotherly clerks" and for people called Cowgill, what could she do but make Basts and Wests all over again? Her Smith is a cabbage, her Tansley a tadpole. Oh, Mrs. Dalloway does "only connect" with the one and Mrs. Ramsay does "connect" in her way with the other, but Mrs. Dalloway's "connection" is only a fancy and whatever happened to that "nice" Mr. Tansley? Why, look at the names they were giving their middle-class characters, these liberal souls: Merton Densher, Hilary Dallison, Henry Galleon. . . . But their lower-class people, their children of the abyss: these they'd call Noaks and Rink and Frant and Frapp and Batch and Bast, yes Bast. Why base? Why bastard? Why Bast?

But "beware of the man who rises to power from one suspender." For did proletarian Wells treat his lower-class folk any better? His Kippses and Pollys have zest right enough, the good humor and good nature of the brave new industrial humanoid, and are eager, as he was, to escape from the traps that a vicious, class-ridden society has set in their way and, all things considered, they're seldom poor sods like the "brotherly clerks" of the Forsters and Woolfs. But he can't help putting them down just a little, has them dropping their h's and speaking the "troof" and living "togever" which is all very cozy but too, too Dickensian for words. Wells knew well enough what they were, these unhappy creatures. They were children who were "thwarted and crippled" by a rotten society, and indeed after three hundred pages of doing a Dickensian number on little Art Kipps and his little wife Ann, he'll explode in a moment of rage and rebellion and "The stupid little tragedies of these clipped and limited lives!" he'll exclaim. "What is the good of . . . pretending that ill-educated, misdirected people 'get along very well,' and that all this is harmlessly funny and nothing more?" Victims they were, victims of "a monster, a lumpish monster" that hung over their lives "like some fat, proud flunkey, like pride, like indolence, like all that is darkening and heavy and obstructive in life." But Wells's heart told him otherwise, told him they weren't defrauded, disinherited creatures, but Dickensian darlings with freckles and curls. "They do very well, the dears, anyhow, thank Heaven!"

No doubt they were awful, these new urban creatures, these poor refugees from the pastoral slums, but was this all they were? Did they have to be cabbages like Morgan's Leonard and Virginia's Septimus or Dickensian sweeties like the Kippses and Pollys? The hero of Hardy's *Jude the Obscure* and the working-class folk of the slums of Christminster: they're the genuine article, undiminished, untarnished, by pathos or sentiment. Bill Price, Henry Straker, Doolittle *père:* Shaw's common people are real human beings, not clowns in a show. They're distinctly themselves, as distinctly themselves as diamonds or nails, and just as enduring. Not *they* are ridiculous. It's their middle-class masters. *They're* not "common." It's their conditions. Was Mrs. Brigstock in Barker's *Madras House* unhappy, inadequate? Why wouldn't she be? She was "the product," said Barker, "of fifteen years or so of long hours and little lunch." Were the children of London in Miss Nesbit's *Five Children and It* naughty and miserable? Why wouldn't they be? Instead of living in the country where everything's different, they live in the city where everything's the same. "Of course," writes Miss Nesbit, "there are the shops and the theatres . . . but if your people are rather poor you don't get taken to the theatres, and you can't buy things out of the shops. . . ." Miss Nesbit may in fact have known more of the Smiths and the Basts and their London conditions than the Forsters and Woolfs. "But how badly you keep your slaves," cries the queen of

Babylon in *The Story of the Amulet.* "They aren't slaves," says one of the children; "they're working-people." "Why don't their masters see that they're better fed and better clothed?" asks the queen, but the children can't answer because, says Miss Nesbit, "the wage-system of modern England is a little difficult to explain. . . ." "You'll have a revolt of your slaves," warns the queen, "if you're not careful." But "you see, they have votes—that makes them safe not to revolt." Arnold Bennett wasn't a socialist like Miss Nesbit. He was nevertheless the soul of sympathy and took notice of things. "The servility that always characterizes the worker in a city of idlers," and the serving-girl now "a charming young creature" but soon to become "a dehumanized drudge," and "the prone forms of the servants [sleeping] in stifling black cupboards under the roof and under the stairs." The easy solutions of humor and sentiment weren't always beneath him and in Samuel Povey of *The Old Wives' Tale* he was "glad to think" of "the vein of greatness which runs through every soul without exception." But Arnold was a democrat in a way that Wells was not and in the heroine of *Hilda Lessways* could extol without laughter or tears the new individual, the new human freedom, "the miraculous human power to make experience out of nothing."

The liberal Barrie, it's true, wasn't all whimsy and sentiment. In *The Admirable Crichton* he'd challenge the English class system itself. When an English party is shipwrecked and marooned on an island, the social roles are reversed. The butler takes over, Lord Loam, his master, becoming his handyman and Lady Mary, the daughter ("any observant spectator can see that she was born to wait at table"), becoming his handmaid. At the end of the play, however, there's a rescue ship and the traditional order of things is restored, the butler reassuming "the humble bearing of a servant" and addressing Lady Mary, who had learned to adore him, as "My lady," and "there is something wrong with England," Lady Mary is forced to conclude. It was shocking of course, such an ending. William Archer even wondered if Barrie was aware of how shocking it was. But the pathos and whimsy were more to the point. The admirable Crichton is admirable enough in his way but is harmless and impotent in the end and nearly a figure of fun: "My lady, not even from you . . . can I listen to a word against England." The servants, Barrie had instructed his players, "go according to precedence but without servility, and there must be no attempt at 'comic effect,' " but they *do* go according to precedence and pose, it's quite clear, no danger at all to the state. "Can't you see, Crichton," the liberal Lord Loam declares, "that our divisions into classes are artificial, that if we were to return to Nature . . . all would be equal." But the admirable Crichton has a perfectly admirable answer: "The divisions into classes, my Lord, are not artificial. They are the natural outcome of a civilized society." But then Barrie wasn't a liberal for nothing. He wanted change all right, but not an excess of it. He wanted things to be different but wasn't quite sure they could be or should be. It was enough perhaps to feel sad and compassionate.

The compassionate Galsworthy was certainly saddened. In his novel *Fraternity* he concluded, with Barrie and Forster, that the gap between the rich and the poor was not to be closed, that classes were ultimate things like rivers and mountains and as final and changeless as God. But then Wells again, who was never a Liberal, was not more enlightened. Of course he hated the England that expected every man to do "his duty in that state of life unto which it shall please God to call him. . . ." Of course he hated "the Argus eyes of [its] social system, the innumerable mean judgments you feel raining upon you. . . ." Like the hero of Dickens's *Great Expectations*, the hero of *Kipps* is betrayed by a venal society. Like him he's ashamed of his "lowness," aspires to gentility, wants to be altered from nice Arty Kipps into proud "Arthur Cuyps, frock-coated on occasions of ceremony, the familiar acquaintance of Lady Punnet, the recognized wooer of a distant connection of the Earl of Beaupres." But Wells who had been wined and dined by the Lady Elchos and Desboroughs and Ribblesdales was himself a bit of a Cuyps, and the ruling classes he had claimed to revile he would come to revere. In *Tono-Bungay* his common people are incurably "common." Marion is "common" and Effie is "common" and Ernest Ponderevo is "common" and even his aunt, for all that she reads Bernard Shaw, is "common," and the Frapps of course, George Ponderevo's poor cousins, are "common." Only George (i.e., Wells himself) isn't common and his lover of high degree, Lady Beatrix Normandy. Consider, dear reader, her name. Lady Beatrix Normandy. How could she be common? In his head a good socialist, Wells was in his heart a good Tory, detesting the birth of the new world of moneyed plutocracy and lamenting the death of the old one of landed "his lordship" and resembling in this his wicked old mother, the snobbish housemaid, who was happy to worship her betters and know her own place and had always despised, Wells would learn to his horror, her own commonplace husband and sons.

"Votes for Women!"

It was "the woman question" in any event that was most engaging the literary conscience in London. It was certainly engaging the conscience of the women of letters. The popular novelist Mrs. Humphry Ward was against it, the suffrage for women. Women already had power over men. Emancipation would spoil it. But for every young actress in town, it seemed at the time, nothing less than complete emancipation would do and no wonder. Something had happened, something amazing. It was Henrik Ibsen. Beerbohm Tree had read Ibsen's *Ghosts* and astonished, indignant, had set it aside. "But this is a woman's play," he had cried. "There's no part for me." And he hadn't been wrong. To do Ibsen wasn't only to serve the new drama. It was also to serve the new woman, to create a new breed of actress eager to play and able to play the powerful new women's parts. Janet Achurch, for example, who had played in the nineties a memorable Nora and Florence Farr a memorable Rebecca West and Elizabeth Robins a memorable Hedda Gabler.

To do Ibsen was also to create a new breed of actress-producer, bold, bitter, combative. With money clandestinely provided by Annie Horniman, Florence Farr took over for a season the Avenue Theatre and there produced in 1894 *The Comedy of Sighs,* a feminist play by one Dr. Todhunter. With provocative lines like "Don't you think a man's love is rather hard to bear?" and "Didn't you find marriage rather a horrid experience?" it so roused the wrath of the pit and the gallery that for over two hours it was jeered at and booed while the play's leading lady, Florence herself, wearily struggled to finish her part. Ten years later the actress Lena Ashwell received from a female admirer a jewel case containing some five hundred pounds and proceeded to lease an old theatre on Great Queen Street as a center for feminist plays. Not many years later Gertrude Kingston would establish on John Street, Adelphi, the Little Theatre which she'd open with Laurence Housman's translation of *Lysistrata.* She would rather have opened with *Pains and Penalties,* Housman's historical drama about Queen Caroline and her unhappy marriage to George IV, but the censor denied it a license on several grounds, among them that its George IV was likely to awaken reminders of a more recent monarch whose private life had inspired, he regretted to say, "certain foolish tittletattle."

But the new drama wasn't just *about* the new woman. It was also *by* the new woman, by playwrights like Cicely Hamilton and Lalla Vandervelde, Mrs. E. S. Willard and Mrs. W. K. Clifford, Lady Colin Campbell and Lady Violet Greville. For sheer will and talent and energy, however, there was no one in London to match the rebellious Elizabeth Robins. Mad about Ibsen, she had produced *Hedda Gabler* at the Vaudeville Theatre and then for the purpose of establishing Ibsen on a permanent basis had started the New Century Theatre. But it wasn't until the suffragette movement came into its own that Robins would come into hers. She not only served with the Pankhursts on the board of the Union but made them a play, *Votes for Women!,* which in 1907 she persuaded Barker and Shaw to produce and which turned out to be the most powerful plea for the movement so far. The plot, to begin with, was a suffragist dream. The heroine who was modeled on Christabel Pankhurst has had an abortion for the sake of a lover too selfish to marry her. When he becomes a force in the Conservative party, however, she threatens to win to the suffragist side the wealthy young woman he now loves unless he agrees to support in the House the bill granting women the vote. What can he do but consent? Nor is this all that she wins. She also wins the battle of the sexes, the bitter struggle between man the aggressor and woman the victim, which dominates the dialogue of the play and accounts for its bitterly militant tone and its anger and power.

Meanwhile the men, if they were for the women at all, were less than forthcoming about it. In Forster's *Howards End* the sainted Mrs. Wilcox is "only too thankful not to have a vote," and though the heroine would be only too thankful to have it, she'll feel the full force of the argument, Mrs. Humphry Ward's argument, that "the woman who can't influence her husband to vote the way she wants ought to be ashamed of herself." J. M. Barrie certainly felt it, the force of this argument. It was, he'd say, *What Every Woman Knows.* The little wife Mag-

gie—she's literally little, almost a dwarf—is the will and the brains behind her fatuous husband's political fortunes and under the circumstances has no need of the vote and indeed, at the end of the play,
poor wee Maggie, "now a little bundle near his feet," says as much:
"Every man who is high up loves to think that he has done it all himself; and the wife smiles, and lets it go at that. It's our only joke. Every
woman knows that." Wells's Ann Veronica does join the Union, it's
true, and storms with her sisters the Parliament buildings, but it's
merely "a phase" in her life, Wells insists, and what she really wants, he
has her confess, is "a proper alliance with a man, a man who is better
stuff than herself." It's certain that Conrad wasn't that strong for the
vote. As his Marlow puts it in *Chance,* "femininity" was a "privilege"
but "feminism" was only "an attitude." Indeed the feminist leader of
the absurd revolutionaries in *Under Western Eyes* is exposed as a fraud
and Mrs. Fyne's feminist doctrine in *Chance*—that a woman should
allow no scruples to stand in her way—must have been for the former
sea captain a positive horror. As for the satirist "Saki," he wasn't inclined to take the business of women too seriously. In a comic poem
he writes of an unhappy suffragette who is "too sincerely hunger-
struck" and elsewhere writes of a Roman emperor who deals with the
problem of his "Suffragetae" by feeding them all to his lions and
wolves.

But then Shaw himself found it hard to take it too seriously. He'd
compose for the London Society for Women's Suffrage a farcical sketch
called *Press Cuttings;* but at its two private showings the audience must
have wondered on whose side exactly the author was supposed to be.
He made fun of the government leaders all right, but he also made
fun, often merciless fun, of the ladies. "The Suffragets are not all
dowdies," says one of his women; "but they are mainly supported by
dowdies." Another has trouble distinguishing the pro-suffragettes from
the antis: "They're all alike when they get into a state about it." But
hold. Perpend. A feminist first but a suffragist second, Shaw may as a
dramatist have done more for the cause than the most ardent apostle
of votes. What was the trouble with women in fiction? Like Conrad's
women, like his Jewels and Natalias, his Floras and Lenas, his Intend-
eds, they were only too womanly. But the secret of Shaw's great success
on the stage was that he had made his women "unwomanly women,"
had made them, like his impudent Anns, like his proud Major Bar-
baras, human, like men. "Whilst all the others were turning out

heroines that were getting womanlier and womanlier and womanlier until they had lost all semblance of humanity . . . he [had] always assum[ed]," he would say, "that a woman [was] just like a man." All too much like a man, cried Frank Harris, who called Shaw's women "distinctly unpleasant, practically unsexed." But Lillah McCarthy who played Ann Whitefield and Shaw's leading ladies thereafter was sufficiently grateful. Away from Shaw's plays, she was told, she could have become "a great tragedienne," but away from Shaw's plays, she replied, she "would never have developed as a woman." Mrs. Pankhurst herself was not unaffected by the Shavian heroine. It was Ann Whitefield, she said, who had "strengthened her purpose and fortified her courage."

"Just like a man"

As for the Edwardian male, if he wasn't altogether for votes for women, he was all for new life and new living for them and would create in effect a new literature, a literature that expressed their new passion for social deliverance. Deliverance, first, from the family, from the towering Victorian father and his sadly obliterated wife and his poor spinster sisters and daughters pining away in his shadow. In plays like *The Voysey Inheritance* and *The Madras House,* Barker would record it, the pathos of their lifeless and loveless conditions, and in a novel like *Hilda Lessways* Arnold Bennett would record it—"I had a sudden vision of it. It has never been done"—the world as seen by a woman and only a woman. They'd create, for that matter, a wholly new creature, a radiantly young and rebellious creature who was ready to burst from her sad and sordid cocoon. Like Barker's freethinking Alice who can say without blushing, "I always do what I know I want to do." Like Bennett's Hilda Lessways for whom "the faculty of men and women to create their own lives seemed divine." Like Wells's Ann Veronica with her passion "to be, to do, to experience" and the courage to abandon for London and life her raging Victorian father. Like, above all, the heroines of Shaw's novels and plays who, like his militant friend Florence Farr, will refuse to have husbands and children, keep house,

and sew shirts but will plan their own lives and make their own living
and choose their own lovers: Hypatia, for example, in the play *Misalliance* who wants, she says, to be "a glorious young beast" and has little
respect for fathers and brothers ("Men like conventions because men
made them. I didn't make them: I don't like them . . .") and has no respect whatsoever for the gruesome home and the family ("Oh, home!
home! parents! family! duty! how I loathe them! How I'd like to see
them all blown to bits!").

They are, true enough, just a little impossible, these Anns and Hy-
patias. Nothing at all seems sacred to them. Wells's Ann isn't seduced
by her married lover. He is seduced, *horribile dictu*, by her: "I want
you. I want you to be my lover. I want to give myself to you." Shaw's
Hypatia is perhaps less immodest, but not very much. "Come, handsome young man, and play with the respectable shopkeeper's daughter." They'd even decline to be surrounded by skirts and by gowns and
the usual heavy Victorian apparel. "I am not accustomed to gowns,"
says the proud Lina Szczepanowska in Hypatia's play: "they hamper me
and make me feel ridiculous." And in *The Admirable Crichton* the
sometimes surprising James Barrie has his young ladies adopting male
clothing and abandoning their girdles and gowns to go hunting, like
men. Lord, how exciting it was, Lady Mary remembers on returning to
stuffy old England. She looks "dolefully" down at her skirt. In *The
Rainbow* and *Women in Love*, Lawrence's Brangwen girls will be active
verbs like Ann Veronica, will defect to careers and to cities from the
same provincial Victorian home and the same enraged Victorian father. No Victorian garb for our Gudrun! No drab skirts going down to
her feet! It'll be a dark blue dress and emerald green stockings or a
dress of green poplin and dark green stockings. But all things considered Lawrence will not be too happy about these developments. As
he'd show in the novels, there'd be trouble ahead for these glorious
nymphs, for his Gudruns and Ursulas, who think that they don't want
to marry. They'll win freedom all right, freedom to live their own lives,
but their freedom will seem in the end like a nightmare. Like Ann
Veronica, they'll need "a man who is better stuff" than they are.

Easier said than done, however. For at the same time the writers
were creating ripping young women, they were also creating unripping
young men, boyish, inadequate, sexless. Like Maugham's Philip Carey.
Like Galsworthy's Bosinney. Like Wells's Art Kipps and his George
Ponderevo. Like Lawrence's Cyril and his Paul Morel. It may have

started with Hardy, with his Oaks and his Yeobrights, his Clares and his Winterbornes, who pale in the presence of his powerful Bathshebas, Eustacias, and Tesses. But by the time of King Edward and his solemn successor, the emasculate male had become, it would seem, epidemic. For James's man Densher is really no match for his gallant Kate Croy. Nor is Bennett's Clayhanger for his strong-minded Hilda. Nor Lawrence's Skrebensky for his powerful Ursula. Nor is Conrad's Lord Jim for his Jewel, his Axel Heyst for his heroic bride Lena. Nor is Hueffer's John Dowell for his Florence, his Edward Ashburnham for his proud Leonora. Why, they're hardly grown men, these wimpish Edwardians. They're sentimental Tommies. They're lost Peter Pans. ("My heart aches, and a drowsy numbness pains/ My sense . . .") This may seem too harsh, too vindictive a verdict to bring down on their heads. Like the hero of *The Way of All Flesh*, they are deeply engaged, these young men, and are all in revolt—Ponderevo, Clayhanger, Paul Morel, Philip Carey—against their Victorian fathers. Just the same, something's gone wrong with their spirit, their sex. They're all of them victims of some failure of nerve, some failure of manhood. They're not, like the girls, active verbs. Shaw was after all as eager to abolish the manly man as he was to abolish the womanly woman. Consider his Marchbanks, his Tanners, his Adolphus Cusins. Consider for that matter the most recurrent of all those Edwardian character types, those charming but otherwise helpless young men who appear in "Saki," Max Beerbohm, and Ada Leverson, not to mention du Maurier's *Trilby* in the tremulous person of Little Billee with "his beautiful sensitive face" and his "easily moistened eyes" and his arms "like a girl's."

For if there was a real difference between men and women, some Edwardians were saying, it was scarcely worth mentioning. "Good Lord," the hero of Barker's *The Madras House* is told, "you can't behave towards women as if they were men." "Why not?" the young hero blithely replies. And why not indeed, said Barker's old friend. Only on the stage were there women, said Shaw. In the real world itself, "there [was] no such thing as a woman." "I am a woman and you are a man," says the man to the woman in his *Village Wooing*, "with a slight difference that doesn't matter except on special occasions." Even Wells who rejoiced in the difference and the special occasions could entertain the idea. "I believe," he could say, "there is very little difference between men and women. . . ." This was none too convincing, however, and in fact it was hard not to notice that the equality he was preaching in public wasn't quite on a par with what he practiced in fiction. Wells's women were clearly the same dear little women, Dorothy Richardson said, "with different shades of hair and proportions of freckles . . . and one vague smile between them all." His New Women, Rebecca West said, were merely the servants of his New Men and his great Endowed Motherhood scheme was but a subsidized form of the old domesticity. "The mind reels," she wrote, "at the thought of the community being taxed to allow [Wells's woman] . . . to perpetuate her cow-like kind."

Discouraging words, no doubt, for the Great Emancipator, but not undeserved. In the earlier novels his women are Dickensian Biddys, like Kipps's "sunlit" Ann. All "warm and welcoming," this "bright and healthy little girl woman" has "soft-looking lips a little apart and gladness in her eyes" and a hat all "Sundayfied with pink flowers." In the later more openly sexual novels there is, to be sure, a difference of sorts, a sexual difference. But they're still the same dear little women, adoring, adorable, like Effie in *Tono-Bungay* who is awfully good to our George, "glancing up ever and again at my face" and making herself "my glad and pretty slave and handmaid." The hero of *The New Machiavelli* is perhaps more advanced than our George. No Effie for him. "Typical of my time," as he thinks, and seeing women at last coming into their own, Remington-Wells finds in his intellectual Isabel-Amber "an equal mate," an equal mate in "the jolly march of our minds together." But it's rot, pure rot! It's sexual pleasure he's after, the sweet rites of romance, and the jolly march of their minds be damned! Equal mates indeed! Even his Ann Veronica, that brave independent, doesn't want to be equal. Like Lawrence's Lady Chatterley who wants to melt "small and beautiful" into the arms of her gamekeeper, "I wish," says Wells's Ann to her lover, "I could roll my little body up small and squeeze it into your hand." But then Wells was but one of many who thought one thing and felt something else. "A woman is not necessarily either a doll or an angel to me," says Conrad's Marlow. "She is a human being, very much like myself." But the problem, as things turn out, is just that she isn't a human being like himself, that "a man [could] struggle to get a place for himself . . . [while] a woman's part [was] passive." Of course he was "speaking here," says Marlow, "of women who are really women."

Rupert Brooke

James M. Barrie

Arnold Bennett

Vanessa Stephen Bell

E. M. Forster

Edward Carpenter

Joseph Conrad

John Galsworthy

David Lloyd George

W. H. Hudson

Cunninghame Graham

Frank Harris

Violet Hunt

Ford Madox Hueffer

Henry James

Augustus John

Rudyard Kipling

Wyndham Lewis

D. H. Lawrence

Katherine Mansfield

A. R. Orage

Christabel Pankhurst

Lady Ottoline Morrell

Ezra Pound

George Bernard Shaw

Beatrice Webb

Bertrand Russell

Virginia Stephen Woolf

H. G. Wells

Rebecca West

William Butler Yeats

"To speke of wo that is in mariage"

But it was marriage and its special problem for women that most attracted the Edwardian attention. Marriage was, it may be, a welcome relief from the horror of family. But why leave one horror to enter another? So they attacked the divorce laws, their difficulty, their unfairness to women. A man could sue for divorce on the grounds of adultery alone while, as the hero of *Tono-Bungay* explains to his unhappy wife, a woman could only sue on the additional grounds of desertion or cruelty. "To establish cruelty I should have to strike you . . . before witnesses," he tells her, but that being out of the question he opts to desert her and when the court orders him to return to her bed and he disobeys, "You get a Decree Nisi," he says, "and . . . if we don't make it up within six months . . . the Decree is made absolute. . . . It's easier, you see, to marry than unmarry." So enlightened Edwardians, like enlightened Victorians, would work to revise what Shaw called "your gratuitously unnatural and vicious English marriage laws," what Carpenter called "the present odious law which binds people together for life." Bennett's *Whom God Hath Joined,* the very first novel devoted entirely to the subject, stressed the baseness not of the laws but of the court proceedings. But the pathos of Galsworthy's *The Man of Property* wasn't just that the heroine was married to a man she abhorred but that, under the cloud of adultery, she couldn't legally win her release and could even be legally raped by her husband. And the pathos of *Lords and Masters,* Edward Garnett's 1911 play, wasn't just that she was married to a man who couldn't or wouldn't feel anything for her, but that the laws were all on his side: "I'll not give you the satisfaction of setting you free." Why, argued Shaw, should adultery be the sole reason for granting divorce? "Imagine being married to a liar, a borrower, a mischief maker . . . or even simply to a bore!" The only sane grounds for allowing divorce, he concluded, was that both or one of the two parties desired it. As for the law that women could only sue for divorce on grounds of desertion or cruelty, he'd make it ridiculous in the play *Getting Married*. "He knocked her down," General Bridgenorth charges his brother, Reggie, "knocked her flat down on a flowerbed in the presence of his gardener." But, as it comes out, poor Reggie has had to arrange this "attack," has had to dig up the dirt with his own hands and soften the flowerbed in question.

Notwithstanding all which, nothing at all was accomplished. In 1903 the Society for Promoting Reforms in the Marriage and Divorce Laws was formed, and soon after that the Divorce Law Reform Union, and in 1906, under Sir Arthur Conan Doyle, the two were united to move the appointment of a royal commission to look into the matter. Maurice Hewlett, who was one of the first to appear at the hearings, was a little hysterical. "No moral cause can be successful," he said, "until a leader has been crucified: someone must go, and it will be me." Edward the King was also a little hysterical. The poor home secretary, Herbert Gladstone, who never seemed to do anything right, had had the bad taste to ask two women to join the commission. Divorce was a subject, His Majesty felt strongly, "which cannot be discussed ...with any delicacy and even decency before ladies." But as things turned out, the novelist's crucifixion was proven unnecessary and the king's apprehension unfounded and three years later the commission produced a few minor proposals which were never, however, made law.

Can nothing be done about marriage, my lord? the bishop is asked in Shaw's *Getting Married*. "You can make divorce reasonable and decent: that is all," the bishop replies. But this doesn't console Shaw's militant Lesbia. "If you will only make marriage reasonable and decent," she says, "you can do as you like about divorce." For the problem wasn't divorce, after all, its unjust laws, its absurd and sordid proceedings. The problem was marriage itself, its unjust laws, its absurd and sordid proceedings. The question was, was there life after marriage for women, and the answer appeared to be no. No, said Wells, whose Ann Veronica wants, naughty maid, to live and love freely and doesn't want marriage at all. No too, said Barker, whose noble young women are just as indifferent to marriage and "If one can provide for oneself or is independent," says his Alice in *The Voysey Inheritance*, "why get married?" Indeed your "ripping" Edwardian girl will have shockingly little to do with the conjugal state. Like the heroine of Bennett's *Hilda Lessways* who wants to live her own life and doesn't "want," she declares, "to get married." Like the heroine of Grant Allen's *The Woman Who Did*, who did, that is, reject marriage, to the consternation of her conventional suitor, and "Surely, surely," he cries, "you won't carry your ideas of freedom to such an extreme. . . ." Like, above all, Shaw's inspired Polish lady in *Misalliance* who'll have nothing at all to do with a husband: "I am strong: I am skilful: I am brave: I am independent: I am unbought: I am all that a woman ought to be . . . and this Englishman! this linendraper! he dares to ask me to come and live with him in this rrrrrrabbit hutch . . . and be his woman! his wife!" As for Edward Garnett, who considered the trouble to be with men, not with women, he said no to marriage a thousand times over. Fathers, husbands, lovers—they were all selfish beasts. You belong to me, says the father in *The Breaking Point*. You belong to me, says her lover who wants her to marry. Caught between the two masculine egos, the poor helpless creature breaks down and drowns herself. You belong to me, says the husband in *Lords and Masters* who would keep her his property. You belong to me, says her lover who would make her *his* property. But this heroine—shades of old Ibsen!—has a little more spunk. "Catherine (turning in the doorway and speaking to both the men): Good-bye! CURTAIN."

But then life after marriage could be no more blissful for men than for women. The freethinking hero of Leonard Woolf's novel is all contempt for the petty legalities of marriage but there's this little affair with a charming but conventional girl and sex of course and pregnancy perhaps and after that, surely, the nightmare of marriage from which, it's assumed, he will never awaken. " 'Dearest,' she whispered. He looked down at her face so close to him, and, shutting his eyes, kissed her." End of novel. End of hero. After *Ann Veronica* and its sordid transgressions, *The History of Mr. Polly* must have seemed like an innocent romp, the jolly old life-loving Wells restoring himself to his friends and his fans. Jovial it is, sure enough, but also a little anarchic and not at all reassuring on the subject of marital bliss. Poor Mr. Polly is more or less insinuated into it, this "unfortunate amoor" as he calls it. And the ceremony itself—he attends in the same outfit that he wore at his father's funeral—is far from encouraging. "Wiltou lover, cumfer, oner keeper sickness and health?" "Pete arf me 'Wis ring Ivy wed.' " The marriage itself is, like so many Wells marriages, a lugubrious business at best, but here, as in his other novels, H.G. can achieve in his art what he couldn't in life. Like Polly himself, he can simply clear out.

Well, "if the world doesn't please you, *you can change it*," as Wells has his Polly proclaim. And could marriage be changed? Could marriage be liberalized? Wells liked with Ellis and Carpenter to think so. Why not, he suggested, the *ménage à trois,* the *ménage à quatre,* the *ménage à . . . ?* "They say you can't love two women at once," says the freethinking Chitterlow in *Kipps.* "But I tell you—" he cries, gesticulating wildly. "It's *Rot! Rot!*" In Wells's *In the Days of the Comet,* there's this meteor encircling the earth and exhaling strange mind-bending gases. The results are miraculous. Two married couples who had been at odds with each other are suddenly altered at the end of the novel. "We four from that time were very close, you understand, we were friends, helpers, personal lovers in a world of lovers." Personal lovers in a world of lovers? What could he mean? Each man sleeping with both women, each woman with both men? Shaw was amused at this fanciful Wellsian invention. "I have never concealed my affection for Jane," he would write Wells. "If the moroseness and discontent which have marked your conduct of late are the symptoms of a hidden passion for Charlotte, say so like a man." Nevertheless Shaw took the idea more seriously than he cared to let on. In the preface to *Getting Married* he may celebrate marriage and deprecate polygamy, but in the action itself he can't help questioning the one and exploring the other and allowing his characters, for all that he didn't respect Edward Carpenter, such Carpenterian jewels as "Oh, how silly the law is! Why can't I marry them both?" and "Married people should take holidays from one another if they are to keep at all fresh." Indeed, a few years later, in his play *Overruled,* he'd be saying with Wells whose libertinism he had not long before been reproving that it was perfectly possible to love a third party and still go on loving one's legal spouse. Nor was Barker in vain Shaw's "heir apparent." Polyandry, says his hero in *The Madras House,* was "as much Nature's way as the other." Mrs. Webb was naturally distraught. Plays about prison reform, about Poor Law reform, and other such topics, these were very good things. But the very odd plays that her Fabian friends were producing . . . Were they not rather "obsessed," she declared after *Misalliance* and *The Madras House,* "with the rabbit-warren aspect of human society?" She was sorry, she said, and so was her Sidney, "to see G.B.S. reverting to . . . anarchic love making" and "everyone wishing to have sexual intercourse with everyone else."

But no need to worry. Neither marriage nor sex was for Shaw the road to the Heavenly City. Sexuality? Farcical, yes, but tragical too. "Do you see this face, once fresh and rosy like your own, now scarred and riven by a hundred burnt-out fires?" cries poor Mrs. George, sex-driven, sex-weary, in *Getting Married*. And marriage, human marriage? *Man and Superman* was, Shaw would say, "an explicit attack on marriage as the most licentious of human institutions." Marriage was, he decided, but the flawed earthly form of that community of saints, that Kingdom of Heaven, that all men and women secretly long for. "The thing one wants most," as his Mrs. George puts it, "has nothing to do with marriage at all." "Marriage," says another voice in the play, "is an abomination which the Church was founded to cast out and replace by the communion of saints." Just the same, Mrs. Webb wasn't wrong to be worried. At the time of *Getting Married* and *Misalliance* Shaw was entering his fifties and suffering a crisis. As an ardent socialist he had long ago sought "the forgetting of being," the surrender of self to the cause of the world, and had long ago given up sex and the flesh for the higher estates of art and the intellect. Like his own Don Juan, he would scale the high ladders of life and storm the pure heavens. "My kingdom was not of this world," he would say. But "the sleep of reason produces monsters" and now with the onset of age they were all flooding back: the body, the blood, sex, longing, desire. Charlotte was anxious, unhappy. Erica Cotterill, Rupert Brooke's young and immature cousin, had a crush on the world-famous playwright, was sending him long and preposterous letters which of course he made fun of but couldn't quite manage to repudiate. A few years later Charlotte would be still more unhappy, more anxious. Shaw would be mad for the beauteous actress, Mrs. Patrick Campbell, but, unable to act on his passion, would suffer rejection and hurt. Ah, the shame of it all, the disgrace! At fifty-five he was as attracted to sex, and as terrified by it, as he had been at twenty and thirty. "The beast with two backs." "Jug jug jug." "Abomination and bitchery." Hence *Getting Married*, hence *Misalliance*, with their critiques of marriage and sex, Mrs. George protesting her body and the erosions of time, Mr. Tarleton protesting his age and the cruel sexual glamour of youth. Shaw still the comedian perhaps but with old tragic tears in his eyes. Like another great poet who had longed for the ultimate, he had rediscovered his meager humanity and found he must "lie down where all the ladders start,/ In the foul rag-and-bone shop of the heart."

"I say we will have no moe marriages"

But if love, like life, was a curse and a care, what then? Live and love freely, the Edwardians were saying in their novels and plays. With or without marriage, sex was a force in the human experience. Embrace it, embrace it. The Jameses and Conrads weren't quite up to it. For them as for Shaw, sexual love was a fearful joy at best. Even they, nonetheless, wouldn't fail to acknowledge its terrible presence. In his Edwardian novels, in *The Ambassadors, The Wings of the Dove, The Golden Bowl,* James's people do on occasion make love with each other. All discreetly of course. Offstage, as it were. Nevertheless. As for Conrad, he'd be willing to enter more hazardous waters. His women will still be those womanly women abhorrent to Shaw, but now with a difference. The heroine of *Chance* will be exposed to the dangers of lesbian love, of incestuous love, and the openly heterosexual lovers of *Victory* will be threatened by a pair of openly homosexual lovers, by the malevolent Jones with "his delicate and beautifully pencilled eyebrows" who "seemed," says his partner, "to touch me inside somewhere."

In the meantime, however, a younger generation than James's and Conrad's would be approaching the amorous passion with much less restraint. Bluestockinged Violet Hunt who took a continental view of the subject may well have been first on the scene. Her *Sooner or Later* was "the first modern novel," Mrs. Lowndes said, "which dealt . . . with the problem of illicit love." But if she wasn't the first, Wells certainly was. From *Love and Mr. Lewisham* on, he would make sex the primary fact in the lives of his people, his married George Ponderevos and Richard Remingtons carrying on as they do and his unmarried Ann Veronicas and Isabel Riverses fleeing to the Continent with the husbands of others and bearing, in Ann's case, a child out of wedlock. Not enough for H.G. that he fight the sex war by enacting his sexual convictions and openly living with his young paramours. To the distress of his Fabian comrades, he must put them in novels and make public stuff of them. It pleased him in fact to reflect that life and art in his time had conjoined, that "young heroines with a temperamental zest for illicit love-making . . . [had] multiplied not only in novels but in real life."

They were, it may be, Wellsie's sexual conceptions, somewhat lacking in charm. The earnest but boring young hero of *Tono-Bungay* refers to "the ferment of sex . . . creeping into [his] being" or, more fetchingly still, to "Dame Nature driving [him] on . . . in her stupid, inexorable way." Sex is elsewhere for poor Ponderevo a form of state service, "the way in which the young people of this generation pair off," he declares with depressing sincerity, "determin[ing] the fate of the nation." He does make allusion, it's true, to its beauty, to "the stupendous beautiful business of love." But how crass to insist on the "business of love" or, for that matter, on his "appetite" for it, an appetite furthermore "roused and whetted." Or to describe his passion as some disgusting old dog that "trails about—even in the best mixed company. Tugs at your ankle." "The beauty which was the essence of it . . . eludes statement," states the hero of *The New Machiavelli*. Alas, it doesn't elude it enough and Wells the great lover wasn't much of a hand at doing love scenes. "We lay side by side and nibbled at grass stalks . . . ," writes his hero. "We've talked away our last half day," he says to his mistress, "staring over my shoulder at the blazing sunset sky behind us." Nibbling grass stalks and staring at sunsets and talking their last precious hours away? This was life, this was love? How young David Lawrence must have winced. He too would celebrate sex, would worship it as the measure of man and the rose of the world. But on Wells's mean terms? But let us not hasten to deride and degrade him. What if he came still wearing old rags and torn cerecloth? He had just crawled out of the stinking fosse, the stinking fosse that was Bromley, the past, the nineteenth century, England.

So there could be love without marriage and sex without marriage, but could there be babies without marriage? Surely not. But some Edwardians thought so and some even said so in novel and play. In Shaw's *Getting Married* Lesbia would love to have babies, but she won't have a husband. "If I am to be a mother," she says, "I really cannot have a man bothering me to be a wife at the same time." But, said other Edwardians, no problem at all. Why bother with husband and marriage! Have a baby anyway! "Good Lord! why hasn't she had a child?" cries the freethinking hero of Leonard Woolf's novel. Ethel is, true enough, an unmarried woman and sadly unlikely to marry. What then? Why not single parenthood? "Wouldn't it be better for her and everyone than the sterile life she's lived?" St. John Hankin the playwright had already made the same modest proposal. In the third act of *The Last of the De Mullins,* he had invited "every unmarried woman of twenty-eight . . . to go straight out and procure a baby at once. . . ." And since Lillah McCarthy, the earnest young actress, had regarded all this as the "most obvious doctrine" and delivered her lines with her usual gusto, she had had "no idea," said Shaw, "of the effect she was producing in the audience." But then Shaw himself, in the preface to *Getting Married,* would propound the same obvious doctrine. Insisting on "the old maid's right to motherhood," why, he would ask, "should the taking of a husband be imposed on these women as the price of their right to maternity?" How very quaint, Max Beerbohm reflected, this lusty new trend in the theatre. The heroine of his *Zuleika Dobson* has no problem at all loving men but she hasn't, says Max, that "quite explicit desire to be a mother with which modern playwrights credit every unmated member of her sex."

Morgan Forster himself had no quarrel with unsanctioned babies in literature. In *Howards End,* middle-class Helen is seduced by lower-class Leonard and though the father is fated to die, a child is providentially born to connect the classes that Forster wishes connected. It's not altogether convincing. Helen's so sexless and Leonard so limp and anemic that it's not only hard to imagine them ever "connecting" and composing a child, it's downright indecent. "Only connect," to be sure. But on such easy terms? Katherine Mansfield who'd had some experience along sexual lines wasn't impressed. "I can never be perfectly certain," she said in the mordant way that she had, "whether Helen was got with child by Leonard Bast or by his fatal forgotten umbrella. All things considered, I think it must have been the umbrella." But the librarian of the House of Lords wasn't amused by "the new craze" in fiction for "the high-bred maiden who has a baby." "I have read," wrote the librarian in question, Mr. Edmund Gosse, "*three* new English novels this autumn of which it is the *motif*" and he couldn't conceive "how an Englishman [could] calmly write of such a disgusting thing." He was, however, consoled. "I am now going to read a few chapters of Mrs. Gaskell to take the taste of *Howards End* out of my mouth."

The question indeed was would marriage survive the new sexual *modus vivendi*? Liberalize marriage? Why bother? Why not wipe it out altogether? G.B.S. certainly thought so. The hero of his novel *An Unso-*

cial Socialist prefers his cottage and corduroys and his socialist mission,
he tells his unlucky wife, to "our pretty little house and your pretty little ways." "There are larger loves and diviner dreams," as his Major
Barbara would later express it, "than the fireside ones." Forster's larger
loves and diviner dreams would be other than Shaw's but he'd understand perfectly. In *The Longest Journey*, in *Howards End*, in *Maurice*,
marriage is a horror, something mean and suburban, Shaw's connubial
bigotry all over again. "Eternal union, eternal ownership—these are
tempting baits for the average man," but not for the hero of *The
Longest Journey* who abandons his wife and his marriage. He can't opt,
to be sure, for an Ideal Friend, for "the love of a comrade." It's too
early for that. But the hero of *Maurice*, unpublished, unpublishable,
certainly can. He'll elect that Uranian love that transcends the limited,
limiting love of a man for a woman, and that will one day, he says, in-
herit the earth. Hence Lawrence's sense that it was—human love, marriage, sex—*"the* problem of today." "You've got to take down the
love-and-marriage ideal from its pedestal," he'd agree with Forster and
Shaw. "We want something broader." But on earth as in heaven a sexless condition, as Shaw would conceive it, and no difference at all between the male and the female? On earth as in heaven neither
"marriage nor giving in marriage," as H.D. would also conceive it? The
men "black beetles" and the women like his Gudrun and Ursula "sisters of Artemis rather than of Hebe" and in either case marriage defunct? It was not to be borne. He would write *The Rainbow, Women in
Love*, would reinstate marriage, redeem it. Not marriage on the sorry
Victorian plan so offensive to Forster and Shaw. Not "the world all in
couples, each couple in its own little house, watching its own little interests, and stewing in its own little privacy. . . ." But couldn't there be
some saving alternative? A little "star-equilibrium?" A union of the
male and the female but with separate identities? Apparently not. See
Women in Love, Aaron's Rod, Kangaroo, The Plumed Serpent: the failure,
that is, of the marital union and the real possibility of the homosexual
connection which was after all, Lawrence said, "as sacred a unison as
marriage." "I believe," he'd say with his Birkin, "in the *additional* perfect relationship between man and man—additional to marriage."

Nor was this all. In *Women in Love* Ursula kneels before Birkin
and lays "her hands full on his thighs, behind, as he stood before her."
"She traced with her hands the line of his loins and thighs, at the back,
and a living fire ran through her. . . ." "She had thought there was no

source deeper than the phallic source. And now, behold, . . . further in mystery than the phallic source, came the floods of ineffable darkness. . . ." Good heavens, what have we here? A repeat of the meeting of Forster and Carpenter's Merrill? Not the womb but the anus the source of life? Not the woman but the man as the "mother," the body, the source of creation? Or more simply, perhaps, Lawrence having his cake and eating it too? His hero not permitted to sodomize Gerald but permitted to sodomize Ursula and this with the strong seal of marriage upon it and the young woman's happy consent. How the vile Norman Douglas must have laughed at these desperate maneuvers to salvage the wreckage of marriage. By the time he was writing *South Wind,* Douglas would be glad to announce that this absurd institution was at last or would soon be extinct. "I don't believe any woman would ever bind herself to one fool of a man if she had her own way," he would say. "She wouldn't marry at all. She needn't, nowadays. She won't, very soon."

"Where do we go from Swinburne?"

But London wasn't just a vortex of new social and political ideas. It was also a vortex of new literary and artistic ideas. The same new energies that quickened the pulses of liberals and socialists, of workers and women, also quickened the pulses of poets and painters, of playwrights and novelists. "Now Swinburne is dead, Meredith dumb, and Henry James inarticulate," wrote Virginia Woolf at the time, "things are in a bad way." But they weren't really, not by a long shot. "About 1908 Letters seemed to come suddenly to life, and the Edwardian revival . . . was with us." So Edgar Jepson was thinking and so also was young Ezra Pound who had just arrived from Philadelphia by way of the Continent. "London, deah old Lundun," Ezra was writing ecstatically, "is the place for poesy" and he wasn't far wrong. It was after all the place for poets of the stature of Hardy and Yeats and of younger poets of the promise of Flint and Hulme, Hueffer and

Lawrence, Richard Aldington and Hilda Doolittle not to mention the Georgians and their happy clan. As things turned out, Ezra's ecstasies may have been premature. What was it, so much of this poesy, he would later recall, but "a doughy mess of third-hand Keats, Wordsworth, heaven knows what, fourth-hand Elizabethan sonority, blunted, half-melted, lumpy?" Tennyson, it's true, was put down by the young as a hopeless backnumber but Swinburne, the long-silent sage of Putney, was still venerated and at Cambridge the young undergraduates, the Woolfs and the Bells and the Stracheys, were walking the Cloisters in the nightingaled moonlight and chanting enraptured the rapturous verses, "From too much love of living/ From hope and fear set free . . ." or "We shift and bedeck and bedrape us/ Thou art noble and nude and antique . . ." No, the new poetry, whatever it was, was still of the future. "The question was still," T. S. Eliot remembered, "where do we go from Swinburne? and the answer appeared to be, nowhere."

To be sure, the poets of the nineties had given their best. For a moment or so Oscar Wilde and his friends had made poetry notorious. But when Edward Garnett's father, the Keeper of Printed Books at the British Museum, had first heard the news of Oscar's conviction, he'd looked over "the great yard of the Museum, with its pigeons and lamps and little lions on the railings," and had sadly concluded: "Then that means the death of English poetry for fifty years." He could have been right. "Good Heavens! Poetry!" cries an Edwardian figure in a Leverson novel. "Do people still do that sort of thing? I thought it had gone out years ago. . . ." Yet Ezra's instincts weren't entirely mistaken. Soon Tom Hulme would be trying his hand at a few sparse imagist poems and Frank Flint would be spreading the word of the symbolist poetry in France and though Pound didn't care for Lawrence's "middling-sensual erotic verses" he was mighty impressed all the same and "I think," he confessed, "he learned the proper treatment of modern subjects before I did." As for Ezra himself, he was bound and determined to resuscitate the dead art of poetry in England, to create a new motive, a new medium, a powerful new voice. One day in the British Museum tea room he'd be scanning Hilda Doolittle's first little Grecophile lyrics and "But Dryad," he'd be telling her, pince-nez in hand, "this is poetry," and "H.D. Imagiste," he'd be signing her work, and calling at once for a new kind of poetry, for a new *mouvemong*.

Where Do We Go from Shakespeare?

But if London wasn't quite ready for poets and poesy, it was ready for everything else. For plays and for playwrights, for instance. Notwithstanding the triumph of Ibsen, the prognosis at the turn of the century would not have been good. The city's West End, the heart of its theatre life, was still the domain of the great actor-managers who demanded long runs and large houses and the fatuous dramas to sustain or maintain them. Of course they put on society plays with upper-class characters and drawing-room dialogue. They were ministering to upper-class people who delighted to witness their lives on the stage and had the time and the leisure to attend matinees. The actor Gerald du Maurier had neither the looks nor the voice to commend him on stage but no matter: "he knew how a gentleman should behave in a club or a drawing-room." And if this wasn't enough to discourage the serious dramatist, there lurked in the wings the menacing shade of the dreaded Lord Chamberlain with his power to withhold His Majesty's license. The connoisseurs of the city were not, to be sure, entirely deprived. They established theatrical societies for the private performing of plays too good for the Strand or too bad for the censor: the Pioneers, the Playactors, the New Stage Club, the English Drama Society, and, most active and famous of all, the Incorporated Stage Society of London whose two or three hundred free spirits would convene on a Sunday evening or Monday afternoon to taste of such forbidden sweets as Ibsen's *Ghosts* and Barker's *Waste* and Shaw's *Mrs. Warren's Profession*. Just the same, they didn't suffice. Poor Bernard Shaw. They played him in America; they played him in Germany; they even played him in the provinces; but they didn't play him in London. William Archer, the doyen of the capital's theatre critics, was entirely disgusted. It was 1904 and at forty-eight his good mentor and friend could still be the greatest, unknown, unacted dramaturgist in all the kingdom.

But in the fall of the year this would change. A company with

Arthur Vedrenne as manager, young Harley Barker as producer-director, and Shaw himself as resident genius would lease for a season of repertory the Royal Court Theatre, a congenial place seating 614 souls and located not far from Sloane Square. Opening in October with Euripides' *Hippolytus* in Murray's translation and following that with Shaw's new *John Bull's Other Island* and that with a brand-new production of *Candida,* the Court was an instant success. In the nearly three years of its active existence, it offered 988 performances of 32 plays by 17 different authors, 28 of these played for the very first time. But the moment, it's clear, was prevailingly Shavian. Of the 12 plays presented that opening season, 4 were by Shaw and of the 32 overall, 11 were his, 4 of them written expressly for the company and among them his most radiant creations like *Man and Superman* and *Major Barbara.* They certainly carried the company. They might be questioned by the Lord Chamberlain, by the chief officer of His Majesty's household, but not, it would seem, by His Majesty himself who commanded a performance of *John Bull's Other Island* and laughed so robustly the chair he sat in collapsed. Whenever Shaw's plays were staged, leaflets were placed in the programs requesting the audience to control its laughter lest it bother the players and spoil the performance. On the opening night of *Pygmalion,* the audience was able for the first two acts to behave but then came the third and Eliza Doolittle's "Not bloody likely" and an explosion of laughter lasting more than a minute and after that all restraint by actors and audience was out of the question. Only Shaw's plays made money, and it was the profit from these that permitted Vedrenne and Barker to put on the work of deserving unknowns.

For the moment wasn't exclusively Shavian and wasn't intended to be. It was meant to revive the dead art of theatre in England, was meant to realize Archer's and Barker's passionate dream of a national theatre. So London's established poets and novelists would be asked to join in the movement and give of themselves to the stage. Shaw wouldn't ask Hardy. He had read the first volume of *The Dynasts* and that was enough: "this mixture of Shelley's Prometheus style, Shakespeare and Wessex torments me," he said. But he'd ask nearly everyone else, Kipling and Conrad, for example, and Hewlett and Wells. He was very urgent about it. He sent Chesterton a scenario to get the man started and offered to pay him a generous one hundred pounds upon its completion, and "I shall repeat my public challenge to you," he taunted his friend; "vaunt my superiority; insult your corpulence. . . ." He even pressed Barker himself into service, though the young man protested that as actor-producer he had all he could handle and that the business of writing was Shaw's and not his. But with time and success the Court no longer would have to recruit. It wouldn't have to seek Galsworthy out. The popular novelist would be seeking it out, would be writing a play with Barker and Shaw precisely in mind. Nor in the end would it have to seek Barker out. For years he'd been working on plays, unplayable plays like his own, Shaw observed, and was only too happy to be seen on the stage. Even Conrad who hated the stage and its players and playwrights may have been tempted a little. Out of one of his stories he composed a one-acter, *One Day More,* which the Stage Society presented in 1905. It wasn't a total success but Shaw was ecstatic. "Dramatist!" he roared at the shrinking author who was nonetheless pleased to be seen by the man of the hour and to find in his mail a letter requesting a play. With time and success the Court would attract, as it fully intended, the young and untried, the St. John Hankins, John Masefields, and Laurence Housmans. When young Gilbert Cannan came down to London, it wasn't to be the novelist he chiefly became. It was to be a playwright and only a playwright.

So they'd flock to the Court as to a mecca of sorts. Under Barker and Shaw it was giving the playwright a wholly new dignity. No more the actor-manager and the play written specifically for the actor-manager and accepted only on the condition that it supply the actor-manager with a one- or a two- or a three-year run. Little chance here for serious drama. Even the best of plays, *especially* the best of plays, were unlikely to carry a run of some two or three hundred nights. So a play at the Court was allowed six matinees on Tuesdays and Fridays (when the commercial theatres were dark) and then, if successful, an evening run of three or more weeks. And that, whatever its profit or popularity, was *that.* Shaw himself neither asked nor expected more. Not for *Man and Superman.* Not for *Major Barbara.* How else give new or young talent a chance? The players themselves were sometimes disgruntled. The great Mrs. Campbell couldn't see the point of preparing the part of Medea for a mere seven performances, and when she did see the point of preparing the part of Hedda Gabler, she wanted the triumphant matinees continued. But they weren't. Messrs. Barker and Shaw wouldn't have it. The Court didn't cater to actors and actresses. As for money, there wasn't any. For *Captain Brassbound's Con-*

version Shaw needed a great Lady Cicely. He made Ellen Terry an offer she couldn't refuse: "£25 and 'find her own gowns' is the sort of thing the Court runs to . . . ," he told her. "What do you think of it?" Ellen didn't think much of it. She turned down the offer.

There were also the rehearsals, the exhausting rehearsals. Entirely the puppets of the play and the playwright, the players were drilled in every gesture, every movement, every intonation, as they'd never been drilled before. Shaw himself did much of the drilling. Barker was perfect for Barker and perfect for Galsworthy but he wasn't perfect for Shaw who found that his style was as different from his "as Debussy's from Verdi's." For though he wouldn't revert to the histrionics of the Victorians, he wasn't therefore content with the drabness of Ibsen. Opera. Mozart, "the true Mozartian joyousness," that's what he wanted. Stagey, was he? Of course he was stagey. "You can't be too stagey on the stage." That was just why he doted on Barker. Stagey, a stager, he could play as no one else could his Marchbanks, his Tanner, his Adolphus Cusins. So too was Lillah McCarthy who arrived on the scene to complete the triumvirate. Gorgeous in green dress and huge picture hat, she had walked into his rooms at Adelphi Terrace one day. "When I was a little girl trying to play Lady Macbeth, you told me to go and spend ten years learning my business. I have learnt it: now give me a part." So without hesitation he gave her the book of *Man and Superman* and she became the Ann Whitefield he was desperate to find and by playing her parts with theatrical flair, "exactly as she would have played Belvidera in *Venice Preserved*," she became for his heroines what Barker became for his heroes. Of course it was hard. Shaw wasn't content to take over the casting from Barker. Demanding, relentless, he also took over the rehearsing and even the staging. But he was wonderful too and a master, was teaching them tricks of a wholly new kind in a wholly new mode, stylish, theatrical, disciplined. And then he was making them famous and special. "We were members of a theatrical House of Lords," Lillah remembered: "all equal and all lords." Poor Janet Achurch who had *made* Ibsen's "Nora" was hurt. Once one of Shaw's darlings, she had never been asked to perform at the Court. But as Shaw very gently informed her, the secret of the Court's great success "was that the plays made the actors and not the actors the plays," wherefore there could be in 1904 no Janet Achurch, no Florence Farr, no Elizabeth Robins, who were trained to play Ibsen but not to play Shaw.

No wonder playwrights were suddenly born or born again. But for Barker and Shaw and the Royal Court Theatre would Garnett the critic and Masefield the poet have turned to the theatre? Would Hueffer and Wells have converted their novels to theatre, Hueffer his *Fifth Queen,* Wells his *Wheels of Chance*? Or would Lawrence have written his colliery plays? Made his "Odor of Chrysanthemums" into *The Widowing of Mrs. Holroyd* and sent it to Barker who didn't, however, accept it? Under the circumstances, the unlikeliest persons were moved to think theatre. Ezra Pound would translate a play of Lope de Vega's on the grounds of its likeness to Shaw's *Arms and the Man,* and Rupert Brooke whose genius was far from dramatic would come down from Cambridge to haunt London's theatre and study its ways and threaten the town with a play of his own. Some twelve years before, Henry James had been jeered from the boards of a London stage and, shattered in spirit, had wandered for hours the dark London streets. Returning to the novel, the blessed novel, he had vowed he would never again be so mortified. But now it was 1909 and "once more, o ye laurels" and he, even he, was emboldened to return to the scene of the crime and was joyously working away on three different plays, one of which Barker himself had commissioned. Shaw and the Court had worked wonders indeed. By the time the Liberals had swept into power, so too had they. Many years later Hueffer would fondly remember "a London of 'Barker at the Court'—a day when if you hadn't seen 'Arms and the Man' with Lilla Macarthey [sic] as Raïna you counted as little as if you had not made the Grand Tour—the days when London began to have the aspect of a 'world-centre' and hope stirred in bosoms and the triumph of all the Arts was just round the corner."

Where Do We Go from Scott, from Dickens?

Hueffer may well at the time have been thinking of a new art of fiction just round the corner. For Edwardian London was exactly the place for novels and novelists as well as for playwrights and plays. James and Conrad, Bennett and Wells, Forster and Hueffer and Galsworthy. *Lord Jim* and *Nostromo, The Wings of the Dove* and *The Golden Bowl, The Forsyte Saga* and *The Old Wives' Tale, Tono-Bungay, Howards End, The Good Soldier.* Not the golden age of British fiction, perhaps, but surely its silver one. At the turn of the century, it's true, the prospects were bleak. Novelists were viewed as second-class citizens of the kingdom of letters, as the mere entertainers of mindless masses. For now that everyone knew how to read, they were turning to trifles. Romances. Ladies' romances. *Hearts Insurgent* and *Red Hearts a-Beating* and *The Furnace of Sin.* Or to historical romances. Feeble rehearsals of good old Sir Walter. The products at best of H. Rider Haggards and R. L. Stevensons, at worst of chromatic titles like *The Red Sword* and *The Purple Robe* and *The Black Helmet.* Arnold Bennett was saddened. The fields of fiction were fallow, he said. Wells also was saddened. His draper's assistant in *The Wheels of Chance* has read Ouida, Corelli, and H. Rider Haggard, but "they didn't seem to have much to do with me," he complains. Frank Harris longed for the day, he wrote in a rage, "When the Rudyards cease from Kipling/ And the Haggards Ride no more."

What to do? How resuscitate the dead art of fiction? Where did we go from Sir Walter Scott, from Dickens and Trollope and Thackeray? Why, open it up, some Edwardian writers were saying. Open it up to new facts and realities, new characters and conditions. "We are not concerned," Forster would regretfully write, "with the very poor," but clearly he was and so too were some of his peers. George Moore and Somerset Maugham, for example, who had published their *Esther Waters* and *Liza of Lambeth,* and Walter Sickert, the British impressionist, who was painting his Camden Town scenes and his Camden Town people. This indeed was romance, the true romance. The romance of the real, of the common and ordinary. Bennett and Wells and their school would certainly think so. They'd be deeply concerned with the grocers and drapers and their servants and clerks, with the gardens they kept and the clothing they wore and their kitchens and closets. In *The Old Wives' Tale,* Bennett's hymn to the middling life of the middle-class folk of the midlands of England, nothing much happens, nothing unusual, nothing heroic. The Poveys pass their first married night in the great family bed; receive their first visit from mother; acquire first a dog, then a child; devise a new way of ticketing their merchandise. . . . But it's all very interesting. It suffices. Dinner at the

Poveys! "Samuel had a mild, benignant air. Constance's eyes were a fountain of cheerfulness. The boy sat between them and ate steadily." A Wordsworthian scene, a pure biblical scene. In *Buried Alive* a world-renowned artist abandons the grandeurs of Europe for the simple pleasures of Putney, where "you had your little house, and your furniture" and your little wife, Alice, with her fresh face and apron and genius for making life comfortable. Breakfast! Were there ever such breakfasts? "Eggs! Toast! Coffee!" and standing against the coffeepot the *Daily Telegraph*, "the ideal companion for a poached egg." Pure paradise it was, this Putney existence. "It seemed to breathe of romance," Bennett says, "the romance of common sense and kindliness and simplicity."

Wells may have overdone it a little, the romance of his untutored drapers and clerks. There was "nothing on earth," he could write, "like starting a small haberdasher's shop.... There are clods alive who see nothing ... in spools of mercerized cotton and endless bands of paper-set pins. I write for the wise...." But alas it was rot, pure rot. Wells had run, not walked, from the meanness of life as a poor counterjumper's apprentice. There must have been some special virtue attaching to breakfast or supper, the Englishman's joy, or to house or to home, the Englishman's castle. For Wells as for Bennett, this, even this, was romance. "Really, old Sid was a wonderful chap, here in his own house at two and twenty, carving his own mutton and lording it over wife and child...." But every dog will have his day and so will ol' Kipps. "I seem to see it," ol' Kipps ruminates, planning his own little house with his own little wife, "sort of cozy like. 'Bout tea time and muffins, kettle on the 'ob, cat on the 'earth-rug. We must get a cat, Ann, and *you* there." O lucky Ann. *Égoisme à deux?* Not quite.

But the commonplace life wouldn't exhaust the expanding matter of Edwardian fiction. When Harmsworth's *Daily Mail* first came out, it exploited at once the new public's passion for debate and discussion, for new facts and developments. It was this passion the popular playwrights would appeal to, the Barkers and Shaws and Court Theatre people, and so would the novelists. The anarchist movement. The feminist cause. The new sciences, the new technologies. The strange new conditions of life in the cities. The strange new relations between men and women and the problems of marriage and sex, which Wells for one was resolved to admit into fiction. There was in fact not very much that Wells wouldn't admit into fiction. In *Tono-Bungay* the new experiments in aerial flight, the bumptious new world of commerce and advertising. In *Ann Veronica* the new rancor of women and their suffragette fury and their violent assault on the House of Commons. In *The Wheels of Chance* and others the mere common bicycle and the joy of escape from that mean little hole in the city or that mean little cot in the country. As for the planning and building of houses, these must have had for the Edwardian mind some special significance. They're involved in the action of *Kipps* and *Clayhanger*, *Tono-Bungay* and *The Man of Property*, and they're almost the subjects of novels like *The Old Wives' Tale* and *Howards End*. There was in fine for these Edwardians no special stuff of romance, no special subject of fiction. Consider, said Bennett, "the very romance of manufacture" or "the romance . . . of a great railway system," not to mention the romance of hotels, department stores, steamships. Everything, rightly considered, was the proper subject of fiction. Everything, rightly considered, was the special stuff of romance.

James thought so too. He was irritated. Novels were restricted, Sir Walter Besant had insisted, to plots and adventures but, James would contend, "the moral consciousness of a child [was] as much a part of life as the islands of the Spanish Main." The irritable Conrad would be even more irritated. They were calling him a "sea-novelist," a teller of tales and exotic adventures, but what nonsense it was! "Far from being adventurous," he argued, his life at sea had involved "hard work and exacting calls of duty, things . . . not much charged with . . . romance." Not for him or for James the easy-way-out of romance, "the romance of yard-arm and boarding-pike" (Conrad), of "golden hair and promiscuous felony" (James). Not for them "the pride of fanciful invention" (Conrad) and "those artistic perversions that come . . . from a powerful imagination" (James). The real, James said, "the romance of the real," was romantic enough. It was enough for Conrad. He may have written of people in faraway places but it was never, he said, to allow himself "a special imaginative freedom." He was content, he said, "to sympathize with common mortals, no matter where they live. . . ." So down with romance and invention. Write out of what you had seen and observed with your own irrefutable eyes. Write for that matter out of experience, out of what you had lived and had known. "J'ai vécu tout cela," Conrad was happy to say. Authors had thought their own lives were too minor, too meager, for conversion to fiction. Not the Edwardians.

"A little mad about letters"

But James and Conrad would go farther than Wells, than Bennett and Galsworthy. How resuscitate the English novel? By all means look for new fictional subjects but also, but also, look for new fictional forms. Study Flaubert and the French. Study Turgenev. Make the novel, as they did, a serious and dignified form of artistic expression. Down with story, down with plot: "break it up, boil it down." Down with omniscient narration, with the all-knowing author, with his telling and preaching. Show, don't tell. Show, don't preach. Dramatize, dramatize. Down, above all, with the author who didn't quite know what he did. Conserve an idea. Compose a scenario. Plan. Organize. Control. Down in short with the English novel, with its "loose baggy monsters," and up with the French and with form, precious form, and "progression d'effet" and of course "le mot juste." In the darkening farmhouses of Kent, Conrad and Hueffer descanted for hours on the wonders wrought by the Flauberts and Turgenevs. How did they do it? How on earth did they do it? C'étais magnifique! C'étais un miracle! "The finest French novel in the English language"? *The Good Soldier*? Hueffer was ench . . . anté. He referred with contempt to the English "nuvvle." He deferred to "my masters and betters in France." In his early days even Wells, British Wells, was a convert of sorts. Covering books for Harris's *Saturday Review,* he was praising the work of Conrad and Crane and Turgenev and "the highest form of literary art." He was talking of a "steady unfaltering progression towards one great and simple effect," of "the bearing of structural expedients upon design" and of "every sentence [having] its share" in that design. Preaching and propagandizing were out, said the man who would soon be the prince of the preachers and propagandizers. The novelist had to realize "that he cannot adopt an art-form and make it subservient to the purposes of the pamphleteer." Wells might as well have been a James or a Conrad and would soon in effect be planning to enter the sacred circle itself. He wasn't condemned "to write 'scientific' romances" the rest of his days, he protested to Bennett. "I want to write novels," he said, "and before God I *will* write novels."

Edward Garnett, one of the Grand Chams of letters in London, had something to do with the new and improved British novel. "Big, purblind, shaggy-haired, baggy-tweed-trousered," he too was a species of Samuel Johnson, gathering about him at luncheons on Tuesdays at the Mont Blanc restaurant some of the city's more illustrious figures: Conrad and Galsworthy, Hueffer and Hudson, Edward Thomas and Cunninghame Graham among them. Indeed he had hatched them, these authors, had nursed them to fame if not always to fortune. As a publisher's reader, his overcoat pockets bulging with manuscripts, he had "discovered" them, had brought into being their first efforts: Conrad's *Almayer's Folly*, Galsworthy's *Man of Devon*, Cunninghame Graham's collections of stories and travels. Despairing of seeing it in print, Hudson had set aside his *Green Mansions* manuscript; but Edward had coaxed it out of his keeping and into the light. He was a tartar indeed. Page by page and word by word he went over Galsworthy's first novel and would later convince him in letters and meetings that the Bosinney of his *Man of Property*—for whom all unknowingly he himself was the model—wasn't the man to commit suicide. Garnett was certainly more to his flock than a publisher's reader. He was a friend, an adviser, a moral and sometimes financial supporter. For all the success of his *Almayer's Folly*, the troubled and troublesome Conrad, just off the ship and a stranger ashore, may not have gone on to write what he wrote or quite as he wrote it without Garnett's hovering presence. "I simply *can't* live without it," he'd write of his mentor's involvement. "As a matter of fact it's about all I have to live upon."

Young Lawrence was at a loss. Hueffer, his new London connection, had run off to Germany with Violet Hunt and left him alone and unfriended. But Garnett, "like a good angel," would take him in charge. He'd have him for weekends at The Cearne, would make much of his talent, would introduce him and his work to the right kind of people. *Sons and Lovers*, he decided, would have to be ruthlessly pruned, but the young genius wasn't quite up to it. You do it, he said. So the excellent Garnett would cut it and barber it and "jolly well" too. Was there in fact anything at all he wouldn't do for good letters? For better or worse, arrange for the collaboration of Conrad and Hueffer. Get published the strange and eccentric like the poems of Davies, the *Green*

Mansions of Hudson, the *Pointed Roofs* of Dorothy Richardson. Himself write the introductions to his wife's translations of Turgenev and so bring home to British business and bosoms the work of the beautiful Russian. At the turn of the century the traditional critics weren't that interested in the work of young writers. But Garnett was different. He praised in print the poems of Frost when few seemed to notice them. He saw and announced the importance of novels like *Howards End* and *The Old Wives' Tale*. In essays and notices he explained and extolled the greatness of Conrad and contributed thus to his growing celebrity. He was in sum what Conrad would call him: "the true knight-errant of oppressed letters." And what Lawrence would call him: "the only man to let a new generation come in."

No doubt Garnett was hurt in the end. At one time their anchor in the great sea of London, he was in a manner let go by his Conrad and Lawrence. He was, it's quite true, somewhat harsh and belligerent, had myopic eyes and thick-lensed glasses, large pouting lips and "grey, jowl-like cheeks." When Jepson suggested that *Victory* was Conrad's best novel, he replied "with a very superior sourness: 'There is too much pressure in it.' " "Oh Mr. Garnett," effused Violet Hunt at the funeral of Hudson, "we never seem to see each other except on these sad occasions. . . ." Mr. Garnett interrupted her brusquely: "I will promise not to come to your funeral, if you will promise not to come to mine." As for Hueffer, Edward could never abide him, his Olympian manner, his too-naked need for success and attention, and his shamelessly self-serving lies. Olive, Edward's sister, delighted in Hueffer's tall tales, his "Huefferisms." But they didn't delight the puritan Edward who felt it behooved him to confront and expose them. Conrad once sent Edward a letter making fun of his labors with Hueffer. He couldn't, said Conrad, take the novel they were working on seriously; but "poor H was dead in earnest! Oh Lord. How he worked! There is not a chapter I haven't made him write twice. . . ." For obvious reasons Conrad asked Edward to burn it, this letter. But Edward didn't burn it. He published the thing. Was this not a little vindictive? Nevertheless he did have his effect on the history of fiction in England. The novel a second-rate form? Inferior to history, biography, poetry, criticism? Not at all, Edward Garnett kept saying and proving. It was, he insisted, as the Flauberts and Turgenevs and the new English novelists were showing, "the most serious and significant of all literary forms the modern world has evolved."

Not that everyone leaped to agree with him. "The novel is not everything . . . ," the crotchety Hudson would cry out. "I don't care for made-up stories that amuse people like you." In the meantime, however, Hueffer was plotting in the rooms of the Mont Blanc a grand revolution. With Garnett and Conrad and Wells around or behind him, he was plotting a new monthly journal named the *English Review*. It was started, Hueffer recalled, with that "copious carelessness of reminiscence" that Wells would deride, in order to serialize *Tono-Bungay* and so give its book publication a boost. To serialize Conrad's "Reminiscences" and so provide that impoverished genius with some ready money. To print poet Hardy's "Sunday Morning Tragedy" which the conservative *Cornhill* had rejected, though in point of fact it was the *Fortnightly* that had been the offender. Perhaps its real *raison d'être*, as Hueffer would elsewhere explain it, was to give "imaginative literature a chance in England," was to give the neglected genius of the Jameses and Conrads a chance. Journals, organs, reviews already abounded— the *Spectator*, for example, and the *Athenaeum* as well as the *Cornhill* and the *Fortnightly*. But staidly conservative, they were less interested in literature than in politics and society, and what little literature they were willing to publish was still sadly Victorian. There was no place at all for the vivid new realism of the Bennetts and Wellses or for the subtle new impressionism of the Jameses and Conrads. Well, the *English Review* would change all that. It would be one English monthly "in which," Hueffer said, "the better sort of work might see the light."

Wells was excited. He agreed to supply half the capital outlay of five thousand pounds and perform half the editorial chores and with *Tono-Bungay* to appear at once in serial form, he was very much with it and for it. Send your stuff to the *Review*, he was urging Violet Hunt: "It's It this year!" "If this Review comes off," he was telling Vernon Lee, "English literature will be saved. Arise! Awake!" Even Conrad, the skeptical Conrad, was deeply involved. "The *ER* may have to stop," he would boldly declare, "but it mustn't fail." He'd invite the editor down to Someries, his wet, gloomy, tree-haunted farmhouse in Kent, for a final editing of the very first number and one dark night in November, to Jessie Conrad's consternation, the editor did descend on the house with manuscripts and proofs and a medieval retinue of subeditor and secretary for an all-night orgy of work and discussion and at a considerable cost, as Jessie complained, in lamp oil and candles. The *Review* was in fact conceived as a group endeavor, as, said Hueffer, "a socialistic undertaking." The contributors were to be paid a guinea a page or, failing that, were to share in the profits. What's more, Hueffer wasn't content to publish the new men of London. He'd insist on enlisting their editorial help. *All*—Garnett and Galsworthy as well as Conrad and Wells—were to be consulted. Hueffer's title as editor would never appear in the *English Review*.

No question about it, though: Hueffer himself was the journal's main man. A small gilt plaque—ENGLISH REVIEW, LTD.—was placed on the door of his Kensington flat at 48 Holland Park Avenue. Located over a poulterer's shop, the entrance was perhaps just a little discouraging, exposing the visitor to "the sickly depraved smell of chickens" and "the suspended carcases of rabbits." But the rickety stairs were lined with Pre-Raphaelite portraits of Christina Rossetti and with Rothenstein drawings of Conrad and others, and the editorial office had the Chippendale bureau at which Christina was said to have sat to her poems and, crammed with manuscripts, a cabinet that once belonged to the Duke of Medina-Sidonia. Then at the head of the stairs, genial and smiling, the editor himself would doubtless be standing in the coat or the cape or the brown velvet jacket that had once belonged to Dante Gabriel Rossetti. His editorial procedures were eccentric perhaps. He was in the habit of losing manuscripts. He had also a habit of performing his labors at night, sometimes in the stalls of the Empire Theatre at Shepherd's Bush where, between the acts or during the dull ones, he would pass on the manuscripts and dictate letters to Goldring, his youthful subeditor. He had also a haphazard manner of making decisions. He read the first paragraph of Lawrence's "Odor of Chrysanthemums" and placed it without further ado in the basket for accepted submissions. Glancing at Violet Hunt's three short stories, he paused in the midst of the second. I'll take it, he said.

No matter. The preposterous fellow worked editorial wonders and his *English Review* would soon be the talk of the town. For never before could so much have been offered to so many for so little. In addition to Hardy's poem, in addition to the first installments of Wells's best novel and Conrad's reminiscences, the famous first number of December 1908 contained stories by James and by Galsworthy, Tolstoy's "The Raid" in Constance Garnett's translation, and articles by Hudson and Cunninghame Graham not to mention a review of Anatole France's *Ile des Pingouins* which the editor had coaxed out of Conrad's reluctant genius at 2 a.m. on the night of their session at

Someries. Nor in the months that followed did its quality slacken. Yeats and Thomas, Belloc and Chesterton, Bennett and Barker: they were all represented in one form or another. A young woman of Nottingham sent in some work of her shy and dispirited sweetheart and lo, the first poems of Lawrence duly appeared in the November 1909 number. Fresh from Paris, an odd young man who was dressed like a Russian accosted the editor, who was having his bath, and read from his manuscript and lo, Wyndham Lewis's "The Pole" duly appeared in the May 1909 number. Fresh from Venice and dressed like a florid Italian, an aggressive American was introduced to the editor and lo, Ezra Pound's "Sestina: Altaforte" would duly appear in the following number. No doubt about it, Hueffer's *Review* was *in*, was *it*. It was "as near to the ideal," Arnold Bennett would say, "as any magazine of pure letters is likely to get."

Hueffer of course was in heaven. A minor "court" figure till now in the noble dominion of letters, he was equal at last to his dreams and pretensions, was at last what the unfriendly Garnett had been all these years: a person of power and position. Over six feet tall, with canary yellow hair and china blue eyes and a fair fresh complexion, he did look the part and, with his drawling speech and his *dégagé* manner, he certainly played it. In his Kensington quarters he'd hold royal court for the great ones of London: for lions of distinction like Hardy and James, for lions of note like Hudson and Bennett, for the latest in lion cubs like Pound and Lewis and Walpole and Cannan. This isn't to mention the great social lionesses, Lady Low and Lady Barlow and Lady St. Davids and even Christabel Pankhurst "looking like a young and pretty Queen Victoria." Splendid in fur coat and topper, he'd drive about town in hired carriages when he'd bless with his presence the literary gatherings. Square Club meetings of such worthies as Masefield and Chesterton. A party for Anatole France at the Bath Club where, with his excellent French and his feeling for France, he'd protect the great man from the bores and intruders. A supper party at "Derwen," the Hampstead home of the Rhyses, Ernest and Grace, where Yeats to his credit refused to recite his "Lake Isle of Innisfree" and Ezra Pound loudly declaimed his "Ballad of the Goodly Fere" and a nervous young Lawrence read at some length his dialect poem "Whether or Not" and would not have stopped there had Hueffer not taken him "under his arm and marched him off murmuring wickedly 'Nunc, nunc dimittis.'" He was trying, provoking, it's true. Pompous and vain

and affected, he could drive people mad with his boastings and fib-
bings. But they were all a mere front, a front for the terror within, for
his sense of his own utter worthlessness, and he was, all his swanking
and bragging aside, a fountain of sympathy. He didn't deceive Jessie
Chambers who noted his "genial warmth," nor Lawrence himself who
called him "the kindest man on earth," nor Joseph Conrad who may in
the end have lost patience with him but would still declare him "a
much better fellow than the world gives him credit for."

The days of his glory were certainly golden. Every morning at
eleven he issued from his apartment, wearing, he recalled, "a very long
morning coat, a perfectly immaculate high hat, lavender trousers, a
near-Gladstone collar and a black satin stock." Followed by his Great
Dane, he'd saunter up Holland Park Avenue to Kensington Gardens;
cross over to Rotten Row to lean on the rails for a chat with the riders;
after traversing St. James Park and the Green Park, enter one of his
clubs to peruse his letters and newspapers. After lunch at his club or
the Carlton, he'd take a hansom cab back to his flat, put in a brief but
genteel stint of good work, and at five or so go to or give a tea party,
after which he would take a bath "and a barber would come in and
shave me." If this wasn't heaven, what was? London was indeed in
those days, for men and women of letters, the country of the blue, "the
great good place."

"A bloody show"

It was even the place for the artists, for the painters
and sculptors. At the turn of the century "London knew little of Paris,"
Vanessa Bell would complain, "incredibly little," and "in those days,"
Leonard Woolf would recall, "we set little or no store by pictures and
painting." As late as 1904 the National Gallery could even see fit to
refuse the gift of a Degas. But now it was 1905 and after years of contempt and neglect the French-inspired British impressionists—Walter
Sickert, Philip Steer, Henry Tonks—were looking at last to be seen and
admired. In 1903 Camille Mauclair's *The French Impressionists* had ap-

peared in translation, the first book in English to treat the new movement with care and respect, and now in 1905 London would witness, for the first time in years, a comprehensive exhibit of the classic impressionists from Manet to Renoir at the same time that Sickert, who was the best of the British and had loved and learned from Degas, would return from the Continent to enliven the scene. Fifteen or so years before, the Steers and the Tonkses had founded the New English Art Club to give impressionist painting in England a chance. But now they were almost as proud and exclusive as the Royal Academicians, and Sickert who was witty and charming and combined, Augustus John said, "old world elegance with the license of artistic tradition," would be called on to rally the young London rebels, the new *réfusés*. In 1907 he'd assemble his Fitzroy Street group; in 1908 help to form the Allied Artists' Association, the London equivalent of the Societé des Artistes Indépendants; in 1911 establish his Camden Town Group, so named for his own predilection for Camden Town kitchens and bedrooms. All the omens were good. When in 1905 Vanessa Bell, inspired by certain Parisian cafés and their lively milieus, started her Friday Club, half the members would be staunch for the old British school but the other half would be strong for the new French impressionists, and when, four years later, Lady Ottoline Morrell and her friend at the time, Roger Fry, would be launching the Contemporary Art Society, it was to purchase the work of avant-garde artists like Sickert himself and his friends and disciples. What Barker and Shaw were for theatre and Bennett and Wells were for fiction, Sickert was for painting in England. He was part of the great reawakening, realistic and liberal, that was shaking Edwardian London.

One early morning in January 1910 there was a chance meeting. On the train down from Cambridge, Roger Fry encountered the Bells, young Clive and Vanessa. Fry who at forty-four was an established authority on Bellini and the early Italians, dilated at length on the classical virtues of form and design which the impressionist painters had sadly abandoned but which, oddly enough, a new school of painters in Paris had of late rediscovered. That very November, he was telling them, he would mount for the Grafton Galleries a show of Cézannes and other bold spirits who had broken out of the impressionist compound. The father and founder of modern painting in England? Fry scarcely seemed fit for the part. "A pleasant gushing young fellow," as Jepson remembered him, "and rather an ass," he had a habit of flinging himself at people's feet. But by 1910 he was seasoned, matured. He had not only lost his wife to the demon of mental disorder but as buyer-consultant for the Metropolitan Art Museum, had dared to confront the great J. P. Morgan and had just lost his job. His charm and vitality were nevertheless undiminished. He was restless and active and behind the large circular glasses his dark eyes were brilliant and quick. It was his voice, however, his rich resonant voice, that people remembered. It was, said Desmond MacCarthy, like Voltaire's, "une voix sombre et ma-jestueuse." "His and Forbes Robertson's," Shaw would say, "were the only voices one could listen to for their own sakes." By the time they reached King's Cross, the Bells were bewitched by the man and his style and ideas. It was possible, it occurred to Vanessa, to be a scholar, a famous authority, and be without pomp and pretension. She had al-ways been silenced by the fearful male figure, by her father Sir Leslie, by her teacher, the terrible Tonks, but Fry was a different sort alto-gether. Back in 1904 Clive had journeyed to Paris to practice historical research on some recondite subject but had remained to discover not only Degas and Renoir but Cézanne and Gauguin and had written in praise of their work. Would he join Roger Fry in his brave new adven-ture? Would he not?

So that summer in Paris Clive would be there when Fry, in the company of Desmond MacCarthy, whom he'd persuaded the Grafton to appoint as secretary, made the rounds of the dealers' establishments. "Wonderful! wonderful!" Fry would exclaim as he sat to examine the Cézannes and Gauguins, the Matisses, Derains, and Vlamincks. By the time the show opened in London on November 5, there were 154 items for MacCarthy to list in the catalog, Manets numbering 9, Cézannes 21, Gauguins 37, Van Goghs 20, Rouaults 6, Picassos 2. But what would they call it, this harvest of wonders, they thought on the eve of the opening? Manet and the "Neo-Byzantines"? Manet and the "expressionists" to distinguish them from the "impressionists"? "Oh, let's just call them post-impressionists," Roger decided impatiently. No doubt he expected an explosion, "a huge campaign," as he said, "of outraged British Philistinism." In the preface he wrote for the exhibi-tion, MacCarthy was almost apologetic. It was disconcerting, he con-ceded, this new sense of things they'd brought over from Paris, but might "a good rocking-horse" not have "more of the true horse about it than an instantaneous photograph of a Derby winner?" Nonetheless, neither Roger nor he could quite have predicted the rage and contempt their paintings provoked. Peals of silvery laughter would come from the ladies poised in front of the pictures and from elderly gentlemen of distinguished demeanor gasps of dismay or howls of derision. Before the portrait of Cézanne's wife, one old chap was suddenly seized by a spasm of laughter and had to be taken outside and walked up and down. And when Strachey went in to see Henry Lamb's portrait of him at the second exhibit, it was to discover a group of purple-faced gentlefolk reviling not the painter but his subject who was lacking, it seemed, a linen collar. Was the show not subversive in fact? The paintings so informal, so grotesquely unfinished, were plainly rebukes to the ruling class which cherished, in art as in manner and dress, formality and finish. Falstaffian Chesterton was indignant. Cubism and post-impressionism he dismissed as "the latest artistic insanities." The old poet Blunt was splenetic. He called the show "pornographic," a manifestation of "that gross puerility which scrawls indecencies on the walls of a privy."

There were those of course who rose to the historic occasion. The art critic C. Lewis Hind was hardly a radical. He had an academic background (Cambridge) and wrote for an academic journal (the *Fortnightly*). Just the same, Matisse's *The Girl with the Green Eyes* was, he decided, the masterpiece of the world. "Whenever he spoke of the verdant charm of that startling girl," it was said, "the tears would well up into his eyes. . . ." Augustus John had referred to the Grafton affair as "a bloody show." It was all over town. But this wasn't, it seems, at all what he meant. Though he hated Matisse and as late as 1907 had never heard of Van Gogh, he was influenced by Gauguin and impressed by Cézanne ("a splendid fellow, one of the greatest") and had discovered the same old Italians and their instinct for form and design as Roger himself. Indeed, John had lately produced in Provence some daring new oils ("rapid sketching in paint") that applied what he'd learned from them. And when he showed them at the Chenil, just a mile from the Grafton, they were treated, these "uncanny notes of form and dashes of color," with the same disrespect as the Gauguins and Matisses with which in fact the critics compared them. John was regarded in those angry days as a more dubious character than the terrible Frenchmen themselves. When he called the show at the Grafton "a bloody show" it was the fuss and the nonsense he was talking about, not the paintings themselves, and when he went to see them a second time he was, as it were, "post impressed."

Meanwhile, the young and advanced were ashamed of the city's behavior. "How insular we are still," the art collector Hugh Blaker complained in his diary. The press had but proven, he said, "that cultured London [was] composed of clowns, who will . . . be thoroughly ashamed in twenty years' time." In a letter to the *Nation*, Arnold Bennett would complain of the same insularity and "in twenty years' time," he would say, "London will be signing an apology for its guffaw." As for Orage and the *New Age*, they were incensed by "the titter and cackle" of London, by its hee-hawing dukes in their stage eyeglasses and its elegant women strolling about saying "How awful! Did you ever? Too killing!" But as things turned out, the secretary Desmond MacCarthy was rather pleased with them all. They were turning up at the Grafton at the rate of four hundred a day and he would be pocketing, by way of commissions, nearly five hundred pounds.

The young artists of London were in any event profoundly affected. Before 1910 and the Fry exhibition, no postimpressionists were known to exist on the islands of Britain, but by 1912 and the second postimpressionist show, it was possible to exhibit no less than nine of them. Young Duncan Grant had been familiar with the new work in Paris but had been quite unseduced by it all. After 1910, however, when he saw the whole thing, thanks to Roger, in one marvelous showing, he was all postimpressionist. Sickert's young rebels had also been familiar with the happenings abroad, but they too had remained unaffected. After the show at the Grafton, however, what could they do but defect? After the fuchsia harmonies of Gauguin's Tahitian productions and the robust vermilions in Matisse's *Girl with the Green Eyes*, the Camden Town scenes of their master seemed dingy enough. Small wonder Sickert was wounded. His Camden Town Group was no sooner formed than it floundered and his Saturday gatherings in good old Fitzrovia would soon be deserted. Vanessa Bell had been glad at one time to buy Sickert, John, Henry Lamb, but after that meeting with Roger a change would come over her. The Sickert would do well enough but the John that hung on their wall would have to be sold in exchange for, perhaps, a Cézanne and, as for the Lamb, "I'm now quite clear what I think of him. It's simply too deadly. . . ."

But the art-quake of 1910 would change everything, everyone, the poets and novelists as well as the painters and sculptors. Why, Roger inquired, were there no English novelists who took their art seriously, who could free themselves from their slavish commitment to representation? With Cézanne and Picasso for guides, it was possible, surely, for writers at last to dispense with the old heavy lumber of Literachoor. There were certainly writers who were glad to oblige. "I have come to connect their ideas with literature," said Bennett after seeing the new painters. He was inclined to believe that if "some writer were to come along and do in words what these men have done in paint, I might conceivably be disgusted with nearly the whole of modern fiction, and I might have to begin again." He didn't of course, but Katherine Mansfield certainly considered it. "They taught me," she remembered of the Grafton's Van Goghs, "something about writing... a kind of freedom—or rather, a shaking free." It even affected the poets. Volumes with titles like *Post-Impressionist Poems* and *Cubist Poems* would soon be appearing and the imagist poets, with a fine disregard for distinctions in matters of schools, would be calling themselves "contemporaries of the Post-Impressionists and the Futurists." The young T. S. Eliot must have seen something in it. When he returned to Harvard from Paris in 1911, he brought with him a Gauguin *Crucifixion* which he hung on his wall. Ezra Pound must also have seen something in it. "Who," he asked haughtily, "takes the Art of poetry seriously? As seriously that is as a painter takes painting?" He wrote a haiku poem he called "L'Art 1910," an imitation, an appreciation, of what he had seen at the Grafton:

> Green arsenic smeared on an egg-white cloth,
> Crushed strawberries! Come, let us feast our eyes.

Postimpressionist theatre? Was it possible, really? Surely not. But Ashley Dukes who wrote drama reviews for Orage's *New Age* was sure that it was. Those who understood what Manet and Cézanne were about, he declared, would have "no difficulty in knowing what Chekhov was about." Pound had called London dead as mutton, but her poets and painters and her playwrights and novelists wouldn't have thought so. Not yet anyway. In 1910 Clive Bell was writing a book called *The New Renaissance* and as late as 1915 Ezra himself was foreseeing "changes as great as the Renaissance changes."

"By George, I believe I've got genius"

Not only was there an Edwardian revival but every Edwardian knew there was one, and the Edwardian writer most of all. Never before, surely, could authors in London have been more aware of themselves and each other and of the honor and dignity of their calling. In Paris, France, they took themselves seriously, they took their work seriously. Why would they not in London, England? So James would ask the ardent young Walpole to address him as "Très-cher Maître" or, for the time being, "my very dear Master," and Hugh who was fresh from the provinces and "simply worshiped men of letters and went for them direct as a kitten goes to a saucer of milk," was glad to oblige. So too, for that matter, was Conrad who had lived in France and fondly affected the manner of France. He addressed the great man as "Mon cher maître" and, with a copy of *The Outcast of the Islands,* sent him a letter in a style oleaginously French: "I want to thank you for the charm of Your words, the delight of Your sentences, the beauty of Your pages!" James invited him to lunch. Conrad was flattered and moved: "so there is something to live for—at last!" Conrad himself would assume in due time the mantle of Master, would allude, with aristocratic simplicity, to "Conrad." For himself at least a legend in his own time. But not for himself alone. For the dilettanti of London too, among them Hueffer, his young friend and collaborator, who also worshiped men of letters and betrayed in Conrad's presence, Violet Hunt said, an "attitude of almost cringing respect." Arnold Bennett who fully admired the man and his work was nonetheless a little disgusted. "When Conrad is mentioned," he complained, "they say, 'Ah, Conrad!' and bow the head." Wells was also a little disgusted. America was little aware of her own Stephen Crane, but "the European reputation, the florid mental gestures of a Conrad," that was another matter. Somerset Maugham was also offended. Henry James? *Cher Maître?* Good lord, how bizarre! It was all very well in Paris or Munich but in stodgy old London? But power corrupts and absolute power corrupts absolutely and Maugham would later inform his leading lady that abroad, in Berlin, they addressed the playwright as "Great and Highly Honored Master" and Miss Irene Vanbrugh, who knew a hint when she heard one, was careful thereafter to call him "Dear Master."

It was perhaps inevitable. As high priests and prophets of a brave new religion called Art, they couldn't help thinking quite well of themselves and their work. "The world divided itself for me," Hueffer was frank to confess, "into those who were artists and those who were merely the stuff to fill graveyards." But though this was all well and good for those who were artists, it wasn't for those who were not and it certainly wasn't for poor Lady Ott. Katherine Mansfield spoke, she complained, "as if she and Murry belonged to some sacred order of artists superior and apart from ordinary people like myself." Nor was it all well and good for the nonwriting husbands and wives of the London community. When Walpole held in his modest apartments near Portland Place his weekly gatherings of great ones, they, the mere spouses, were pointedly *not* invited to come. An acid of bitterness entered their souls, but so it must be. They weren't *creators*. For sheer self-importance, however, there was no one to match Percy Grainger, the composer-musician, for whom as for Hueffer the masses were merely the stuff to fill graveyards. "I, & folk like me," it pleased him to think of the fortunate few, "are the strange reward for all the cruelty & injustice done to the poor and the under-refined." This was in fact the finding of James's *Princess Casamassima*. As a mere proletarian, as one of London's untutored millions, the hero of the novel is a political radical, but after his exposure to the grandeur of Europe he's willing to grant that the misery of the masses may well be justified by the art and the culture their misery makes possible.

It may indeed have gone to their heads, this cult of the artist. Henry James, whose monologues rumbled and rambled in their anguished pursuit of the right word and the total effect, couldn't abide interruption. "He gets angry with me," said Violet Hunt, "because he says I won't let him finish his sentences." But Violet adored him for or in spite of it and so too did Desmond MacCarthy. "I know, my dear fellow, you are getting fidgety," MacCarthy affectionately imagined him saying in the throes of a long peroration; "but wait—and we shall enjoy together the wild pleasure of discovering what 'Henry James' thinks of this matter." Conrad's sense of himself was perhaps less endearing. "Now then, Goldring. Mind! No paragraphs. I know *what you journalists* are." Goldring, who wasn't a journalist but Hueffer's assistant and a poet, was furious. Conrad, he complained, "never for a moment forgot his greatness," he was "chained, so inexorably, to his Importance." As for Frank Harris, who had "a marvelous speaking voice—like the organ at Westminster Abbey," he was not, it would seem, self-effacing. He thought nothing of delivering great booming lectures on "Shakespeare, Shaw, and Frank Harris."

But que voulez-vous? They were giants in those days. Poets and playwrights and novelists, they weren't just ordinary men. They were MEN OF LETTERS. It was a phrase they used. Conrad could speak of protecting "the dignity of letters" and Yeats of protecting his integrity "as a man of letters" and "You do not talk like a poet," Yeats was once told, "you talk like a man of letters." So when Pound came to town it was as a man of letters that he'd offer himself. "He breathed Letters, ate Letters, dreamt Letters," his friend Percy Lewis would later recall. "I have always considered "the profession of a man of letters a third order of the priesthood!" Lionel Johnson remembered Cardinal Newman informing him. But Johnson's remembrance wasn't reliable. He was inclined to invent conversations with illustrious men and had never, not ever, met Cardinal Newman. Men of letters? They were more, the Edwardians. They were MEN OF GENIUS. It was another phrase they used. "By George, I believe I've got genius," cries the "hero" of Somerset Maugham's *Of Human Bondage*, and though it doesn't turn out to be so, he had every right, as a man of his time, to think that he had. Tom Hulme? "He affected everyone as a man of genius." Virginia Woolf? "Like Picasso she emanated simply and unmistakably a sense of genius." Joseph Conrad? A little touchy, a little testy, perhaps, but all could be forgiven "because of his obvious genius." Augustus John? "Everyone felt in the imperious manner, flaming eyes and eloquent cadenced voice . . . that demonic spiritual endowment we call genius." On a dusty road on the Romney marshes, Henry James once described to MacCarthy the deeps of the depressions he had had to descend. The aridities! The agitations! " 'But,' and he suddenly stood still, 'but it has been good'—and here he took off his hat, baring his great head in the moonlight—'for my genius.' "

Geniuses or not, the Edwardians certainly dressed like geniuses. It wasn't just Conrad with his Englishman's bowler and monocle or Hueffer with his top hat and tails and his air of a *chargé d'affaires*. There were also the poet-and-painter bohemians, Augustus John with his brigand's hat and his green velvet collar and his single gold earring and young Percy Lewis, just over from Paris, with his ample black cape and Russian-looking coat without revers and his long dark locks ("romantically disordered") falling from under a steeple-crowned hat that gave him the look of a Russian *muzhik*. Strachey ridiculed Rupert Brooke's long golden hair and silk shirt and loosely knotted foulard tie. But lovesick for Lamb he himself would soon be appearing *à la bohème*, discarding his collars and other bourgeois apparel for a dark Italian cape and a black Carlyle hat. But Lytton was nothing compared to Pound whose changes were legion. There was always the cane with which he seemed on the street to make passes at enemies, real or imagined, and the one turquoise earring which Agnes Tobin, the American expatriate, had provided him. But when young Lawrence saw him he was wearing a Panama hat and a blue cotton shirt and "a tie of peach-blossom tint," and when Hueffer saw him in Germany he was in "bright green shirts with glass buttons" and when he saw him in London he was in a blue shirt and pink coat and green billiard-cloth trousers. Hueffer's Goldring wasn't impressed by "his whole operatic outfit of 'stage poet' " but it thrilled Brigit Patmore to see him on Kensington Church Street with his hat pulled over one eye and his cane swinging boldly before him.

Ezra was stagey all right but hardly more stagey than the obese Gilbert Chesterton. "A mountain of a man" with a tiny pince-nez and a head full of curls, he'd be seen about town in a huge-brimmed hat and a great heavy cape, in the one hand a stout wooden sword, in the other a tankard of beer. No doubt it expressed his childlike simplicity, his harmless affection for the good old Falstaffian past. But it wasn't entirely naive, uncontrived. Devised by his wife who created his costumes, and by Gilbert who referred to himself as "that Falstaffian figure in a brigand's hat and cloak," it was a shrewd piece of self-advertisement. Henry James wasn't moved by the man or the image. " 'The unspeakable Chesterton' . . . ," he called him, "a sort of elephant with a crimson face and oily curls." He was even too much for the impudent Harris who, not without reason, found him "a talent divorced from life." Perhaps less absurd but no less self-conscious was Robert Bontine Cunninghame Graham, the Scottish laird who was said to descend from King Robert II of Scotland and to boast in his veins the glamorous blood of Spain and of Italy. Graham had ridden with the Moors in Morocco and with the gauchos on the Argentine pampas and riding now in Rotten Row, bravely attired and bravely mounted on an Arab stallion or an American mustang or a barebacked Mexican steed (the reports were various), he brought to dreary old London, they said, "the *panache* of [Athos], the most noble of Dumas's Three Musketeers." He was remembered by one with "a long whip in one hand, a lasso in the other . . . and his steed galloping *ventre à terre.*" Jacob Epstein who dubbed him "Don Roberto Quixote" imagined him fondly with Colt revolvers at his belt and bringing "a whiff of the American Wild West into London studios and drawing-rooms." Even Conrad, the reformed romantic, the ultimate skeptic, would feel to the end his ineffable glamour. "May you ride," he would write Graham at last, "firm as ever in the saddle, to the very last moment, *et la lance toujours en arrêt.* . . ." As for Hueffer, romantic and royalist, he dedicated his novel *Mr. Fleight* to the man, to "R. B. CUNNINGHAME GRAHAM/ Of Right King of Scotland/ Known to this Dully Revolving World as A/ Revolutionist/ And in All Realms of Adventure/ Most Chivalrous." .

But then it was, it would seem, this Edwardian age, an age of impersonations. If they had no personas to hand, ready-made, the Edwardians were quick to invent them. Wells, who abhorred the imagined "reality," came down rather hard on his peers and contemporaries. He reviled Conrad's pose of "a romantic adventurous unmercenary intensely artistic European gentleman carrying an exquisite code of unblemished honor through a universe of baseness. . . ." Hueffer was worse. Conrad had one persona but Fordie, who had a hole, it was said, where his ego should be, had only too many. "What he really is or if he is really, nobody knows and he least of all; he has become a great system of assumed personas and dramatized selves." And indeed they were characters all, the Edwardians were, Wells himself no less than the others. Conrad and Hueffer, Graham and Shaw, Harris and Hudson, Kipling and Chesterton, Mansfield and Woolf, Pound and H.D., John and "Dorelia," Lady Ott, Strachey, Henry Lamb: they were less like people you'd meet on the street than like people you'd meet in a novel, a Dickensian novel, Dostoevskyan even.

No surprise they felt free to refashion reality, James rearranging his brother's letters in accord with his passion for beauty and order; Hardy using his second wife's name to write and to launder his own "biography"; Hueffer readjusting his reminiscences on the grounds that his sense of the facts was more true in the end than the facts themselves. Frances Chesterton was worried. She and Gilbert hadn't a penny to their name, no, not a *sou*. So Gilbert went to the publisher Lane, outlined a novel he was planning to write, demanded at once twenty pounds in advance, and, returning to Frances, poured the twenty gold sovereigns onto her lap. The trouble is, the story's pure fancy. Gilbert went to see Lane by appointment and by this time had nearly completed *The Napoleon of Notting Hill* and was carrying part of the manuscript with him. He and Frances herself had invented the story to enrich the Chesterton legend. Conrad's life was a miracle, surely. Romantical man, he had fought a duel in Marseilles and been almost fatally wounded, had joined the British Merchant Service as an ordinary seaman and amazingly risen to captain, had heroically decided to abandon the sea for another career on shore, had elected to write not in French but in English for which he had felt a special affinity. Alas, none of it true, or not altogether. No duel had been fought. He had tried to commit suicide and not too efficiently. His career on the waves had not been exemplary. He had failed his first tests for both first mate and captain, had been fired as the second mate on one ship and been forced to resign as the first mate of another. His decision to abandon one troubled ship for another, the marine for the literary one, was never that final. After *Almayer's Folly* was written he was still looking out for a sea berth and only a bequest from his uncle would tip the scales in favor of writing. As for his soul's a priori devotion to the language of England, he first thought of writing his novels in French which was, after Polish, the language he felt most at home with.

Of course they wrote masterpieces, the literati of London. As men and women of genius, what else would they do? "I shall have been a failure," James decided, "unless I do something *great!*" "No man has a right to go on as I am doing," said Conrad, "without producing manifest masterpieces." Some doubt perhaps about Wells's *Kipps* which was "not so much a masterpiece," James said, "as a mere born gem," and some doubt too about Lawrence's *Trespasser* which was only, said Hueffer, "a rotten work of genius, one fourth of which is the stuff of masterpiece." But no doubt at all about Hudson's *El Ombú*. "You have written," Garnett gravely informed him, "a masterpiece." So when Hugh Walpole came down to London he was naturally convinced he'd been born to write masterpieces. In the throes of writing *Fortitude* he was consoled by the thought that it was destined to be "not only my masterpiece but the masterpiece of my time." Little wonder they wrote in an anguish of spirit. Everything they did had to bear on its page the mark of the masterpiece. James referred to "the divine diabolical law" under which he labored. Conrad was sure he was "under the patronage of a Devil," for "unless beguiled by a malicious fiend what . . . creature would be mad enough to take upon itself the task of a creator?" "Pray for me these days," he would scrawl in the margins of his letters to Hueffer and Violet, by which they would know that the sage of Pent Farm was enduring those hells reserved for the makers of master-pieces.

"I shall change the world for the next thousand years"

Not every Edwardian, it's true, was seduced by the siren songs of greatness and genius. Morgan Forster, whose sense of his own unimportance was most un-Edwardian, didn't think much of the "greatness" idea unless they were speaking of Dante or Shakespeare, and Virginia Woolf who had heard in her childhood the booming oracular voices of genius, Meredithian, Jamesian, considered the genus "now entirely extinct." "We need not always be thinking about poster-ity," she'd say, and "as for 'genius,' " she'd later declare, "even I have done with that." Lawrence had done with it too, or said that he had. "I hated," he said, "being an author, in people's eyes." It annoyed him when the grandiloquent Hueffer introduced him to people "as a ge-nius." It made him feel shy and uncomfortable. Not that he wouldn't be tempted, like Christ by the Devil. Seated at night before a blazing log fire at Garnett's The Cearne, and "feasting," it was said, "on the ge-nial eloquence of our host as he warmed to the theme of Lawrence's genius"—"Lawrence's genius, you see . . ."—well, how could a young man not think much more of himself than he did? But somehow he managed. Not for him the airs and pretensions of the grandees of let-ters. "I never," he insisted, "starved in a garret . . . nor did I struggle in sweat and blood to bring forth mighty works, nor did I ever wake up and find myself famous." Even Conrad, for all that he worshiped the artist as genius, wasn't always convinced. In such of his figures as

Kurtz, de Barral, Peter Ivanovitch ("He is a man of genius"), he'd bitterly assail the type of the great man, and, as for the man of letters who claimed "exclusive superiority for his own amongst all the other tasks of the human mind," he hadn't much use for the fellow. James himself didn't take himself seriously, not always. Traveling in America and delivering a lecture en route, he made fun of himself as "a mountebank 'on tour' " and, sitting for a large formal portrait, described himself as "very big and fat and uncanny and 'brainy.' "

It certainly wasn't for the Shaws and the Bennetts and Wellses to make much of themselves. Good socialists all, it sufficed them to take a pragmatic view of the religion, nay, the business, of art. In Bennett's case, all too pragmatic, it was felt in some quarters. As an artist "with strong mercantile interests," as he put it himself, he was quite unembarrassed and defended in print the professional author who labored "for food, shelter, tailors, a woman, European travel, horses, stalls at the opera, good cigars, ambrosial evenings in restaurants. . . ." He was "speaking of human beings," he added morosely: "I am not speaking of geniuses with a mania for posterity." "I am in a way," Shaw conceded, "a man of genius," but his success as a dramatist was nevertheless, he'd continue, "the result of perfectly straightforward drudgery." "Only do, for Heavens sake, remember," he admonished one playwright, "that there are plenty of geniuses about" and that "the real difficulty is to find writers who are sober, honest and industrious." Not that he hid his light under a bushel. "I am not 'one of the Shaws,' " he announced: "I am actually THE Shaw." *Man and Superman*? "STUPENDOUS. Really and truly." *Major Barbara*? "a MAGNIFICENT play, a summit in dramatic literature." Compare Pinero with him, as William Archer had done? Pinero, poor man, just didn't belong and "you are just torturing him by dragging him into *my* arena." But if he took himself as an artist this seriously, it's not always certain. "I have never claimed," he declared, "a greater respect for playmaking than for the commoner crafts." The making of plays was not after all, he'd insist, his only or even his principal object in life. "My theatrical activity," he'd tell his biographer in 1905, "has been confined to the last ten years of my life (and has played no very absorbing part even in those ten years)." By 1908 he had written five novels and sixteen plays, but he had also served on countless committees, delivered a thousand lectures, written a million words for the journals. So not for him the magisterial manner and mode of the masters of letters. Criticism? No problem at all.

Desmond MacCarthy once struck from one of his pieces on Barrie a sentence he thought would offend the wee man. "Shaw," he said, "would have been perfectly indifferent."

As for Wells, he was no more given to grandeur than Shaw. "Little sense of contemporary Greatness among the Elizabethans," he noted in *Boon,* his angry assault on the London establishment. It was wholly, he said, a Victorian phenomenon and was now, thank heaven, declining in fashion and "the less we hear about authors the better." He and Bennett, a kindred spirit and friend, could laugh at themselves and the very idea of greatness. Bennett to Wells: "Either you have in supreme degree the journalistic trick of seeming omniscience, or you are one of the most remarkable men alive. . . ." Wells to Bennett: "I am glad to tell you that your modest surmise is correct. There is no illusion. I *am* great." Galsworthy was doubtless an admirable man, modest, considerate, but when young Frank Swinnerton met him at first, he couldn't help feeling, under the inspection of the grave grey eyes and the rimless eyeglass and the sense so discreetly conveyed of a man of distinction, just a little bit lowered in spirit. Bennett and Wells produced no such effect, "never gave the impression of being 'literary men.'" Galsworthy couldn't bear to read the reviews of his books. They made him nervous, he said. But like Shaw, Bennett and Wells took criticism not like men of letters but like men of the world. "It's awfully good, you know," Arnold would stammer one morning at breakfast, after consuming every word of a hostile review. "It's . . . devastating." Wells in fact liked what he called "the new (undignified) criticism": the mode of the *English Review* ("the street-boy style") and of the *New Age* ("literary carbolic acid"). He would have approved the new doctrine propounded by Hulme who wanted to speak of poetry in "a plain way, as I would of pigs."

In the London of Edward VII, however, there was evidently more than one species of megalomania. To perfect not the forms of art with the Jameses and Conrads but the social and political forms of the world, this, and no less, was the Shavian and Wellsian endeavor, *their* religion of art, *their* delusion of grandeur. Shaw denounced in a lecture the utter fatuity of the West End audience. "What about the audiences at the Court?" a heckler cried out. "That's not an audience," Shaw quickly retorted; "it's a congregation." Nor was he speaking in jest. "The theatre is as holy a place as the church," he would say, "and the function of the actor no less sacred than that of the priest." The end of philosophy, Marx had said, wasn't just to record reality but to change it. The end of the theatre, Shaw could believe, was no different. "We can change it: we must change it: there is absolutely no other sense in life than the work of changing it." The trouble with Shakespeare and Dickens and Scott was that they accepted the current reality, the current morality. It was also the trouble with James. "People don't want works of art from you," he belabored the poor wounded novelist: "they want help." Wells wouldn't have quarreled with this. If the world didn't please you, you could change it, as his own Mr. Polly would say. Shaw notwithstanding, however, the theatre wasn't, said Wells, the way. Books, novels, literature—these were the true religion, the real chance for a change in the human condition. "All you . . . ," he would sing, "who print books and collect books, and sell books and lend them . . . all you are priests . . . offering consolation and release to men and women. . . ." Dorothy Richardson was translating Andreyev, whose twilight view of civilization had been all the go at the turn of the century. But Wells wasn't interested. The end of the world? What nonsense! He was working on the solutions. It was his job as a novelist to work on solutions. Lawrence himself would soon be working on them. "I shall change the world for the next thousand years," he'd be promising Frieda. Arnold Bennett? "I hate Bennett's resignation," he'd declare after reading his *Anna of the Five Towns*. Joseph Conrad? "I can't forgive Conrad," he said, after reading his *Under Western Eyes*, "for being so sad and for giving in." No wonder Conrad felt out of it all. When, at a dinner with Shaw, Bennett, and Wells, he heard them expounding on writing as "action," he soon left the table to catch, as he told them, an earlier train. "They all made me feel so dowdy," he said. But he needn't have fretted. There was more than one way to change the condition of things. The novel was, like the sea itself, Conrad said, "a scene of great endeavor and of great achievements changing the face of the world." Thus the Edwardians. Whether Jamesian and Conradian or Shavian and Wellsian, it was never their defect that they doubted their place or their power in the order of things.

"Don't know yah"

But the world outside. Did it take them as seriously as they took themselves? They didn't always think so. It pained them—the Jameses and Conrads, the Hudsons and Hueffers—that they didn't qualify as gentlemen, that as artists they stood no higher in the eyes of the best British people than the butler and governess. They would be recognized by the gentry. They would be recognized *as* gentry. "Fun, isn't it, for middle-class people like you and me to find ourselves hob-nobbing with all these swells." So one fool of a woman had said to James at Londonderry House where all was ablaze with ribbons and royalty, decorations and diamonds. But the distinguished American wasn't amused. He didn't like to be called middle class. Not one bit. Nor would Conrad have cared for it. He referred to himself as "a Polish nobleman, cased in British tar" and was pleased to affect the monocle and beard, the bowler hat and checked suit, of the English country gentleman. Write for money? He wouldn't think of it. Always short of funds and always resentful of it, he would nevertheless go rigid with fury at the merest suggestion that "anyone, not merely himself, but any writer of position, could possibly write for money." So at least it was said by Hueffer who longed himself to belong to the gentry and boasted he was "a 'baron' five times over" and "had no need to earn a living," he said, "by my pen," and indeed his lordly airs and graces were maddening alike to his friends and his foes. "Not sure," said Pound, "that the beastly word gentleman hasn't caused you more trouble in yr/bright li'l life than all the rest of the lang." No wonder the Spanish hidalgo was a figure beloved of Edwardian London. Cunning-hame Graham seemed to young Goldring "like a Spanish hidalgo" and impressed Jacob Epstein by "his air of Hidalgo of Spain." Old Hudson wore what it pleased them to call a "grey hidalgo's beard" and the handsome Fabian Sydney Olivier looked to Shaw "like a Spanish grandee." Who wasn't in fact in London in those palmy days a Spanish hidalgo? "With his pointed face and neat black moustache," said John Buchan of Lord Basil Blackwood, "he had the air of a Spanish hidalgo."

Fresh from Nottingham, young Lawrence was in any case duly impressed. "Oh, how that glittering taketh me," he'd be telling his sweetheart after feasting on roast beef and brussels sprouts, plum pudding and champagne, at the elegant table of Violet Hunt and hearing the imperial Hueffer murmur in parting that he was on his way to a party at Lady St. Helier's. Hueffer was splendid, he rhapsodized: "He knows W B Yeats and all the Swells. . . . I have met a gentleman indeed in him, and an artist." By the time he got back to Croydon where he taught school and lodged with Jones, the school's admissions officer, he was affecting a different accent. "That's not your usual form of talk," Jones would interrupt him in the kitchen. "I don't understand what you mean," Lawrence would answer him haughtily. He was restless and fretful. "I'm not keen a bit on being a swell," he would say, but perhaps he protested too much. A letter from Jessie's mother offended him frightfully: it was addressed to "Mr. Lawrence" instead of to "D. H. Lawrence. Esq." As for Jessie herself he feared she wouldn't be up to his new conditions. She would seem, would she not, he asked the poet Rachel Annand Taylor, just "a little provincial" in the realms of the Hueffers and Hunts? He was, the lady decided, "a terrific snob." To be sure, he made fun of himself and the life, reenacting for young David Garnett's amusement "a shy and gawky Lawrence being patronized by literary lions." All the same, he wasn't for nothing a free-born Englishman. "Aren't the folks kind to me," he'd write in Uriah Heep fashion of his hosts in the city. "I really do honor your birth," he would tell Lady Ottoline. "Let us do justice to its nobility. . . ."

This glittering didn't take everyone. It didn't take Forster. After the success of *A Room with a View,* he lunched with Lady Ottoline at Bedford Square and dined with Sir Edward Grey who was all affability and was introduced to the monocled Marsh who gave him a key to his rooms in Gray's Inn and was eager to launch him in London society. Morgan, however, didn't care to be launched and on the eve of publishing *Howards End* dreaded the prospect of fame and the inevitable social commotion. But if the glittering didn't take Morgan, it took nearly everyone else. It had long ago taken old Hardy who couldn't resist for a moment the joys of the London season. Leaving behind him Emma Lavinia, who had never let him forget she had married beneath her, he'd shyly present himself at the gates of the great. Lady Treves, Lady Powis, Lady Milnes-Gaskell, Ladies de Ros and de Grey, Ladies Spencer and Stanley, Ladies Hoare and St. Helier, Ladies Portsmouth and Londonderry: they were like magic, like music, to Hardy, these magniloquent names, which it pleased him to drop like rich pearls in the prose of his second wife's sham "biography." Eddie Marsh's sense of these social encounters—"I never heard him say anything that couldn't have been said by the most self-effacing parasite"—was doubtless unkind, but when old Meredith died and it became widely known that he had, poor soul, been the son of a tailor, Hardy's response was less than magnanimous. Not three weeks dead, he was telling Mrs. Lowndes, and already all Meredith had tried for so long to conceal had come out. Better to tell the whole truth, he was saying, whatever the cost. Disingenuous man, he knew something himself of Meredith's plight and had endured it no better. His homely old mother, the widowed Jemima, was never permitted to enter Max Gate though, at the very end of her life, when she seemed little more than "a beady eye peering from a heap of bedding," she was sometimes wheeled out in a Bath chair to observe the arrival of guests at a garden party and it wouldn't in fact be long—"Such and so little is the mind of man!"—before her son would leave out of his quasi-biography the less flattering sides of the family history, its roots, for example, in the humblest peasantry. James Barrie was nothing if not a good liberal. A poor little man from a wee Scottish village, rank and class could mean nothing to him, the author besides of *The Admirable Crichton*. But then he met Millicent, Duchess of Sutherland, who wrote novels and was, it was said, one of the most beautiful women in England. A few months later he was calling her Millie. A few years later he was collecting duchesses and walking the lawns and the terraces of their big country houses. He was naturally amused by it all. "Dear Duchess," he'd write the great lady, with that pawky Scotch humor of his, "May I come to dinner on Thursday or Friday? I am dining beside a duchess on Sunday. I want to come very much either of these days. On Sunday I am dining with a duchess. I was away for the week-end at Berkhamsted, and next week-end I am dining with a duchess. . . ." He was human, it seemed, all too human. Millie fascinated him. Duchesses fascinated him. The romance of the peerage, the glamour of it: who after all could resist it?

It even took the young Turks, the bold young bohemians. It didn't matter that Wyndham Lewis was all for an aristocracy of the arts, that he denounced as defunct the old aristocracy of money and birth. "In the presence of a beautiful woman of title," he always assumed, Augustus John said, an "attitude of respectful servility." Katherine Mansfield

was another. It didn't matter that she too was the artist as rebel, that,
dark and intense, she haunted the fringes of the culture she hated, like
an angry French governess. She just couldn't resist it, the glamour of
Garsington, and it was an "endless miracle," she'd write Lady Ott, "to
know that you exist and that you are *you*," and when she went walking
with her on those beautiful grounds, had the look, Frieda Lawrence
would wickedly tell her, of "a maid going out with a grand lady." It certainly took Ezra Pound, the *haut monde* of London. For all that he
played to the hilt the American boob, the Buffalo Bill, the "cowboy
songster," he was glad to appear at Alice Meynell's famous Sunday
night suppers or at Sir Lawrence Alma-Tadema's distinguished establishment ("full of splendor and bad taste"), or at Lady Glenconner's to
deliver a lecture on Provençal poetry. He even developed, Aldington
said in disgust, like any other base American person, "an almost insane
relish for afternoon tea" and insisted on meeting his imagist friends "in
the rather prissy milieu of some infernal bun-shop full of English
spinsters." Not very surprisingly, Ma and Pa Pound weren't too welcome when they visited in London their son, the celebrity, "poor Ezra
not knowing," according to Lawrence, "what to do about them." "If
gold ruste, what shal iren do?" For how could Hugh Walpole ever confess, he who was now so near to the hearts of the great—Henry James,
Lady Lovelace, Lady Russell—that once he had worked with the dockers in Liverpool and had once even preached the Gospel of Christ in
the open air? Of course he never confessed it. He couldn't. It was out
of the question.

It would be different with the socialist crowd. The gold and the
glittering wouldn't take them. But be damned if they didn't. Young Alfred Orage didn't want his name pronounced like "porridge" as it was
back home in crass Huntingdonshire. He was, he maintained, of
Huguenot stock. It should be pronounced like the French for "storm."
Ora-a-a-ge. But Shaw's comic sense was aroused. He persisted in calling him "Orridge." Barker? Harley Barker? As a professional name it
just wouldn't do, the fussy young actor-producer decided. He'd change
it to "Harley Granville Barker." But Shaw's comic sense was aroused. I
find it hard to adjust, he wrote Barker's wife Lillah, to her husband's
"new name, which sounds harley appropriate" and went on to refer to
"'Arley" and "Barley" and to say that "if the Shulamite is a success, it
may mean that Hainley—there! this comes of calling a man Harley
when his real name is Barker—that Ainley may soar into impossible

terms. . . ." It may have been just as absurd as G.B.S. made it of course, but alas he wasn't himself in the end, for all of his genius, immune to the English disease. That his widowed grandfather on his mother's side had taken to bed a second bride he was frank to confess, but that the marriage had been of the shotgun variety he neglected to mention. Nor did he mention that Vandeleur Lee, the third of the *ménage à trois*, was a fearful *Catholic* and that, under his influence, he, Bernard Shaw—he would keep it a secret for some eighty years—had had to consort in his youth with the offspring of *Catholic* tradesmen. Nor for that matter did he have much to say about his mother's connection with the great Vandeleur. She may have occupied the same house with him for some seventeen years, and when he left Dublin for London may have abandoned her husband and followed the man ("her man" as Shaw phrased it) with an unseemly haste. Shaw would nevertheless argue, implausibly enough, that her relations with him were purely professional and not at all sexual. All of which didn't prevent him from taking great pains, a griddle of pains, to establish that he was the son of George Carr Shaw and in no way the son of the Other Man. As a good Marxist, however, it wasn't his habit to hide the grim social effects of a capitalist world. He never concealed his utter contempt for the enormous snobbery of "the Shaws," as his family referred to themselves, and observed without obvious grief their inevitable decline to the shabby gentility of a landed family lacking in land. His mother's grandfather may have been in his way a country gentleman but his wealth he derived, Shaw disclosed, less from his land than from the pawnbroker shop he secretly owned in the Dublin slums. "I sing my own class," Shaw would write: "the Shabby Genteel, the Poor Relations, the Gentlemen who are no Gentlemen." Not so his frock-coated Fabian friend and confederate. Hubert Bland would glare out at the world through a monocle and claim descent from the oldest of "Old Catholic" families but his grandfather was, it turned out, but a plumber and house painter.

And if they were species of snobs, these distinguished Edwardians, what else could they be? This was snob country, wasn't it? "My God, how workmen smell," said Vita Sackville-West when Sissinghurst was under repair. "The whole house stinks of them. How I hate the proletariat." How Maynard Keynes hated them too. "I must go to tea now," he'd write Duncan Grant, "to meet some bloody working men who will be I expect as ugly as men can be." As for Mrs. Woolf, Joyce's

Ulysses, great as it was, was nothing to her but the "illiterate, under-bred book . . . of a self-taught working man . . . egotistic, insistent, raw, striking, and ultimately nauseating." But the problem wasn't just Bloomsbury. It was Britain, Great Britain. I hope she likes being Mrs. Bernard Shaw, said one of Charlotte's old friends: "He began as an office boy in Townshend French's agency office in Dublin, and now he is distinctly somebody in a literary way, but he can't be a gentleman." Even Conrad, for all that in Poland he belonged to the *szlachta,* wasn't sure that in England he ranked as a gentleman. "Poor queer man," as Henry James called him, he was only a sailor, some exotic sea creature washed up on the shore, and was not, surely not, "one of us." Did Lady Ottoline really intend to pay him a visit? James held his hands up in horror. "But, dear lady . . . but dear lady . . . ," he cried in a fright. "He has lived his life at sea—dear lady, he has never met 'civilized' women."

So if lower-class people like Hardy and Lawrence and Bennett and Wells could enter at last the brave new republic of letters, it wasn't quite home. It was still the same England. The gentleman's paradise. "Don't know yah. Don't know yah." Publish Arnold Bennett! Mrs. Lowndes remembered the publisher Heinemann exclaiming. I might as well ask him, he said, to publish the work of a grocer. An apocryphal story perhaps. The lady was never a fountain of truth. The effect she described was nevertheless the effect Arnold everywhere made. He reminded Maugham of "a managing clerk in a city office" and Chesterton of "a man who having come to London for the Cup Final has never gone back" and Shaw of "a fourth-rate clerk from the Potteries and out of work at that." Arnold wasn't, it's true, much to look at. With his drooping eyelids and his half-open mouth and his cluttered discolored front teeth, not to mention the cowlick standing straight up at the back of his head, he was never an ornament. He stuttered, moreover, and, to make matters worse, stuttered in dialect, the same heavy dialect he'd brought down from the north and was never to lose. Maupassant? Not at all. It was "Mopesun" for Arnold.

And then his apparel, his appalling apparel. He was a famous novelist. As "Jacob Tonson" he was a celebrated columnist for a celebrated journal. But when he entered the *New Age* office at Chancery Lane it was likely to be in "a broad check suit with a vivid yellow waistcoat, a bright tie with a large horseshoe pin . . . and a grey bowler hat." This isn't to mention the fobs and the quiffs he adored, his "gastric jewelry" as Wells affectionately called them. Lady Ottoline, no shabby dresser herself, was delighted. "His elaborate pleated and embroidered shirts were always," she said, "a pleasure to me" as were also the "little vain gestures" he made when she admired his flowered silk ties and fancy gold pins. Bertie Russell, her lover, couldn't bear to be in a room with the fellow. He was "vulgar," he said. But Lady Ott to her credit didn't agree. Showy he was but not vulgar, she said. Still, Lady Ott was one of a kind and Arnold was never a hit in the very best circles. When Somerset Maugham met him in Paris he considered him "cocksure and bumptious and . . . common. I don't say this depreciatingly. . . ." But Clive Bell who also met him in Paris and introduced him to his fine artist-friends did say it depreciatingly. With "his thumbs in the arm-holes of his waistcoat," he affected Clive as "the boy from Staffordshire who was making good," indeed (misquoting Eliot) as

> "One of the low on whom assurance sits
> Like a silk hat on a Bradford millionaire."

Maugham did give him his due. Though Arnold was "never what in England is technically known as a gentleman," he said, "he was never vulgar any more than the traffic surging up Ludgate Hill is vulgar." But though this was all very well if you fancied the traffic surging up Ludgate Hill, if you didn't it wasn't. Arnold didn't wear shoes. He wore boots. He was fond of rice pudding which he ate every day.

No wonder he and Wells were for long fast friends. Refugees from the same dreary province of shopkeepers and housekeepers, they were not to find in the homes of the great a true habitation and name. Wells was famous and fortunate. He was everywhere known and revered. But a varmint he had been, a varmint he was, and a varmint he always would be. He was frowned on by Belloc who called him "provincial." He didn't have, it was clear to Miss Dorothy Richardson, the instincts of a gentleman. Let him try to dismantle the Fabian movement, Mrs. Webb would declare: "It takes gentlefolk to run a political body in England." Percy Lewis would find him a "rather unromantic pepper-and-salt figure." At the Vienna Café near the British Museum he'd witness the great man in action, "springing about in a suit too tight for him, as he inducted ladies into chairs and did the honors," and inspiring in one of Percy's associates a witty remark: "Whenever I see H. G. Wells I feel uncomfortably refined." So, it would seem, did Virginia Woolf. "A slab of a man formidable for his mass," Wells was, she decided, "the pattern of a professional cricketer." He had, she noted—she was a keen observer of the social scene—"the cockney accent in words like 'day.' " To her credit, however, Virginia was frank to acknowledge her snobbery. It was one thing, she thought, to have luncheon with Lady Oxford, quite another to have dinner with Wells and sit at his table with Bennett and Shaw, when she couldn't help feeling, she said, "like an old washerwoman toiling step by step up a steep and endless staircase." Lawrence was more sympathetic. He was saddened by Wells, by his need and his hunger and his feeling of not being at ease in the world of his "betters." "He always seems to be looking at life," Lawrence said of his books, "as a cold and hungry little boy in the street stares at a shop where there is hot pork."

Lawrence, poor sod, would know all about it. He was cold and empty himself and hungrily stared at the same shop window. Back home in school, he had been dropped by a boy who had discovered he was only the son of a miner. Now in London and a promising writer, he was still, it would seem, the son of a miner. Mrs. Taylor could feel his appeal, his naiveté; but "there was," she couldn't help thinking, "some slum in him." As a boy David Garnett had worshiped his father's young protégé but would later learn better. Lawrence looked, he'd discover, "like a mongrel terrier among the crowd of German Alsatians and Pomeranians." "You could find him," he'd say, sounding like Kipling or Conrad, "in every gang of workmen, the man who . . . is saucy to the foreman, who gets the sack . . . and is the cause of a strike, and is always cocky, cheeky and in trouble." David would even find Lawrence's physical features repellent. His nose was "too short and lumpy." Thick-matted and a "bright mud-color," his hair was "incredibly plebeian, mongrel and underbred." For by this time David had defected to Bloomsbury which didn't much care for people like Lawrence. Upon people like Lawrence, as upon people like Murry and Katherine, there fell, Virginia would say, "the shadow of the underworld." It fascinated her too, this "Underworld." Katherine Mansfield fascinated her. But she was, she confessed, "a little shocked by her commonness" and couldn't help wishing that her first impression "was not that she stinks like a—well, civet cat that had taken to street walking." In the London of Edward VII, however, who wasn't a snob? Hueffer

would after his death be put down by the critics for his social pretension, but Wyndham Lewis would be quick to defend him. "Seeing
what England is in the matter of social snobbery, it is difficult to see
how *one* snob more would make any difference."

"The parish of rich women"

Nevertheless it wasn't unkind to its writers and
artists, snob country wasn't. Did the lions want to be hunted? There
were those who were eager to hunt them. Milords and miladies, His
and Her Graces, with "the lust of authorship" in them, as Violet Hunt
said, or, in the absence of that, the lust of the acquaintance of authors.
The Duchess of St. Albans who had Hardy to dinner endeared herself
to the grateful old man by "taking a diamond pin from her neck and
telling him it had been worn by Nell Gwynne," and Lady Essex,
"among the fashionable cosmopolitans in London," was happy to seat
at her table, in the company of the great Henry James, that other distinguished American, Mrs. Edith Wharton, who'd meet on the occasion "Mr. H. G. Wells, most stirring and responsive of talkers," and "Sir
Edmund Gosse, who always showed me great kindness." Millicent,
Duchess of Sutherland, wasn't for nothing named Meddling Millie. Interested in everything from infant mortality to the teaching of Gaelic,
she would later appear in Bennett's *The Card* as Interfering Iris, the
Countess of Chell. But her noble dinners and Friday "at homes" were
quite irresistible. Once she "got used to the splendor," Chesterton's uneasy wife found them "jolly enough," and as for Will Rothenstein, more
at home in such ducal surroundings, he found them "not only the
most splendid but the most delightful parties I ever went to." James
Barrie was doubtless the life of her parties. The wonderful things he
could do with a penny and stamp! He'd lick the stamp, place it face
down on the penny, then flick it aloft till the penny stuck on the ceiling. It was charming. The duchesses smiled. This isn't to mention a
host of others like Lady Colefax, "an unabashed hunter of lions,"
whose Argyll House was becoming a center for leonine Londoners, and

Lady Low whose drawing room supplied Ezra Pound with his first social contacts, and Lady Russell, once Forster's Gräfin von Arnim, who
formed at her house the Pharos Club for the edification of the city's
intelligentsia. As for Lady St. Helier who "took a frank and indefatigable interest in celebrities," she was determined, it seemed, to have them
all, more or less, in her Portland Square mansion: e.g., Hardy and
Galsworthy, Mrs. Wharton and James, Sir Philip Burne-Jones and
Princess Marie-Louise of Schleswig-Holstein. Not that everyone answered the call. One successful young writer had the effrontery to turn
down one of her invites. He "hated," he said, "dining out" and was
"hard up" in any case "and would she lend him £5?"

It was indeed the golden age of the London hostess and the London salon. Mrs. Olivia Shakespear, for one, who'd have Ezra to dinner
when, smoking and hugging his ankles, he'd sit on the hearth rug that
the great Willie Yeats had but recently occupied. Ada Leverson, for another, who had known Oscar Wilde in his prime and was the only person in London to receive the poor man when he left Reading Gaol,
and was the good friend in fact of all painters and writers. Item: Mrs.
George Steevens who at Merton Abbey, just eight miles from London,
gave dinners on Tuesdays for indigent artists like Maugham and Beerbohm. Item: the Sangers, Charles and Dora, at one of whose Fridays in
their rooms on the Strand ("high above the hustle and bustle and roar
of traffic"), Lady Ott, at the time very shy and unknowing, first met
Desmond MacCarthy who was kind and encouraging, she said, and
Lytton Strachey whom, notwithstanding his falsetto voice and small,
dismal mustache and long, spidery body, she found sympathetic. Item:
Miss Ethel Sands, the wealthy American painter, at one of whose
weekly salons in Lowndes Place, Lady Ott would meet Walter Sickert,
Augustus John, and Prince Antoine Bibesco, and at one of whose
weekends at Newington, her country estate near Oxford, Lady Ott
would meet Henry James who "admired," she remembered, "the shape
of my head" and whose elaborate speech it pleased her to call "golden
stuff." She had attended so many brilliant salons—among them Clive's
and Vanessa's at 46 Gordon Square and Virginia's and Adrian's at 29
Fitzroy Square—she resolved to have one of her own. Thus her famous
Thursday "at homes" at 44 Bedford Square with its pale grey walls, yellow taffeta curtains, and urns of golden chrysanthemums, where on
one brilliant occasion Lytton Strachey, no sooner arrived, was rushed
into the arms of the prime minister himself and where, on another,

Virginia would introduce Rupert Brooke to "an aristocracy of letters as exclusive as the Apostles of Cambridge," the company also including Winston Churchill "very rubicund, all gold lace and medals," and Augustus John "very sinister in a black stock and a velvet coat." "Conversation, talk, interchange of ideas—how good it was!" Lady Ott would remember. "I felt greedy for friendship and launched recklessly on the sea of London . . ." and "with such zeal, such enterprise as I then had," she bravely recalled, Moll Flanders in muslin, "nothing daunted me."

It wasn't for every poor artist and writer of course, this "parish of rich women." At the beginning at least it wasn't for Wells. At a special dinner to introduce him to such VIPs as Asquith and Shaw, that normally ebullient talker fell "rather silent." "He tried hard to be clever," they said, but couldn't quite "let himself go." For all his airs of the man about town, Willie Maugham was so stricken by shyness that he made calls on his hostesses fervently hoping they wouldn't be home, and at one time was so short of money that he traveled by bus in white tie and tails and made himself miserable over the tips that would have to be paid to the butlers and footmen. But for happy Hugh Walpole it was heaven, pure heaven. He'd report to James on the wonders of his country-house visits, to the Ashley Combe of old Lady Lovelace, for instance, "the most beautiful house I've ever stayed in," and, though lonely in Rye and depressed at the time, James would reply with affection and humor, "Great must be your glories and triumphs and rounds of applause, and I break into solitary clapping here, late in the sultry night, when I hear of your lawn tennis greatness." Hence Mrs. Webb's distress and anxiety. Once the "bitter opponent of wealth and leisure," Bernard Shaw was "now the adored one of the smartest and most cynical set of English 'society.' " But she needn't have worried. The prince of the Fabians would not be seduced. When Lady Charm or Disarming sent him cards announcing that she'd be "at home" on this day or that one, he'd gaily reply, "So will G. Bernard Shaw." At their Heartbreak Houses, you'd find in your bedroom a few plays by Barker and Shaw and a few stories by Wells and Galsworthy. But it was show, all show. They weren't serious people, he said, these drawing-room socialists. "They refused the drudgery of politics."

As regards the parish of great men, they were many of them enlightened souls and as eager to read and receive the literati of London as the parish of women. Mrs. Webb didn't expect to like Arthur Balfour, the Conservative chieftain, but she couldn't resist him. He was a man, she discovered, "of extraordinary grace of mind and body—delighting in all that [was] beautiful and distinguished—music, literature, philosophy...." As for the Liberal leaders, they were writers themselves, men of letters in fact, the light belletristic essay their specialty. C. F. G. Masterman, Churchill's undersecretary at the Home Office, did publish in 1909 his important *The Condition of England*, but Augustine Birrell had been a scribbler of notes and reviews for the journals, light literary exercises that his friends and detractors alike would come to call "birrelling." Even Asquith, the PM himself, had put in his time as literary jack of all trades for the dear old *Spectator*. He turned out to be, as a matter of fact, the head of a family of littérateurs. At Lady Ott's Thursdays the young man "crackling with epigrams" would be Raymond Asquith and at Walter Sickert's assembly of Camden Town artists, the "solitary figure in a corner" brooding "over a glass of port" would be young Herbert Asquith "in poetic travail." As for Mrs. Asquith herself, Virginia Woolf wouldn't care for her writing. "Expecting life & smartness at least," she'd perused Mrs. Asquith's love letters but had found them "flat & feeble & vulgar & illiterate" and not worth the eightpence she'd paid for the magazine in which they'd appeared. Some years later Mrs. Asquith, now Lady Oxford, would have Mrs. Woolf to lunch to ask for a favor: "When I die, I would like you to write a short notice in the *Times* to say you admired my writing...."

They were wild about artists and writers in any event, the political people. Balfour went to see Shaw's *John Bull's Other Island* not once, not twice, but five different times, and the following year he'd see *Major Barbara* and be overwhelmed by "the horrible force of the Salvation Army scene." Indeed, when the Barker-Vedrenne management came to a close, royalty itself was in grief. "The King and Queen," Shaw was told by Vedrenne, "have sent me a diamond scarf pin." There was nothing in fact that the people in power wouldn't do for the poets and playwrights of London. Churchill presided over a public dinner for Ellen Terry's stage jubilee and Lord Esher, an aide to the king, took an active part in the Shakespeare Memorial project and Asquith himself decided to honor the stage and to offer knighthoods to Barrie, Pinero, and Beerbohm Tree. Frank Harris was lunching at the Savoy when the PM took a seat at a table nearby. Harris had something in mind and, brash and brassy as ever, took it to Asquith. "There's a real poet half-starving in London...," he told him. "He is too proud to take money from me, but you could make him prouder by helping him . . . his name is John Davidson." "I never heard of him," said the PM, but "let me quote you a verse or two," Harris went on, and began to recite, in thumping blank verse, "My feet are heavy now, but on I go,/ My head erect beneath the tragic years" and so on in heroical vein. "Very fine indeed, very fine and inspiring," the PM responded, the poet's name appearing sure enough on the next pension list.

They wined them and dined them, the great people did, and they even befriended them. Sir Edward Grey wasn't too proud to call Hudson his friend and appear at his weekly "at homes," and Charles Masterman wasn't too proud to call Bennett and Wells his friends and join Hueffer and Violet Hunt on a tour of the Rhineland, nor was he too proud to call Chesterton and Chesterton's cronies his friends and have them to supper at a Soho restaurant and a night of carousing that lasted till dawn. There was hardly in fact a political figure that Chesterton didn't connect with. At the home of the Webbs he'd see Winston Churchill and David Lloyd George and at the home of Mrs. Grenfell would see Arthur Balfour and the great Austen Chamberlain. Invited to dine at the Buxtons' he'd run into Asquith, and invited to dine at the Asquiths' he'd enjoy, he'd report, "the hearty humors" of the PM himself. After golfing together at Stoke Poges, Churchill and Somerset Maugham of all people became lifelong friends, Churchill admiring the playwright's wit and urbanity and the playwright admiring the minister's freedom from cant. On a weekend at Sir Wilfred Blunt's Newbuildings, Churchill offered Granville Barker a seat in the next general election and he would have made, Blunt believed, a first-rate MP, for he was "a man of much political intelligence, besides being an excellent fellow and man of the world." Lawrence was ashamed. Invited to tea by the Herbert Asquiths ("jolly nice folk—son of the Prime Minister"), Lawrence had introduced Frieda, at the time his mistress, as his wife. He apologized. It was a form of "false entry," he said. But young Asquith, who was all admiration and would frequently have them to dinner thereafter, couldn't have cared less. "Far removed from the dust of politics," Lawrence lived, as he'd say, "more deeply in revolt against the values of the day than any political leader." No question about it. In these halcyon years, the artists of London were scarcely neglected.

Indeed, if they weren't quite of the establishment they were frequently with it, would join with the dukes and the generals, with the

Lords and the jurists and the cabinet ministers, the revered social clubs of the city. On Pall Mall, for example, the grand solitude of the venerable Athenaeum where, with the support of Lord Crewe or Fitzmaurice or Rosebery, such gifted commoners as Hardy and James and Barrie and Wells would win their election, under the impressive Rule II, as persons "of distinguished eminence." Then just round the corner, on Adelphi Terrace, overlooking the Thames, the famous Reform Club where James had discovered he could rent him a room, a "refuge in winter," for as little as fifty pounds a year, and it was here he'd invite to dinner for two his ecstatic disciple, Hugh Walpole ("He was perfectly wonderful"), and do Conrad the honor ("dear Henry James") of introducing him to the dramatist Jones. It was certainly here, after leaving his "funny French wife," that Bennett would walk from Cadogan Square past Buckingham Palace for luncheon and politics with his good fellow liberals and here that Violet Hunt would have her "at homes" for old friends like Hudson and Wells or for new ones like Lawrence and Pound and here that Hueffer would invite his young protégé, Lawrence, who had, however—"I've not got a decent suit"—to decline. The Carlton Club nearby on Pall Mall would not be involved. It was purely political and Tory at that. But always available was the National Liberal Club where ambitious young people like Hueffer and Wells could meet with rising politicians and publishers. Wells would make fun of it all, the social ambition, the social climbing, of the young men of letters. They were "almost like gentlefolks," says his innocent Kipps. "On the one hand essentially Low, but by factitious circumstances capable of entering upon those levels of social superiority to which all true Englishmen aspire...." But then these meetings with Balfours and Churchills, these luncheons and dinners at the Athenaeum, at the Reform Club, would work their effect and Wells, little Wells, would be singing a far different tune. "The literary life is one of the modern forms of adventure...," he'd be singing. "One meets philosophers, scientific men, soldiers, artists, professional men, politicians of all sorts, the rich, the great...."

Of Publishers and Agents

The publishers, it's true, didn't always work in the authors' best interests. In the good old days they had acted as mediators between writers and printers and still liked to think of themselves as the writers' best friends. But the good old days were dead now and gone and their tendency now was to treat them as useful commodities, as mere portable property. Somerset Maugham rather liked William Heinemann. He was said to be hard on young writers, but if they "stood up to him and wrung better terms out of him," Maugham reported, "he would laugh heartily and say, 'Well, you're not a bad businessman.'" This was not reassuring, however, and the publisher Unwin was notorious for driving hard bargains and Heinemann himself was, Henry James said, "the most swindling of publishers," and as for Lawrence, who felt he had been unfairly used by the man, "publishing people [were] more sickly than lepers." Not that the authors themselves were utterly helpless. With his Olympian claims to high social station Hueffer felt for his publishers the lordly contempt he was sure that, as merely commercial creatures, they richly deserved, and with his primitive zest for money and markets Wells was inclined to change publishers as often as he took off his clothes. As for Conrad, he was positively indecent, even downright dishonest, in his dealings with them. To William Blackwood, who had treated him kindly, he would send an official letter informing him coolly that from this time forward his financial affairs would be in the hands of an agent, one Mr. Pinker. He made no mention of the three hundred pounds he had borrowed from the publisher who was never in fact to see them again. There are even grounds for believing that he blithely deceived him in the matter of *Lord Jim*. Blackwood had contracted for a sketch, a short story, for serialization in *Maga,* but Conrad would seem to have known that a longer work was involved and, in serial form, a more profitable one from his point of view. As for the American publisher McClure, there's no doubt at all he was swindled. Conrad said so himself. "I've obtained a ton of cash from a Yank," he confessed, "under, what strikes me, are false pretenses.... He *thinks* the book he bought [*The Return*] will be finished in July while I know that it is a physical and intellectual impossibility.... He sends on regular checks which ... looks uncommonly like a swindle on my part."

Just the same, the Wellses and Conrads were less the rule than the exception, and the authors of London were under some disadvantage in coping with publishers. They'd need the Society of Authors which, led by Sir Walter Besant, had begun to attack with some force the greed of the publishing houses and to offer authors its service as a species of agency. Even more especially they'd need the literary agent, an entirely new citizen in the duchy of letters. Pioneered by one A. P. Watt, they'd come to include the great J. B. Pinker who would represent writers as various as Conrad and James and Bennett and Maugham and Wells. Of course they were hurt and affronted, the publishing people, who regarded themselves as the authors' real representatives and literary agents as mere interlopers. Fisher Unwin certainly thought so. When Somerset Maugham took on an agent, Unwin was annoyed and Maugham soon left him for Heinemann. Arthur Waugh, the chairman of Chapman and Hall, was also annoyed. Do you not think, he wrote Pinker who had just taken charge of Bennett's affairs and transferred his business to Methuen, "do you not think that, considering the relations which have obtained between Arnold Bennett and myself ... it would have been ... more in accordance with the courtlier traditions of publishing if you had said some word to me before taking Bennett away ... ?" As for Heinemann, he was also annoyed by this brutal betrayal of the courtlier traditions. Devoted to publishing and its civilized mission and convinced that the Society of Authors was no more than a writers' trade union, he helped form in 1906 the Publishers' Association and from 1909 to 1911 served as its president. As for those agents, those detestable agents: they were beneath his contempt. When James gave his business to Pinker, there was, James reported, "a lively row." "Once an author gets into the claws of a typical agent," said Heinemann bitterly, "he is lost to decency."

The authors themselves for that matter weren't always convinced that agents were necessary. Andrew Lang, a man of letters of a late Victorian gentility, hated to think that his fellows were so inept as to need their assistance and Shaw who felt the same way would later denounce them as the "favorite resort of persons who have not ability enough either for ordinary business pursuits or for literature." Indeed, the Soci-

ety of Authors, for all that it fought against publishers, was ready to
fight against agents as well. They were, the Society felt, no better than
mercenaries who corrupted the friendly relations that ought to obtain
between writer and publisher. Just the same, by 1911, May Sinclair was
noting, most of the members of the Society of Authors were taking
their business to agents and for very good reasons. The courtlier traditions of publishing, it seemed, were no longer in force. Edward Garnett
who had worked for at least five publishing houses had no illusions
about these traditions. "While publishers posed as patrons of the art,"
he complained, "they honored most those who sold most." The shrewd
Arnold Bennett had no doubts about it at all. He was entirely persuaded, he said, "that every author of large and varied output ought to
put the whole of his affairs into the hands of a good agent."

Not that these courtlier traditions were dead altogether. An author's first social contact with literary London was likely to be with
publishers and their advisers and readers. Worldly, urbane, Frederick
Macmillan took a special delight in entertaining his writers at home
and much of the pleasure Heinemann took in publishing authors had
to do with the cordiality of their social relations. Conrad may have
ridiculed Unwin's Jewishness, the sharp business dealings he considered Semitic. Nevertheless he and Jessie exchanged social visits with
the Unwin family and the only guests, really, whom the Conrads had
to their house in the early days were publishers' readers like Garnett
who was Unwin's and Pawling who was Heinemann's and Meldrum
who was Blackwood's. Ezra Pound's first London contacts were certainly professional. It was Elkin Mathews, the publisher-bookseller,
who introduced him to Rhys who introduced him to May Sinclair who
introduced him to Hueffer who would publish his poems in his *English
Review* and it was Mathews who took him along to the old Poets' Club
which met once a month at the United Arts Club and featured such
stalwarts as Shaw and Belloc and Chesterton and it was at Mathews's
bookshop on Vigo Street that he first made the acquaintance of Hulme
and Flint and the younger set generally.

There were even those publishers who took seriously their writers,
their art and their genius. Blackwood was more than a publisher to
Conrad. He was a friend and a confidant, responding with care to
Conrad's accounts of his woes, financial and literary, and treating with
real understanding the problem of *Lord Jim* whose chapters were
threatening to multiply all but indefinitely. As for Elkin Mathews,

whose Vigo Street bookshop was a gathering place for new poets in London, he was all generosity to desperate young prospects like Pound. When Pound published in 1909 his *Personae* and later that year his *Exaltations*, Mathews gave him exactly the terms he gave Maurice Hewlett who was after all an established author. "Ah, eh, ah, would you, now, be prepared to assist in the publication?" the diffident Mathews had asked him. "I've a shilling in my clothes," Ezra had answered, "if that's any use to you." "Oh well," Mathews had said. "I want to publish 'em. Anyhow." Even old Heinemann wasn't wholly the ogre that James and Lawrence had made him to be. A mercurial little man with bright eyes, wide mouth, and bald head, he was entirely devoted to letters, Violet Hunt said, and their meetings would end, she'd remember, "in an academical discussion about literature." James and Conrad he published, it was said, more for the honor than the profit and he would gladly have published Wells's "dangerous" *New Machiavelli* if only to protest the publishers' cowardice and the press's mistreatment of poor *Ann Veronica*. When the circulating libraries banned Hall Caine's *The Woman Thou Gavest Me,* he was frightened to death, for the risks were enormous, but he didn't capitulate and by issuing the novel helped to defeat the librarians' attempt to control the production of books. Violet Hunt, as a matter of fact, preferred dealing with Billy, as she called him, to dealing with Pawling, his partner-adviser. The Jorkins to Heinemann's Jarndyce, Pawling was business, all business, but Billy could "always be carried away...into accepting a masterpiece that would not earn its royalty." So Pawling was happy to see his partner off to Prague or to Leipzig for some publishers' conference where he was free to dilate on the wonders of literature and do the least possible damage to the profit and prestige of the firm. When Heinemann died in 1920 he left half his estate to struggling poets and other artistic unfortunates.

If the publishers weren't always the writers' best friends, the agents certainly were and no one of them more so than "Jy Bee" as they called J. B. Pinker. "Jy Bee" loved driving a four-in-hand and riding to hounds and after a fall would return to his office in Arundel Street with the telltale green stain on the back of his head. But there wasn't a trace of the social pretender about him. A short, sturdy, clean-shaven man, self-made, self-educated, he shook hands shoulder-high in the old-fashioned way, spoke distinctly in a hoarse whisper, and laughed, when he laughed, without moving a muscle. His was, in fact, a force or a rectitude which made publishers blanch and editors glower and made money for clients. For James, for example, who could see in his future only "a gloomy vista of pinched discomfort" until Pinker appeared and all became "gas and gingerbread" with a gazebo in the garden and apartments in Chelsea and all the china he wanted. Of course this was Hueffer again, no reliable witness, and poor James in fact would never grow wealthy. But Hueffer was essentially right. Pinker *was* the fairy godfather for the Bennetts and Conrads and Maughams if not for the Jameses. Indeed he was more. He was their friend, their confidant, their benefactor. The "prince of agents," as Violet Hunt called him, he agreed, in an arrangement rare for the time, to pay Arnold Bennett fifty pounds a month while he went off to Paris to write the Great English Novel, *The Old Wives' Tale,* and thereafter, with his loans and his friendship, nursed him along from a meager obscurity to a prosperous celebrity. His relations with Conrad were even more generous. He advanced him money on the promise of manuscript to come, and since it was slow to materialize or didn't at all, by 1908 Conrad was in debt to his patron to the tune of some sixteen hundred pounds, or the equivalent in royalties of two novels. It came to the point where Pinker became in effect his banker and accountant, assuming not only the contracts of his books but full control of his money and his merest domestic expenditure.

Of course there were quarrels, and some of them bitter. The more Conrad received the more he resented it; the more Pinker disbursed the more he resented it. Every request for money, every delay in the production of manuscript, brought a lecture from Pinker and sometimes a refusal; every lecture from Pinker, every wretched refusal of funds, brought a torrent of hurt indignation from Conrad: "Were you as rich as Croesus and as omnipotent as all the editors rolled into one . . ." One day at the end of January 1910 Conrad went up to London carrying the copy of *Under Western Eyes* that Jessie had just finished typing. At the publisher's office there was a heated argument, no doubt over money, and Conrad, enraged, pushed out the arms of the huge leather armchair he sat in. At his next port of call, the office of Pinker, there was yet another fierce argument, still over money no doubt, Pinker demanding at one point that he should, if he could, speak in English. By this time beside himself, Conrad stormed out of the office and spent the night at Galsworthy's where, "incredible as it seemed, he pushed the foot out of the bed in an excess of nervous energy." Returned home the next day he sent Pinker a wire: "Have you a complete copy of *Western Eyes*?" And when the agent's one-word answer, "No," came back, the author was so strangely elated that his wife was suspicious. Would this madman her husband go so far as to burn his own novel? She wasted no time. She locked "that mighty pile," as she named it, in the drawer of the table. The next day the author would lapse into delirium. "Speak English . . . if I can . . . what does he call all I have written? I'll burn the whole damned . . ." And Conrad indeed would for months be disabled and Pinker get from him no novel at all and for the next few years would be coldly addressed as "Dear Sir." And so it would go till the financial success of *Chance*, and all would be well once again.

For all their fussing and feuding in fact, they respected and even revered one another. "Those books," Conrad said, "which, people say, are an asset of English literature owe their existence to Mr. Pinker as much as to me." He was, he once said, "the Pinker of agents." Nor was their relation entirely commercial. That relation, Conrad remarked, "is not of business but of intimate friendship in the last instance." "In case of my early death," Conrad would write him, "my wife would be perfectly safe in your hands," and when Pinker himself was the first one to go, his sons motored to Canterbury to make his old friend the first one to know. "Agents are created by God to be beaten down." So Hueffer had said with Pinker in mind. For Lawrence he was "that little parvenu snob of a procurer of books." But not for James and Bennett he wasn't and not, not, certainly, for Conrad. The publishing world of Edwardian London may not have been the best of all possible worlds but quite clearly it wasn't the worst.

"Fit audience find, though few"

Henry James, true enough, was tired and dispirited. Since 1900 not one of his books had paid back its advances. "My books make no more sound or ripple now," he sadly reported, "than if

I dropped them one after the other into mud." He thanked Cunninghame Graham for praising his recently issued collected works, the New
York Edition, on which he had lavished so many years and all he had
learned of the art of the novel; alas, those twenty-three plum-colored
volumes just weren't selling and his first royalty check was an embarrassing $211. "My productions affect me as mostly dropping into a
bottomless abyss whence no echo comes back to me. . . ." He had never
of course been caviar to the general, to people like the philistine Pem-
brokes in Forster's novel who had "tried to read out a long affair by
Henry James" but "simply couldn't remember from one week to another what had happened," nor for that matter to people like the ill-
natured Hudson who referred with contempt to the Master's "dear last
style which he abhorred the critical world for not liking," or even the
good Arnold Bennett who would "feel bogged down in his books" and
after 150 pages of *The Ambassadors* would sadly conclude that he
couldn't go on. Still, even so, even now, the old man was hardly forgotten, was hardly ignored. As the great novelist in Hugh Walpole's *Fortitude*, he was "so famous that American ladies used to creep into his
garden and pick leaves off his laurels." He was already, Will Rothenstein said, "one of the great pundits, to whom ladies sat listening in
adoration" and whose "dicta, elaborate, wise and tortuous, were re-
peated in clubs and drawing rooms." So at her fine country house at
Newington, Ethel Sands would offer a party to surround the great man
with affection, and when at the end of the season Edith Wharton arrived for tea at Cassiobury, the country estate of Lord and Lady Essex,
it was to find among the Balfours and the Sargents and "the very
flower and pinnacle of the London world" the distinguished figure of
James himself, and Pound would refer in one of the Cantos to another
high social occasion, the Princess Bariatinsky

> holding dear H.J.
> (Mr. James, Henry) literally by the button-hole . . .
> and saying, *for once*, the right thing
> namely: "Cher maître"
> to his checqued waistcoat . . .

"It was the thing to do," as Mr. C. Lewis Hind would declare it. "It was
always the thing to do. I can never remember the time when Henry
James was not a Feature and a Figure in London life."
    That Feature and Figure didn't at once make a powerful Impres-

sion. With a round heavy body set on short stumpy legs and a habit of speech portentous and ponderous, his effect was at times just a little absurd. But he was more, much more, than the portly Pickwickian presence he may have suggested. After removing his beard at the turn of the century, he'd reveal to the world, in the massive head, the pale marble eyes, the clean-shaven cheeks and wide saturnine mouth, a figure of almost ecclesiastical power and persuasion. He didn't in fact look like an American at all or even an Englishman. It was a Frenchman he looked like, or a Roman or Rothschild. "Priest—fine eyes—magnificent head—strong voice." So Max Beerbohm recorded him. He breathed, Hueffer said, "the air of a divine," was "the most masterful man" he had ever met. He had in fact the power to hurt, to be dangerous. Interrupted at a tea party by a devoted young host, he turned upon him, said Hueffer, and "indicted his manners, his hospitality, his dwelling, his work, with a cold fury in voice and eyes." Lady Ottoline Morrell called him "a kind and penetrating spirit" but, she meditated later, "should I now call it kind?" For, though it gave her a thrill of keen pleasure, she remembered how with "a sudden quick thrust of phrase [he] would hold up his victim pinned on the point of his sword."

There were those, to be sure, who found his speech and his humming and hawing preposterous enough. "You don't suppose . . . it has been whispered to me . . . you know swift madness *does* at times attend on the too fortunate, the too richly endowed, the too altogether and overwhelmingly splendid. You don't suppose then . . . I mean to you too has it been whispered? . . . that . . . well, in short . . . That-he-is-thinking-of-taking-to-politics?" Thus James to Hueffer on the dread possibility of Wells's abandoning literature. "My dear Virginia they tell me, they tell me, they tell me, that you—as indeed being your father's daughter, nay your grandfather's grandchild, the descendant I may say of a century, of a century, of quill pen and ink, ink, inkpots, yes yes yes, they tell me, ahmmm, that you, that you, that you *write* in short." So Virginia, visiting Rye with Clive and Vanessa, would mimic the talk of her father's old friend. But Desmond MacCarthy found it all fascinating, found it rather like "watching through a window some hydraulic engine, its great smooth wheel and shining piston moving with ponderous ease through a vitreous dusk." Its Polonian value wasn't lost, that's certain, on the poet who would himself "by indirection find directions out." "The massive head," Ezra Pound would remember, "the slow uplift of the hand, *gli occhi onesti e tardi,* the long sentences piling themselves up in elaborate phrase after phrase, the lightning incision, the pauses, the slightly shaking admonitory gesture with its 'wu-a-wait, wait a little, something will come' . . ." It was, he said, this great Jamesian performance, "all unforgettable."

James was not at any rate wholly forgotten by the young, by "the gallant and intelligent young" as he called them. By the ardent Hugh Walpole who named him "by far the greatest man I have ever met." By May Sinclair, for another, who worked at her desk with a signed Henry James above her—the Master "has influenced *me* considerably," she'd say, "and I'm not a bit ashamed of it." By Dorothy Richardson, for still another, who didn't want to write in the manner of the day, in the coarse, dingy manner of the Bennetts and Wellses, for where in all this was life itself?, and it was, she would call *The Ambassadors,* "the first completely satisfying way of writing a novel." Even skeptical Bloomsbury which was out to demolish exactly the world that he worshiped found it hard to resist his appeal. As Cambridge undergraduates, Strachey and Woolf had read aloud in their rooms his Mandarin prose and indeed had conducted themselves like figures in a Jamesian phantasmagoria, "writing and talking," said Leonard, "as if we had just walked out of *The Sacred Fount* into Trinity Great Court." One night in Rye, young Strachey would be haunting the streets of the town and scanning the windows of Lamb House and would catch just a glimpse of the venerable head and next day in the Mermaid Inn would witness the great man himself and call him "colossal" and "I long to know him," he'd say. Morgan Forster was rather less worshipful. Lamb House seemed to him stuffy and precious. Leaving it one evening he observed in the shadows a young worker leaning on a wall and smoking a cigarette and this, he'd assert, was reality itself, the reality that Lamb House excluded. Just the same it was "a funny sensation," he said, seeing "a really first class person" and this is what it felt like, he'd think, to be "in the presence of a Lord." James was a Master indeed, a Monument in fact, had known in his time the Dickenses and Thackerays, the Eliots and Trollopes, the Flauberts and Turgenevs, and had fought all his days for the cunning and craft of his form. "O poet of the difficult, dear addicted artist . . ."

Forster or no Forster, a new generation of young Cambridge students would still be invoking James's shade. Three of them would write him a letter one day. Would he do them the honor of passing a week-

end in Cambridge? He would, yes, he would, he replied, "in an enormous letter even more complicated than a novel." So for forty-eight
hours in June 1909 there would be breakfasts and dinners and room-
fuls of respectful young men who smoked and fell silent or conversed
in a language or on topics so entirely their own that the old man was
often bewildered. But "I *liked* it," he said, "the whole queer little commerce, and *them*, the queer little all juvenile gaping group. . . ." What's
more, he met Rupert Brooke—it was the event of the weekend—
whose golden good looks made the usual impression. Was he, the Master asked Desmond MacCarthy, a very good poet? No, not very,
MacCarthy replied. "Well, I must say," the old gentleman thereupon
said, "I am *relieved,* for with *that* appearance, if he had also talent it
would be too unfair." On one happy occasion he reposed in a punt on
velvet cushions while he gazed up "through prominent half-closed eyes
at Brooke's handsome figure clad in white shirt and white flannel
trousers." Poor Wells, he was naturally chagrined. James was so *there,*
so *immovably* there! "You see, you can't now talk of literature without
going through James. James is unavoidable. James is to criticism what
Immanuel Kant is to philosophy—a partially comprehensible essential,
an inevitable introduction." Even Pound who would venture to BLAST
from existence every remaining Victorian saint would be careful to
leave unmolested the Master. "Henry's *Anschauung* never precisely my
own," he would say. But if "London [was] possible in 1908" it was because H.J. with Browning "HAD smacked the teak-heads with their
flails. . . ." No, the Master was not quite neglected. He had his admirers.
"You stand," his friends Beerbohm and Gosse would remark in a
poem, "marmoreal darling of the Few."

"My God! Is it you?"

Nevertheless James wasn't wrong to be vexed and discouraged. It was all very well being the darling of the Few but would it
not have been still better to be, like the Shaws and the Chestertons, the
Wellses and Bennetts, the darlings of the now-lettered Millions? For

this lusty new audience considered, the age had to be for its popular idols the true golden age. Sir Walter Besant was ecstatic. Your new man of letters could expect, he'd exult, to earn as much money as a doctor or lawyer and as much social respect as a bishop. Arnold Bennett was also ecstatic. "Never before . . . ," he'd propose, "did so many average painstaking novelists earn such respectable incomes" and Arnold was in fact out of sorts with "the dilettante spirit" which denied "the connection between art and money and . . . [made] a literary virtue of unpopularity." He wouldn't be one of them. He'd buy him a yacht with a crew of eight "just to show these rich chaps," as he said, "that a writer can make money too." In fact, he'd acquire by the time of his death a fortune of £68,000. And his was by no means the largest. Galsworthy's amounted to £88,000, Hardy's to £91,000, Kipling's to £150,000 and Barrie's to £200,000. Conrad and Shaw, it's true, were not quite luxuriating. In 1904, on the eve of his great efflorescence, Shaw reported that he'd averaged no more than 500 a year and before his own efflorescence of 1913 Conrad, who was always in debt and not at all happy about it ("I am sitting on my bare ass in the lee scuppers"), had averaged no more than 600. But considering that Dorothy Richardson made but 50 a year as a medical secretary, that Orage made as little as 80 as a teacher and Lawrence 95 and that Keir Hardie, the tireless Labour MP, never made more than 200 a year, Shaw's 500 and Conrad's 600 weren't quite pittances. Even so, Shaw would soon come into his own, laying his hands, in one season alone, on £13,000, and after 1913 and the publication of *Chance* Conrad's income would allow him that indifference to detail to which as a gentleman he was surely entitled. As for Wells, he had no problem at all. Between 1893 and 1896 his annual income was transfigured from less than 400 to more than 1,000 pounds and after the appearance in 1915 of *Mr. Britling Sees It Through*, which made him richer by £50,000 in the first eighteen months alone, he was never to worry about money again.

To be sure, not every Londoner had his good luck. Edward Thomas made a paltry five pounds a week, and when Davies's wooden leg gave way his friends had to raise the few meager pounds to buy him a new one, and when in 1901 the poet Arthur Symons got married to a wealthy young lady of luxurious tastes he reviewed for the *Star* some one hundred plays and received for his pains a mere five pounds a week. As for the underground world of the Murrys and

Mansfields, a check for a pound or even a few shillings from some wretched journal could seem like a fortune, and Katherine who loved cigarettes had seldom the money to buy them and "Yes, I *am* tired, my dear . . . ," she'd confess, "tired . . . of eating hard-boiled eggs out of my hands and drinking milk out of a bottle." They were for a fact just a little embittered. Thomas blamed the world for his wretched condition and Davies complained that while a painter like John could make fifty pounds for the work of an hour, a poet like Yeats was lucky to make a few guineas for a lyric that had taken him weeks to compose. Not that poverty was thrust upon them. In the bohemian circles of the Davieses and Mansfields, it was the mark of their pride in their art that they shunned the middle-class office and the horrors of regular employment. When his friends got for Davies a small sinecure in the British Museum, the tramp-poet was not at all grateful. "They expected me to work. I have never worked in my life. *That's* what your friends do for you!" But Thomas his patron wasn't displeased. He understood perfectly. The man was a poet and wasn't to work as other men do. Pound would have understood also. Gaudier, his friend, was an artist in marble and stone and this was indeed hard labor enough. His primitive workshop, Arch 25, was one of the railway arches approaching the Putney Bridge. Trains roared above him. The concrete floor was muddy and wet. But this was the way things were done in Montmartre where, for the sake of their craft, the young artist-rebels preferred to be poor and in rags and the direst distress.

Nevertheless, if work wasn't for them, the bohemian people, work was available and not badly paid. Even old Grub Street had altered. The professional writer was no longer the hack of the George Gissing novel, wretched, impoverished, a figure of fun or derision. He was now the good citizen of letters, like solid John Buchan, assistant editor of the old *Spectator*, or like Middleton Murry, editor of the *Athenaeum*, and making as much as eight hundred pounds a year. This new man of letters would enter his study in the morning "as regularly as a barrister goes to chambers" and was likely to find on his desk two or three books for review and a publisher's manuscript sent for an estimate and work of his own no doubt to get on with, i.e., an essay he'd promised some journal or "a life of some dead-and-gone worthy" or even, perhaps, an unfinished novel, a minor masterpiece, of his own. Little wonder they multiplied like flies in the summer. In 1891 six thousand Englishmen called themselves authors. Ten years later their numbers had swollen to eleven thousand and ten years after that to fourteen thousand.

The same revolution that produced a new kind of reader also produced a new kind of writer. Would the folk not think it was silly of him, the son of a miner, to want to write poetry? the young Lawrence asked. What did it matter? his sweetheart replied. And it didn't. Not any more. Orage was the son of a poor village schoolteacher, Gilbert Cannan of a badly paid shipping clerk, Edward Thomas of a Board of Trade staff clerk, Middleton Murry of a War Office copy-clerk. Shaw himself, the autocrat of a hundred London committees, was a refugee from the petty bourgeois bohemia of Dublin, and almighty Wells, the autocrat of a hundred dining and drawing rooms, couldn't trace his ancestry, he was proud to confess, beyond his grandparents, one of them an innkeeper and the other the "head gardener to Lord de Lisle at Penshurst Place in Kent." No wonder they were often such popular figures. Themselves of the populace, it was to the populace that they frequently gave themselves, Shaw and Wells addressing hundreds of lectures to workers ardent for knowledge, Bennett writing books of instruction like *Mental Efficiency, Journalism for Women: A Practical Guide, How to Live on Twenty-four Hours a Day.* Where indeed but in them, in their Edwin Clayhangers, their Paul Morels, their Lewishams, Kippses, and Pollys, could the new proletariat see its own image, read its own legend? If *Jude the Obscure* was a masterpiece, it was, Wells decided, because Hardy's protagonist was "the voice of the educated proletarian, speaking more distinctly than it [had] ever spoken before in English literature."

So it wasn't just that they made lots of money, could join a good club, could have a nice house in the city and a place in the country. It was also that they were widely known and acclaimed. They were stars and celebrities. Pundits. Politicos. They made the news and, in the popular press and the lecture halls, gave their views on the news. So, jaunty and jubilant, Shaw addressed everyone everywhere on just about everything and Galsworthy, grave man that he was, "delivered himself sonorously in public on animal welfare and human suffering." As for Wells, it didn't matter that his voice was meager and hoarse and sometimes came out a squeak or a squeal and that he addressed his audience with his head down and his hands spread out on the table like, Shaw wickedly observed, a butcher selling meat at the counter. It didn't matter at all. He was rich and famous and everywhere heard and admired. Poor Bennett was under some disadvantage. He had a bad stammer and had to make do with articles in the dailies and weeklies. Nevertheless, his fame was not unacknowledged. "My God! Is it you?" the manager of a Brighton hotel would cry when the great man presented himself at the desk. So why wouldn't Conrad and James feel a little aggrieved? They were geniuses, too, but alas they were geniuses who didn't sell well and whose names were unknown and whose private adventures and public opinions never appeared in the press.

"Mon cher confrère"

But if they weren't loved of the populace, they weren't alone. They were loved of themselves, were loved of each other. Surrounded as they were by hosts of uncomprehending Philistines, by hordes of horrid anthropophagi, they were wonderful with each other. Generous. They weren't ashamed, Violet Hunt would remember, "to exhibit enthusiasm for other men working in the same line." They even took pride, it was said, in extolling the work of their enemies. "After all, my dear Goldring," as Hueffer would say, "dog does not eat dog." Hence logs might roll but heads would not. "From first to last it *never* fails," Wells would write Bennett when *The Old Wives' Tale* came out. ". . . Go on, great man!" Wells was, Bennett would declare on his part, when *The New Machiavelli* came out and came under attack, "one of the greatest forces for real progress in the world today." This was hardly astounding. They needed each other, did Bennett and Wells. They were the day-boys of the London school of artists and writers. But what could they possibly have seen to admire in a writer as different from them as was Conrad? Frank Harris, editor of the *Saturday Review,* was impressed by Conrad's first novel, but the person he had asked to review it was not, so he turned it over to Wells who "descended from his 'Time-Machine,' " as Conrad would gratefully say, "to be kind as he knew how." Because he was Polish, Conrad wasn't much help as a model, Mrs. Woolf would decide, but the provincial Bennett who was lacking her Bloomsbury taste and discernment was never in doubt for a moment. In a letter to Conrad he spoke of "the *passionate* comprehension which some of us have of your work," and Conrad was moved to reply that it was "indeed a rare happiness for a craftsman to evoke such a response in a creative temperament so richly gifted. . . ."

What, for that matter, could writers like Conrad and James have seen to admire in a writer like Wells? Such a novel as *Kipps* was hardly their cup of tea. Nevertheless, "the book, my dear fellow," Conrad would write him, "is simply admirable in its justness and its justice" and "the book has, throughout," James would write him, "such extraordinary life" and "everyone in it, without exception . . . is so vivid and sharp and *raw*." No doubt it would trouble the Master, this Wellsian rawness, "the co-existence of so much talent with so little art." But he couldn't deny him. The work of the man was "more brimming with blood," as he put it, "than any it is given me nowadays to meet." It was with Shaw and Yeats as with James and Wells. For Yeats, Shaw was all that was evil in life and in letters: "a sewing machine that clicked and shone," and that, still more appallingly, "smiled, smiled perpetually." For Shaw, on his side, Yeats was all that was sadly mistaken in thought and in theatre: Shakespeare, Tragedy, Blank Verse. Rot, all rot! Notwithstanding, the two great men sat side by side in their boxes, accepting if not quite approving the plays of each other, or in Florence Farr's drawing room—she had loved and been loved by them both— reciting their plays to each other. It was the spirit of the age. Amplitudes, generosities, magnanimities. Shaw and Chesterton had disagreed over so many things over so many years. The relative values of Family and State, of Beer and Abstention, of Beef and Vegetarianism . . . No matter. Chesterton could remember nothing from Shaw that didn't "come," as he'd say, "out of inexhaustible fountains of fairmindedness and intellectual geniality." Wells was estranged. Shaw and the Fabians had done him great wrong. No problem, however. At the time of the *Ann Veronica* crisis, when every man's hand was raised against him, Wells had from Shaw a letter of sympathy. He was touched. "Occasionally you don't simply rise to a difficult situation but soar above it. . . ." Old friend of Shaw though he was, the dour William Archer was no Shavian. "You are a great force wasted." " 'Man and Superman' rather dashes my hopes." "The years are slipping away . . . and you have done . . . nothing original, solid, first-rate, enduring." But what did it matter? "I have never wavered in my admiration and affection for you . . . ," Archer would write him at the end of his life, and Shaw in his turn would reciprocate, still feeling, three years after the death of his friend, "that when he went he took a piece of me with him."

They were more in fact than merely professional, these Edwardian relations. They were social and personal. Who after all did the Blooms-bury circle, the Bells and the Stephens and Stracheys, know but one another? Who did the *New Age* circle, the Orages and Murrys and Mansfields, know but one another? James and Conrad, Hueffer and Garnett and Wells: what a disparate lot! Too disparate surely for lasting connections. Yet in the early years of the century they were all for a while in more or less close social contact. With James at Rye and with Hueffer at Winchelsea a few miles away or at Aldington just fourteen miles off and Conrad nearby at the Pent Farm near Hythe and Wells at Sandgate not many miles to the east and Garnett at Limpsfield not many miles to the west, there was by horse trap or motor car, a lively concurrence of people and minds. Wells would bicycle from Sandgate to Aldington to discuss with the amiable Hueffer *la vie littéraire* or *la vie politique*. At the same time Hueffer and his wife and his children would drop by for two weeks or so at the Conrads' old farmhouse and Conrad and his wife and his children would drop by for two weeks or so at the Hueffers' old cottage, the husbands relaxing between sessions of authorial labor to play games with the children, and, one Christmas day, when the Hueffers were living in Winchelsea, the great James him-self would stop by the cottage with toys for the children. What a piece of good fortune it was! For when Conrad came to see Hueffer at Winchelsea, the prospect of meeting the James he revered was en-chanting to him. "Conrad haunts Winchelsea," James would write Wells at the time, "and Winchelsea (in discretion) haunts Rye," James and Conrad proceeding together ahead of the party on afternoon walks and conversing in French, with the Master addressing monsieur his disciple as "Mon cher confrère" and Conrad "almost bleat[ing] with the peculiar tones that Marseillaises get into their compliments, 'Mon cher maître.' "

Conrad would abhor coteries but would nonetheless go for the best of his friends to the artistic and literary folk, to Hudson and Ep-stein and Galsworthy, to Arthur Symons and Cunninghame Graham as well as to Garnett and Hueffer. When he referred to Galsworthy it was always "dear Jack" and always with tenderness and "could you conceive for a moment," he'd say, "that I could go on existing if Cunninghame Graham were to die?" At one point or another Conrad's feeling for

Garnett—"dear old fellow"—who had helped and befriended him was no longer as warm as it had been. As his best reader and critic, Edward was doubtless as downright as ever and Conrad, a celebrity now, was proud and impatient. Even so, it was at the end as it had been at the beginning. Edward: "That will be delightful—to come & sit & smoke & interchange our wisdom & our affection." Conrad: "I am proud after all these years to have understood you from the first." Edward: "It is your heart that speaks." Shortly before Conrad's death, Edward paid him a visit "and something moved me as we said good-night, to put his hand to my lips. He then embraced me with a long and silent pressure." The next morning, time to depart, Conrad "suddenly snatched from a shelf overhead a copy of the Polish translation of *Almayer's Folly*, wrote an inscription in it and pressed it into my hands." The date he wrote in it was the date of their very first meeting thirty years earlier.

Not every Edwardian friendship was quite as impassioned as Conrad's, but very nearly. Lytton and Clive weren't talking. The writers, Lytton and Virginia, resented the success of the artists, Roger, Vanessa, and Duncan. Virginia was jealous of Lytton, of Forster, of . . . No matter. Ten and twenty and thirty years later, they were still meeting and talking and delighting in each other's lives. One gloomy day in the country Lytton and Clive stood staring out at the rain and the gathering darkness. "Loves apart," Lytton said, "whom would you most like to see coming up the drive?" No need to wait for an answer. "Virginia of course," Lytton said. In the meantime what jolly fun to belong to that gaggle of Fleet Street inebriates, Chesterton, Belloc, Maurice Baring, Charles Masterman, Auberon Herbert! Those boisterous dinners at old Soho restaurants and those roisterous parties at Auberon's rooms near Buckingham Palace or at Baring's wee house on Lord North Street, Westminster, and those flagons of wine and those tankards of beer and the jesting and singing that went along with them. There was the time they boiled eggs in Beerbohm Tree's hat and the time they rendered "Drake's Drum" at Auberon Herbert's with such lusty vocality that King Edward himself had to beg them to cease and desist and the time when at four in the morning three of them mounted three chairs and conducted an argument that threatened to go on forever. "O born in days when wits were fresh and clear,/ And life ran gaily as the sparkling Thames. . . ."

So it wasn't surprising the novels these Edwardians were writing were *of* or *about* one another. Who else's lives did they know after all? For Auberon Quin in his *Napoleon of Notting Hill* Chesterton would go, it was thought, to Max Beerbohm; for her St. John Hirst in *The Voyage Out* and her Neville in *The Waves* Virginia Woolf would naturally turn to her friend Lytton Strachey; and for Beatrice Normandy in *Tono-Bungay* and Carlotta Peel in *Sacred and Profane* Wells and Bennett would go in their turns to the seductive Miss Violet Hunt. For his Bosinney in *The Man of Property* Galsworthy would go for his model to Garnett and for the literary critic in their *Inheritors* Hueffer and Conrad would go for their model to the same friendly figure, and was Hueffer himself not the model for Densher in James's *The Wings of the Dove*? Hueffer liked to think so and say so but, in point of fact, he wasn't. It was Morton Fullerton, James's Parisian friend and Mrs. Wharton's lover. The *roman à clef* was something indeed of a Georgian convention. Lawrence's *Women in Love* with its portraits of Katherine and Murry and poor Lady Ott would count as its masterpiece, but its manifestations would be many: May Sinclair's *The Creators* reconstituting Hueffer and James; Leonard Woolf's *The Wise Virgins* Virginia and Vanessa; H.D.'s *Bid Me to Live* Aldington, Lawrence, and Pound; Hueffer's *The Simple Life Limited* Conrad and Garnett and Wells. It was Hueffer, in fact, who made the most use of his friends, Violet Hunt appearing not only in *The Good Soldier* as the terrible Florence but in *The New Humpty Dumpty* as the admirable Lady Aldington and in *Mr. Fleight* as Augusta Macphail, chief editor of a literary journal whose poetry editor, an emerald-shirted, obsessively talkative young man, could only have been Ezra Pound.

Of course there were circles, coteries, cliques. Bloomsbury for certain but, in addition, constellations of poets and painters, playwrights and novelists. Orage, for example, and his *New Age* people, Garnett and his Mont Blanc associates, Chesterton and his Fleet Street companions, Walter Sickert and his Fitzroy confederates, and Hueffer and his gang of the *English Review,* not to mention Marsh and his Georgians, Pound and his Imagists, Lewis and his Vorticists, and Hulme and his Soho adherents.

It was a small world, however, this Edwardian world, in more ways than one, and its circles, for all their variety and number, intersected each other. So Arthur Symons would attach himself to figures as various as Yeats and Conrad and John, and Katherine Mansfield whose connection was first with Orage and his circle would also connect with

Lady Ott and hers and with Lawrence and his. As for the protean
Pound, he was bound to appear anytime anywhere in the various suburbs of letters and art. At a Fleet Street table of Chesterton's Square
Club. At the Tour Eiffel table of Hulme's poet's club. In the offices of
the *New Age* or the *English Review*. At the dining room tables of the
Violet Hunts and the Lady Glenconners. So, one way or another, they'd
all come together, the great ones of London, and in no narrow way.
They managed to link all the arts with one another and with everything else for that matter. Bloomsbury, for example, eclectic Bloomsbury. In addition to novelists like Woolf and Forster, it included
painters like Fry and Grant and Vanessa and in addition to them the
historian Strachey, the Fabian Leonard, the critic MacCarthy, the econ-
omist Keynes and the philosopher Russell. Thus also the Soho of
Hulme. In addition to Hulme who was now more philosopher than
poet and Lewis who was as much a painter as a novelist and Pound
who was a musician as well as a poet, it included sculptors like Epstein
and Gaudier and critics like Ashley Dukes and Middleton Murry.

There was nothing at any rate they wouldn't do for one another.
Pound hated the country. Not for him the forest of Arden. Nevertheless he'd spend months in Yeats's Stone Cottage in Sussex as an
amanuensis of sorts. It wouldn't profit him; it would certainly bore
him; but it was, he drolly decided, his "duty to posterity." And this
wasn't just Pound's road. It was the Edwardian road. Poor Barrie was
deeply distressed. His wife's suit for divorce was impending and with it
the usual publicity, the usual rumor and scandal. But they rallied
round him, James, Gosse, Archer, Wells, among others. They sent a
joint letter to every editor on Fleet Street beseeching him "as a mark of
respect and gratitude to a writer of genius" to spare him the pain of
exposure. At the turn of the century the young novelist Wells was re-
covering from a serious illness. Two magisterial figures descended one
day from their bicycles and knocked at his door. All solicitude, James
and Gosse went over the state of his health and, very tactfully, the state
of his funds. A week or so later Barrie dropped by for tea and for talk
that touched on the same tender subject. The young writer was naturally flattered, but what on earth were they up to? They were acting, it
seemed, for the Royal Literary Fund which gave special grants to authors in trouble. Davies was in trouble. He was always in trouble. But
Thomas would find him a cottage at the Weald and provide for the
rent, Edward Garnett agreeing to pay for the coal and the light and ar-

ranging a grant from the Royal Literary Fund and a Civil List pension. Conrad was in trouble. He was always in trouble. But no need to worry. There was the generous Galsworthy who was always good for a loan or a handout. There was Wells who, hearing that Pinker, discouraged, was about to withdraw his financial support, persuaded the man to continue his good ministrations. There was Miss Agnes Tobin, the American poet, who urged John Quinn, the wealthy New Yorker, to purchase the novelist's manuscripts and relieve his distress. There were also his friend Rothenstein who got him a grant of five hundred pounds from the Royal Bounty and James and Gosse who, hearing that a lamp had exploded and demolished the text of *The End of the Tether,* procured him a grant of three hundred pounds.

Above all there was Hueffer, the implausible Hueffer, who was young and unknown at the time, a mere minor figure at best. Conrad was lonely, dyspeptic, unsure of himself as a stranger in England, as a writer of English, and was suffering acutely from writer's block. Why shouldn't he ask the young man to collaborate with him? So Hueffer who adored men of genius was happy to serve him as, he'd say in his bitterness later, "his cook, slut and butler in literary matters." The collaboration was less than successful, produced no best-sellers; but when the gout-ridden genius was down and depressed, Fordie would rush to his side, take down his dictation, copy out parts of his manuscripts, and even, in times of emergency, do some of the writing itself. He helped him convert the story "Tomorrow" into a play, helped him compose the essays that would make up *The Mirror of the Sea,* and when the manuscript of *The End of the Tether* was destroyed, it was to Fordie and Winchelsea that Conrad went for help and support. But then Conrad himself had his magnanimous moments. From the publisher Blackwood he arranged an advance for his friend Stephen Crane, got him to publish Hueffer's *Cinque Ports* and also perhaps Jack Galsworthy's first work. He certainly helped Norman Douglas along, reading and placing his work in the *English Review,* getting him a job as the editor's assistant, and encouraging Dent to publish *Siren Land* when no one else cared to. The Edwardians would for that matter make the supreme sacrifice: they would read one another's manuscripts. Wells would read the manuscript of *Romance,* Hueffer's and Conrad's joint endeavor, and Galsworthy the manuscript of *The Secret Agent,* and Conrad not only the manuscripts of Galsworthy's first novels and Garnett's drama *The Breaking Point* but, at the Master's request, the scenario of *The Wings of the Dove*. Not surprisingly, then, they'd dedicate their books to one another, Hueffer his early *Poems for Pictures* to Garnett, Davies his *New Poems* of 1907 to Thomas, Pound his Cavalcanti translations and Lawrence his first book of poems to Hueffer, Galsworthy his *Jocelyn* to Conrad and his *Fraternity* to Barrie, Chesterton his *Napoleon of Notting Hill* to Belloc and Lawrence his *Sons and Lovers* to Garnett, Conrad his *Nigger of the "Narcissus"* to Garnett, his *Nostromo* to Galsworthy, his *Secret Agent* to Wells. They admired one another. They cared for one another. They were good to one another. Hueffer was right. London *was,* as he said, "a kind place to people who were reputed to be writing masterpieces."

And not only to the older and more established reputations. To the young too, and the unknown, to the lonely newcomers from the provinces and the Continent and even the colonies. It wasn't for the young Gilbert Chesterton to seek out the elders of London's great Zion of letters. They sought him out. A review in the *Daily News* brought an invitation from Mr. John Masefield at 1 Diamond Terrace in Greenwich ("Will you and Mrs. Chesterton come to see us next Tuesday evening?"), and a number of articles in the *Daily News,* including one on Scott's *Ivanhoe,* brought a letter from Shaw who was eager to know all about this new star in the firmament, and an ardent defense of the poetry of Tennyson in the same *Daily News* brought a summons from Putney Hill where Mr. Swinburne and Mr. Watts-Dunton, both alike lovers of Tennyson, would be happy to receive and embrace the anonymous author. Pursue the great Beerbohm? It wouldn't be necessary. Max would be only too glad to do the pursuing. "I have seldom wished to meet anyone in particular," he'd write Chesterton from the Savile Club, "but you I should very much like to meet" and would he not "lunch with me here next Wednesday or Saturday at 1.30?" The young man was naturally surprised by his London reception. After being taken by Garnett to lunch ("a gorgeous repast") and being asked for first look at his novel in progress, he couldn't help wondering "where the jealous, spiteful, depreciating men of letters we read of in books has got to."

He didn't in fact appear to exist, this mythical beast. There was Hueffer who, in the glory days of the *English Review,* made much of *les jeunes* as it pleased him to name the young and aspiring, and helped to provide them, at Violet Hunt's famous South Lodge, with a happy "oasis in a city of solitude." So it wasn't for Lawrence to blush unseen and waste his sweetness. His generous patron not only printed his poems and his stories at once but, as Ezra Pound said, "put him over," sending him to Heinemann with a letter that helped get his first novel published and taking him with him to parties and teas to encounter such worthies as Yeats, Rhys, and Wells. Fordie, it's true, would leave him ere long in the lurch. "I cannot say that I liked Lawrence very much," he'd confess. He was much too demanding, insistent, "disturbing," Fordie said, and in any case he'd have business abroad, an affair of the heart, that would take him to Germany with Violet, his lover. But all would be well. The ubiquitous Garnett would hasten to fill in the void and serve as the young writer's mentor and friend. As for little Hugh Walpole, he'd get nothing but kindness and care from the "folks" as Lawrence called the London elite. From the good Thomas Hardy ("a little nutcracker faded man with a wistful smile and a soft voice") who had Hugh to tea and was "nice about *Maradick*," Hugh's latest novel. From Mrs. Lowndes who had him to dinner and introduced him to writers of note and even read, in an act of pure friendship, his manuscripts. From Bennett and Wells who called him, affectionately, "Hughie" and fondly referred to him as "the child." From, most affecting of all, the Master himself, who had him to Lamb House for weekends and plied him with avuncular advice and affection ("It isn't written *at all*, darling Hugh") and invited him to the first London performance of Maeterlinck's *Blue Bird* at the Haymarket Theatre, where he sat in a box with the author himself and it was all, as he said, "like a fairy-tale." He even got it, this tender loving care, from the great Gosse himself who took, it was said, "a fatherly interest in him" and persuaded Lord Stanmore to make him his secretary. A few years later Hugh would be down, quite down. An American publisher, he would tell Arnold Bennett, had rejected his *Fortitude*, had called this, his "masterpiece," "a hopeless book, dull, heavy, unreal." But Arnold, magnificent, would come to the rescue. He'd seat himself down at a table nearby and write out a letter to the publisher Doran. "Here is Hugh Walpole, a young English novelist in whose work I believe. I want you to publish his three next novels. . . . If you do not do this you shall never again publish a novel of/ Yours,/ Arnold Bennett."

"We are not amazed"

There loomed at the gates, to be sure, a terrible presence. It was Gosse, Edmund Gosse, later Sir Edmund, "the official British man of Letters," as Wells would derisively call him. Browning and Tennyson, Morris and Swinburne, Hardy and James, Beerbohm and Chesterton and Somerset Maugham: there wasn't a mogul of letters, major or minor, he hadn't encountered or wouldn't encounter. He had traveled to Paris and become for the French their English connection, had traveled to Norway and become for Ibsen and the young Scandinavians their English connection. He had an instinct in fact for all that was current in avant-garde letters: Baudelaire and the Decadents, Mallarmé and the *Symbolistes*, John Donne and the Metaphysicals. And indeed it was frightening, the range of his interests. In letters and lectures, in historical surveys and formal biographies, in the views and reviews of the journals and papers, in volumes of poems like *In Russet and Silver* and *On Viol and Flute* and collections of essays like *Critical Kit-Kat, Books on the Table, More Books on the Table,* "he lisped in numbers for the numbers came." So it wasn't for nothing that Ezra Pound called him "the pewking Gosse." A force in the land as he was, he cast over London a terrible shadow, a menacing pall. Bad enough that as one of the time's leading critics he wielded the power of life and of death over innocent authorship. But as librarian for the House of Lords he would mediate now between the government itself and the aspirants of letters, would advise the prime minister as to who would or wouldn't receive from the Royal Literary Fund financial assistance. When George Gissing died, leaving behind him an impoverished wife and two children, he'd interrogate Wells. This man Gissing had been all right, had he not? Nothing unsavory in his life and behavior, nothing bohemian? The Fund was not after all for men of that ilk.

Gosse was indeed, as everyone knew, the complete toady and snob. His vocation was Literature but his love was Society and the higher the better. Arthur Benson was appalled. It was sickening, he said, "the difference of his behavior when he is with people of consequence and when he is not." Virginia Woolf was repelled. This "little dapper grocer," as she called him, had been fawning all over her Honorable friend, Vita Sackville-West. Evelyn Waugh, the publisher's son, would remember the man as "a Mr. Tulkinghorn, the soft-footed, inconspicuous, ill-natured habitué of the great world," and he "longed," he'd confess, "for a demented lady's maid to make an end of him." This was not, it turned out, an uncommon sentiment. He was, it would seem, "a dangerous enemy" and "looked askance," it was said, "at budding talent." He denounced Morgan Forster as "coarse in morals," dismissed Ezra Pound as "that preposterous American filibuster and Provençal charlatan." Would he not take an interest, he was asked, in a gifted young writer who needed support? "I have not been invited," he coldly replied, "to take an interest in him." He wore gold-rimmed spectacles. He had a bristling mustache and parted his hair in the middle. He looked, in fine, like the dean of a liberal arts college in Ohio or Texas. Henry James was his friend and admirer but "the most lurid thing in my dreams," he would tell him, "has been the glitter of your sarcastic spectacles."

"Hooray, Fordie's discovered another genius"

But then Gosse, thank heaven, wasn't the only grand cham of letters in town. Besides Garnett and Hueffer who fancied themselves as the patron saints of the young and obscure, there was also the great James himself who considered that greatness was not inconsistent with kindness and viewed his relation to the new generation of writers as "quasi-paternal." As for Shaw, there was no one quite like him for kindness and greatness. What was the point of a repertory theatre, of a national theatre, if it wasn't to give to the young and untried their place in the sun? He'd produce his play *Getting Married*, he told the Haymarket Theatre people, only on condition that they'd produce in advance two plays by unexercised talents like Housman and Masefield. He'd do all he could to help Jacob Epstein who was young and impoverished but Charlotte was outraged. She would not have the thing in her house, Jacob's barbarous bust of her husband. Shaw was inclined to agree—it was "Neanderthal Shaw"—but he wasn't unduly concerned. Jacob did need the money. Sir Hugh Lane was perhaps less forgiving. When he saw Jacob's bust of his aunt Lady Gregory, he threw up his hands in horror. "Poor Aunt Augusta," he cried. "She looks as if she could eat her own children."

To be sure, they were good to one another, the young ones of London, caring, considerate. The penniless Gaudier wasn't likely to perish for lack of attention in his dank, noisy workshop. Hulme and Pound would commission his figures, put them out for display in their London apartments, praise and advertise them in their essays and articles. As for Orage of the *New Age,* it wasn't his policy to pay his contributors as much as a penny and in fact he was moved in his humor to nickname his journal the "No Wage." Somehow or other, nevertheless, he managed in the desperate hours to come up with moneys for needy young talent. "He did more to feed me," said Pound, "than anyone else in England." Aside from Hueffer and Ezra himself he may have done more to sustain the young writer than anyone else. Not from him came the heartless rejection slip but a letter of kind explanation or warm commendation and sometimes an invite to the office near Chancery Lane where, reposing behind his battered rolltop desk, he'd enchant his young listener with the lyrical charm of his voice and his smile and his warm hazel eyes flecked with gold. "How sensible I am," poor dying Katherine Mansfield would write him, "of your wonderful unfailing kindness to me . . . you taught me to write, you taught me to think. . . . My dear Orage, I cannot tell you . . . how often, in *writing,* I remember my master."

Even Augustus John, for all his bohemian rages and silences, was at bottom a good sort of fellow. If he did succumb to Lady Ott's blandishments, he may have had more motive than one. A leading light in the Contemporary Art Society, the amorous lady had the power to dispense to deserving young artists the largesse of her money and influence, and how could he otherwise come to the rescue of indigent friends like Epstein and Lamb? Arthur Symons, that refugee from the Wesleyan chapel, that passionate poet of the sinister nineties, was for very good reason devoted to John, to his "lust and life and animality." On a visit to Italy the pint-sized poet had suffered a breakdown. Eluding his wife, he had "walked and walked and walked—always in the wrong direction," and caught and manacled and returned to London, had been diagnosed as a victim of "general paralysis of the insane" and given two months to live, two years at most, "not shriving time allow'd." John was all generosity. Everywhere he went he took with him the doomed little Don Juan ("I cannot sin, it wearies me. Alas!"): to the Empire, to the Russian ballet, to Claridge's for luncheon, to the Carlton for dinner, to the Café Royal for absinthe and cigarettes and for ranting recitations of his latest effusions in verse which were, said John, "all hell, damnation and lust." "Drawn blinds and flaring gas within,/ And wine, and women, and cigars." "As I lay on the stranger's bed/ And clasped the stranger woman I had hired." One wonderful evening, in front of a restaurant, there was even a brawl in the course of which John was knocked to the ground and, *hors de combat,* carried home in a cab. ("I will arise, and leave these haggard realms.") As things turned out, John's entertainments were not entirely necessary. Symons would live, in good health and good spirits, for another thirty-six years.

But then London was kind even to strangers and foreigners and to American ones at that. It was the first place to show him any human kindness, said John Cournos who had just arrived from New York City. And it was certainly the first place to show Ezra Pound any kindness. May Sinclair for one was kindness itself. To give the young fellow a start in her world, she'd gaily introduce him to the editor of the *English Review* as the world's greatest poet to the world's greatest editor, and so Ezra was published and praised and was even made fun of in the pages of *Punch* as "Boaz Bobb, a son of the Arkansas soil" and as "the new Montana (U.S.A.) poet, Mr. Ezekiel Ton." At a Dutch dinner in Soho for poets, most of them Georgians, Richard Aldington was incensed. They were putting down Ezra. He rose to his feet. "Ezra Pound," he announced, "has more vitality in his little finger than the whole lot of you put together." He stalked from the room. As the author of *Personae* Ezra doubtless deserved it, the acclaim, the attention. But would he in any other time, in any other clime, have fared half as well? To be sure, he was never lacking in push. With a cane in his hand and a blue ring in his ear, he wasn't reluctant to knock on doors. But the doors they swung open, swung open at once. The American West come to grimy old London, "a somewhat Dakota Dante" as Hilda Doolittle called him, he was just the man they were waiting for. They had colonized America once. Now let America colonize them. Hueffer remembered it all with the warmest emotion. If his American friends "had all become Londoners," it was, he said, because London had been "the great, easy-going, tolerant, loveable, old dressing-gown of a place that it was then."

London was above all the scene of the literary "discovery." They took pride, they took pleasure, the London crowd did, in "discovering" that rara avis, the "genius." It was you, was it not, who sent Lawrence's poems to the *English Review*? said Violet Hunt to Jessica Chambers. Jessie allowed as it was. "But you *discovered* him," the lady exclaimed in a rapture. Unless it was the editor himself who had made the "discovery." At a dinner at the Pall Mall Restaurant, Fordie'd announce to Belloc and Chesterton and company that that very day he'd uncovered a poet of uncommon promise named Lawrence and "Hooray," Wells would shout from the very next table, in the general direction of Lady Londonderry, "Fordie's discovered another genius!" It aroused, in fact, a touch of bad feeling at times. "To be a really great writer," Edgar Jepson would say, "you had to be discovered by a Leading Literary Critic," but when Edward Thomas made much of Pound in the *English Review*, the *gens des lettres* were annoyed. He had landed a big one all right, but he had landed it, unhappy man, before they had. Hueffer who was a well of self-doubt couldn't stand the condescension of Garnett, the discoverer of Conrad and Hudson and Galsworthy, and Garnett, when Hueffer came into his own and became the discoverer of Lawrence and Lewis and Pound, couldn't stand his. So those Tuesday luncheons at the old Mont Blanc were less than convivial. Edward "terribly snappy" across the table. A row about something Ford hadn't put in the *English Review*. Since Edward felt an almost *"physical* antipathy" to Hueffer—he was, he said, "too blond for him"—"a sort of fleshly dislike upset our talks."

Spots on the Sun

Not all in fact was pure cordiality, not even in paradise. Two geniuses in one room could be one too many. When a meeting of minds was arranged and Hulme was conducted to Conrad's hotel just south of the Strand, things didn't pan out. Before thirty minutes had passed the great conversation had languished and the two were to part. It turned out no better when Wells brought Shaw to see Conrad. "I nearly bit him," said Conrad who detested the playwright's "oracular vanity." "What do you think he told me?" Conrad complained. "He told me that his father drank like a fish! Imagine my feelings on being presented with this revelation of his private life on our first meeting!" A second encounter at the home of the Wellses' was no improvement. "You know, my dear fellow, your books won't *do*." Thus Shaw to Conrad with his customary frankness and freedom. But the touchy aristocrat wasn't used to such frankness and freedom. White with fury, he followed Wells out of the room. "Does the man want to *insult* me?" he hissed. Wells was amused. He thought there might be a duel. But he did his best to appease the proud Pole. It's humor, he told him, *English* humor.

Conrad, it's true, was notoriously difficult, thin-skinned, fractious. But so more or less were they all. At a party in Chelsea Augustus John was in deep conversation with an actress of large and flamboyant dimensions. Would she, he asked, care to sit for him? He would engage, he assured her, a much larger studio. Enter, alas, the abrasive Frank Harris with his broad-chested build and brass-knobbed waistcoat. "Why not take the Crystal Palace then?" he proposed in his loud booming voice. Everyone laughed. Everyone that is except John and the actress. Hard to imagine Lawrence and Pound in closest conjunction but it did in fact happen. After one of Violet Hunt's "at homes" Pound took Lawrence to sup at Pagnani's and then to his Kensington quarters, Lawrence missing the last train to Croydon and spending the night at his host's. His first impression of Pound wasn't bad: "jolly nice . . . rather remarkable—a good bit of a genius." But that first impression didn't last and soon he'd refer to "Pound's David Copperfield curls" hanging "like bunches of hop-leaves over his ears" and to his theatric apparel which suggested, he thought, a "sort of latest edition of jongleur." As for Pound, his feelings for Lawrence were just as ephemeral. He thought much of the artist. "There is no English poet under forty," he said, "who can get within shot of him." But he didn't think much of the man. "Detestable person." Hard though it may be to imagine Lawrence and Pound in one room, it's harder still to imagine Lawrence and Pound and Hueffer and Yeats in one room, but that too was destined to happen. One night at the Rhyses, Yeats would dilate at some length on the virtues for the reading of verse of Florence Farr's marvelous psaltery when Pound, himself no mean monologuist and craving attention, would snatch from the table a handful of tulips and with some ostentation devour them.

Et Ego in Arcadia

Well, these were but vapors. Human they were, all too human. And in spite of it all, they were still, the Edwardians, gregarious souls. Somerset Maugham would complain that they didn't live in London as the writers of France lived in Paris, that they didn't mix with their kind as the French did with theirs. But he was surely mistaken. Could authors and artists in any other time, in any other place, have communed with each other more often, more ardently? They joined clubs. They were always joining clubs. The Adelphi Club, for example, where Pound and his friends heard "the Eagle," as they liked to call Yeats, give a lecture on young Irish poets, and the Chelsea Arts Club where, at a dinner, Bennett was aghast at the shamelessly flattering speeches the artists addressed to one another. The Writers' Club too, where Violet Hunt held bimonthly luncheons for twelve, Bennett and Maugham and Wells among them, and, not to be confused with it, the Authors' Club where Bennett would make himself comfortable in a seventh-floor bedroom and do much of his work in the library but would have the misfortune to attend the club's banquet for Sir Beerbohm Tree which was, he protested, "an appalling orgy of insincere sentimentality." Also, the old Savile Club on Piccadilly, "the Mecca," it was said, "of every young writer," where poor shrinking Hardy once thought of resigning for the disgrace of publishing *Tess* and where Wells would later resign (or be forced to resign) for the disgrace of his affair with the daughter of Pember Reeves who had introduced the cad to the club in the first place but awaited him now with a gun and a temper. Maugham's brother Frederic, a lawyer, belonged to the Savile but Maugham himself couldn't have cared. After his sudden success as a popular playwright, he was invited to join the fashionable Garrick Club, which "damned him," he said, "in the sight of the intelligentsia," as it very well might seeing that J. M. Barrie was also a member, and "what a fine place that Gerrik Club is, to be sure," Wells would mock it in *Kipps*: "Footmen in powder they got—not waiters, Ann—footmen!" There were clubs too for ladies, for ladies of letters. The Albemarle Club, for example, "rather desolately vast," as Henry James thought, where May Sinclair invited her idol to tea in what he described as "a dim and dumb literary circle as of pale ink-and-water. . . ." The recently founded Lyceum Club, for another, located near the Savile, a center for ladies who wrote or who wanted to write, like Lady Russell, once the Gräfin von Arnim, who invited the ubiquitous Walpole to meet with her there or, perhaps with less reason, like the first Mrs. Hardy who was vain and eccentric and fancied herself as a writer in a class with her husband.

This isn't to mention the more informal literary groups that gathered in cafés and restaurants. The Dramatists' Club, for example, which was founded by establishment figures like Pinero and Barrie to do battle with theatre censorship and which met every month to eat lunch at the famous Criterion and also to blackball new playwrights like Bennett and St. John Hankin, to the open distress of Shaw who called them "a clique of old stagers." The Square Club was another. Founded in honor of Fielding and named for his Parson Square, it was patronized, it was said, by "old fogies," by Belloc and Chesterton, by the darkly handsome de la Mare who regarded the monthly dinners at Simpson's on Fleet Street "with an air of childlike pleasure" and by the sedately handsome Galsworthy with "an air of placid self-content." It was, presumably, not so regarded by Pound who, new to London society, however, would keep at the time a low profile or by Hueffer who, now advanced to a more adventuresome company of writers, would survey "the literary friends of his callow youth with a sinister and mocking wariness." Jepson would call it "the literary club of the Edwardian revival" but, all things considered, that honor would fall, if it fell at all, on Garnett's Tuesday meetings in "a very smelly private room" in Soho's Mont Blanc which Edward had chosen for its central location and "its utter emptiness" and, at from tenpence to a shilling and one pence, the saving cheapness of its luncheon fare. Here Edward would gather some of the city's most notable figures, Hudson and Hueffer, Thomas and Davies, Belloc and Chesterton, and even, from time to time, Conrad and Galsworthy.

This doesn't include Hulme's little poets' club. Not the fussy group of 1908 whose Gosses and Hewletts and Sir Henry Newbolts dined once a month in the United Arts Club on St. James's Street and recited their poems and their papers in evening dress and published a sedate little volume of verses called *For Christmas MDCCCCVIII*. It may not have been as utterly boring as Ezra Pound found it. In the midst of a heated discussion with Shaw, the bushy-haired Chesterton was said to have shattered a chair. All the same it wasn't the way they did things in Paris and Frank Flint, the Francophile poet and critic, made fun of its Christmas anthology, of its "after dinner ratiocinations" and "its suave tea-parties in South Audley Street." Poor Hulme, its secretary and, it was said, a most troubled and troublesome one, was first enraged and then embarrassed. He seceded at once. Joining Flint, Florence Farr, and "a few congenial spirits," he started another poets' club, more informal, more bohemian, meeting on Thursdays in the Tour Eiffel to talk about Japanese *haiku* and Provençal songs and the new "vers libre" and soon to be joined by other congenial spirits, among them Victor Plarr of the old Rhymers' Club of the nineties and, just six days after *Personae* came out, young Ezra Pound who, in red straggling beard and florid Italian dress, declaimed his "Sestina Altaforte" with such roaring gusto ("Damn it all! all this our South stinks peace") that the diners adjacent were alarmed and affronted and waiters were summoned to surround the offending party with screens.

And indeed they were scarcely in need of the *salons littéraires* of the great ones of London, the Lady St. Heliers, the Duchesses of Sutherland. They'd fashion their own *salons littéraires*. Aside from Soho whose French eating houses were still largely unknown and unvisited, restaurants were scarce, and aside from the occasional ballet or opera or play, entertainments were scarce. So for cocoa and cigarettes or for brandy and buns or for dinner and good conversation, they gathered together, the illuminati of London, in their drawing and dining rooms. On Thursday evenings in Bloomsbury of course, all, it seemed, were at "at home," Clive and Vanessa on Gordon Square and Virginia and Adrian on Fitzroy Square and Lady Ott on Bedford Square where young artists and writers shyly shook hands and rubbed shoulders with barbarous men of the world. But on Sunday at four Edmund Gosse was "at home," at 17 Hanover Terrace for men of distinction like Hardy and James and Sickert and Beerbohm, the host apprehensive that George Moore would say something outrageous, and that very evening the poet Mrs. Alice Meynell was "at home" for "all literary London," for Yeats and Pound and Augustus John among others, and there Miss Agnes Tobin of San Francisco heard what she called "the best talk of the day," though the opinion of Mrs. Meynell that "the greatest living Englishman" was Mr. G. K. Chesterton was, in the view of Mrs. Harriet Monroe of Chicago, "a preposterous opinion." On Monday evening in his bachelor quarters over a bootmaker's shop, Yeats was "at home" for the London elect and in a dimly lit room, its walls richly hung with Pre-Raphaelite paintings, the talk could be good and the company lively, though "one grew a little weary," Richard Aldington said, "of spooks, fairies, elementals, sorcerers, Lady Gregory and the feud with George Moore." On Tuesday afternoon Violet was "at home" at South Lodge for her writing and suffragette friends, May Sinclair for one and the beautiful Brigit Patmore for another, and on Tuesday evening at eight Ezra Pound, eager no doubt for a "gang" of his own, was at home in his tiny Kensington flat at 10 Church Walk for young neophytes like H.D. and Aldington. The next afternoon, on Wednesday, old Hudson and Emily would of course be "at home" in their Bayswater lodgings for faithful admirers like Garnett and Thomas and Sir Edward Grey and on the afternoon of the Saturday Walter Sickert was "at home" in his Fitzroy Street studio for John and for Lamb and for various defectors from the New (but now old) English Art Club. "Through all the ages," Tom Hulme liked to think, "the conversation of ten men sitting together is what holds the world together." So, on Tuesday evenings at 67 Frith Street in Soho, the fine Georgian house of his friend Mrs. Kepplewhite, he'd gather about him his gang of originals, Lewis and Pound and Gaudier and Epstein and, from time to time but rather out of the picture (he had just lost control of the *English Review*), poor nervous Hueffer. Hueffer himself—"unspeakably

gregarious," "incorrigibly hospitable"—was no social nonentity. In the
days of his glory when the *English Review* was a force in the land, he
was ever "at home" in his Holland Park Avenue flat and was pleased to
prepare for the happy few, for Hardy and James, for Bennett and Hudson, the most elegant dinners, and even after his falling from grace he
and Violet would make South Lodge their headquarters-in-general for
ribald young rebels like Lewis and Pound, feeding them "lavish crumpets and sandwiches, nut bread and plum cake" and giving them the
run of the communal garden across the way for violent tennis matches
and putting up with Ezra's outrageous contempt for the rules of the
game and his habit of hurling his angular body into Violet's delicate
and not indestructible chairs. Violet's senile old mother quite hated
him. She took to hiding his tennis shoes. Violet herself was resentful.
She insisted he use her plain kitchen chairs.

Was there in fact, in all of London, a place, a corner, a niche or
cranny where artists and writers didn't assemble? On St. Martin's Lane
the vegetarian restaurant, the St. George, where, every odd Wednesday,
Edward Thomas would meet fellow poets like Davies and de la Mare.
On Fleet Street the wine shop, El Vino, where at six every evening,
under a huge cask of sherry, the inimitable Chesterton, sometimes
joined by his brother and friends, would pour out a torrent of epigram
and paradox to the delight and amazement of the gathering throng.
Across from the British Museum the second floor of the Vienna Café
where museum officials and readers and poets convened for coffee *mit
schlag, real* schlag, and for talk, *real* talk: Ernest Rhys and George
Moore and, for the first time encountering each other, Ezra Pound and
Percy Lewis. Across from the *New Age* office the smoking room of the
ABC shop where on Mondays the editor met with his staff and contributors, with Bennett and Wells, with Belloc and Chesterton, with
Pound and Tom Hulme and Katherine Mansfield, to read proof for the
Thursday number and, that accomplished, to engage in such heady
talk that nowhere in London, they said, was its like to be heard. Unless
in the old Café Royal on Regent Street, as Augustus John fondly recalled it, "with its gilded caryatids and painted ceiling, its red plush
benches and marble tables, its conversational hum mixed with the clat-
ter of dominoes." It may well have been, as one of Conrad's friends
saw it, "the *rendezvous* of impecunious foreigners and artistic snobs"
and "if you want to see English people at their most English," Sir Beerbohm Tree would report, "go to the Café Royal where they are trying

their hardest to be French." Nevertheless it still marked the spot where whole London worlds intersected, where in addition to Harris and his seedy disciples, Orage and his crowd, John and his cronies and Hulme and his myrmidons met to commune and carouse and be joined on occasion by Walter Sickert whose "natural majesty" lent, it was thought, "an extra weight to the proceedings." Harold Monro's Poetry Bookshop was more than a bookshop. Located at 35 Devonshire Street in a small eighteenth-century building just a five-minute walk from the British Museum and across the way from a roaring brothel, the bookshop was also a poetry center and a meeting place for young versifiers and sometimes, for those visiting poets of slender resources, a *pied-à-terre*. Above the bookshop itself was a lecture room where poets recited their lyrics on Tuesdays and Thursdays and at the top were a few spare bedrooms where birds of passage, Hulme, Robert Frost, Wilfred Owen among them, found a roost and a roof. It was there that Hueffer's Goldring would meet Marinetti, the futurist founder, and there that Aldington would come upon "quantities of people in very different social sets" and there too that Pound would be asked to hear Gosse, Hewlett, and Lascelles Abercrombie reciting their verses which invitation, *imagiste* that he was, Ezra would doubtless decline. No surprise they'd remember these days as arcadian days. Lady Low, Lady Londonderry, and Mrs. Maynell, the Tour Eiffel, the Café Royal, and the ABC restaurants, the dinners, the clubs and the meetings and the friends and the foes. Never before, surely, had life been so good for young artists and writers, so rich and rewarding. "Those who cannot remember London then," as Hueffer would say, "do not know what life could hold."

"O God, give me fame"

Not that everyone felt it this way. It was exciting enough, this landscape of Gosses and Garnetts, of Hulmes and Orages. But it may have been just a little bit hectic, just a little frenetic. After the success of *Howards End* Morgan Forster was rather discouraged. "I knew I shouldn't and I don't enjoy fame." After visiting Walpole who had written "a novel, is writing another, and if cut would reveal diminishing eggs, like a fertile hen," he had no reason to feel any different. "No other age," he decided, "can have produced such a mannikin of letters." Young Lawrence was likewise discouraged. The literary world seemed to him from the start "a particularly hateful yet powerful one." But this for Lawrence was putting it mildly. Popularity. The bitch goddess Success. The business of Fame. The machinery of Sell. Literature as an Institution, as a vast and elaborate Edifice. In novels and stories—*Women in Love, Aaron's Rod, Lady Chatterley's Lover*—he'd bitterly mock it, its Gudruns, its Café Royal bohemians, its Hermione Roddices, its Sir Clifford Chatterleys, its careerists and climbers and their factions and cliques. Lady Ottoline, the Hermione Roddice of *Women in Love,* was herself disenchanted by *la vie littéraire* and its stresses and strains. The Murrys, for example, were they not after all rather frightful, frightening? So star-struck. So consumed with ambition. So obsessed with their writing. So hungry for fame. She wished, Lady Ottoline said, she had known Katherine Mansfield "before the ambition of being . . . a great writer, and of using people for that end, had become such an absorbing game." Murry invited her ladyship once for a stroll in the moonlight at Garsington. How charming, romantic! He meant, she was sure, to make love. But this wasn't at all what he meant, not at all. "If *we* believe in you," he was telling her in that moonlight, that serious moonlight, "it shows you are of value." The lady of course was wounded, was mortified. The cheek of the man! The gall! "I bang the door of my life in your face," she wrote in her diary.

Murry, it turned out, was his own best archivist. He saved every scrap of his paper, and why would he not? Posterity, it seemed, was watching and waiting, her face wreathed in smiles. She was awaiting young Percy Grainger as well. "My letters shall be admired," he was writing his lover, "by a yet-unborn generation" and when they broke up and she married another, "What will you do with my letters to you?" he anxiously wrote her. "Do not destroy them. . . ." Ill as she was, despondent, embittered, Katherine Mansfield herself never wrote the most intimate pages without being aware that, as she put it herself, "these letters will one day be published, and people will read something in them, in their queer finality." After Katherine died, Virginia Woolf was certainly sad. Why bother to write? "Katherine won't read it." But she also felt glad and a little relieved. One rival the less.

For Ezra of course it was heaven, pure heaven, the literary life. Tea at the Rhyses. A talk with May Sinclair. A reading of his poems at Mrs. Fowler's and of the chapters of his book, *The Spirit of Romance,* at the home of the Shakespears. With the sculptor Derwent Wood to a supper at the Chelsea Arts Club and soon after that to the Bechstein Hall to hear Mrs. Wood singing songs from the Continent, some of them translated for the evening program by Ezra himself. In what seemed like no time at all, the happy American was running the show at Yeats's Monday séances, distributing the Chianti and cigarettes and laying down law on matters aesthetic and generally dominating the shadowy, candlelit room. Ezra was furious. Invited to a Yeats Monday evening, his American friends the Cannells kept answering the poet's rhetorical questions and disrupting his monologues. "I told you that being interrupted was the one thing WB can't stand." "Why did he ask questions, then?" "Because the rhythm calls for a rising inflection . . . any Imagist poet ought to understand that!" In town for a week to be shown by Ezra "the wonders of our dusky and marvellous city," William Carlos Williams was taken one night to hear Yeats deliver a lecture, Edmund Gosse presiding, on some of the young Irish poets, but somehow or other it wasn't, thought Williams, much fun. It was, in truth, a disaster. As it drew to a close and Yeats was attacking the English for neglecting those young Irish poets and driving them all to drunken and lecherous lives, Gosse angrily banged the bell on the table before him. Yeats paused and tried to go on as if nothing had happened but again Gosse banged on his bell. Yet once again Yeats, now red in the face, would try to go on but again Mr. Gosse, also red in the face, would bang on that bell. There was now consternation and bitter confusion and "You let him browbeat you," the ladies were protesting to Pound. But so ended the lecture. It was all very thrilling, this rich London life, Williams thought, but how on earth ("It would have killed me in a month") could poor Ezra stand it? Not that everyone did. Bennett who detested the dilettanti of London kept his distance at Thorpe-le-Soken in Essex and Kipling who hated "the long-haired literati of the Savile Club" kept his distance at Burwash in Sussex and even James, albeit he loved the great Babylonian place and its social amenities, kept his distance in Rye and saw "nothing whatever, thank heaven," he'd be writing from Boston, "of the 'littery' world." John Buchan did regret he'd never been close to the company of writers but he had to confess that he "rarely found a man of letters" as interesting to him "as members of other callings." Shaw would have known what he meant. He avoided "literary and artistic people like the devil," he said, for what after all would it profit him? "The greengrocers and bootmakers and builders and publicans (Gasthauswirths) with whom I sit on committees . . . are far better company."

"Shall we not seek for newer ways of sinning?"

But the solidarity of artists and authors wasn't just social. It was political too. Clubs and club dinners were all very well, but that lively sense of themselves and their craft was perhaps better served by those groups and committees it pleased them to form. A British academy of letters, for example. Ardently Francophile, Gosse suggested to Hardy the creation of an English Academy on the model of the Académie Française and designed to preserve "the purity of the language and a high standard of style." Installed as the Academic Committee of the Royal Society of Literature, it would consist, to begin with, of thirty savants as selected by a council headed by Maurice Hewlett, that thirty including, in addition to Hardy and Gosse and Hewlett themselves, such masters of letters as Conrad and James and Pinero and Yeats. Yeats was delighted in fact. It would save us, he'd say, "from the journalists, who wish to be men of letters, and the men of letters who have become journalists." But there were troubles, alas, from the start. Excluded from the elect, Mrs. Humphry Ward challenged the authority of Hewlett's committee, and though Shaw the next year would be invited to join, he too at the time was resentful, calling those who had chosen each other a "collection of old-age pensioners" and condemning a list that omitted not only his own eminent self but Barrie's and Barker's and Kipling's and Chesterton's.

Hueffer and Wells in the meantime kept a safe and superior distance. Renegades that they were, they would have nothing to do with this pompous academy business. The young and rebellious were even more antipathetic. In 1913 Pound's *imagiste* party, H.D. and Aldington and Dorothy Shakespear, sauntered into the Caxton Hall where Masefield and Beerbohm were about to be hallowed as members and Mr. James Stephen of Ireland awarded a prize for his new book of poems, *The Crock of Gold*. The report of the *Times* was of course reverential:

> Mr. Binyon said the Comic Muse had no more loyal, no more serious votary, than Max Beerbohm. . . . He had made serene fun of the most august reputation; not even Emperors, not even editors, had escaped his vivacities. (Laughter.) The ambitious aspired to be his victims. (Laughter.) . . . Mr. Yeats, announcing the award of the Polignac prize, said:—"The Crock of Gold" had given him more pleasure, he thought, than it could give to another man . . . because it was a proof that his own native city of Dublin had vigor and lived with a deeper life. . . .

But the report of the *New Freewoman*, as delivered in all probability by Aldington, was quite something else:

> Mr. Binyon began by praising the Muse of Comedy . . . in a tone of dull melancholy. . . . But Mr. Binyon was shamming. He came out; he made a joke; it was a good one. Mr. Yeats who, up till that time had been writing his speech for the press . . . turned round and smiled, and waved a delicate hand. . . .
>
> Mr. Yeats? Ah, Mr. Yeats. Mr. Yeats explained . . . that he had no manuscript to read from. He had given his to the press. He smiled benignly, and recited his memorized speech perfectly. . . . He spoke of spirits and phantasmagoria. He spoke of finding two boots in the middle of a field and the owner of the boots listening for the earth-spirits under a bush. . . .
>
> Mr. Yeats concluded the performance by giving Mr. Stevens [sic] a hundred pounds. We could not hear Mr. Stevens promising to be a good boy and not spend it all in toffee and fairy-books.

Well, it was perhaps too late for a British Academy. By the time the Gosses and Hardys got round to it, the idea itself would seem, like the maiden aunt, like the man of letters, to be quite obsolescent. It wasn't in any case the only sign of the wakening consciousness of the lettered of London. Founded in 1853, the Society of Authors had only

68 members in 1884 but by 1902 it had swollen to 900 members and by 1914 to 2,500. It was never, it's true, an effectual force. As an agent for authors in their battles with publishers, it was no match at all for professional agents nor was it likely to be when the Gosse who served on the Society's Council also served as adviser to Heinemann and, not unexpectedly, was accusing poor writers of "unbridled greed." As for the censorship, the Society couldn't or wouldn't do much, and when in 1908 40 members conducted a meeting in the Criterion restaurant, it wasn't only to protest the Society's inaction but to establish an independent society, the Dramatic Authors' Society, more likely to attack with élan the Lord Chamberlain's power.

For it was monstrous, surely, that a playwright's livelihood should depend on a mere "court official," on the king's censor of plays, the Lord Chamberlain, and, more specifically, on the Lord Chamberlain's deputy, the examiner of plays, Mr. Redford, a onetime bank-manager who had the authority to grant or deny, at his will or his whim, the necessary license. He had already denied it to Ibsen's *Ghosts,* to Maeterlinck's *Monna Vanna,* to D'Annunzio's *La Città morta* and, closer to home, to Shaw's *Mrs. Warren's Profession,* and now he'd deny it to Garnett's *The Breaking Point* on the ground it dealt with premarital pregnancy and then Barker's *Waste* on the ground it involved "casual coupling" and then to Shaw's *Blanco Posnet* on the ground it derided the Almighty himself ("He's a sly one, he's a mean One . . ."). The novelists, to be sure, didn't have His Majesty's examiner of plays to contend with, but they did have just about everyone else: the librarians, the booksellers, the printers, and, above all, the publishers, who wouldn't let Maugham use the word "belly" in *Liza of Lambeth* or Joyce the word "bloody" in *Dubliners* or Lawrence the word "bellyful" in *The White Peacock.* Violet Hunt wanted to conclude *The White Rose of Weary Leaf* with her heroine, unborn baby and all, killed by the fall of a chimney, but it wasn't to be. Billy—the publisher Heinemann— was "dreadfully shocked" and poor, pale, underfed Amy "had to live to bear her illegitimate child and die in the odor of sanctity. . . ." And indeed it was a serious business enough, the disapprobation of Cyclopean folk like the National Vigilance Society. Already in 1888 the publisher Vizetelly had been tried and fined for publishing Zola and the very next year, despite a petition signed by Hardy and Gosse and Havelock Ellis among others, had been sentenced to three months in prison.

But the spirit of 1906 was already upon them, the playwrights and novelists of London, and when Garnett's *The Breaking Point* was rejected that year, the author was less than obliging. He brazenly published his play as *A Censored Play: The Breaking Point* and with it a furious letter addressed to the censor himself. What's more, he enlisted the help of his eminent friends who signed angry petitions and sent angry letters. Conrad perhaps wasn't wholly persuaded. The imbecile censor was surely more right than he knew when he vetoed D'Annunzio, "that dreary, dreary saltimbanque of passion," and Maeterlinck, "the farceur who has been hiding an appalling poverty of ideas . . . in wistful babytalk," and even Ibsen himself, "of whom like Mrs. Verloc of Ossipon, I prefer to say nothing." Nevertheless, a friend was a friend and a principle a principle and he faithfully delivered to the *Daily Mail* a ferocious attack on the censor. But it wasn't until Mr. Redford refused in 1907 to approve Barker's *Waste*—and this on the eve of its Savoy performance so that the Court Theatre movement itself was brought to an end—that literary London banded together. They formed a committee—Gilbert Murray and Galsworthy and, for secretary, young Gilbert Cannan just down from Cambridge—to deal once and for all with the problem and at Leinster Corner, Barrie's London abode, they prepared dark plans and petitions. Drafted by Galsworthy and signed by some seventy writers, a letter of protest was sent to the *Times* and, led by Barrie himself, a deputation of concerned British authors appointed itself to call on the prime minister.

King Edward, who viewed with alarm the continuing erosion of monarchical power, wasn't likely to surrender his Lord Chamberlain's rights in the matter, confirming the Shavian suspicion that the only way to get rid of the censor was to get rid of the monarchy. But the prime minister, by this time Asquith, was a little more disinterested and in 1909, when Shaw's *Blanco Posnet* was banned, he appointed a joint committee of the two houses of Parliament to consider the question. Shaw was quite indefatigable, perhaps to a fault. He thrust himself upon the chairman of the committee, planted anonymous notes and articles in friendly journals and papers, wrote circular letters to scheduled witnesses instructing them how to behave at the hearings. What's more, he composed an eleven-thousand-word statement he planned to pronounce at one of the hearings—his *Areopagitica* as he jestingly called it—printing 250 copies at his own expense and distributing them to committee members and fellow dramatists and gentlemen of the press. But in vain, all in vain. He was the star of the hear-ings all right, but he wasn't permitted to read out his statement nor to present it as evidence nor for that matter to influence at all the com-mittee's conclusion. At fifteen meetings it had heard forty-nine wit-nesses. It had heard Shaw declare that it wasn't the law he opposed but the absence of law. It had heard James declare, in a letter read into the proceedings, that it condemned British theatre "to ignoble depen-dences, poverties and pusillanimities." It had even heard the inept Mr. Redford make a fool of himself. But no matter. At the end of it all the committee declined to abolish the Lord Chamberlain's power which would not in fact be removed until 1968 when dust had long closed the eyes of Edward and Redford and even old Shaw.

On the contrary, the crusade to enfranchise the stage would create at the time a countercrusade, a crusade to deliver the nation from "the new immorality." The National Vigilance Society, the National Social Purity Crusade, the YMCA, the Girls' Friendly Society, the Church of England's Mothers' Union, and so on and so forth: they were all multi-plying and buzzing like flies in the heat and by 1910 would be uniting to form a convention of London Societies Interested in Public Moral-ity. When in 1908 Jacob Epstein had unveiled in the Strand, on the walls of the British Medical Association building, the daring new series of statues which embodied, he said, "the great primal facts of man and woman," there were those who found them only too primal. But when, the next year, Wells published his *Ann Veronica*, the reaction was even more strident. Bad enough that the heroine should break with her fa-ther and take up with the socialists and the suffragettes; but that the hussy should then, on top of all this, seduce a young man, a young married man, and bear him a child and run off to the Continent, this was all too much for the good Canon Lambert. Let his daughter read such a book? He'd just as soon send her "to a house infected with diphtheria or typhoid fever." It was certainly too much for St. Loe Stra-chey, editor of the venerable *Spectator*. Self-restraint? Self-sacrifice? "Such things have no place in the muddy world of Mr. Wells' imagin-ings." What was it, this world, but a world of "scuffling stoats and fer-rets, unenlightened by a ray of duty or abnegation"? Mr. Strachey would make a decision. The *Spectator* would no longer advertise books of this sort. And this wasn't all.

At a meeting of the Circulating Libraries' Association, the man-agers agreed to follow his lead. They set up their own watch committee, applied their own censorship. In the twelve lending libraries of Glasgow, writers like Fielding and Smollett and books like *Anna Karenina* and *Jude the Obscure* would not be available. New products like Hall Caine's *The Woman Thou Gavest* would be banned altogether and a volume of essays by Henry James, profanely entitled *Italian Hours*, would be eagerly sought as an "improper book," as, in fact, "a sex novel of Italian life." One dark day in December 1910 two plainclothes inspectors from Scotland Yard entered the premises of John Lane's Bodley Head press which had recently published an English translation of Sudermann's *Song of Songs*. They were bringing no charges, they told him, but a certain party had lodged a complaint that the novel in question was not, shall we say, *comme il faut,* and if such were the case then the publisher himself would surely be liable. Lane was naturally shaken. He sent copies of the allegedly dangerous book to fourteen distinguished authors, Hardy and Bennett and Wells among them. Shaw was as usual a shining light. "If Germany may read Sudermann and we may not," he responded, "then the free adult German man will presently upset the Englishman's perambulator and leave him to console himself as best he may with the spotlessness of his pinafore." But others of the fourteen were less than supportive and Lane had perforce to withdraw the offending volume.

Strachey and company did in fact have their effect. After the scandal of *Ann Veronica*, Macmillan was reluctant to publish *The New Machiavelli* and spent all of six months locating for his troublesome writer another publisher who turned out to be the more reckless John Lane. When the novel was published, the *Spectator* wouldn't acknowledge it, some of the libraries refused to receive it, and the city councils of Manchester and Birmingham disallowed it. As for young Lawrence, not yet the victim he was destined to be, he was properly chastened. At the publisher's request he not only removed from *The White Peacock* "all the offensive morsels" but asked that the manuscript of his second novel be promptly returned to him. It was rather erotic, he said, and "I don't want to be talked about in an Anne [sic] Veronica fashion." Just the same, the literary community didn't wholly collapse. Hewlett and Gosse were ready to fight a class war on the issue. Was it "for the tradesmen," quoth Hewlett the one, "to dictate their terms to the Authors?" Was it "for the reading class in this country," quoth Gosse the other, to surrender itself to "a group of commercial gentlemen?" In June 1911 Frank Harris's notorious "Notes on Morality" came out in the *English Review*. It was quite good-natured and even engaging but it did announce it, as Harris's considered opinion, that "Be yourself," "Be wilful," and "Never conform" should supplant the Ten Commandments, that sexual excess was much less harmful and much more agreeable than sexual restraint, that Nature ("the deep-breasted Mother") had "no liking for the Sunday-school scholar" and clearly preferred those "hot-blooded, vigorous personalities who scatter abroad [their] sins and seeds...." Worse still, Harris let drop by the way that since the sexual passion was "the more natural in women than in men," it should be regarded in their case "with even greater leniency." Strachey's *Spectator* would not of course allow this to pass. Harris's statement about women was tantamount, Strachey declared, to a "recipe to make prostitutes." As for the *English Review*, he went on, the *Spectator* wouldn't "see garbage being dumped on the nation's doorstep," would no longer deign to publish its ads and its notices. The *Review* replied with a protest signed by some ninety-five writers, but Harris, calling it "Strachery," roared and roared loud. "There is," Harris roared, "a pit fouler than any imagined by Dante, a cesspool bubbling and steaming with corruption.... That pool is English morality, and one of the foul bubbles on it is the *Spectator*." Forster may not have been on his side. "Try the English Review—" he'd write Leonard Woolf apropos of his novel, "I know of no other magazine that will pay for erections and excrement." But Wells and Shaw were delighted, the one rubbing his hands with glee and "magnificent idiot," the other exclaiming, "I must support him at any cost."

For, truth to tell, a new spirit of joylessness was threatening the land. They had already made it illegal to sing or to play the piano in public houses and now they were trying to make it illegal for children to accompany their parents inside and were even attempting to reduce the number of pubs in the country. By 1910 the Reverend James Marchant was assembling his Crusade for Social Purity and was urging young people not only to cease reading modern fiction but to practice strict abstinence and to start with cold baths. But now they were ready, the writers and journalists, to fight the new meanness of spirit, and with Hubert Bland for their leader and Cecil Chesterton for their secretary they were founding the Anti-Puritan League which was now holding meetings and sponsoring dinners and joyously singing a naughty new ballad, "Shall we not seek for newer ways of sinning?" As for Chesterton the Elder, he was already beside himself. Rich men could drink in their clubs whenever they chose but they'd limit the hours when the poor workingman was permitted to drink and even the number of pubs available to him. G.K.'s paper, the *Daily News,* was a puritan organ but this furious Falstaff declined to be daunted. In a bar across the street from the newspaper's office, he'd take wicked pleasure in working away with a bottle of burgundy at the ready before him. In the meantime the Reverend Stewart Headlam had conceived a most novel idea. He had conceived the Church and Stage Guild in the hope, as he said, that every chorus girl would be able to convert one curate at least. It was a notion that Rebecca West could not have resisted. The admirer of Shaw and the lover of Wells, she wanted a new woman's movement that called not alone for the vote or for jobs or for equal pay but for the freedom to live and live fully. What women now needed, she boldly declared, was "a militant movement for more riotous living."

"On the whole the most possible form of life"

So if one couldn't love it, this London, so anarchic, so dissonant, so urgent, how on earth could one leave it? It was the capital city of the English-speaking world, of the learning and letters Shaw was so bound and determined to conquer. Yeats detested the place, the dirt, the delirium, but he nevertheless made Woburn Buildings his London address for some twenty-four years. London was after all the sole scene of his occultist interests, of his literary fame, of his social and sexual successes. Sore disillusioned, Frank Harris would abandon old London and settle in Nice where he'd hope to get on with his writing. But he'd soon be back and for months at a time. The Riviera was all very well, all very pretty and pleasant, but it didn't quite give him "the stuff for new stories or portraits like the stirring life in London." "You may call it dreary, heavy, stupid, dull, inhuman, vulgar at heart and tiresome in form," as Henry James put it, but it was also, wasn't it, "the biggest aggregation of human life—the most complete compendium of the world" and hence for the novelist, it was, he was sure, "the right place." It was even possible, it was thought in some quarters, to love London dearly. It was sooty and smelly, dingy and dusky, a maelstrom, a vortex, but then too it was Life, Life, Force, and Energy, and Life, Force, and Energy were in those days all the rage. "Mud! London was full of mud . . . ," Hugh Walpole would write. "And yet he loved it, London and its dirt and darkness." The charm of "rural" Richmond was all well enough, Virginia Woolf would complain, but one did want "serious life sometimes" and so off to the city she'd go "for the sake of hearing the Strand roar" or to "the dusky streets in Holborn & Bloomsbury" for the sake of "the tumult & riot & busyness of it all." In his rural retreat James was sometimes disconsolate. "It's all rather dismal," he'd wail, "and I don't see life." "Come down! Come down!" he'd appeal to his London friends, to Gosse, to Walpole, to Violet Hunt. And down they would come with their tales of the scandalous life. Indeed he often regretted his flight from the capital. For all that he cherished his "poor frowsy tea-and-toasty Lamb House," he could sometimes feel he'd had more than enough of "the so amiable but so jejune little city" outside and would long "for the blessed Kensington fields," for "the electric metropolis and the fringe of 'South Belgravia.' " An Englishman first and a Londoner second, Kipling—"But I am sick of London/ From Shepherd's Bush to Bow"—would not be consoled. Hueffer, however, was something else again. To have been born an Englishman was no great matter, he'd say. But he would have been deeply offended "if, after accusing me of being English, you should suggest that I was born anywhere but within sound of Bow Bells."

To be sure, not all of them lived within sound of Bow Bells. Like James they'd defect to the country, to some picturesque cottage or Tudor mansion or Elizabethan farmhouse. But their business there was never country business. James scarcely sought in Rye what Thomas and other New Lifers had sought in their pastoral hovels and huts. Hueffer may have gardened a little but not for long and not very well, and what would our Conrad have done with a spade or a pitchfork? Bennett, the squire of Hockcliffe, made no bones about it. "I want a nice garden (and shall have one) and a horse that will go (and have got one) but I don't want to be troubled with the details." In any case they were never far from London, from the trains that carried them directly and quickly to the heart of the British metropolis and its aching de-

lights. James's Rye was but an hour and a half away and Hueffer's Aldington cottage no more than an hour and Conrad's Someries house
just forty-five minutes on the Midland line and Yeats's Stone Cottage
in Sussex, "a most perfect and most lonely place," as he called it, was
"only," he said in addition, "an hour and a half from London." As for
Bennett's Hockcliffe, it was, he noted with some satisfaction, "on a certain main-line at a certain minimum distance from London." Shaw
doubtless spoke for them all. "Can you suggest a country seat for us,"
he would ask, "within an hour of Charing Cross?"

At that they'd sometimes repent of their pastoral follies. Hueffer
would abandon his rigorous wife and his rigorous life in the country
for the pleasures of Kensington and, doubtless exhausted by his trials,
domestic, political, Wells would abandon Sandgate for the pleasures of
Hampstead. After eight years in that mean little cottage in Kent even
Davies, primitive man, would remove to great London to receive the
attention he was sure was his due. In the meantime the fog and the
darkness and rain were descending on Rye and the lights of Lamb
House would wink and burn low. Not just the death of a dearly loved
brother but dyspepsia, shingles, palpitations and terror and shortness
of breath: all were assailing the Master at once and with them the
darkest depression, "the blackest most poisonous melancholy," and at
times he had scarcely the spirit to rise from his bed in the morning.
His nephew Harry came to him from America. In his oak-paneled
bedroom the old man panted and sobbed. Harry sat by his side, held
his hand. But all would be well in the end. No more "the era of Rye hibernations," no more the "beastly solitudinous life." Back to London,
thank goodness, he'd go, to dear Cheyne Walk and two large rooms
overlooking the Thames and to friendships and clubs and the latest
amenities in taxis and telephones. "The remedy of London," he'd call
it, the remedy of "pavement, lamplight, shopfront . . . and numerous
friends' teacups and tales!" The old man breathed a sigh of relief. "Yes,
dear brave old London," he'd say, "is working my cure."

As for the young refugees from the towns and the villages, from
the provinces and the colonies, they couldn't but love it. For the
Wellses and Bennetts, the Orages and Cannans, the Mansfields and
Pounds, London was freedom, variety, tolerance. With its music halls,
lecture halls, restaurants, galleries, drawing rooms, theatres, bookstores,
it was the place where all things were possible and few things forbidden and the range of experience all but unlimited. Dorothy Richardson

was enthralled. Mystics and scientists, Quakers and vegetarians, free-thinkers and anarchists, Anglican bishops and Cambridge philosophers: who couldn't she meet, what couldn't she know? Eric Gill, the libidinous one, was also enthralled. In a matter of two or three days he and his wife and his mistress could listen to Rothenstein lecture on art and religion, Wells on the Samurai, Shaw on "The New Theology" and Orage on "Nietzsche versus Socialism." Even young Lawrence, lonely and homesick, could still be enthralled. By the Royal Academy where he looked at the Sargents, Millaises, and Bastien Lepages. By the secondhand bookstalls on Surrey Street where he picked up a copy of Synge's *Playboy*. By Covent Garden where he heard Wagner and Strauss and Puccini and even by Croydon where he heard *Il Pagliacci* and *Cavalleria Rusticana* and decided ("it's so reckless") he liked Italian opera best and "Damn Wagner, and his bellowing at Fate and death." London was more, it would seem, than a world. It was worlds.

For the freedom to see and hear and enjoy wasn't all that excited the London newcomer. It was also the freedom to meet and to mingle with all kinds and classes of people. Back home in the hinterland, nothing had changed. The squire and the vicar were still the divinities of their own little worlds, and everyone else, the tenants and tradesmen and servants, like their fathers before them, went on bowing and bobbing and tipping their hats or tugging their forelocks. But in literary London it was different. Be a poet or painter, write a novel or play, run a newspaper column or edit a journal, be a person of genius in short or, failing that, a person of letters, and down sure enough went the barriers of custom and class. Orage always hated his origins, the remote little village in Huntingdonshire which was still something straight out of Fielding or Austen. The squire and the vicar and the squire's eldest grandson were all grace and benevolence. They had taken the clever but penniless boy and helped him along, the squire paying for some of his schooling and the vicar teaching him French and the squire's eldest grandson tutoring him in the manor house library. But the promising boy would become in his time the outrageous young man who took him a wife and made socialist speeches and wore a soft felt hat and a flame-colored tie. Would they pay for an undergraduate course at Oxford, he would ask them? Not on your life, they'd reply in effect. So he left them for London which was, he said, "like coming out of an egg." Back home in the village he was nobody and would always be nobody, a poorly paid teacher at best, like his father.

But in London he'd soon be somebody and rubbing shoulders with somebodies like Shaw and the Webbs and Bennett and Wells.

"It's fang-de-seeaycle that does it, my dear, and education and reading French. . . ." For it might not be all for the best, this new freedom of London, it was felt in some quarters. By the author of *Women in Love*, for example. Up north in the Midlands "where their social standing was so diverse," Gudrun, the schoolteacher's daughter, feels awkward meeting with Hermione Roddice, a baronet's daughter, but in bohemian London where she has friends, Lawrence says, "among the slack aristocracy that keeps touch with the arts," she can meet her "on terms of equality." As Lawrence's Birkin sourly observes, "class-barriers are breaking down!" But if Lawrence was doubtful of these London developments, no one else seemed to be. "Wales England wed; so was I bred; 'twas merry London gave me breath." So Ernest Rhys sang and so sang they all. "To have the freedom of London," Dorothy Richardson said, "was a life in itself." It lifted one "out of one's narrow circumstances," said Wells, and into a world of knowledge and power.

By this time indeed it was *de rigueur* to love London, to acknowledge in novels and poems and in etchings and oils its terrific existence. They had done it before, the poets of the nineties: Henley in *London Voluntaries*, Symons in *London Nights*, John Davidson in *Fleet Street Eclogues* and *The Thames Embankment*. But theirs had been Wordsworth's city, the city of spiritual light: "the high majesty of Paul's/ Uplifts a voice of living light, and calls." Or Bawdy L'Air's city, the city of dreadful night: "the dreary rain, the depressing mud, the glaring gin shop, the slatternly shivering women. . . ." The new poets and painters would be different, less sentimental, less melodramatic. Returned from the Continent, Walter Sickert would be painting not only the music halls dear to the decadents but also the plain, shabby world of his Camden Town cockneys. ". . . Avoid the drawing-room and stick to the kitchen," he'd be telling his friends and disciples who'd name themselves the Camden Town Group and later the London Group.

As for the poets, it was a little too early for Eliot but when he did come to town they'd be ready to greet him. "All great art is born of the metropolis," Pound was saying already. "Take, as it were, a walk down Fleet Street," Hueffer was advising them, or "a ride on top of the bus from Shepherd's Bush to Poplar." "For some unknown reason," said Goldring, who couldn't have been in the know, James Elroy Flecker was still writing poems about London—"The Ballad of the Londoner,"

"The Ballad of Camden Town"—but he was writing them as if he had never ridden a bus in his life or taken a walk down Fleet Street. Hueffer, however, called the first of his volume of poems *Songs from London* and Goldring whose first book of poems he called *A Country Boy* would soon be publishing a volume called *Streets* and Harold Monro, who was otherwise Georgian, would write poems with titles like "London Interiors" and would go for his idiom to the world of the suburbs: "The hall smells of dust"; "The dingy garden with its wall and tree"; "It is sad in London when the gloom/ Thickens, like wool." London was certainly interested in seeing and knowing itself. Chesterton wrote an introduction to a book called *Literary London,* Symons contributed *London, A Book of Aspects,* and Bennett wrote for the *Nation* a "Life in London" series. Hueffer's first popular work was neither a poem nor a novel but *The Soul of London,* a prose celebration of sorts, and James contracted with Macmillan to produce a volume called "London Town" which, though never launched, inspired him to read such recent town studies as Besant's *Survey of London* and Stow's *Survey of London.*

How resuscitate the dead art of fiction in England? Why not by looking at London, Arnold Bennett suggested, "as though it were a foreign city" or as though one were seeing the place for the very first time. So Edwardian London would sometimes be other than purely Dickensian. It would also be Galsworthian or Wellsian, Chestertonian or even Conradian, and Hueffer would later refer to "the London novel" and to Henry James as its "Master" for *The Princess Casamassima,* for one, was in fact the result, as James said himself, of "the assault directly made by the great city upon an imagination quick to react." In novels like Conrad's *Secret Agent* and Chesterton's *The Man Who Was Thursday* and James's *The Wings of the Dove,* London would still, it's true, be Baudelaire's city of madness and death and despair. "Satanic," Forster would call it in *Howards End.* But it wasn't satanic for Chesterton whose *Napoleon of Notting Hill* he called "my little romance of London" and which he might also have called his little romance of the suburbs of London, Kensington, Battersea, Hammersmith, dear Notting Hill. "The suburbs are commonly referred to as prosaic . . . ," Chesterton said. "Personally I find them intoxicating." Nor was the city satanic for Bennett in novels like *Buried Alive* which was all about Putney and *The Roll Call* which was all, he said, "about London," "a city so incredibly strange" that it seemed to breathe of romance, Arnold said, with its trams and its trains and its tube that "always filled him with wonder. . . ." They were perhaps repulsive, the data of London. Eliot's "stockings, slippers, camisoles, and stays." But not for Arnold they weren't. He loved them enough to recite them in *Buried Alive:* "Illuminated calendars, gramophones, corsets, picture postcards, Manila cigars, bridge-scorers . . ." Even Wells's *Tono-Bungay* and *New Machiavelli,* for all that they denigrate London, also praise it and honor it, and though his freethinking heroes and heroines have sometimes to leave it behind them, it's not without sorrow and doubt: "It seemed to me we must be going out to a world that was utterly empty. All our significance fell from us—and before us was no meaning any more." "To speak against London," as Forster would note, "[was] no longer fashionable. The Earth as an artistic cult has had its day. . . ."

PART THREE
London Declined

"Pity spareth so many an evil thing"

Of course it wasn't to last, the Edwardian euphoria, the euphoria of 1906. By 1910 and the death of the king, Liberals and liberalism were fast losing heart and momentum and the party that had won by a landslide in 1906 was lucky to win by a hair in 1910. It had come into power with the greatest mandate in party history but it hadn't fulfilled it. It had managed to provide for old-age pensions, compensation for injury, minimum wages for sweated workers, an eight-hour day for the miners, and now would try to insure the men against unemployment and sickness. But it wasn't enough. By 1910 the rich were richer and the poor were poorer than ever before, and by 1910 it was no longer a secret. It had been brought home to men's business and bosoms by B. S. Rowntree's *Poverty: A Study of Town Life*, by L. Chiozza Money's *Riches and Poverty*, by the last volume of Charles Booth's *Life and Labour of the People of London*. No doubt they regretted the poor, the Liberals did, but alas they didn't regret them enough to change at the root their conditions. They were disabled by history. Committed to the survival of the fittest, to laissez-faire and as little state intervention as possible, they could hardly consider that radical redistribution of money and power that alone might have worked a saving reform. The Liberals were, truth to tell, in a bind. If they did what was needed, they must anger their capitalist friends and drive them into the camp of the enemy Tories. If they did anything less, they must anger their working-class friends and drive them into the camp of the new Labour party. Arthur Balfour was undisturbed by the Tory debacle of 1906 and the specter of Labour. "It will end, I think, in the break-up of the Liberal Party."

So Chesterton would work for that party in 1910 as he had in 1906 but his heart would no longer be in it and he'd soon give it up altogether. He couldn't endure it, he said, "its invariable alliance with the employer, its invariable hostility to the striker," and he'd have, he decided, to resign from the *Daily News* "before the next great measure of social reform made it illegal to go [out] on strike." His friend Hilaire Belloc wasn't less disillusioned. He had run and had won as a Liberal in 1906 but by the second election of 1910 he too could bear it no longer. Parliament was a fraud and a failure, a betrayal of democracy, not its fulfilment. It forced good men to vote not as their conscience but as their party dictated and was governed in any case by unholy alliances of families and friends and "I am relieved to be quit," he would tell them in parting, "of the dirtiest company it has ever been my misfortune to keep." When their friend Charlie Masterman came in with the Liberals in 1906, he was thought "a young Moses who was to lead the people to a new way of life" and how wonderful it was, his wife Lucy remembered, "when London seemed full of exciting people and my husband . . . was hoping the way was open to getting rid of . . . the blackest pits of poverty. . . ." But by 1914 all had changed. He'd become a mere minister, a mere party creature, weak, ineffectual, and old party members would dismiss him at last as a man with "a heart of gold and a head full of feathers." It may have been worse. His old idealism, John Buchan believed, "disappeared in the rut of office and was replaced by a mild cynicism," by what Chesterton called a "luxuriant gloom," and though his *Condition of England* was full of real care for the suffering poor, there was also about it a note of discouragement, a "feeling . . . of helplessness in the face of events."

And indeed they tended to be, these Liberal reformers, the darkest-dyed pessimists. Like Gissing, like Galsworthy, they pitied themselves even more than they pitied the poor, pitied themselves for the meaningless world that the industrial revolution, that the Darwinian revolution, had left them. They felt so much pity in fact they could barely feel anything else, so much pity they were powerless to act or even believe in the value of action. For it wasn't society that did it, was it? 'Twas life and nature, human life, human nature. Useless to hope or to act. So in *The Admirable Crichton* Barrie can deplore the British class system but be quite content to deplore it. On a desert island or in England, it was all the same, the immutable Law, the unchanging Way of the World. So in *The Island Pharisees* Galsworthy can deplore the fatuity of the rich and the wretchedness of the poor but all he can do is deplore them. It doesn't occur to him that the one may have something to do with the other. So in *Of Human Bondage* Maugham can deplore the poor sods of the slums, their hunger and pain and despair, but what can he do but deplore them? Life, rotten life, was the problem, "the natural order of things." No mention at all of a rotten society, the social disorder of things. Forster's Miss Schlegel does give it a try. Only connect the rich and the poor, the Wilcoxes and Basts. But alas they cannot and will not connect and Margaret and Morgan eventually make do, as good Liberals must, with personal relations and personal solutions. Like the hero of *Of Human Bondage* who finds peace in the end picking hops in the country, Margaret and her sister find peace in the end gathering hay. The dear grassy path to heaven on earth.

So of course they'd look down, these liberal folk, on Shaw and his "chaos of clear ideas." He thought, poor soul, that personal salvation meant nothing at all apart from the general salvation and that much could be said for a walk in the country or a cottage in Kent but he couldn't for the life of him think what it was. Fact is, they didn't much feel for the poor, the Liberals didn't. "There is something about human nature that is awfully repulsive," said the sensitive Galsworthy after smelling the slums. But so in the end said they all. Said Forster the creator of Bast, and Hugh Walpole the creator of West, "little West," and Virginia Woolf the creator of Septimus Smith and Miss Kilman. Hence the Liberal party and its looming defeat and its near disappearance from political view. They didn't know the poor. They didn't care for the poor. They certainly didn't know what to do with the poor. Lord Alfred Douglas, the betrayer of Wilde, was no saint but he did have his moments: "If the saviors of the poor are to come out of the ranks of the John Galsworthys of this world," he declared, "heaven must help the poor."

But then Shaw and his Fabian friends were not to perform any better than the Liberals. The great Wellsian boom that had promised so much—a socialist party, a socialist regeneration—turned out to be but the great Wellsian bust, and the Fabian fate was in doubt. For if Wells and his youthful supporters didn't win the great battle of 1906, neither, it seemed, did Shaw and the Society itself. Its force was divided, its energy spent, and out of the void that remained there was hardly a voice to be heard. Hubert Bland was aging and ill and the other old guardsmen were otherwise occupied, Shaw by the theatre, Olivier by a post in Jamaica, the Webbs by their national committee to abolish the Poor Laws. The Webbs were doing in fact precisely what in activist Wells they had sadly deplored as un-Fabian. No more permeating, no more gradualizing. They were touring the country, crusading, converting, evangelizing. Old Bland was disgusted. The Webbs were preempting, he said, the members' attention and the Society itself in the meantime was languishing, stale, apathetic, inactive. There were resignations from the executive committee, Wells's in 1908, wife Jane's in 1910, Bland's in 1911 for reasons of health and Granville Barker's for reasons of general discouragement, and, most telling of all, the great G. B. Shaw's to make room, he explained, for younger and livelier wits but really because he was tired of it all and at last had lost faith in its future. No doubt his marriage to Charlotte, the "green-eyed millionairess," had loosened his bonds to his socialist past. But he had also delivered a thousand harangues all over London, all over the land, and to what avail? Where were those millions of underpaid, underfed workers who, according to socialist theory, were ready to rise in revolt? Shaw was scarcely a socialist at all in the Sidney Webb sense. The Wagnerian hero or the Nietzschean Superman would seem more to his liking than the uncharactered fellow who occupied Sidney Webb's thoughts. He was in fact given to mocking the creatures he was pledged to believe in. Morell, the socialist clergyman in *Candida,* turns out to be hollow and fraudulent and Dick Dudgeon in *The Devil's Disciple* isn't ready, it seems, to die for the cause and Gunner, the young Marxist in *Misalliance* is, generally speaking, a ridiculous sort and no threat at all to the governing classes.

Resignations? There were outright defections. It wasn't just Wells who was estranged by the Fabian Society's "hygienic aridities." The young who had flocked to the colors in 1906 were also estranged. "The socialists are so stupid," Lawrence was saying, "and the Fabians so flat" and "Oh, the Fabians," Rupert Brooke was drawling, "I would to God they'd laugh & be charitable" and at a general meeting of *New Statesman* subscribers at the Kingsway Hall, Lytton Strachey couldn't help noting how lachrymose Beatrice looked and how far from a gentleman Sidney Webb seemed and how utterly meaningless Shaw's address was and, all things considered, what a bleak little tableau the trio composed on that platform. As for the Fabian doctrine, the less said the better, the young people were saying. Nationalize power and industry? Exchange one machine for another, for a capitalist state a collectivist one? No thank you, my dears. Romantic socialists now, they would localize power and industry, would put them in the hands of the workers, their unions or syndicates. Chesterton, who had called Wells's Samurai terri-

ble prigs (Rebecca West called them "stuffed bishops"), declared himself a "distributivist," proposed a society of peasants and craftsmen
and, if they promised to be good, a few lonely merchants, and Eric
Gill, on Gilbert's Distributist principle, would betake himself and his
family to Ditchling to found a community of artists and sculptors
where small could be beautiful or at least picturesque.

A Platonist and Theosophist as well as a socialist, Orage was never
at heart a good Fabian. If he did help to found the Fabian Arts Group,
it was to free the Society from the terrible tyranny of the statistical
Webbs or, as Eric Gill said in an outbreak of wit, "to deprive Fabianism
of its webbed feet." And if he did take over the New Age it was to make
it, it seemed, the servant of every socialist cause but the Fabian one,
the evangelism of Wells to begin with and then, when the syndicalist
movement began to be heard, the romance of guild socialism. The editor was for that matter as interested in art and letters as in socialist
doctrine. By 1908 he'd remove from the New Age masthead the term
"socialist" and print Chesterton's "Why I Am Not a Socialist" and quietly announce that his pages were open not alone to socialist leaders
but to "leaders of thought." By 1909 he'd recruit Bennett to run the
"Jacob Tonson" column and Flint to review the latest in poetry and
young Ashley Dukes to review the latest in drama from the Continent
and by 1910 he'd have Sickert reviewing the latest in art from abroad.
They tell us, he said, "the old Socialist buccaneers," that "The New Age
is too damned literary, or too damned aesthetic or too damned something or other," but under his guidance it was "losing," he said, "its
bony statistical aspect and putting on the colors of vivid life." He
wasn't nice to the Webbs. He referred to them in his weekly as Mrs.
Sidney and Mr. Beatrice Webb. By 1911 he had gone, it would seem, all
the way. He was printing not Shaw and his friends and not even Wells
and his friends, whose work he was openly disparaging now, but new
angry young men like Pound and Lewis and Hulme and such new ex-
otica as vers libre, cubism, and psychoanalysis. So Shaw and the Webbs
would be founding the New Statesman in 1913. The New Age of Pound
and Picasso wasn't quite after all what they'd bargained for.

But the young weren't defecting alone from the Fabian fount.
They were defecting from socialism itself. They were even defecting
from the New Age. Rediscovering religion and mystery, they were turning against their old secular masters, their Wellses and Shaws, and their
"dreaming of systems so perfect that no one will need to be good." Eric

Gill who had seen much of Orage and designed for him the type-heading of the *New Age* was deciding, his "Stonehenge" at Ditchling notwithstanding, that the Church of Rome was "the right answer to modern England and also to Morris and also to Wells and Shaw. . . ." and Ashley Dukes, Orage's theatre critic, was "casting off socialism and the Fabians and the *New Age*" and was adopting the "heroic values" he associated with Hulme. Orage himself would eventually abandon the *New Age* and all that it stood for, would go over to Fontainebleau and the vulgar mysticism of Gurdjieff and "The Institute for the Harmonious Development of Man," and Katherine Mansfield who was also a convert would tell her old mentor that of all her short stories there was none "that I dare show to God." No surprise, then, that Shaw was despondent. He'd quarrel with his old friends the Webbs on the part he should play in the *New Statesman*. He wanted the freedom to take up positions contrary to theirs: they didn't. He was perfectly willing to write articles for them, but he wanted them printed unsigned: they didn't. Before very long he was no longer a regular contributor. The Fabian Society itself, to be sure, was far from extinct. By this time it could claim nearly four thousand members. But they weren't attractive, it was felt in some quarters. They came down from Oxford and Cambridge and settled in Chelsea and talked rather gravely of the fate of the empire as if it was theirs to decide. They had longish hair and white fingers and smoked Algerian cigarettes. They wore red ties and ate triscuits for breakfast and served at their meetings lemonade and wine (unfermented) and chestnut sandwiches buttered with nut tose. Hubert Bland died April 14, 1914. Pease was the only one of the old guard to appear at his funeral. Bland felt that Fabianism had failed. So, more or less, did they all. The Fabian moment had come all right but, like the great Liberal moment, it would seem to have gone.

"My bolt as a real playwright is shot"

It was in art as in politics. For the most part a Fabian enterprise, the Court Theatre movement went the same sorry way as the Society itself. Flushed with success, Barker and Vedrenne would invade the West End, would lease the Savoy for the season of 1907. But it wasn't the small, warm, congenial place the Court Theatre had been, as its stark empty stalls would soon be reminding them, and as for the plays, Galsworthy's *Joy* was a failure and Barker's own *Waste*, on the eve of its opening, was banned by the censor and, dull and dispirited, Barker's productions of Shaw didn't have the old fire and conviction. By March they would have to close down, six thousand pounds in the red. In 1910, it's true, they'd attempt a revival. Barrie wasn't content with a crass *Peter Pan* popularity. He would march at the front with the Barkers and Shaws and the avant-garde crowd. He would ask Mr. Frohman, the producer of a hundred commercial successes in New York and London, to sponsor a season of repertory, and Mr. Frohman who worshiped James Barrie and adored *Peter Pan* would be only too glad to oblige. He'd do anything, everything, for the sake of good theatre, he said: "plays by anybody and everybody, conversational plays and literary plays, plays with plots and plays without plots. . . ." Money? No problem at all. His London theatre, the Duke of York's, would be closed for expensive repairs and remodeling. Nothing but the best for the best of directors and playwrights. But even before the king died in May and out of respect the theatres were inconveniently closed, Mr. Frohman's bold spirits were failing him. His opening number, Galsworthy's *Justice,* was a resounding success but Shaw's *Misalliance* and Barker's *Madras House* were financial disasters and, staggering under losses to which he was quite unaccustomed, the great impresario would be beating a frantic retreat. There'd be no revival of Shaw's *Man and Superman,* no production of *The Outcry* which Mr. Henry James had been commissioned to write, no staging of Euripides' *Iphigenia in Tauris*. Repertory be damned! Mr. Frohman would settle for runs of the proven successes like Housman's *Prunella* and Pinero's *Trelawny*. So came to an end the great Court experiment and Barker's brave dream of a national theatre. Scarred and embittered, he'd think of leaving a country that offered authors and actors so little encouragement, but loathing the stage and its vulgar connections, he'd turn to producing and lecturing on Shakespeare. He "threw off the dust of battle and became," said a disgruntled disciple, "a mere professor." Even the old Court imperium of Barker and Shaw and Lillah MacCarthy would soon be dissolving. Bad enough that Barker should divorce the unhappy Lillah to marry Miss Helen Huntington of the American Huntingtons, the rich railway Huntingtons. Since the heiress detested alike the socialist crowd and the theatre crowd, Barker felt obliged to dissociate himself from the fatherly Shaw who envisioned him as his natural successor and Shaw, hurt, disappointed, would console himself with Swinburne's reflection that "Marriage and death and division/ Make barren our lives."

But by this time in any case murmurs and mumblings had been heard in the land. From the young and advanced they received now as dramatists, these Court Theatre people, the same curses and blows they'd been receiving as liberals and socialists. Barker and Galsworthy? Good heavens! They weren't artists at all. They were realists (and drab ones at that) or preachers (and dull ones at that) and had sold their birthright, Max Beerbohm would say, for a pot of message. "The interpretation of life [was] not," said young Ashley Dukes, "a lecturing business" and by making it "their personal pulpit" they were, he said, "misusing the stage and frustrating the actor and boring the audience." "Mr. Galsworthy's views!" cried another. "How devastatingly present they always are." "Ridden by his ideas" and "harried by his ideals," the man had "no spaciousness, no ease, no geniality." Max Beerbohm and Lady de Grey attended a revival of Barker's *Voysey Inheritance* but it wouldn't, they concluded, revive. "The characters aren't in the least interested in each other," said Beerbohm, "—only in their ideas." "Everything will be all right," Lady de Grey remarked scornfully, "if we all go on the London County Council."

Old Shaw, to be sure, had his points. He was witty, ebullient, a dramatist born. All the same, his art and aesthetic were as crass, it was felt, as his politics. Orage was affronted. Shaw didn't have soul. "For a soul," said the soulful editor, "he substituted an idea." Ashley Dukes was also affronted. "He nationalizes his men and women. . . . He ex-

propriates their imagination. He municipalizes their emotion. He con-
fiscates their surplus value." At 67 Frith Street he was rarely discussed.
He wasn't in touch, it would seem, with the "heroic values" that
worked in the bosoms of Hulme and his friends. The old boy was, it
was clear, quite over the hill. *Blanco Posnet?* It was mournful, Rupert
Brooke noted, "to see the beginning of senile decay in that brilliant intellect." *Misalliance?* He "kept us on the rack for 3 hours last night,"
Virginia Stephen complained; "his mind is that of a disgustingly preco-
cious child of 2. . . ." "We seem to have left him behind as a dramatist,"
Rupert Brooke thought. Sadder still, Shaw himself was inclined to
agree. "I have done my turn," he was telling his friends. "I am getting
too old now for melodrama—even Shavian melodrama," he wrote
apropos *Getting Married,* and as for his *Misalliance,* it was "nothing
but endless patter," he sadly confessed: "my bolt as a real playwright is
shot."

At the time, to be sure, Shaw was entering the soul's dark midnight, was questioning himself and his life and his art. His new plays
he was calling experiments. Comedies of ideas, argument, talk. *Getting
Married* he subtitled "A Conversation," "A Disquisitory Play." *Misalliance* he subtitled "A Debate in One Sitting." But the new generation
of Orages and Dukeses would not be persuaded. They were worshiping
new idols, new images, tragedy, poetry, soul, "heroic values," were entirely oblivious to the valor of comedy, to what Shaw would call the
"proud overbearing gaiety that carried all the tragedies of the world
like feathers and stuck them in my cap and laughed." Masefield's
Tragedy of Pompey the Great was "a good sign," young Percy Lewis considered: "there's no Shaw Barker nonsense about it." A better sign yet
were the Abbey players who had first come to London in 1904 but
didn't carry the day till 1907 when they brought with them Synge and
the *Playboy.* The old poet Blunt wasn't terribly impressed. The house,
he complained, was half empty and a good deal of the brogue wasn't
easy to follow, and the *Playboy* itself didn't seem to him more than a
"harmless bit of broad farce." But the young bloods of London were
enchanted entirely, Orage and the *New Age* calling it one of the better
plays of their time and Ashley Dukes remembering with emotion on
stage "the gaunt ill-dressed figure of Synge . . . facing the Irish hooli-
gans with the unseeing eyes of a dreamer." For here indeed was no
Fabian preaching or praying, and after the drabness of Barker and
Galsworthy, Synge was a riot of color and Yeats a feast of heroics and

poetry. As for Shaw and his unabashed staginess, what a treat were the Abbey productions, their natural simplicity. They scarcely moved at all on the stage, these Irish players. The speaker of the moment might be granted a gesture but otherwise they stood stock-still or moved with a natural clumsiness as though quite unconscious of being stared at in public. Indeed it was talk, all marvelous talk, and London adored it, the words and the sounds and the rich Irish cadences. "We learned Irish idioms, adopted Irish accents, hurried again and again to hear *The Playboy.* . . ."

A few years later the Orages and Dukeses would have something else to set against Barker and Shaw and their theatre. It was Chekhov, it was *The Cherry Orchard*, which in May 1911 the Stage Society let London see for the very first time. It wasn't, it seemed, caviar to the general. From the second act on, the bored or bewildered drifted out of the old Aldwych Theatre or stayed on to scoff or to snigger. But the young cognoscenti who were weary of Barkers and Shaws and familiar with Hauptmanns and Wedekinds, they knew what it meant, this new play, and remained to be moved and instructed and to bid the scoffers and sniggerers, as Ashley Dukes did, to mend their bad manners. Bennett and Shaw must needs see the play as a tract, as "one of the most savage and convincing satires on a whole society . . . ever seen in a theatre," but this, said Ashley Dukes with determined obtuseness, was not what it meant, was not at all what it meant. It was art, he said, art in the mode of Flaubert, and had nothing to do with the dull social drama of Ibsen and his English successors.

Just a month after Chekhov it was the turn of the Russian Ballet and its barbaric music and dance to conquer the town. Rupert Brooke would often go down to see it and Ezra Pound would take Olivia Shakespear and her Dorothy and Lady Ottoline never seemed to see it enough and would say to an uncomprehending Nijinsky, "Quand vous dansez, vous n'êtes pas un homme, vous êtes une idée." Lytton Strachey made fun of her "gaping and gurgling [before him] like a hooked fish." But he too had been hooked at the time, sending Nijinsky "a great basket of magnissime flowers, which was brought on to the stage and presented to him by a flunkey." Leonard Woolf, just back from Ceylon, would never remember a time when the London intelligentsia went night after night to a theatrical performance as it did in this summer of 1911. Even Alexandra, the queen mother, was a passionate convert, moving from her box to an orchestra seat the better to witness

Nijinsky's great leap at the end of *Le Spectre de la Rose*. As for Ashley Dukes, the message of the ballet seemed to him unmistakable: "It was possible," he'd declare, "to speak of the art of the theatre." And indeed after Synge and Yeats, after Chekhov and Diaghilev, what was there to say for the theatre of Barker and Shaw? Not, it would seem, very much. The heroes and saints of 1905 had become the villains and devils of 1911 and "it is the Court people," Shaw would be saying this year, "who are 'the old lot.' "

"The old lot"

But it was in the nature of Edwardian things to falter and fade. It was 1909 and Bennett and Wells were dear to the hearts of the young and emancipated. Wells had just fought his heroic last stand against Shaw and the Webbs and now *Tono-Bungay*, the best of his novels, was being serialized in Hueffer's *Review* and "read, *read* Tono-Bungay," Lawrence was exhorting his friends: "it is a great book." In the meantime Bennett's just-published novel, *The Old Wives' Tale*, was being everywhere praised for a masterpiece and as "Jacob Tonson" in Orage's *New Age* he was widely admired for his slashing attacks on philistine England, its ridiculous censorship, its deplorable ignorance of the new art and drama abroad. But then it was 1910 and the year of Cézanne and Matisse and all of a sudden the weather turned round. Orage who had long honored Wells and published his articles was referring now to the "adiposity" of his prose and "What!" he'd expostulate, "a man can be in the front rank of a literary art and never have learned to write!" He was in fact calling in question all that had made Mr. Wells what he was. "Who demanded," he was asking, "that the artist should 'follow' life? No artist, it is certain." "Mr. Wells," he was saying, "knows no more of sociology than Mr. Bennett knows of life." Yes, not even Bennett, his own "Jacob Tonson," would be spared his disdain. By 1911 he was no longer writing for Orage and his journal and his place was being taken by young men like Pound who condemned "the unspeakable vulgo," the contemptible crowd, who "whore[d] after their Bennetts and their Galsworthys. . . ." What had happened to Sickert and his realist painting and to Barker and Galsworthy and their realist theatre had also happened to Bennett and Wells and their realist fiction.

Ford Madox Hueffer may well have been pleased. His heroes and saints were the Jameses and Conrads, the artist-impressionists, not the Wellses and Bennetts, those slovenly realists. But if he was pleased, it couldn't have been for long. In 1909, with his *English Review* a success and, with it, his intention of "giving a shove to Impressionism in its literary form," he was full of high hope. Surely now the merits of Conrad and James and the novel of France would be obvious to even the most besotted defenders of the primitive, plot-ridden novel of England. But it wasn't to be. It was 1910 and for him as for Bennett and Wells the weather turned round. A marvelous editor but a deplorable manager— "he seemed like an infant in charge of a motor-car"—he lost control of his wondrous *Review,* lost his post and his money, nearly three thousand pounds, and lost in the process the respect of his friends and contributors who resented his lordly indifference to finance and detail. Wells who had agreed to do half the editing and pay half the expenses soon declined to do either, and Conrad who was deeply involved in the journal's inception ("The early E. R. is the only literary business that . . . 'came home to my bosom' ") was quick to jump ship and even deny he had served at the helm: "I have been in no sense associated with the E. R. . . ." On the verge of a breakdown, his ego in tatters, Hueffer tried not to weep, tried not to be bitter and bruising but, wounded man that he was, he wasn't quite up to it. His heart full of childish self-pity and impotent rage, he wrote long rambling letters presenting himself as another King Lear, as a virtuous man who had given his all for his country and been badly betrayed for his pains by his *soi-disant* friends and "I will do such things—/ What they are yet I know not, but . . ." Frank Harris was unsympathetic. "The man's an ass," he declared categorically. Forster was unsympathetic. "A fly-blown man of letters," he called him. But Lawrence who had reason to know Hueffer's warmth and good nature wasn't fooled for a moment: "he daubs his dove-grey kindliness with a villainous selfish tar, and hops forth a very rook among rooks: but his eyes, after all, remain, like the Shulamites, doves eyes."

And what of his new English novel, his impressionist novel? That cause, alas, seemed lost and forever. For London's young rebels who had seen the new paintings and would call themselves Vorticists and would do for their art what Cézanne and Picasso were doing for theirs, old Ford and his heroes were strictly old hat. Percy Lewis would take him aside. "What is the sense of you and Conrad and Impressionism," he'd tell him. "... This is the day of Cubism, Futurism, Vorticism." Verisimilitude? Vicarious experience? Good heavens, this wasn't what people wanted at all. "They want to be amused. . . . By brilliant fellows like me." Efface yourself? Make people believe there's no author at all? "What balls! What rot! . . . What's the good of being an author if you don't get any fun out of it?" So when Fordie mentioned Conrad's name to a lively young novelist, he was told "he had never heard of the feller" and when he mentioned to Lawrence that he might read with profit Flaubert's *Bouvard* the young man just "grunted with absent-minded half-contempt" and indeed when they heard that Cunning-hame Graham had called Henry James "Henrietta Maria," Pound and his clamorous crew were said to have whooped with delight. It was all very sad. When Bloomsbury planned to visit "old Henry James" in lit-tle brown Rye, Vanessa Bell hoped that he wouldn't be "too monumen-tal and difficult" and she couldn't read James, Virginia would admit at the time, without feeling "embalmed in a block of smooth amber." "For an hour," Rupert Brooke would confess, "I have tried to put my-self in the frame of mind in which a middle-aged maiden would write to a literary Colonel. But it is vain. I am not Mr. Henry James."

"And what rough beast . . .?"

But it wasn't just Cézanne and Matisse and the mod-ernist spirit at work. Already on the horizon a little cloud had ap-peared, a shadow or shape no bigger than a man's hand. A fabulous darkness? A rough beast slouching toward Bethlehem to be born? It was Chekhov. It was Dostoevsky. It was the Russians, "them Russians." Even in England the Russian phenomenon wasn't unheard of. Tolstoy was known and revered and Turgenev who, by the turn of the century, had been put into English, all seventeen volumes of him, by Constance

Garnett, was adored by the Jameses and Conrads for the art of the novel he'd mastered in France. But with Dostoevsky and Chekhov it was different. In the 1880s and '90s six volumes of Dostoevsky had been translated and published and in 1903 and 1908, at Edward Garnett's suggestion, two volumes of Chekhov's short stories, but they were incomplete and by 1906 no longer in print and, in any case, hadn't entered the mind of John Bull who wasn't likely to relish their hyperborean humors nor their morbid interest in people who ate cabbage soup and beat each other to death. It was in Paris in fact, not London, that Englishmen first came under the Muscovite spell. There Augustus John had read Dostoevsky in bad French translations and had spread the good word to Ida, his wife, and to young Henry Lamb who together discussed, every night after dinner, the work of this strange new appearance in fiction. Back in England, in Cambridge, at James Strachey's table, John would discourse on his Russian discovery and Lamb would persuade the amorous Lytton to read *The Possessed* and "Colossal! Colossal!" Lytton would write him and "It's mere ramping and soaring genius," he'd declare. He didn't, perhaps, care much for the Christianity parts of *The Brothers Karamazov*, but it belonged nonetheless, he'd assure Leonard Woolf, with the greatest of novels and "The Agamemnon is childish compared to it." It was in Paris for certain that Duncan Grant, his little cousin, came under the spell. The result was immediate, was striking. Returning to London he painted a picture of Marjorie Strachey seated on a sofa with her face in her hands and by her side on the sofa a half-opened copy of *Le Crime et le Châtiment*. It was also in Paris that Percy Lewis, no doubt affected by John, would come under the spell. By the time he got back to London he was "spiritually a Russian" and it was partly at least "as a Russian," he recalled, "that I wrote my first novel, *Tarr.*"

By this time, however, Russia already was crossing the Channel. It wasn't until 1911 and *The Cherry Orchard* was seen that Chekhov became a cult figure in London, but in Moscow to cover the Russo-Japanese war, Maurice Baring had seen *Uncle Vanya* performed and had sent back to London a glowing report, and in 1908 a second volume of Chekhov's short stories had had its effect and "we have no writer . . . ," "Jacob Tonson" was saying, "who could mold the material of life . . . to such an end of beauty," and perhaps thus instructed, the *New Age* would soon be printing translations of Chekhov and imitations by young English authors like Mansfield and Lewis. In the meantime the Dostoevsky of Paris was well on the way to becoming the Dostoevsky of London. In 1909 Baring's *Landmarks of Russian Literature* devoted half its pages not to the famed Turgenev but to the obscure Dostoevsky and argued, indeed, that Turgenev was no more to Dostoevsky in Russia than Charlotte Yonge was to Charlotte Brontë in England. At a party that year Bennett was told that *The Brothers Karamazov* was no major achievement. He turned to Mrs. Garnett. What did she think? It was, she replied, his masterpiece. So the next year he'd be telling his audience that he had just read *The Brothers Karamazov* in French and that it was for a fact "one of the supreme marvels of the world" and "now, Mr. Heinemann, when are we going to have a complete Dostoevsky in English?" and was it not his duty to get "Mrs. Constance Garnett to do it?" So in 1912, for the very first time, London would have *Karamazov* in English and Dostoevsky become the cult of the decade. Bennett wasn't quite ready to grant that the sainted Turgenev was inferior to Dostoevsky. "In spite of the recent wave of enthusiasm for Dostoevsky," he could say, "I am still of opinion that nobody alive or dead has written finer novels than Turgenev." But in 1917 when he collected and published his *New Age* columns, he chose to delete this sentence. Dostoevsky was, as they said in those days, "the top of the tree."

He was certainly the top of the tree for London's young writers and readers. Here at last was an author with soul, an author who didn't reduce the mystery of life to a Fabian formula. One evening in 1912, the year of *The Brothers*, Mansfield and Murry and Cannan and Swinnerton would agree that that Russian book was the greatest thing ever written, and in the Rhineland that summer Jessica Chambers who had just lost her Lawrence to Frieda was burying herself in the book and finding in it, she believed, "the wreckage of my life." As for the Anglo-Indian passengers on a slow boat to India, they didn't quite know what to make of Morgan Forster and his three Cantabrigian friends. They weren't joining at all in the planned entertainments but were lolling about and loudly comparing Dostoevsky with Tolstoy. By 1920, in any event, Mrs. Garnett would have finished translating the complete Dostoevsky and Middleton Murry would have sat down and written in five Dostoevskyan weeks his book on the Russian colossus and Koteliansky would be translating, with the various help of Lawrence and Cannan and the Murrys and Woolfs, the works of the great Russian writers. It was everywhere powerful, this Muscovite virus.

Percy Lewis wasn't the only one trying to look like a Russian. Henry Lamb insisted on cossack boots and Katherine Mansfield's host at a party insisted on calling her "Yekaterina" and as for "Yekaterina" herself, she'd smoke Russian cigarettes, drink Russian tea in glasses, and promise her lover Russian cherry jam for his tea. "Dear Madam," she'd write Mrs. Garnett: "my generation (I am 32) and the younger generation owe you more than we ourselves are able to realize. These books have changed our lives. . . ."

It wasn't easy of course to Russianize the plain life and art of the English but they did do their best. Mansfield's first *New Age* stories were all too Chekhovian and Lewis's all too Dostoevskyan and in her novel *The Judge* Rebecca West tried in vain, Wells said, "to beat Dostoevsky at his own game." Even good British Bennett wasn't untouched. *Crime and Punishment* "depressed me about my own work," he confessed, "which seemed artificial and forced by the side of it"—hence *Hilda Lessways*, his effort to capture the dark Dostoevskyan note. Not every young person, it's true, felt this mania for the matter of Moscow. In the midst of *Les Frères Karamazov*, Forster was, he admitted, "a little disappointed." Was it too heavy, too formless? No, that wasn't it. "It seems sketchy . . . ," he remarkably said. As the author of *The Trespasser*, Lawrence was thought to be Dostoevskyan but it couldn't have been his intention. *Crime and Punishment* was "a tract, a treatise, a pamphlet," he complained, "compared with Tolstoy's *Anna Karenina* or *War and Peace*." In an outburst of Anglo-Saxon pride, he denounced Tolstoy as well as Dostoevsky and Flaubert and the French as well as the Russians. "They are all . . . ," he said, "so very *obvious* and coarse, beside the lovely, mature, and sensitive art of Fenimore Cooper or Hardy." But then Lawrence who loved to play Ishmael was as usual a minority of one. In 1905 Shaw had hardly heard of the feller. "I hear that there are several dramas extant by Whatshisname (Tchekoff, or something like that). . . ." But in 1913 when he started to write *Heartbreak House*, his "Fantasia in the Russian Manner on English Scenes," it was exactly old Whatshisname who served as his model.

So it wasn't surprising that Hueffer was dismayed and dejected. For him and his friends who believed in Flaubert and Turgenev and the beautiful novel of France, it was a disaster, this passion for Chekhov, for Dostoevsky, for everything Russian. The *English Review* had been a smashing success and in 1913, when Conrad published his *Chance*, one of their members had even achieved, *mirabile dictu*, best-seller status. The omens were good. They were on the verge, it appeared, of full recognition at last. But the year of the Conrad was also the year of the Dostoevsky and the weather turned round. At *The Cherry Orchard*'s first showing James was perplexed. During the second intermission, he tried to explain, Maugham reported "how antagonistic to his French sympathies was this Russian incoherence" and well it might be, Maugham sourly observed, "when his dramatic values were founded on . . . Dumas and Sardou." But a Chekhovian incoherence was as nothing compared to a Dostoevskyan one. Did he not feel, Hugh Walpole was asking him, did he not "feel Dostoevsky's 'mad jumble' . . . nearer truth and beauty than the picking and composing" of the novelist as artist? No, "Beloved little Hugh," he did not, the Master replied, and went on to denounce the mere "fluid pudding" of the Tolstoys and Dostoevskys. Of course they tried to make Conrad a mysterious Slav. H. L. Mencken made much of his "Slavonism" and with the best of intentions Edward Garnett found in *Under Western Eyes* not the rational Turgenev but the accursed Dostoevsky. But Conrad, enraged, wouldn't have it. "Slavonism" indeed! "Does he mean by it primitive natures fashioned by a Byzantine theological conception of life, with an inclination to perverted mysticism? Then it cannot possibly apply to me." Like Dostoevsky, was he, "the convulsed terror-haunted Dostoevsky"? The Russian sounded to him "like some fierce mouthings from prehistoric ages" and his people like "damned souls knocking themselves to pieces in the stuffy darkness of mystical contradictions." It helped, sad to say, to strain Conrad's friendship with Garnett, this whole Dostoevskyan matter, and with poor Mrs. Garnett whom he blamed in his heart for it all. But then Garnett himself wasn't wholly converted. Though he was one of the first to extol Dostoevsky, his heart was, like James's and Conrad's, with Flaubert and Turgenev, and Dostoevsky he described with no obvious pleasure as a "Russian Dickens." He must for that matter have been just as appalled as Hueffer and company by the gathering darkness and the sudden eclipse of the novel they cherished. Like Asquith and the Liberals, like Sickert and the British impressionists, like Barker and Shaw and the theatre of ideas, they had seen, they must surely have thought, the best and the last of their time.

"O O O O that Shakespeherian Rag"

As for the open sex warfare of 1900–1914, it did take its toll. There were serious losses, heartbreaking casualties. One day in July 1909 at Black Lake Cottage in Surrey, Mr. Barrie was approached by his gardener. Hunt was indignant. Mrs. Barrie had unjustly complained of his work. Not only that, she was carrying on with young Mr. Cannan. Early one morning had he not had to remove a ladder from under a window? Trained as a barrister but now a promising author who was working with Barrie's committee to abolish the censorship, Gilbert Cannan had not read his Stendhal in vain and, like Julien Sorel, had chosen in thus operatic a fashion to enter his hostess's bedroom. Barrie was naturally appalled. He took the next train to London. But Mary, his still-pretty actress-wife, declined to abandon her lover and be forgiven her sins, nor would she consent to a quiet and genteel separation. She would have a divorce, would marry her Gilbert, her Gillie, and would live and love and be happy at last. It wasn't just that Barrie was sexually incompetent, was the boy who wouldn't grow up. It was the little man's meanness, his mute Scottish hostility, his pale haggard face, his dark haggard eyes. It was the rich but terrible dinners when her chatter annoyed him and he put her down in front of the guests. It was the lies of the fantasies he lived by, his fatuous dreams of charming young mothers and ineffable children like Mrs. Darling and Peter Pan. It was above all his disturbing obsession not with a woman but with a family, the Davies family, the mother and the five little boys, whom he'd come upon in Kensington Park quite by accident and whom, uninvited, he'd visit day after day and whom, unsolicited, he'd lavish with gifts and affection. It was something in fact of a nightmare. The poor father Arthur, who was mild and unmoneyed and in any case soon to be stricken with a cancer that ended his life, must sit helplessly by whilst this strange little creature took over his house like a terrible curse. It was more than Mary Barrie could bear. Childless, she wanted children, her own. Loveless, she wanted to love and be loved. So she didn't contest in October the divorce for which the shattered playwright petitioned the court and six months later, when the divorce became final, she married her Gillie in the Holborn registry office.

As for Gillie himself, who at twenty-four was twenty years younger than she, it may not have been the consummation he devoutly desired. For an enlightened young person such as he was, marriage was, don't you know, out of fashion and so was divorce for that matter. Would he consider, he had asked Mr. Barrie, the liberal playwright, would he consider, as one civilized man to another, a *ménage à trois*? Mr. Barrie spoke not a word. His friend, Maurice Hewlett, who thought of himself as a freethinking aristocrat in the tradition, perhaps, of Thackeray's wicked Lord Steyne, was a touch disappointed. Marriage? Divorce? This wasn't the way things were managed abroad. Jim was behaving *"impossibly,"* he feared. It surprised him to find him not "more of a gentleman." But then the lovers themselves, it appears, were just as naive. To the amusement of Wells, who was an expert on such city matters, they kept strictly apart during the six months' period prescribed by the law and were sexually abstinent. "Sillies you are!" the great one would tell them. "Go & live together & get Babies as soon as you can like two sensible people. One could think there was Magic in Marriage."

Slender and tall, gallant and courteous, Gilbert was a considerable catch for a woman unhappily married and near middle age. With his large blue eyes, corn-colored hair, and Duke of Wellington nose, he had the conceited good looks of a matinee idol and carried himself with a tragical Hamlet-like air. What's more, as a budding young playwright and novelist he had great expectations. Would his star not burn as bright in the end as that of Barrie himself? "Oh! Heaven. It is too much," he would write after visiting the wrinkled old Meredith. "The great man his soaring done and the little young man with wings trembling to the flight." Not surprisingly, under the circumstances, he wasn't well liked by his peers who found his pretensions not easy to bear: the "deliberately portentous manner," the crooked inscrutable smile, the conversation that seemed to turn everything into a lecture. He presented himself as one of the young and advanced but Bloomsbury wasn't impressed. Ottoline called him "a rather vacant Sir Galahad." Strachey called him "an empty bucket which has been filled up to the brim with modern ideas—simply because it happened to be stand-

ing near that tap." There may in fact have been something wrong with
the fellow. He had, it was noticed, a staring but unseeing eye.

Lady Ott thought the marriage in any case doomed from the
start, he, "towering above her always looking with his pale, romantic
eyes into space, and shaking his fair hair and tilting his large thin nose
in the air," and she, "so determined to keep herself young and
sprightly" and looking, with her "carefully preserved complexion, like a
very competent lady house-decorator," chatting away "in a loud harsh
voice about what she and Gillie had done." "It made one raise one's
hands," Lady Ottoline said, "like Henry James, in horror." The marriage
was certainly not what poor Mary envisioned. There was the woman
he kissed on their honeymoon and the serving girl he got pregnant
and other sordid adventures not excluding the company of creatures
like Murry and Katherine. Would she, he asked her one day, share his
bed and his body with another for whom he now felt a most powerful
affection? Mary was outraged. A monogamous marriage to the great
J.M.B. had been sickening enough but a polygamous marriage to the
unfortunate Gillie. . . . She had him committed. In 1917 there were bitter proceedings and in 1918 a separation and though Barrie was generous and bequeathed to her money for life, she died without holding a
child of her own. As for Gillie, he died thirty years later in a home
called the Priory. Under his bed, in a large cardboard box, they found,
dusty, moth-eaten, his barrister's wig.

When Lady Dilke invited Violet Hunt to dinner, she asked her if
she'd mind sitting next to Mr. Ford Madox Hueffer. Violet said that
she'd like it. "Lots of people wouldn't," Lady Dilke said. This amused
Violet. She was already Fordie's lover. They had been eating Irish stew
together. Will you marry me if I'm ever divorced? he had suddenly
asked her. He had been depressed, had been talking of suicide. At
forty-six more than ten years his senior, she was eager to marry and
under the circumstances how could she resist? The daughter of London celebrities, a painter-father and a novelist-mother, as well as the
niece of Holman Hunt, the famous Pre-Raphaelite, Violet was something of a celebrity herself. As the author of *Sooner or Later* and *The
White Rose of Weary Leaf*, she was widely admired as an English Colette. On the boulevards of Paris she was seen with the likes of Bennett
and Maugham, and at home in South Lodge entertained swells like
Lady Houston and Mrs. Pankhurst, James and Hudson and Kipling
and Wells. Already a legend, she had lived and loved in her day. Even

now, middle-aged, she was not unalluring with her curious green eyes and her "sparrow-brown hair, plummy and softly drifting. . . ." Nevertheless the marks of time and experience were on her. "A thin viperish-looking beauty with a long pointed chin and . . . burning brown eyes under hooded lids," she affected young Derek Patmore as "a handsome witch" and, with her brilliant but caustic wit—"Violet prefers her worst epigram to her best friends"—and the presence of unexplained spots on her forehead and wrists, was no longer a wholly desirable commodity. Hence her need, her dilemma: with all the anguish of the fading freethinking beauty, she longed for the bliss of a husband and home.

The problem was Fordie's wife Elsie, an Anglo-Catholic of the "bloody Mary" rather than the "Merrie England" type. "Tall, high-breasted and dark, with a bold eye and a rich, high color, like a ripe nectarine," and wearing the richly stained garments of the William Morris style, she indeed had the look of a Pre-Raphaelite Judith. Ford may have outgrown the romance of their childhood and marriage, but she hadn't and wouldn't. He may have defected to literary London and, except for the weekends, abandoned their picturesque cottage at Aldington with its low ceilings and windows and thick-leaden window panes but she hadn't and wouldn't. She summoned the Conrads to her Aldington cottage. In her shapeless gown with its girdle of rope and its large wooden beads, she denounced "all literary people" and vowed to expose "the whole literary world." Tall, blue-eyed, and blond with an upper-class manner and drawl, Hueffer was not unimpressive. But he had put on weight; the "pale lemon moustache" was straggling, untidy, and the smooth pink cheeks were at times "the color of raw veal." A little adenoidal, his mouth would hang open disclosing rabbit teeth discolored from smoking and making his speech so muffled and fluffy it was an effort to listen and suggesting to Lewis a "lemonish pink giant . . . with his mouth hanging open like a big silly fish." More fatally perhaps he was shy and sentimental and, like his Edward Ashburnham in *The Good Soldier*, was attracted and attractive to women. One night at the Shepherd's Bush Empire he picked up a poor, strayed creature to whom he offered purely spiritual counsel and a shelter of sorts in his Kensington flat. Everywhere they went they went together, and everywhere they went there went with them a slight scent of scandal and sex. He called her his "secretary." She called him "Papa." Unhappy libidinous man, he had even made love, on at least one occasion, with his wife's younger sister. Hueffer indeed was the lord of mismanagement. In October 1909, after two ill-advised weeks in Normandy, he and Violet got off the 10:45 train from Paris at Charing Cross and who should they find on the platform to greet them but Elsie herself, "the irate goddess," and beside her her lawyer? "It's all up, old girl!" Hueffer stated lugubriously. "You will see. There'll be no divorce."

Poor Violet! Poor Fordie! Accomplished scandalmongers the both of them, they were now to become the rich stuff of scandal themselves. There were rumors in London. There were even paragraphs in the papers. "I can't breathe in situations that are not clear," cried the mortified Conrad. "I abhor them." As for James who had invited Violet down for a weekend of gossip, his was the most unkindest cut of all. He canceled the invite, deeply deploring "the lamentable position in which I gather you have put yourself" and which affected him, he said, as "painfully unedifying." He once called her his Purple Patch. She was now, it appeared, a Patch too Purple for him. A few months later Violet went shopping on Kensington High Street. Suddenly, before her horrified eyes, loomed a shabby wee man with a sandwich board bearing a legend in CAPITAL LETTERS. It read, for the whole world to see, MR. HUEFFER TO GO BACK IN FOURTEEN DAYS. Disconcerted, ashamed, Violet rushed home. Elsie, it seemed, had petitioned the courts for the restitution of her conjugal rights and Mr. Justice Bargrave Deane had ordered the truant back home and to pay his wife in the meantime a modest allowance of three pounds a week.

The baronial Hueffer was deeply offended. All along he had been paying her that much and much more. So, Quixotic man that he was, he mounted his high horse. By heaven, he wouldn't pay up. He would go to gaol first or, as he preferred more romantically to call it, to prison. Maybe then Elsie would repent of her ways and grant him his freedom. On the morning appointed, Violet packed his bag and dropped him off in a nearby slum and bade him a fond farewell. Ten days in Brixton Gaol. Dialogues with burglars and frauds. Needle and thread and sacking for the making of mailbags. A diet of gruel and stews, of meat a little high and loaves of bread a little soggy in the center. On the fourth day Violet paid him a visit. Behind a thick plate of glass he loomed up at her. His face didn't look like his face. His voice didn't sound like his voice. She couldn't make out what he said. He was, it would seem, just a little hysterical. His incarceration ended,

she'd take him home to South Lodge to be properly installed as her senile old mother's respectable guest and soon she'd be hiring an open
carriage in which, "all veils and tocque and parasol" and a chastened
Hueffer beside her in top hat and tails, she'd drive about Kensington,
paying her calls and leaving her cards. Alas, Fordie's martyrdom wasn't
complete. There'd be stations to pass on his way to the cross. Was his
father not German? Did he not descend from the "baronial" Hueffers?
So he and Violet would settle in Germany to claim German citizenship
and obtain the divorce denied them in England and return to London
in triumph as Mr. and Mrs. Hueffer. The trouble was they weren't Mr.
and Mrs. Hueffer at all. Doomed from the start, they had given their
hearts and their hopes to another quixotic adventure. The other trouble was that they nonetheless presented themselves to the papers and
journals as "Mr. and Mrs. Hueffer," to the bitter resentment of Elsie
who took them to court and demolished their claim and their virtue.
It was, of course, the scandal, the shame, in every tabloid in town. Poor
Violet so hungry for marriage, so zealous to keep her good standing in
town, was denied the one and lost the other. In 1916 Fordie would
leave her. Until her death in 1942 she'd list her name in the London
directory as Mrs. Ford Madox Hueffer.

The Barries and Hueffers belonged, to be sure, to an older, more
conventional set, to a generation raised in the seventies and eighties.
But the new sexual freedom their successors would seek to secure and
what they called with it the "modern marriage" was never a total success. There was the case, for one, of poor Hilda Doolittle. When she
became pregnant, husband Richard elected to start an affair with
young Mrs. Patmore, and when the marriage collapsed he elected to
live with a sad-eyed, bohemian beauty, and when, the year after that,
Hilda was pregnant again, Cecil Gray, the composer who was thought
the responsible party, refused to acknowledge his parenthood and
Richard gallantly threatened to have her arrested if she registered the
child in his name and "my only real criticism," Ezra would say, as he
stood at her bedside, "is that this is not my child." No wonder in *Bid
Me to Live*, the *roman à clef* she'd write many years later, Hilda would
sadly regret the new life in London, "the web of sophisticated love-
making," as she bitterly called those *ménages à trois* involving not only
her and Richard and their lovers but Lawrence and Frieda and theirs.
"Funny, in the old days," Hilda would write, "people asked us to a
dance . . . now they simply say, will you sleep with me." There was also

the case of Katherine Mansfield who after arriving in London in 1908 would fall in love with one young man and then proceed to seduce, or be seduced by, his brother, and pregnant thereby would soon appear in the drab Paddington registry office, wearing for the happy occasion a black mourning dress, to marry not one of the brothers but Mr. George Bowden, whose self and bed and hotel she'd abandon the very next morning. In the short unhappy life that followed there would be miscarriage and abortion, gonorrhea and drugs and tuberculosis and "we made love to each other," she would say at one point, "like two wild beasts." "Why don't you make me your mistress," she'd ask a new friend, J. Middleton Murry, but Jack who was shy and sexually inexpert said no, before he surrendered at last and became her partner and later her husband. For a time at Lady Ottoline's Garsington, a weird exchange of hands and hearts seemed impending, the hostess eyeing young Murry and Bertie Russell, her lover, eyeing Katherine. But by this time Bertie, the reformed Quaker, had acquired, it was said, the manners and morals of an alley cat, "Priapus in the shrubbery/ Gaping at the lady in the swing." Offering to share his London apartment with T. S. Eliot, he promptly seduced the poet's young wife of two months and won to the bargain the young husband's gratitude: "I am sure you have done *everything* possible, and handled her in the very best way; better than I."

The new gospel of freedom worked no better for unauthorized babies than for unauthorized lovers. Anthony West, the son of H. G. and Rebecca, was raised to call his mother "Aunty" and the man he knew only as a visiting friend he was raised to call "Uncle" or "Wellsie." Ezra Pound's son by his wife would be given away to Olivia, his mother-in-law, and his daughter by his mistress, Olga Rudge, to a peasant woman they'd happened to meet in the maternity ward. Hilda Doolittle's illegitimate daughter was boarded out in various nurseries or with the mother of a wealthy friend and companion. They called her "Perdita." Angelica Bell, the daughter of Vanessa and Duncan, wouldn't know until she reached seventeen that her father wasn't Clive after all and when still only twenty would be seduced ("appropriately enough, in H. G. Wells's spare bedroom") by the middle-aged man Bunny Garnett who had once been her father's homosexual lover. Bunny in fact had made at her birth an eerie avowal. The day would come, he had said to her parents, when he'd marry their child. Twenty-four years later, at fifty, to Vanessa's distress, he would keep his strange promise. So it wasn't emancipation some Edwardian women would desire in the end but emancipation from emancipation, Florence Farr abandoning the world for Buddhist Ceylon and Katherine Mansfield surrendering her will to the charlatan Gurdjieff and Angelica Bell calling freethinking Bloomsbury a "precarious paradise."

"Telegrams and anger"

And indeed it would come to an end, the old geniality, the old generosity, of Edwardian London. Even before the war and the postwar it would come to an end. What had created the Victorian unity but the old British code of respect: of the young for the old, of women for men, of servants for masters. But the bitter divisions that Forster projected in *Howards End* would become all at once the grimmest realities and by 1914 Wells would be noting "a steady rotting in political life, an increase in loudness, emptiness and violence. . . ." At the turn of the century Cunninghame Graham had regretted the political apathy of the masses in England, their reluctance to rise in revolt against their heartless oppressors. But after 1910 he wouldn't need to regret it. Underpaid, overworked, these wretched men who were pale and unfed and so utterly abject they seemed scarcely human began to behave in a new and intemperate fashion. Bitter and mutinous, they were coming out of their underground caves, these Wellsian Morlocks, and were asking, demanding, minimum wages and eight-hour days and seemed willing to take the most unseemly steps to achieve them. Not enough that they battle the single employer, the hard-faced owner of the mine or the mill. They would now join together to battle whole industries. Not enough that they battle whole industries. They were now ready to battle in one federation the government itself, the nation itself. There was even among them a new militant breed, Syndicalists, Amalgamationists, who were thinking of strikes that would culminate in one great millennial strike and would make them, the workers, the owners and masters and bring to an end the centuries of suffering and servitude.

So in the summer of 1911—the hottest summer in living memory—there were anger and violence all over England. The seamen and firemen of Southampton would call for a general strike and the railwaymen of Liverpool, joined by the tramwaymen, dockers, and carters and by workers in sympathy all over the land, would be striking, and so would the transport workers of London, and casks of butter from Denmark and piles of fruit from the tropics and sides of meat from the Argentine and New Zealand would be rotting away on the docks. Henry James was appalled. No rain for weeks and the thermometer mostly at ninety "and famine threatening strikes (at London and Liverpool docks) with wars and rumors of wars. . . ." But the next year and the next year again there would be more of the same. In 1912 a million workers walked out of the mines and brought the whole country near to collapse, and in 1913 the transport workers of Dublin closed down the docks and the city itself and sympathy strikers in Liverpool threatened to bring that port to a halt. The year after that, embittered by failure, frustration, fatigue, the workers were thinking of even more massive assaults on their masters. They were thinking of forming a Triple Alliance, the railwaymen, miners, and transport workers, and were planning a strike on a national scale for a living wage.

It was hard not to see in all this a class war in the making. In 1911 in Liverpool and in 1913 in Dublin there had been riots and arson and destruction of property and thousands of workers battling the police and hundreds arrested. The will of the Lord, was it, their hunger, their poverty? What cant, what Victorian cant! It was the will of the owners, of the great malefactors of wealth and of power. "Poor but honest?" "The deserving poor?" "The respectable poor?" Convention be damned and respectability too! Poor was poor and hunger was hunger and there was an end on't. As for the masters, they were just as embittered, just as obdurate. "Of course I'm feudal," Mrs. Frankau had said when she urged that the miners be forced back to work. But hers were exactly the sentiments of the owners themselves who were feudal enough and wouldn't relent on the question of wages and hours or even the unions' right to exist. They were almost the sentiments of the Liberal government which was pledged to oppose the aggressions of power and wealth but was also pledged to oppose the unseemly pretensions of the poor and the pushy who were, after all, always with us. "Then your blood be upon your own head," the exasperated prime minister was said to have muttered as he left a meeting with the trade union leaders, and he had Winston Churchill, his Home Office secretary, to see that it was on their head. The fire-eating Winston, who loved an emergency, would mobilize every regiment in the land and send them to the docks and the streets with orders to shoot so that one day in Liverpool two men were killed and two hundred wounded.

But class warfare wasn't the end of it. There was also sex warfare. The same intransigence, the same ugly violence, that invaded the workers' movement also invaded the women's. Before 1912 they hadn't been quiet. They had broken windows, stormed cordons of police, harassed Tories and Liberals alike. But in 1912, when Asquith's government reneged once again on promises it never intended to keep, the Pankhursts would make violence itself a program, a policy. "The argument of the broken window pane," Mrs. Pankhurst would declare that February, "is the most valuable argument in modern politics" and on March 1 she and the faithful would set out to prove it. Taking a taxi to 10 Downing Street, she would pick up a stone and break one of the windows and, just at that moment, in the major streets of the city's West End, hundreds of well-dressed, middle-class women would take hammers out of their muffs or their bags and in one great crescendo shatter the windows of the luxury stores and emporiums. Three days later, when nine thousand police were assembled there to prevent a recurrence, the same numbers of women in Knightsbridge and Kensington were seizing their hammers and wreaking destruction.

The thing was too bad but there was much more to come and that even worse. Christabel who had fled to Paris to escape arrest would make a decision. She was no longer leading a protest. It was a rebellion. She was no longer conducting a political campaign. It was a military campaign, guerrilla warfare in fact. It wasn't just that telegraph wires were cut and street lamps broken and mailboxes stuffed with smoldering waste. She instructed her soldiers to flee from arrest where before they had sought it. What's more, she gave orders for housebreaking tools and inflammable matter to be gathered and soon women in twos carrying cans of petrol and paraffin would be stealthily crossing strange landscapes at night toward shadowy targets of choice, untenanted mansions and halls, places of historical interest, even churches. In 1913 alone property valued at £500,000 was destroyed and in the first seven months of 1914, 107 buildings were put to the torch. Nothing at all was spared the new rancor or rapture. Mr. Lloyd George's country house at Walton Heath? It was bombed. A teahouse at Kew Gardens? It was burned. Cricket pavilions and the grandstands of race courses? They were fired. The delicate greens of the golf links? Scarred with acid they were and "Votes for Women" and "No Votes No Golf" written upon them. "I naturally feel very scalped and disfigured," Henry James said. Miss Mary Wood, who had never heard of the novelist, had entered the Royal Academy with a meat cleaver under her cloak and inflicted grave damage on Sargent's great portrait of him. But another occasion had a darker and more tragic significance. At the Epsom Derby, in His Majesty's presence, Miss Emily Davison, inspired or deranged and thinking a death would bring to an end the subjection of women, rushed out of the crowd and onto the home stretch and under the hooves of the fatal horses. Royalty itself wasn't spared by the furious women. "You Russian Tsar," one of them shouted at the king in His Majesty's Theatre, and at Covent Garden three of them, locked in their boxes, screamed at him through their megaphones not wholly intelligible messages. It was not very womanly and not at all ladylike but then, like the mutinous miners and dockers and railwaymen and indeed like the Bloomsbury women, Vanessa and Virginia ("alarming girls"), and the ardent young women who followed the lead of the rebellious Wells, they had had it with the gospel of respectability. Know your place? Acknowledge your betters? Play the game? They hated their place and they hated their betters and, all things considered, the old game was no longer worth playing.

But then even their betters, the high Tory leaders, didn't think it worth playing. It was March 1914, and with the veto power of the Lords so sadly diminished, the Liberal government was free now to legislate home rule for Ireland. The problem was that it wasn't. Estranged by its bitter defeats, the Tory party was prepared to do what no opposition had done in more than two hundred years. It was prepared to commit treason. With an angry Ulster ("Ulster will fight and Ulster will be right") arming and mobilizing and ready to resist to a Protestant death any government effort to join it with Catholic Ireland, the Conservative leaders were contriving to aid and abet it and to frustrate by craft and conspiracy the will of a legitimate government. Bonar Law, their new chieftain, was secretly meeting with Sir Henry Wilson who, as head of the War Office and commander-in-chief of the army, was betraying the government he had promised to serve, and both were in touch with Sir Edward Carson who stood at the head of the Ulster rebellion and its "provisional government." In 1912

Sir Edward had formed the Irish Covenant which had pledged "all means which may be found necessary to defeat the present conspiracy to set up a Home Rule Parliament in Ireland." Now in 1914 and in England itself, Lord Milner was forming a British Covenant promising action "falling short of violence or active rebellion, or at least not beginning with it." The result was predictable. When the government ordered the army in Ireland to move to the north, the unthinkable happened, the unspeakable. Committing what amounted to mutiny, the generals and their officers resigned their commissions or threatened to do so and refused in short to obey. With civil war pending both in Ireland and England, the government was, or chose to be, helpless. The country was no longer run by the party in power but by the opposition party with the army behind it.

The bitterness was inevitably fierce. In the good old days before the anger and telegrams, all had been sweetness and light. When in the nineties Herbert Asquith and the beautiful Margot Tennant had been joined in sweet matrimony, the ceremony had been attended not only by two onetime Liberal prime ministers but by Arthur Balfour, the future Conservative prime minister, and Margot in fact would later beg Balfour to persuade her father to increase Herbert's income so he wouldn't have to resign from the Liberal bench. Why, it wasn't unusual for these heads of the two major parties, after even the most violent debates in the House, to leave arm in arm and smiling and laughing. Happy, moneyed, successful, they were members alike of the same ruling class and were interested alike in preserving the rights of the same ruling class. The House of Commons was after all but "the best club in London" and politics was, it was said, but "a drawing-room game, almost a drawing-room comedy." Of course they debated ideas and creeds, did the Tories and Liberals, but it wouldn't disturb their *entente cordiale*. After 1909, however, the weather turned round. New creeds and conditions came into play and soon all was ashes and acid. In 1910 and the time of the great constitutional crisis, Tories like the Earl of Balcarres were attacking the Liberals with upper-class rancor and rage, sneering at Asquith's "middle-class sentiment" and at little Lloyd George "who isn't educated" and at Charlie Masterman who had "the aspect of a seedy biblewoman and a cockney accent which throbs in your ear." What's more, they were attacking each other with even more rancor and rage, those who had voted against the government reviling those renegade Lords who had voted for it. At the Carlton Club they were ready to greet them with shouts of "Judas!" and "Traitor!" and, "boiling with rage," Lady Halsbury was refusing to shake the hand of Lord Lansdowne and the *Globe* was expressing the fervent desire that no one at all would take men of his kind by the hand, that "their friends [would] disown them [and] their clubs expel them. . . ." It was the same four years later when the issue of Irish Home Rule was in question. Lady Londonderry was quite unforgiving. She declined to enter those houses that opened their doors to Home Rulers. Lord Curzon was also quite unforgiving. He declined to invite the PM and his wife and their daughter to the splendid ball he was giving. Margot was hurt to the quick, but his lordship was adamant. It "would be impolitic," he told his tearful informant, to invite "the wife and daughter of the head of a Government to which the majority of my friends are inflexibly opposed."

"Now the leaves are falling fast . . ."

It was in art and letters as in society and politics. The same anger and truculence that entered with the strikers and suffragists and the Lords and the Ulstermen to disrupt and embitter the political life of the city also entered to disrupt and embitter its artistic life. It wasn't quite unexpected, perhaps, the rage and the outrage of the Academicians at the first postimpressionist show, of old dinosaurians like Sir William Richmond who declared that this P.I. business was "all *Rot, clear Rot*" and that Roger Fry was at the head of a bunch of wild asses, "exactly his right place." But what of the art critic Robert Ross who was no dinosaurian and had lived and survived the deplorable nineties and befriended and defended poor Oscar Wilde and could still find it possible, nevertheless, to denounce Matisse as a madman and Van Gogh as "a typical matoid and degenerate" and the whole Grafton show as of no interest at all "except to the student of pathology"? And what of the painters themselves who had stood in their day at the barricades and fought the good fight against the pomp and the prejudice

and were wincing now in the teeth of the new wind of change? Walter
Sickert did his best to be generous, to make do with a situation that
looked more and more like a natural disaster for him and the impressionist cause. He was an old friend of Fry's and though he disliked Van
Gogh and considered Picasso "a *faux fauve*" and despised Matisse who
was full, he said, of "the worst art-school tricks," he respected Cézanne
and was seeing more and more to admire in Gauguin, in addition to
which, as he saw it, the sound and the fury of Roger's big show didn't
quite signify nothing. Whatever brought the brutes to the park to look
at the animals couldn't be utterly worthless: "John Bull and his lady,
who love a joke, walk up, and learn a few things, some of which have
been known in Europe for a decade and some for a quarter of a century." Indeed he took to assuming a "blasé, 'known-them-all-years-
ago' " attitude. For though he tried hard "to smile on all that smile,
and show/ There is a comfortable kind of old scarecrow," he couldn't
quite manage it. He began to discredit those "meaningless patterns"
and to say harsh things about Epstein's figures, and the more Roger
made of Cézanne, the more Walter found in Cézanne to disgust him.
Cézanne indeed! What was the man after all but "a curious and pathetic by-product of the Impressionist group"? Poor Sickert, it was all
very sad. Once the darling of the young and advanced, now set aside as
a stodgy old senator. "Now the leaves are falling fast,/ Nurses' flowers
will not last;/ Nurses to the graves are gone,/ But the prams go rolling
on."

Sickert at least had tried to be civil and civilized, but Roger's old
friends of the once New English Art Club wouldn't even try. Would
Will Rothenstein join him, Roger would ask, in a second postimpressionist show that would also exhibit new English artists of every degree? No, my dear sir, he would not. Annoyed by his sudden eclipse as
doyen of the arts and offended by Fry who could be willful and arrogant ("The poor things lose their heads altogether") and in any case
hating the new modernist business, Rothenstein would have nothing to
do with it. ("Roi je ne suis; prince je ne daigne.") As for Tonks who
was dour and tendentious, he too would have nothing to do with it
and threatened to resign from the Slade if they didn't stop talking up
cubism ("It is killing me," he groaned), and it must have been hard,
right enough, that his New English Art Club once denounced as advanced should now be denounced as defunct. He circulated caricatures
of Roger and Clive, Roger as Christ, his hair flying wild and his mouth

open wide, proclaiming the religion of "Cézannah," and Clive standing by, his St. Paul, in silly attendance. But then the Bloomsbury people responded no better, scarcely flocked to the sides of their Roger, their Duncan, their Clive, their Vanessa. They were writers and thinkers and were miffed that the painters had stolen their thunder. "Gauguin and Van Gogh were too much for me," said E. Morgan Forster. "I don't think I ever saw anything so stupid . . . ," declared Bertie Russell. And Virginia and Lytton? "Now that Clive is in the van of aesthetic opinion," Virginia remarked, "I hear a great deal about pictures. I don't think them so good as books." She certainly didn't think much of Roger's selection. "A modest sample set of painters," she coolly observed. Lytton didn't think much of them either. Enamored of Lamb and loyal therefore to the tribe of Augustus, he dismissed Fry's collection as "coagulations of distressing oddments." As for the English contingent, Vanessa, he said, was pathetic and Duncan a fish out of water and Wyndham Lewis unspeakably dreary. Besides, he was jealous of Roger, "a most shifty and wormy character," and of Clive, the abominable Clive, whose loud and arrogant voice as he went about lecturing people at the second exhibit was altogether too bad. "I had to disown him," Lytton told Lady Ott.

It was the same with the old camaraderie that had once united, for all of their differences, the Jameses and Conrads, the Hueffers and Wellses and Garnetts. Flushed with his failures and in fact very nearly demented, Hueffer would quarrel with all of them and in novels like *The Simple Life Limited* and *The New Humpty Dumpty,* would ridicule everybody who had somehow aroused his distemper. In the character of Pett, "the little cockney" who considers himself "the high priest of the world," he'd ridicule Wells, and in the character of "Mr. Parmont, the London critic" who attacks the establishment but is seen about London in "a white stand-up collar," he'd ridicule Garnett, and in the character of Parmont's protégé, the novelist Simon Bransdon, who had changed his name from Simeon Brandetski and, "convinced he led a dog's life," is nonetheless "one of the laziest men that ever breathed," he'd ridicule Conrad himself, who was often disabled by gout and depression, but lazy? James had esteemed the earlier Conrad but not the Edwardian one, the Conrad of *Nostromo, The Secret Agent,* and *Under Western Eyes,* calling them "wastes of desolation" and declining to join Mrs. Wharton in a *Festschrift* for him. In "The Younger Generation," his majestic assessment of the work of his juniors, he'd do less than

justice to his "poor dear J.C.," setting the man who was now in his
fifties and by this time himself an established *cher maître* beside
striplings like Walpole and Lawrence. *Chance* was *done,* no doubt
about that, James had grandly conceded, but was it not, perhaps, just a
touch *over*done? Conrad was hurt. "This," he would say, "was the *only*
time a criticism affected me painfully." But then Conrad himself was
by this time detaching himself from his old friends and companions.
Poor brain-damaged Hueffer? "He's a megalomaniac who imagines
that he is managing the Universe." Edward Garnett who had praised
Under Western Eyes but had mentioned in passing what he felt was the
novel's hatred of Russia? "You are so russianized, my dear, that you
don't know the truth when you see it—unless it smells of cabbage-
soup. . . ." Conrad, like James, had thought highly of Wells, had expected, like James, his triumphant artistic emergence, had dedicated
The Secret Agent to him, "The Biographer of Kipps and/ The Historian
of the Ages to Come." But no artist, alas, H.G. was, it seemed, a mere
propagandist who wouldn't let art "contain his convictions" and "the
difference between us, Wells," he would tell him, is that "you don't care
for humanity but think they are to be improved. I love humanity but
know they are not!"

Conrad a lover of humanity? Perhaps. But by this time, in any
case, H.G. himself would be divesting himself of his Edwardian attachments. Like Hueffer exacerbated by failure, by the collapse of his Fabian
adventure, the chagrin of his aching affair with Miss Reeves and, hard
upon that, the scandal of *Ann Veronica,* he'd become, like Hueffer, the
Ishmaelite and would raise his hand against friends and detractors
alike. Like Hueffer in *The Simple Life Limited,* he'd deride in *Ann
Veronica* the rustic school of Fabian socialists who keep a shop for
fruitarians and debate at some length whether Shaw should go into
Parliament which, naturally enough, "brought them to vegetarianism
and teetotalism." In *The New Machiavelli* he'd turn on the Webbs
whom he'd denominate "prigs at play," and "of all the damned things
that ever were damned," as he'd say, "your damned, shirking, temperate,
sham-efficient, self-satisfied, respectable, make-believe, Fabian-spirited
Young Liberal is the utterly damnedest." The literary establishment
would be next. Not for him the Academic Committee of the Royal Society of Literature which Gosse and James were bidding him join. "I
would rather," he'd tell the affectionate James, "be outside the Academic
Committee with Hall Caine, than in it with you and Gosse and Gilbert

Murray and Shaw." In point of fact he was already building a bomb, was already writing the papers he'd publish in 1915 as *Boon,* his sardonic assault on the great lords of letters in London: on Gosse, that "almost malignantly ambitious organizing energy," on Conrad whom America preferred to her own Stephen Crane for, "you see, she can tell Conrad 'writes.' It shows."

But, most tellingly of all, on the ineffable James who, like Conrad, had been urging him for years to write novels their way, not his way. Lord knows, he had wanted to write them their way, not his way. But now, he decided, it was his way he wanted to write. A scenario in art was not less obnoxious to him than a scenario in life or in politics and he "was disposed," as he said, "to regard a novel as about as much an art form as a marketplace or a boulevard." So in *Boon* he'd justify his way, the way of the journalist who wanted to change things, and ridicule James's, the way of the artist who didn't want changes at all. "He doesn't find things out. He doesn't even seem to want to find things out. You can see that in him; he is eager to accept things—elaborately." For what in effect was the Jamesian novel, said Wells, but much ado about nothing? "It is a magnificent but painful hippopotamus resolved at any cost, even at the cost of its dignity, upon picking up a pea. . . . Most things, it insists, are beyond it, but it can, . . . with an artistic singleness of mind, pick up that pea." "Ought there to be such a thing as a literary artist?" asks one of his characters. "Ought there in fact to be Henry James?" asks another. James, poor soul, was distressed. He had loved H.G. and admired him, his verve and vitality, his "impossible cheek." In "The Younger Generation," it's true, he had done to H.G. just what he'd done to J.C., had not only lumped him with untested beginners fifteen years younger but had put him down as a sad disappointment, as an awful warning of the perils and penalties of artistic indifference. Nonetheless the copy of *Boon* Wells left in the porter's box at his West End club was more impossibly cheeky than the Master could bear. H.G. was not, it would seem, to the manner born. One of the new literary plutocrats, he tended to be "low" on occasion, a bit of a Magwitch, and cared not a jot for custom and ceremony.

It was the spirit of the age. A new generation of angry young people was out of all patience with the old high Victorian good manners. But though there'd be freedom as never before, freedom from form and convention as never before, there'd also be rudeness as never before, rancor as never before, blasting and brawling and bombardiering as never before. Pity indeed the poor stranger unwary enough to pass through the Bloomsbury gates on a Thursday at 29 Fitzroy Square. Her hand would be taken all right but by hosts who made it a point not to smile. She would be greeted and welcomed all right but with a studied gaucherie of manner, "an expression of blazing defiance" or "a few carefully chosen banalities," that was meant to demoralize. And if she was truly unfortunate, she was likely to become, before the evening was over, the butt of the company's "merciless chaff." "Of course, you Miss Cole are always dressed so exquisitely. You look so original, so like a sea shell. There is something so refined about you coming in among our muddy boots and pipe smoke, dressed in your exquisite creations." This from the lips of the lovely but wantonly wicked Virginia. At which point Clive himself might join in the fun— "Why is it you dislike me so, Miss Cole?"—until poor Miss Cole, by this time the unwitting center of everyone's eyes, was reduced to a shambles of tears and distress. No, they didn't suffer fools gladly, these Bloomsbury people, the stately Vanessa whose silence was always uncompromising, the insolent Keynes whose rudeness was said to be freezing and terrible, the venomous Strachey whose wit was incisive and his sallies insulting and who liked with his baleful eyes and high-pitched voice to play Mephistopheles.

But then they didn't suffer one another more gladly. Clive, it appeared, was widely despised and not the least by his friends. Virginia would refer to his "bawling voice," Leonard to "his fat little mind," and Lytton with disgust to the "fat little hand" he saw stroking a statue in the Grafton Gallery. Indeed they were ruthless, malicious, Leonard and Lytton. In *The Wise Virgins* Leonard would describe Clive as "one of those men so small mentally and morally that anything which took place in his little mind . . . seemed to him to be one of the great convulsions of nature." And the unsparing Lytton? "Clive presents a fearful study in decomposing psychology," he'd be writing his brother. "Fallen into fatness and a fermenting self-assurance," the man was "a corpse puffed up with worms and gases." Even Forster, dear man though he was, wasn't spared their contempt. "He is limp and damp," Virginia observed, "and milder than the breath of a cow." "He's a mediocre man," Lytton said more unkindly, "—and knows it . . . and in the meantime he's treated rudely by waiters and is not really admired even by middle-class dowagers." Lytton may have felt from the first an aversion for Keynes. "Keynes sits," he could say, "like a decayed and amorous spider. . . ." But after Maynard stole Duncan away from him, there'd be no doubt whatsoever about it and he'd subtly and secretly make Keynes's life miserable, spreading malice against him and calling him loveless and lustful and a "safety-bicycle with genitals." But then Lytton himself was not always adored. One of Woolf's undergraduate friends called Strachey and Co. "the most offensive people I have ever met" and Bertie Russell thought "loathing for him quite pardonable. . . ."

No wonder Bloomsbury would come to be feared and detested. No one was safe from its "genial brutality." Will Rothenstein was taken aback. He was of the opinion, he announced at a dinner, that poetry, though regarded by many as a vague, highfalutin art form, was the clearest expression of man's thoughts and ideas. Who was he, Strachey cried out in his peevish falsetto, to meddle with matters that were none of his business? Katherine Mansfield was wounded. In a game they were playing one night after dinner, she was compared to "some rather exotic scent such as stephanotis or patchouli, and although her name was not mentioned, we all knew and she knew who was meant. It was dreadful." Katherine would have loved to have entered this circle of beautiful people but she may have been just a little afraid of them. It wasn't for nothing that she or Murry or both would call them the "Woolves." "They profess to live by feeling," she'd write, "but why then do they never give a sign of it—and why do they do their very best to ridicule feeling in others? It is all poisonous." Not even Lytton who adored Lady Ott could spare her the edge of his satire. "Lady Omega Muddle," he called her and cruelly described her as "infinitely antique, racked in every joint, hobbling through the buttercups," and though his Bloomsbury friends enjoyed to the full her lavish attentions, they reacted no differently and "it's beastly of them," it was said, "to enjoy Ottoline's kindnesses and then laugh at her."

Well, this may have been Bloomsbury's way but it wasn't just Bloomsbury's. "To be devastatingly witty . . . and abominably rude; to pretend not to understand a name, a simple remark or a line of argument . . . to lambast . . . the bourgeois habits of the day . . .": all this, according to one observer, was the Edwardian way. It was Katherine's way for that matter and Middleton Murry's and the way of the *New Age* people in general. When the nation mourned the death of its Rupert Brooke, Orage wasn't one to let sentiment stand in the way of his judgment. "Dead," he wrote in his weekly, "he is as bad a poet as he was alive." When Murry devastated the Georgian poets in a merciless article and helped bring to an end their short-term celebrity, "You have really wiped the floor with them . . . ," Katherine shrieked. "Oh with what arrows, to spear those sparrows, to their very marrows!" She certainly gave no quarter to the Forster of *Howards End*. He was "a rare fine hand" at warming the teapot, she said. "Feel this teapot. Is it not beautifully warm? Yes, but there ain't going to be no tea." To be sure, they were just as hard on each other, the Orages and Murrys. They were old friends. Katherine's and Murry's first work had been printed under their auspices. No matter. When they started *Rhythm*, their pretentious and immature little journal, Orage and Beatrice devoted a full page to attacking their work and "Mediocrity," Beatrice announced, "is not a product to treat with indifference, but to destroy wherever possible. . . ." In one of his numbers, Murry called James Stephens a greater poet than Milton, nay, one of "the greatest poets the world has ever known." This was more than Frank Harris could stand. He rushed into Dan Rider's bookshop off St. Martin's Lane and loudly rebuked the rash boy who promptly burst into tears and fled from the room with Katherine after him, crying "Oh, he'll kill himself," and Harris left behind all agape and crying "Good God!" Violence itself wasn't out of the question at times. The floor at the Orages' was once littered with beads. Katherine and Beatrice had assaulted each other with necklaces. Gaudier once rushed into the office of *Rhythm* demanding instant payment for something or other and threatening physical force. He was as good as his word. He tore two drawings from the wall and slapped the terrified editor's face.

But for swashbuckling fury and frenzy there was no one in London like Pound and Lewis and Hulme and, as Hueffer described them, their "explosive-mouthed gang of scarce-breeched filibusterers." "What's the good of being an island," young Percy Lewis would say, "if you are not a *volcanic* island." And volcanic he was for a fact and cantankerous and quarrelsome. Committed to Picasso and cubism and founding for the cause a Rebel Art Center at 36 Great Ormond Street, Percy squabbled and broke in the end with just about everyone. With Sickert and impressionism of course but also with Gauguin and postimpressionism and with Marinetti and futurism ("accelerated impressionism") and, it goes without saying, with Fry and his Bloomsbury bunch, with "this family party of strayed and Dissenting Aesthetes," whom he'd scorn for their dilettante ways and their lifeless decoctions. By 1914 he'd come into his own. Forming with Pound and Gaudier a gang they thought of as Vorticists, he wrote, managed and published the first of two volumes of a large, angry, "puce-colored monster" called BLAST. BLAST, DAMN OR CURSE, it declared in bold capital letters, ENGLAND and ITS CLIMATE FOR ITS SINS AND INFECTIONS and OH BLAST FRANCE and SENTIMENTAL GALLIC GUSH. Blast also WILD NATURE CRANK and "bowing the knee to wild Mother Nature" and CURSE WITH EXPLETIVE OF WHIRLWIND THE BRITANNIC AESTHETE and damn STYLISM and FUTURISM and damn GYPSY KINGS and ESPADAS. BLAST above all the British establishment in its myriad forms: Tonks and the Bishop of London, St. Loe Strachey and Sidney Webb, Elgar and Galsworthy and "socialist-playwright." BLESS on the other hand England's MACHINES. Bless the HAIRDRESSER who "attacks Mother Nature for a small fee." Bless also, though for reasons not clear, the Pope and Cunninghame Graham, James Joyce and Granville Barker, Frank Harris, Castor Oil, and Mrs. Belloc Lowndes.

They were a ruthless, uncompromising lot, Lewis and company. They had a rage for some order or other no doubt, but for the moment the accent was more on the rage than the order. Lewis promised the editor of the *Times Literary Supplement* a thorough horsewhipping if he dared to let Hueffer, who was now obsolescent, review one of his books. One night in a bar Augustus John heaped drunken abuse on Lewis's person. If this ever happened again, he informed John in writing, he would certainly break his Borrovian head. There was this concert performance at the Doré put on by the great Marinetti and who should turn up to heckle and threaten him but Percy and friends, Hulme and Gaudier and Epstein along with a cousin of Wadsworth the painter who was, as it happened, "very muscular and forcible." Pound wasn't there for the occasion but, "a born revolutionary" as Percy would call him, he was eager to enter the great wars of art and "where he detected the slightest hint of a fractious disposition, expressing itself in verse or pigment, he became delirious." Good poetry was doubtless important to him but not, it would seem, more important than victory. He offered Harriet Monroe and *Poetry (Chicago)* six poems by Rabindaranath Tagore and, as he told her by way of a clincher, "nobody else will have *any*." One Thursday evening at 10 Church Walk where he entertained his young imagist friends and where the exchanges were flippant and the tropes cabalistic, a young man had the temerity to read aloud one of his poems. He was to regret it. There followed a silence. "Nearly as bad as Milton," somebody drawled. Someone else sniggered. On occasions like these, it was said, Ezra would assume a half-recumbent position with his eyes "at the cat-like angle, glittering out of a slit."

And in fact he was almost as captious as Percy himself in his battles against what he called "the arthritic milieu" that controlled things in London. "My one present consolation," he could say of the writing of *Patria Mia*, "is that I am making six enemies per paragraph." At the performance of a Barrie one-acter, he and Hueffer made a point of groaning so loud "as to be heard all through the theatre." He was even said to have challenged a reviewer of the *Times* to a duel on the unassailable grounds—"I cannot imagine any better reason," said poor fatuous Hueffer—that the person had expressed too high an opinion of Milton. The truth of this story may well be uncertain. It was Hueffer's. But it's certain that Ezra Pound, being of sound mind and body, did throw down the gauntlet to Lascelles Abercrombie, the eminent Georgian, who, "A lover of the meadows and the woods,/ And mountains; and of all that we behold/ From this green earth," had been advising young poets to study their Wordsworth. Dropping one evening by 10 Church Walk, John Cournos found Ezra typing a letter. "Dear Mr. Abercrombie: Stupidity carried beyond a certain point . . . I hereby challenge you . . . My seconds will . . ." But Mr. Abercrombie, a tiny bespectacled person, was equal to the occasion. "Knowing that Nature never did betray/ The heart that loved her" and that he was for that matter entitled to choose his own weapons, he boldly accepted the challenge. Let us bombard each other, he said, with the unsold copies of our books. Unhappy Hueffer, so fond and so foolish, and now that he'd lost the *English Review* a king uncrowned, would know the disillusion of Lear or perhaps more exactly an unfrocked priest, the disillusion of Falstaff. Penniless now and disheartened and betrayed as he thought by the old guard of London, he would throw in his lot with Lewis and Pound and the young Janizaries who were out to destroy the old palace guard and their works and their ways. But though he was with them Hueffer was never quite of them and, eyeless in Gaza, would be treated with scorn and contumely. "Poor fat Ford," Pound would sadly allude to him. "How fat you are!" the young painter Nevinson would tell him directly. "*Tu sais, tu es foûtu*," Percy Lewis would speak in his ear. "*Foûtu!* Finished! Exploded! Done for! Blasted in fact!"

To be sure, they were just as hard on one another, these Vorticist people, as they were on their foes, and the time was to come when they'd be merrily blasting and bombardiering each other. Three buccaneers were all very well but three buccaneers on one poop deck? Besides, the vicious and heartless attack—"eye-gouging," Ezra Pound called it—was now a matter of policy, an essential part of the anti-Victorian program. It proved you were serious, it proved you meant business. Lewis, who thought of himself as the "Enemy," called Eliot a "pseudoist" and Pound a "revolutionary simpleton," but Eliot himself was not offended. "At no time," he said, "do I remember his wit as having any savor of malice." The hysterical Gaudier did threaten at Hueffer's, it's true, to give Bomberg the painter a punch on the jaw, and when Pound commenced to expand on the merits of Epstein's *Rock Drill* the sculptor turned on the poet and "Shut up," he shouted, "you understand nothing." No problem, however. What were these rages, these ructions, but signs of a total commitment to art? Percy wasn't happy with Hulme who was falling under the spell of the egregious Epstein and, what was worse, was making eyes at Miss Lechmere who was Percy's dear friend and the backer in fact of his Rebel Art Center. As for Hulme, he wasn't happy with Pound who was claiming as his what wasn't. His imagist theories, for example, and F. S. Flint's symbolist ones. How long, the dangerous Hulme was asked, how long would he tolerate the impossible presence and posture of Pound? He already knew, he replied, exactly when he'd have to kick the fellow downstairs. Lucky for Ezra that time never came, but it did come, alas, for poor Percy Lewis. "Remember," he roared at Miss Lechmere at a table in an ABC restaurant, "Hulme is Epstein and Epstein is Hulme," and rising from the table—I will have to kill him, he said—he rushed out of the restaurant and down Piccadilly and then into Frith Street with the frantic Miss Lechmere behind him crying "Please don't kill him, please don't." She needn't have worried. When he climbed the stairs and entered the room and went for Hulme's throat, he was instantly seized by the burly philosopher and dragged down the stairs and hung upside down on the tall iron railings of Soho Square. So much for London, for Edwardian London. So much for the Edwardian revival. So much for the brave new frankness and freedom and for the *entente cordiale* that had made the great city a lively republic of letters.

Small wonder there were wars and rumors of wars. After a century of selfish individualism, after decades of vulgar and decadent peace, the West, the savants were saying, was a sick civilization, sick, sinking, near done-for, and nothing remained to save its poor carcass from a fatal decay but a war, a "remedial" war. For Marinetti, war was "the only health-giver of the world." For the intelligentsia of Europe— Ortega, Alain-Fournier, Henri de Montherlant—it was a culture's last chance for redemption. As for England, it wasn't just Hudson who longed for a war as "the only remedy for the present disease." There was Kipling who thought that a sacrificial war was the only hope of a national regeneration and William Archer, not Shaw's William Archer but another, who argued in *The Great Analysis* of 1911 that for the establishment of a far better world some "great catastrophe" would have to take place and "since I love England as much as I detest her present lethargy," said Wells, even he would be praying, with the hero of *The New Machiavelli*, "for a chastening war." Nor were these the delusions of elderly lunatics. In his celebrated sonnets of 1914, Rupert Brooke would welcome the war as a chance to replenish the national spirit. "THIS WAR IS A GREAT REMEDY," Gaudier would be writing insanely from France where a short time later—no remedy for him—he'd be killed at the front. Percy Lewis was also convinced it would be a great remedy, would "shatter the visible world to bits, and build it nearer to the heart's desire." He was soon disabused of his faith in the war's therapeutic potential, however. He was sent to the front. Shaw was heartbroken of course. It confirmed his suspicions, this remedial war, that for thirty years he had labored in vain for a better world order. He bravely condemned the war and its makers and received for his pains the contempt of his peers. Henry James, whose political intelligence may well have been zero, was ashamed and embarrassed and "the huge performing frivolity of G.B.S. on our actual tragic stage affects me," he said, "as an indecency beyond all forgiving." He was quick, on the other hand, to lavish his praise on the "Splendid Rupert" and his banal but beloved war sonnets and couldn't say enough for our friends and allies, the starving French workers, "when one thinks what wonderful little persons they mostly are." Eliot, it seems, would be right about James. His was indeed "a mind so fine that no idea could violate it."

"Rome fell. Babylon fell.
Hindhead's turn will come."

Meanwhile there was Paris, beautiful, enchanting Paris, with its art and adultery, its concerts and courtesans, its cafés and cabarets! *La belle époque* at its height! Was London really the great beating heart of the universe? There were those who had been to Paris in France and didn't quite think so. The foreigner Conrad, for example, and Hueffer who fancied himself as more European than English. One night at the Empire, hearing Englishmen laugh at those coarse lower-middle-class jokes, one of them leaned over to the other and "Doesn't one feel lonely in this beastly country!" he said. For the Victorians, of course, it hadn't been beastly at all. Wasn't Paris a sink of iniquity, a den of decay and debauchery? Besides, what was there to see beyond English shores, what was there to know? Wordsworth and Tennyson, Browning and Arnold, Scott, Dickens, and Thackeray. Was there anything else? But for the poets and painters of the nineties and increasingly thereafter for enlightened Edwardians there *was* something else. For Arthur Symons, for one, who had discovered the joys of the Parisian café and would like to see London adopt it "and so redeem England from the disgrace of being the only country where men have to drink like cattle, standing." For Clive Bell, for another, who for a year had observed the new art of the glorious city and had studied to live in a hotel without bath and to eat at the Chat Blanc and to sit at the marble-topped tables of the Café du Dome and to speak not Strachey's classical French but the French of the streets, and after discovering Cézannes and Matisses had returned to a London that could still be amazed, good heavens, by Monets and Manets. For Arnold Bennett, for still another, whose five years in Paris had spoiled him, he thought, for the *longueurs* of London, for what could be said for a city whose only response to the wondrous new painting was laughter or rage and whose only response to a book like *The New Machiavelli* was the ludicrous chatter and gossip of its *soi-disant* pundits and whose dilettanti of letters were so obsessed with their Jameses and Conrads that they had no idea at all what "a bit of sheer luck for England" a writer like Wells really was. This wasn't the way things were managed in Paris. And it wasn't just Symons and Bennett and Bell. Others had crossed the Channel and had noted the difference: not just those thousands who had happened on du Maurier's *Trilby* or Puccini's *Bohème* and had fallen in love with a new and improved Latin Quarter but serious seekers like Percy Lewis and Norman Douglas, Roger Fry, Lytton Strachey, and Duncan Grant. Augustus John had gone there in 1905 with a wife, a mistress, a dog and four children and "I think," he had written from Montparnasse, "I shall be a supernaturalist in Paris and in London a naturalist," and Somerset Maugham, the year before that, had gone over to dine and carouse with rowdy expatriates like Gerald Kelly the painter and Aleister Crowley, the sexual evangelist, and "poor dear old London," as Hueffer would put it after the war, what was it now but "a Paris without effervescence"?

Paris wasn't, to be sure, for everyone. By 1909 passionate Francophiles like Clive and Vanessa were thinking of moving to Paris (London, said Clive, had "no aesthetic intention"), but Virginia, no Francophile, was less than encouraging, and "To go from London to Paris," she may have believed, with Camilla in Leonard's *Wise Virgins,* "is like going from the twentieth century, which is alive, straight into the nineteenth, which is dead," and all things considered, she seems to have thought, "I'd rather live in Peckham," and so for that matter, for all he loved France, would Strachey himself and "I think I should burst into tears," he'd be saying, "if I woke up and found myself on the Pont Neuf." But then Virginia and Lytton were nothing at all if they weren't perverse and after 1910 all the young lions of London, it seemed, were commuting to Paris. Aldington would go there with Pound and H.D. and it was love at first sight, and as a mere undergraduate Murry had gone there to talk the night through at the Deux Magots, fall under the spell of a Scottish *Fauviste,* and bring back to the boglands of London, as the founder of *Rhythm,* the Promethean fires of Montparnasse. And indeed the great exodus that was now but a trickle would soon become, when the great war was over, a flood. Then they'd go not for weeks but for years, Hueffer and Pound and Lawrence and Douglas and Aldington and a host of others, and the ashen and acrid London of the twenties and thirties would then be upon us and what Lawrence Durrell would call "the black death" of England. On June 28, 1914, Hueffer stood on the edge of the curb in Piccadilly Circus and looked all about him. How splendid the day was! The sky above the Fountain was high and bright, and the flowers the flower girls had brought made a mountain of color and the Season, with a week still remaining, was still at its height. He felt free, Hueffer said. It was over. Finished. "Tout fini." He had done all he could, could do no more. He didn't know it, he said, but he was taking his last look at London—"our London/ my London, your London"—as a Londoner.

Notes

Note: The letter "q" in a citation indicates a quotation from the page referred to; the letter "n" indicates the source is a footnote on the page referred to.

Pp. 3–6. On James and Queen Victoria's death and funeral, see Leon Edel, *Henry James, The Master: 1901–1916*, V (New York, 1978), 86ff (hereafter Edel, *James*); see also Leon Edel, ed., *Henry James, Letters*, IV, 1895–1916 (Cambridge, Mass., 1984), 180, 184 (hereafter James, *Letters*). "As well a well-wrought urn . . .": Donne, "The Canonization." "Falling towers . . .": Eliot, "The Waste Land."

Pp. 9–10. "Ah, London . . .": Leon Edel and Lyall H. Powers, eds., *The Complete Notebooks of Henry James* (New York, 1987), 218 (hereafter James, *Notebooks*). ". . . like swallows went": Yeats, "Coole Park, 1929." ". . . no Londoner": Ernest Rhys, *Everyman Remembers* (New York, 1931), 314. ". . . that of a Londoner": Ernest Rhys, *Letters from Limbo* (London, 1936), 140. ". . . a Londoner afterward": Rhys, *Everyman Remembers*, 309–310. "dust and smoke": *ibid.,* 257. ". . . smoke of the underground": Richard Aldington, *Life for Life's Sake* (New York, 1941), 58. ". . . like a stable": Rhys, *Everyman Remembers,* 229. ". . . the vast city": D. H. Lawrence, *The White Peacock* [1911] (New York, 1950), 326. "bewildering Babylon": James, *Letters,* 279. ". . . unexplored wilderness": Gerard Jean-Aubry, *The Sea Dreamer: Joseph Conrad* (New York, 1957), 78q.

Pp. 11–12. "enthusiastic pedestrians": Joseph Conrad, *Chance* [1913] (New York, 1957), 32. ". . . behaving naturally": Geoffrey Keynes, ed., *Letters of Rupert Brooke* (London, 1968), 164 (hereafter Brooke, *Letters*). taking the train to Purley: Harry T. Moore, *The Priest of Love: A Life of D. H. Lawrence* (New York, 1981), 131. "the windy downs": Douglas Goldring, *Trained for Genius: The Life and Writings of Ford Madox Ford* (New York, 1949), 121. . . . outside city limits: William Rothenstein, *Men and Memories* (New York, 1932), 100. ". . . by the rural Pan": Matthew Arnold, "Lines Written in Kensington Gardens." "on solid, rural earth": Conrad, *Chance,* 45. the footpaths of England: *ibid.,* 32. ". . . if not restrained": *ibid.,* 34. "its deer parks and downland . . .": H. G. Wells, *The History of Mr. Polly* [1910] (Boston, 1960), 21. ". . . of their lives": *ibid.,* 22. "love of the earth": E. M. Forster, *Howards End* [1910] (New York, 1955), 119. ". . . led Jefferies to write them . . .": *ibid.,* 120.

Pp. 12–15. "I am partial to fisher-folk": Augustus John, *Chiaroscuro: Fragments of an Autobiography* (New York, 1952), 70–71. "a short, dark man . . .": David Garnett, *The Golden Echo* (New York, 1954), 121. . . . designs on his body?: David Garnett, *Great Friends* (New York, 1980), 62; see also Richard Stonesifer, *W. H. Davies: A Critical Biography* (London, 1963), 120. "He went along country roads . . .": Wells, *Mr. Polly,* 175. "and dusty tramp. . . .": *ibid.,* 174. . . . to study the

Romany life: Michael Holroyd, *Augustus John: A Biography* (New York, 1975), 299.
". . . outlast pyramids": *ibid.*, 328q. there were difficulties: *ibid.*, 295. there was this
horse . . . : *ibid.*, 303. "I was given a crust of bread . . .": Lady Ottoline Morrell,
Memoirs: A Study in Friendship, 1873–1915, Robert Gathorne-Hardy, ed. (New
York, 1964), 154 (hereafter Lady Ottoline, *Memoirs*). The trip would not be a total
disaster: P. N. Furbank, *E. M. Forster, A Life* (New York, 1977) I, 154ff.
Toad . . . his gypsy caravan: Kenneth Grahame, *The Wind in The Willows* [1908]
(New York, 1969), 45ff. ". . . the primitive life": *ibid.*, 49. ". . . with carts for ever":
ibid., 53. ". . . a Nomad tribe": Lady Ottoline, *Memoirs*, 128. "like a Renaissance
prince": Richard Shone, *Bloomsbury Portraits: Vanessa Bell, Duncan Grant and
Their Circle* (New York, 1976), 34q. "like a sea-anemone": Holroyd, *John*, 277q.
"rather méfiant": Lady Ottoline, *Memoirs*, 101. ". . . sit to me?": *ibid.*, 121.
". . . with passion": Brooke, *Letters*, 200. ". . . the John family": *ibid.*, 175. ". . . disquieting, emphatic": Malcolm Easton and Michael Holroyd, *The Art of Augustus
John* (Boston, 1975), 62q. "Dorelia" was . . . : Holroyd, *John*, 147. like "a sheer tinker . . .": *ibid.*, 261q. "boring Borrovian . . .": W. K. Rose, ed., *The Letters of Wyndham Lewis* (London, 1963), 70, 70n.

 Pp. 16–21. "Thou, Nature . . .": Shakespeare, *King Lear*. ". . . and so furiously?": Edward Garnett, ed., *Letters from W. H. Hudson, 1901–1922* (New York,
1923), 161. "so grand the silence . . .": Jan Marsh, *Edward Thomas: A Poet for His
Country* (London, 1978), 42q. "as I was pausing . . .": *ibid.*, 46q. wore "Liberty
dresses": *ibid.*, 12. ". . . putting an end to it": *ibid.*, 71q. . . . revolver in hand: *ibid.*,
24. "Weep no more . . .": Milton, *Lycidas*. ". . . sensitive face": Garnett, *Golden Echo*,
120. ". . . fine chiseled features": Rhys, *Everyman Remembers*, 255. ". . . face was
his": Ernest Rhys, *Wales England Wed: An Autobiography* (London, 1940), 195.
". . . and cottagey": Garnett, *Great Friends*, 60. . . . and his honey-bees: Rhys,
Wales England Wed, 195–196. . . . and hot buttered scones: Garnett, *Great Friends*,
58. . . . with plasmon powder: *ibid.*, 62. ". . . in the wide inglenook": Clifford Bax,
Some I Knew Well (London, 1951), 178–179. ". . . testicles & guts": Marsh, *Thomas*,
50q. "unwillingness to live . . .": Charles Norman, *Ezra Pound* (New York, 1969),
37q. "touch of bestiality . . .": Mark Holloway, *Norman Douglas: A Biography*
(London, 1976), 189q. "Marsh-marigolds . . .": Marsh, *Thomas*, 5q. . . . come up
to his elbow: Ford Madox Ford, *Portraits from Life* (New York, 1937), 54. ". . . after
Hudson married her": *ibid.*, 53. . . . lost her voice: Rothenstein, *Men and Memories*, 62; see also Ford, *Portraits*, 55. "Tower House": Violet Hunt, *I Have This to
Say* (New York, 1926), 30. ". . . curtains and antimacassars": Rothenstein, *Men and
Memories*, 62. moving from flat to flat: Jessie Conrad, *Joseph Conrad and His Circle* (London, 1935), 87–88. ". . . her husband's shortcomings": *ibid.*, 88. ". . . her
distinguished husband": Hunt, *I Have This to Say*, 30. "the gloomiest verdict . . .":
Rothenstein, *Men and Memories*, 62; but see also Garnett, *Great Friends*, 26.
". . . the world could imagine": Ford, *Portraits*, 56. ". . . the wrong way": *ibid.*
". . . animal about him": Rothenstein, *Men and Memories*, 63. ". . . as rocks are":
Ford Madox Ford, *Return to Yesterday* (New York, 1972), 34. "not altogether
human": Holloway, *Douglas*, 191q. ". . . down the broad valley": Ford, *Portraits*, 54.
". . . look after birds": Rothenstein, *Men and Memories*, 161q. ". . . man of the
woods": *ibid.* ". . . & the Almanac": *ibid.*, 63q. ". . . innumerable multitude": Ford,
Portraits, 54q. ". . . his chosen friends?": Rothenstein, *Men and Memories*, 162.
". . . than he does": Richard Curle, *Caravansary and Conversation: Memories of
Places and Persons* (London, 1937), 182q. ". . . nothing about people": Garnett,

Great Friends, 30q. "... the present disease": Edward Garnett, *Letters from W. H. Hudson,* 183. "... will purge us": *ibid.,* 201–202. "... lace-up boots": Garnett, *Great Friends,* 28. "a disappointment": H. Montgomery Hyde, *Oscar Wilde* (London, 1976), 51q. "... American married life": *ibid.,* 65q. "choirs of birds...": Michael Holroyd, *Lytton Strachey: A Biography* (New York, 1980), 418q. "... imbecile mountains": R. F. Harrod, *The Life of John Maynard Keynes* (London, 1951), 106n. "... are repulsive": Leonard Woolf, *The Wise Virgins* [1914] (New York, 1979), 63–64. "... kind of existence": Zdzislaw Najder, *Joseph Conrad: A Chronicle* (New Brunswick, N.J., 1983), 200q. "No outdoors for him....": Jacob Epstein, *An Autobiography* (New York, 1955), 75. "... this pretentiously rural place": Clifford Bax, ed., *Florence Farr, Bernard Shaw and W. B. Yeats* [Letters] (Dublin, 1941), 6–7. "... it's there for": "Saki," *The Chronicles of Clovis* [1911] in *The Complete Works* (New York, 1976), 133.

Pp. 21–25. "... the garden's lovely": popular song. "... and quite idyllic little farm": Margaret Drabble, *Arnold Bennett* (New York, 1974), 87q. Shaw's friends the Salts: Margot Peters, *Bernard Shaw and the Actresses* (New York, 1980), 63; see also Dan H. Laurence, ed., *Bernard Shaw: Collected Letters, 1898–1910,* II (New York, 1972), 489 (hereafter Shaw, *Letters,* II). "... or a weald": Mrs. Cecil Chesterton, *The Chestertons* (London, 1941), 70q. ... in Beaconsfield not far away: Dudley Barker, *G. K. Chesterton: A Biography* (London, 1973), 188. ... near Winchelsea: Peters, *Shaw,* 236. "... on a little theme": Aldington, *Life,* 110. One day in September...: re the Georgian movement, see Marsh, *Thomas,* 88ff, and Stonesifer, *Davies,* 96ff. "policeman of poetry": Stonesifer, *Davies,* 97q. "simpering simplicity"?: *ibid.,* 100. "... my little oil": Aldington, *Life,* 111q. "... to be brutal": Marsh, *Thomas,* 92q. ... to Wordsworth: Stonesifer, *Davies,* 99–100. "... the why and wherefore of life": Marsh, *Thomas,* 103q. "mine be a cot": Walter Allen, *The English Novel* (New York, 1957), 343q. ... twenty-three pounds: John Carswell, *Lives and Letters: A. R. Orage, Beatrice Hastings, Katherine Mansfield, John Middleton Murry, S. S. Koteliansky* (New York, 1978), 277. Thomas's farmhouse...: Garnett, *Great Friends,* 60. Davies's small cottage...: *ibid.* No system of drainage...: Thomas Moser, ed., "From Olive Garnett's Diary" in *Texas Studies,* Fall 1974, 520. ... adored the discomfort: Maisie Ward, *G. K. Chesterton* (New York, 1943), 247. ... that badly blocked sink: Jeffrey Meyers, *Katherine Mansfield: A Biography* (New York, 1978), 105. "It is a very grey day...": Vincent O'Sullivan and Margaret Scott, eds., *The Collected Letters of Katherine Mansfield,* I, 1903–1917 (Oxford, 1984), 123 (hereafter Mansfield, *Letters*). "It is very cold here...": *ibid.,* 153. contracted arthritis...: Meyers, *Mansfield,* 107. The Thomases' Ivy Cottage...: Marsh, *Thomas,* 44. When Arthur Symons...: Edmund White, "The Critic, the Mirror and the Vamp": *Times Literary Supplement* (hereafter *TLS*), November 13–19, 1987, 1240. ... stark moments: Holroyd, *Strachey,* 345, 501. "... low-ceilinged hole": Omar Pound and A. Walton Litz, eds., *Ezra Pound and Dorothy Shakespear: Their Letters, 1909–1914* (New York, 1984), 170 (hereafter Pound and Shakespear, *Letters*). "... about five days too much": *ibid.,* 171. Davies's old uncle...: Garnett, *Great Friends,* 61.

Pp. 25–28. "O Lord! I suppose...": Woolf, *Wise Virgins,* 88. "I am the land...": Kipling, "The Recall." "colonize the countryside": Jefferson Hunter, *Edwardian Fiction* (Cambridge, Mass., 1982), 164q. H. Rider Haggard...: *ibid.,* 168. "wonderful land": *ibid.,* 160q. "my favorite foreign country": Lord Birkinhead,

Rudyard Kipling (London, 1980), 243q. the thirty-three acres of "Bateman's": *ibid.,* 239. As for Maurice Hewlett . . . : Hunter, *Edwardian Fiction,* 168. It was in art as in life . . . : *ibid.,* 191–192. Even the musicians . . . : *ibid.,* 168. "the spirit that dwells . . .": Joseph Conrad, *Lord Jim* [1900] (Boston, 1958), 159. "The little church on a hill . . .": *ibid.,* 6. "the cozy ambushed English life": D. H. Lawrence, *Aaron's Rod* (London, 1922), 212. "Rather parochial . . .": Norman Douglas, *South Wind* [1917] (New York, 1925), 432–433. "One has the sense . . .": James, *Letters,* 256. "Merrymakings. Lads and lasses . . .": H. G. Wells, *Tono-Bungay* [1908] (New York, 1935), 258. . . . isn't wholly converted: *ibid.,* 259. the Heir of Hockcliffe: Drabble, *Bennett,* 88. ". . . which we shall dominate": *ibid.,* 192. a Dalmatian and a dog cart: *ibid.,* 88. Was the voice of the tommy . . . ?: Angus Wilson, *The Strange Ride of Rudyard Kipling* (New York, 1977), 236. "Ow can I ever take on . . .": *ibid.,* 235q. By the end of the war even . . . : G. E. Mingay, "New Patterns of the Plough", *TLS,* January 25, 1985, 96.

Pp. 28–32. "The Fellowship of the New Life": see Norman and Jeanne Mackenzie, *The Fabians* (New York, 1977), 21ff; Marsh, *Thomas,* 30ff; Robert Skidelsky, "The Fabian Ethic," in Michael Holroyd, ed., *The Genius of Shaw* (New York, 1979), 114ff. Back to nature . . . to the farm: Skidelsky, "Fabian Ethic," 114–115. "romantic agriculturists": Goldring, *Trained for Genius,* 160q. "and other Cockneys": *ibid.* "a real old farm . . .": Frank MacShane, *The Life and Work of Ford Madox Ford* (New York, 1965), 30. a gaggle of socialist rustics: Najder, *Conrad,* 237; see also Ford, *Return,* 40ff. ". . . made of bullock's horns": Goldring, *Trained for Genius,* 65. "Gas and Water Socialism": Ford, *Return,* 41. . . . of the peasant: Garnett, *Great Friends,* 39. "Yaws . . . yaws . . .": *ibid.,* 40. ". . . poultry farm and bees": Wells, *Tono-Bungay,* 197. "They are wonderfully beautiful . . .": Woolf, *Wise Virgins,* 88. ". . . philanthropic bunkum": Forster, *Howards End,* 205. ". . . and see it whole": *ibid.,* 269. ". . . such a crop of hay as never!": *ibid.,* 343. "a Saxon goddess": W. Somerset Maugham, *Of Human Bondage* [1915] (New York, 1963), 598. ". . . by keeping fowls": Drabble, *Bennett,* 87q. ". . . and was ashamed": *ibid.,* 86q. "a ripping time": James T. Boulton, ed., *The Letters of D. H. Lawrence,* I, 1901–1913 (New York, 1979), 316 (hereafter Lawrence, *Letters*). "like the 15th century": *ibid.,* 314. . . . only grow radishes: Drabble, *Bennett,* 87. . . . perhaps a few ducks: Garnett, *Great Friends,* 39. "drink of the mead . . .": Hunt, *I Have This to Say,* 51. "They got very muddy . . .": Wells, *Tono-Bungay,* 205. On a smallholding at Millthorpe . . . : Marsh, *Thomas,* 31. "vast vegetable pie": Skidelsky, "Fabian Ethic," 115. the homemade woolens: Skidelsky; see also Marsh, *Thomas,* 31. were the sandals: *ibid.,* 31. "A singularly unhealthy . . .": Goldring, *Trained for Genius,* 160q. ". . . organize the docks": Marsh, *Thomas,* 30q. "The Noble Savage . . . impostor": Shaw, *Letters,* II, 490, 348. . . . would sad Sue Bridehead!: Thomas Hardy, *Jude the Obscure* [1895] (New York, 1966), 180–182. "One hears . . .": Wells, *Tono-Bungay,* 68. "It is my belief . . .": Sir Arthur Conan Doyle, "The Adventure of the Copper Beeches," in *The Complete Sherlock Holmes* (New York, n.d.), 323.

Pp. 35–36. "London, the bloody world!": Ford, *Return,* 221. "the queen city . . .": Robert Pearsall, *Frank Harris* (New York, 1970), 31q. "the great beating heart . . .": James, *Letters,* 34. "the roar of London . . .": Arnold Bennett, *Buried Alive* [1908] (New York, n.d.), 202. "giant London . . .": H. G. Wells, *The New Machiavelli* (London, 1911), 11. "intelligent without purpose . . .": Forster, *Howards End,* 108. "the end of the world": Lawrence, *Women in Love* [1920] (New

NOTES

York, 1960), 54. poor homesick Yeats who . . . : *The Autobiography of William Butler Yeats* (New York, 1965), 103. "a witless old giantess . . .": Wells, *Tono-Bungay,* 92. "to be born in London . . .": Ford, *Return,* 221.

Pp. 36–44. "Implacable war": Philip Magnus, *King Edward the Seventh* (New York, 1979), 505. "We want to draw a line . . .": Barbara Tuchman, *The Proud Tower: A Portrait of the World Before the War, 1890–1914* (New York, 1966), 372q. fifty-three new creatures called Labour . . . : George Dangerfield, *The Strange Death of Liberal England* (New York, 1961), 10; see also Tuchman, *Proud Tower,* 365. now voting Labour: Sir Charles Petrie, *Scenes of Edwardian Life* (London, 1965), 233. ". . . quite passed away": Magnus, *King Edward,* 429q. Churchill would do . . . : Wilfred Scawen Blunt, *My Diaries, Part Two, 1900–1914* (London, 1920), 305 (hereafter Blunt, *Diaries*). ". . . to copy the French!": *ibid.,* 435q. . . . were in ecstasies: Carswell, *Lives and Letters,* 26. "Bliss was it . . .": Wordsworth, *The Prelude,* Book Eleven, 108–109. devoured prodigious amounts: see Petrie, *Scenes,* 42, and Magnus, *King Edward,* 332–334. one-third . . . starved to death: Samuel Hynes, *The Edwardian Turn of Mind* (Princeton, 1968), 55; see also Mackenzie, *Fabians,* 317. heads and tails of fishes: Ward, *Chesterton,* 221. under the Waterloo bridge: Lawrence, *White Peacock,* 321. and, in the meantime, the children: Tuchman, *Proud Tower,* 356. "broken boots . . . a lump of bread": Lawrence, *Letters,* 124. When the novelist Gissing . . . : Anthony West, *H. G. Wells: Aspects of a Life* (New York, 1984), 270–271. All good people . . . : see "The Nicest Set of People" in Mackenzie, *Fabians,* and Hynes, "The Fabians: Mrs. Webb and Mr. Wells," in *Edwardian Turn of Mind.* "gruesomely respectable": Peters, *Shaw,* 36q. labored to "permeate": Shaw, *Letters,* II, 252–254. "a Socialist Tammany Hall": Ford, *Portraits,* 120. "the only repository of statesmanship": Edgar Jepson, *Memoirs of an Edwardian* (London, 1937), 28. . . . a little exclusive: Mackenzie, *Fabians,* 322; see also Norman and Jeanne Mackenzie, *H. G. Wells: A Biography* (New York, 1973), 184–185. "You're the cleverest member . . .": *The Autobiography of Bertrand Russell* (Boston, 1967), 107q. Their socialist goal . . . : Ben Pimlott, "Thinking in Combination," *TLS,* November 23 1984, 1331q. They had just recruited . . . : Mackenzie, *Wells,* 184ff, 194ff; Dan H. Laurence, "1906–1907," in Shaw, *Letters,* II, 595–598; Archibald Henderson, *George Bernard Shaw: Man of the Century* (New York, 1956), 250ff; Hynes, "Fabians," in *Edwardian Turn of Mind,* 87–131. Short and slight . . . : Mackenzie, *Wells,* 230. . . . a new order of Samurai: *ibid.,* 190. hardly a Marxist . . . : West, *Wells,* 284. He delivered a paper . . . : Mackenzie, *Wells,* 185. ". . . into the dustbin": *ibid.,* 195q. "This Misery of Boots": *ibid.,* 196q. "The Faults of the Fabian": *ibid.,* 196q; for text see Hynes, *Edwardian Turn of Mind,* Appendix C. "giggling excitement . . .": Mackenzie, *Wells,* 197; see also Henderson, *Shaw,* 252–253q. all too Fabian: *ibid.,* 251–253; Mackenzie, *Wells,* 214; Mackenzie, *Fabians,* 332. . . . endowed as mothers: Hynes, *Edwardian Turn of Mind,* 112ff; also Mackenzie, *Wells,* 190, and *Fabians,* 334. "This Misery of Wells . . .": Henderson, *Shaw,* 251. ". . . that ends Wells": *ibid.,* 253. ". . . balance the old gang": Shaw, *Letters,* II, 220, 254. . . . a Fabian party: Michael Holroyd, *Bernard Shaw, 1898–1918,* II (New York, 1989), 129. ". . . interesting again": Shaw, *Letters,* II, 536. ". . . go clog dancing": Shaw, *Letters,* II, 613. humiliate the Old Guard: Henderson, *Shaw,* 254. that day in December 1906: *ibid.,* 254–255; see also Mackenzie, *Wells,* 216ff, and *Fabians,* 336ff. a lively two thousand: Mackenzie, *Fabians,* 342. Bennett among them and . . . : Lovat Dickson, *H. G. Wells: His Turbulent Life and Times* (New York, 1969), 116. to the distress of Constance Garnett: Carolyn G. Heilbrun, *The*

Garnett Family (New York, 1961), 69; see also Garnett, *Great Friends,* 182. the wives of the Old Gang: West, *Wells,* 290, 294. Even Beatrice Webb . . . : *ibid.,* 305. "the wee, fantastic, Wells": Mackenzie, *Fabians,* 343q. his political taste: Holroyd, *Strachey,* 399. the Fabian Nursery: Mackenzie, *Wells,* 226; Dickson, *Wells,* 121, 130. the Samurai Press: Joy Grant, *Harold Monro and the Poetry Bookshop* (Berkeley, 1967), 16ff. ". . . of your ideas": Carswell, *Lives and Letters,* 24. "in a holy war . . .": W. H. Auden, "Voltaire at Ferney." . . . the city's first socialist weekly: Wallace Martin, *The New Age Under Orage, Chapters in English Cultural History* (New York, 1967), 5; re founding and operation of *New Age,* see *ibid.,* 23–24; Carswell, *Lives and Letters,* 32ff; Mackenzie, *Fabians,* 344–345; John Gross, *The Rise and Fall of the Man of Letters* (New York, 1969), 227ff; re history of Orage and *New Age,* see also Philip Mairet, *A. R. Orage: A Memoir* (London, 1936), and Paul Selver, *Orage and the New Age Circle* (London, 1959). . . . five hundred pounds: Martin, *New Age,* 1, 24; Carswell, *Lives and Letters,* 32–33. a romantic socialist: *ibid.,* 25; Gross, *Rise and Fall,* 228. "An Independent Review . . .": Carswell, *Lives and Letters,* 35. first called "An Independent Socialist Review . . .": Martin, *New Age,* 24. the great Chesterbelloc affair: Carswell, *Lives and Letters,* 38ff; Martin, *New Age,* 35. a penny a number: Carswell, *Lives and Letters,* 35. five thousand copies . . . twenty thousand: *ibid.,* 38, 41. a pestilence of anarchists: see Tuchman, *Proud Tower,* ch. 2, on history of the movement. . . . hotly pursued: Ford, *Return,* 112. Conrad wasn't wholly unsympathetic: Frederick Karl, *Joseph Conrad: The Three Lives* (New York, 1979), 395. London . . . anarchic enough: Hunter, *Edwardian Fiction,* 232. . . . Kropotkin to dinner: Tuchman, *Proud Tower,* 74. Teachers' Guild: Gloria G. Fromm, *Dorothy Richardson: A Biography* (Urbana, Ill., 1977), 26. ". . . distinguished refugee": *ibid.* "Dostoevsky's corner": Najder, *Conrad,* 237. "be an anarchist": Yeats, *Autobiography,* 141. . . . harmless enough: Fromm, *Richardson,* 26. and the Rossetti children: Ford, *Return,* 111–112. the case of Francisco Ferrer: Carswell, *Lives and Letters,* 46ff; see also Blunt, *Diaries,* 292. an unconfirmed rumor . . . : Selver, *Orage,* 86. ". . . in the streets": Lady Ottoline, *Memoirs,* 166. Catholic Belloc . . . : Carswell, *Lives and Letters,* 48. Cunninghame Graham . . . on horseback: Cedric Watts and Laurence Davies, *Cunninghame Graham: A Critical Biography* (Cambridge, England, 1979), 228–229. ". . . to Ferrer's murder": Selver, *Orage,* 57. ". . . what this leads to": Furbank, *Forster,* 178.

Pp. 44–47. "Go . . . rouse London": Dudley Barker, *Prominent Edwardians* (New York, 1969), 195q; the women's movement, see also Midge Mackenzie, *Shoulder to Shoulder: A Documentary* (New York, 1975); Dangerfield, *Strange Death;* Hynes, *Edwardian Turn of Mind,* 200ff. By 1900 . . . 100,000 . . . : Carswell, *Lives and Letters,* 16. Pitman's shorthand: Arnold Bennett, *Hilda Lessways* [1911] (London, 1975), 54–55. "by earning twelve pounds": *The Plays of J. M. Barrie* (New York, 1956), 752–753. But in truth . . . : Drabble, *Bennett,* 57–58. . . . a tyrannical boss: Bennett, *Hilda Lessways,* 60. tenpence per one thousand words: H. G. Wells, *Love and Mr. Lewisham* [1900] (Oxford, 1983), 174. She returns as . . . : H. G. Wells, *Ann Veronica* (New York, 1909), 268ff. The valiant Sophia . . . : Arnold Bennett, *The Old Wives' Tale* [1908] (New York, 1911), 43. "I don't think teachers . . .": Lawrence, *Women in Love,* 201. from the lower-class ranks: Carswell, *Lives and Letters,* 16. Miss Dugdale . . . as a teacher: Robert Gittings, *Thomas Hardy's Later Years* (Boston, 1978), 123. "as a fancy": Michael Millgate, *Thomas Hardy: A Biography* (New York, 1982), 463q. fill the Queen's Hall: Barker, *Prominent Edwardians,* 210. heckle the Liberal candidates: *ibid.,* 226. "Women's Parliaments": Mackenzie, *Shoulder to Shoulder*, 58; Barker, *Prominent Edwardians*, 210. by the "London Cossacks": *ibid.* Sunday, June 21, 1908 . . . : Mackenzie, *Shoulder to Shoulder*, 78–80; Barker, *Prominent Edwardians*, 215. At the end of the month: Mackenzie, *Shoulder to Shoulder*, 80–83; Barker, *Prominent Edwardians*, 215–216. "I cried, my dear . . .": Mrs. Chesterton, *Chestertons*, 141q.

Pp. 47–51. "O brave new world/ That hath such people in't": Shakespeare, *The Tempest*, V, i, 183–184. "was betrayed into poverty . . .": *The Young Rebecca: Writings of Rebecca West, 1911–1917*, selected by Jane Marcus (New York, 1982), 155 (hereafter West, *Young Rebecca*). The newspapers, for example . . . : Petrie, *Scenes*, 52ff. ". . . members of the poor generally": Drabble, *Bennett*, 165q. "fine blue cover . . .": E. T. (Jessie Chambers), *D. H. Lawrence: A Personal Record* (Cambridge, England, 1980), 156. "link with the world . . .": *ibid.* four hundred publishing houses: Gross, *Rise and Fall*, 199. "All that is greatest . . .": Bennett, *Buried Alive*, 124. . . . twenty-eight pounds and a penny: Gross, *Rise and Fall*, 205. The cheap reprint edition . . . : *ibid.*, 206. Grant Richards . . . World's Classics: Ned Polsky, "Publishing History," *TLS*, May 18–24, 1990, 527. Buchan . . . the publisher Nelson: Janet Adam Smith, *John Buchan and His World* (New York, 1979), 51–52. *Everyman's Library*: Gross, *Rise and Fall*, 206ff; see also Hugh Kenner, *A Sinking Island: The Modern English Writers* (New York, 1988), 30ff. "like a good lyric": Gross, *Rise and Fall*, 208q. "to foster a taste . . .": *ibid.*, 210q. the Democratic Shilling: *ibid.*, 208. Plutarch in three volumes . . . : *ibid.* The spines with their . . . : *ibid.*, 208–209. . . . a little intimidating: *ibid.*, 209. a new set of publishers: John Sutherland, "The Great and the Cheese-paring," *TLS*, April 27–May 3, 1990, 442. ". . . and enlargement of life": Moore, *Lawrence*, 95q. ". . . sunshine of literature": H. G. Wells, *Kipps* [1905] (London, 1968), 297. "Literature . . . is the way": H. G. Wells, *Boon* (London, 1915), 222. ". . . culture—horrible": Forster, *Howards End*, 145. the absurd Leonard Bast: *ibid.*, 54. ". . . a thinking man": Bernard Shaw, *Misalliance*, in *Complete Plays with Prefaces*, IV (New York, 1963), 189. "If I'd had money . . .": Arnold Bennett, *The Roll Call* (New York, 1918), 70. ". . . I know nothing": H. G. Wells, *The Wheels of Chance* [1896] (London, 1984), 112. "bookish intentions": see Bennie Green, "Introduction," in Wells, *Love and Mr. Lewisham*, ix. Had his mother . . . : West, *Wells*, 169, 184–185, 190ff. "Rabooloose": Wells, *Mr. Polly*, 18. Lady Horner's son . . . : Lady Ottoline, *Memoirs*, 147. Lawrence and their daughter . . . : Moore, *Lawrence*, 94. Should Jessie read . . . ?: Philip Callow, *Son and Lover: The Young D. H. Lawrence* (New York, 1975), 100, 123. Hueffer was impressed: Ford, *Return*, 376–377.

Pp. 51–55. ". . . like Travel and Books": Wells, *Kipps*, 142. . . . but Devon or Cornwall: Fromm, *Richardson*, 25. gateways to freedom: Drabble, *Bennett*, 47. "the glorious and the unknown": Forster, *Howards End*, 12. the paid holiday: Petrie, *Scenes*, 47. the modern bicycle: West, *Wells*, 228; Drabble, *Bennett*, 69. cost as little as four: Eugen Weber, "Freedom of the Wheel," *TLS*, February 26–March 3, 1988, 209. cycling all over it: see Wells, *Wheels of Chance*. one's manhood: Wells, *Wheels of Chance*, 7. John Galsworthy was . . . : Weber, "Freedom of the Wheel," *ibid.*, 209q. . . . and rivers and animals: Wells, *Wheels of Chance*, 30. "the first weasel . . .": *ibid.* ". . . all the best people": *ibid.*, 144. ". . . all cyclists nowadays": *ibid.*, 173. Arnold Bennett took trips . . . : Drabble, *Bennett*, 69–70. Leonard Woolf and his brother . . . : Leonard Woolf, *Sowing: An Autobiography of the Years 1880–1904* (New York, 1960), 191. when the Webbs came down . . . : Dickson,

Wells, 94. and even the Hudsons . . . : Garnett, *Great Friends*, 28. As for the Hardys . . . : Millgate, *Hardy*, 388–389. Even James . . . : James, *Letters*, 82; see Kenner, *A Sinking Island*, 71. Bennett dislocated an elbow: Drabble, *Bennett*, 70. Emma Hardy . . . : Millgate, *Hardy*, 389. and Hardy himself . . . : *ibid.*, 419. "a Homeric spill followed": Bernard Shaw, *Collected Letters, 1911–1925* (London, 1985), 200 (hereafter Shaw, *Letters*, III). . . . the road with his face: Peters, *Shaw*, 229–230. ". . . whirling bicycle machinery": Bax, ed., *Florence Farr, Bernard Shaw and W. B. Yeats*, 39–40. . . . as early as 1897: Birkinhead, *Kipling*, 236. . . . in a steam motor car: Hunter, *Edwardian Fiction*, 160. whose Lanchester . . . : Birkinhead, *Kipling*, 237. . . . to church in a Bath chair: Millgate, *Hardy*, 484. J.M.B. didn't himself . . . : Denis Mackail, *The Story of J.M.B.: A Biography* (London, 1941), 313–315. As for the Shaws . . . : Shaw, *Letters*, II, 822–823. ". . . one-cylinder puffer": Najder, *Conrad*, 378. four-seater Humber: *ibid.*, 390. . . . end up in ditches: *ibid.*, 378; see also J. C. Retinger, *Conrad and His Contemporaries* (New York, 1943), 68. "chariot of fire": James, *Letters*, 443. "as jubilant as a child": Edith Wharton, *A Backward Glance* (New York, 1934), 248q. "I hear with fond awe . . .": Najder, *Conrad*, 387q. "a huge extension of . . .": James, *Letters*, 483. "stink pot": Petrie, *Scenes*, 92. a law was repealed: Fromm, *Richardson*, 24. ". . . roar of a huge Car": Hunter, *Edwardian Fiction*, 46q. "the reek of petrol . . .": *ibid.*, 225q. "throbbing, stinking car": *ibid.*, 47q. . . . make Englishmen think: *ibid.*, 36. "to make Mr. Kipling think": Ford, *Return*, 16. King Edward himself . . . : Magnus, *King Edward*, 519. from Pall Mall to Windsor Castle: Bennett, *The Roll Call*, 15.

Pp. 55–60. ". . . chapter of cruel accidents": Shaw, *Letters*, II, 672. ". . . no meaning in life": Allen, *English Novel*, 392q. ". . . an inhospitable shore": Russell, *Autobiography*, 286. "the eternal Error": Najder, *Conrad*, 184q. ". . . and nothing matters": *ibid.*, 219q. "Live all you can . . .": Henry James, *The Ambassadors* [1903] (New York, 1958), 163. "No Jump about the place . . .": Wells, *Tono-Bungay*, 55. life . . . a subject: Dickson, *Wells*, 99. . . . stared at and glared at: Forster, *Howards End*, 125. . . . the hatless persuasion: Wells, *Ann Veronica*, 13. "plenty of cranks . . .": Lawrence, *Women in Love*, 101. ABC teashops: West, *Wells*, 210–211. One day in 1910 Frida Strindberg . . . : John, *Chiaroscuro*, 103–104; 116–118; Holroyd, *John*, 398ff. the Cave of the Golden Calf: Holroyd, *John*, 442; see also Pound and Shakespear, *Letters*, 270–271n. fashioned by young Eric Gill: Fiona MacCarthy, "The Word Become Flesh," *TLS*, December 25, 1992, 14. "in kneedt of money . . .": Pound letter to Patricia Hutchins during making of her *Ezra Pound's Kensington* (Hutchins collection in the British Museum). the bunny hug and the turkey trot: Theophilus E. M. Boll, *Miss May Sinclair: Novelist* (Rutherford, N.J., 1973), 89. Katherine Mansfield: Meyers, *Mansfield*, 37. ". . . draw a line *somewhere*": John Tytell, *Ezra Pound: The Solitary Volcano* (New York, 1987), 104q. "impoverished artists": Noel Stock, *The Life of Ezra Pound* (New York, 1974), 197. the Crab-tree: Holroyd, *John*, 443; see also Garnett, *Golden Echo*, 237–238. ". . . a fight for living": Shaw, *Misalliance*, in *Complete Plays*, IV, 143. "to live a Free Life . . .": Wells, *Wheels of Chance*, 117. ". . . an active verb": Shaw, *Misalliance*, in *Complete Plays*, IV, 142. ". . . at your own life!": Woolf, *Wise Virgins*, 191. ". . . beastly bits of tulle": Smith, *Buchan*, 48q. ". . . dissenting spinster": Frank Tuohy, *Yeats* (New York, 1976), 65q. "oh, nao . . .": Millgate, *Hardy*, 390q. ". . . live one's own life!": Wells, *Love and Mr. Lewisham*, 233. "I can't believe . . .": Russell, *Autobiography*, 98q. ". . . life with a big L": Woolf, *Wise Virgins*, 84q. Led by Vanessa herself . . . : Virginia Woolf, *Moments of Being: Unpublished Autobiograph-*

ical Writings (New York, 1976), 162–163. When Leonard Woolf went off...: Leonard Woolf, *Beginning Again: An Autobiography of the Years 1911 to 1918* (New York, 1972), 33ff; see also Leon Edel, *Bloomsbury: A House of Lions* (New York, 1979), 176. with their Christian names: Woolf, *Sowing*, 119–120. "I say, what's your Christian name?": Bennett, *The Roll Call*, 103. "How do you do, Gudrun?": Lawrence, *Women in Love*, 112. hat, stick, and gloves: Douglas Goldring, *South Lodge: Reminiscences of Violet Hunt, Ford Madox Ford and the English Review Circle* (London, 1943), 46–47; see also Petrie, *Scenes*, 43. Vanessa despised...: Virginia Woolf, *Moments*, 148ff. "pouring tea and talking like a lady": Edel, *Bloomsbury*, 177q. Now they were free...: Virginia Woolf, *Moments*, 167ff. ... and languished in basket-chairs: Lady Ottoline, *Memoirs*, 149. who sat round a fire...: *ibid.*, 121. "Deplorable, deplorable!...": Quentin Bell, *Virginia Woolf: A Biography* (New York, 1972), I, 99q (hereafter Bell, *Woolf*, I). "What a nuptial 'solemnity'!": James, *Letters*, 437. "...third-rate Clive Bell": *ibid*. "...in a duck pond": Furbank, *Forster*, 163q. "Tell Virginia...": Edel, *James*, 393q. "Look at them...": Lady Ottoline, *Memoirs*, 125.

Pp. 61–63. "...That dare not speak its name": "I am the Love that dare not speak its name," a line from Lord Alfred Douglas's poem, "Two Loves." Vanessa, unchaperoned: Shone, *Bloomsbury Portraits*, 27. How shocked...: *ibid.*, 26–27. "Semen?" he asked.: Bell, *Woolf*, I, 124q. "Sex permeated...": *ibid*. side by side in their bedroom: Frances Spalding, *Vanessa Bell* (New York, 1983), 63 (hereafter Spalding, *Vanessa*). his most indecent poems: *ibid.*, 63–64. as Gauguin girls: Bell, *Woolf*, I, 170; see also Woolf, *Moments*, 178–179. But at Oliver Strachey's...: David Gadd, *The Loving Friends: A Portrait of Bloomsbury* (New York, 1974), 57–58. ...in Byron's pool: Bell, *Woolf*, I, 174. "it's quite alright, George...": *ibid.*, 175q. "amiable absurdity": Edel, *Bloomsbury*, 98q. taken to Duncan Grant: Holroyd, *Strachey*, 292ff, 379ff; see also Gadd, *Loving Friends*, 177ff, and Edel, *Bloomsbury*, 145ff. ...recanted their "vows": Bell, *Woolf*, I, 141. ...Adrian would probably reject him: *ibid.*, 129q. ...buggery in Bloomsbury?: Woolf, *Moments*, 172. "I imagine a great orgy...": Nigel Nicolson, ed., *The Flight of the Mind: The Letters of Virginia Woolf*, I, 1888–1912 (London, 1975), 473 (hereafter Woolf, *Letters*). "...of an alligators tank?": *ibid.*, 445. quite unashamed, the buggers of Bloomsbury: Noel Annan, "Portrait of a Genius as a Young Man" (Maynard Keynes), *New York Review of Books*, July 19, 1984, 36ff. "Oh these womanizers...": *ibid.*, 37q.

Pp. 63–68. "Th' expense of spirit...": Shakespeare, *Sonnet*, 129. "...your whore soon": Spalding, *Vanessa*, 90. flirting with sister Virginia: *ibid.*, 72ff; see also Bell, *Woolf*, I, 132ff; Edel, *Bloomsbury*, 152ff; Gadd, *Loving Friends*, 50ff. "the terrible ructions...": Woolf, *Letters*, I, 449. "My dear Virginia...": Bell, *Woolf*, I, 133q. "nothing shocking...": Woolf, *Moments*, 174. set off for Constantinople: Bell, *Woolf*, I, 168ff; Spalding, *Vanessa*, 94ff; Edel, *Bloomsbury*, 166ff. ...doing mosaics: Denys Sutton, ed., *The Letters of Roger Fry*, I (London, 1972), 40 (hereafter Fry, *Letters*). took command on the spot: Spalding, *Vanessa*, 96; see also Virginia Woolf, *Roger Fry: A Biography* (New York, 1976), 170–171. his friend, Lady Ott: Sandra Darroch, *Ottoline: The Life of Lady Ottoline Morrell* (New York, 1975), 99. ...left her in tears: *ibid.*, 107–108; see also Lady Ottoline, *Memoirs*, 195–196. "...my feeling all of it so much": Fry, *Letters*, 349. ...with the satyrlike Duncan: Spalding, *Vanessa*, 133ff; Edel, *Bloomsbury*, 212ff; Shone, *Bloomsbury Portraits*,

86ff. . . . if Duncan gave her a child?: Spalding, *Vanessa*, 139. ". . . paint me at the same time?": Shone, *Bloomsbury Portraits*, 89. "he wanted to shave . . .": Spalding, *Vanessa*, 102. . . . very civilized: Edel, *Bloomsbury*, 195–196. . . . they'd laugh at: Angelica Garnett, *Deceived with Kindness: A Bloomsbury Childhood* (New York, 1985), 103. . . . howling in anguish: *ibid.*, 104. Duncan's daughter: Garnett, *Great Friends*, 188. Bertrand Russell . . . at Bedford Square: Darroch, *Ottoline*, 86ff; Russell, *Autobiography*, 314ff. "There is always a tragedy . . .": Lady Ottoline, *Memoirs*, 169q. no longer cared for his wife: Russell, *Autobiography*, 222. . . . destroy her affection: Darroch, *Ottoline*, 88q. . . . his love was dead: Russell, *Autobiography*, 223. . . . and with scant satisfaction: *ibid.*, 227. "Oh the pity of it! . . .": Darroch, *Ottoline*, 88q. "The Day of Judgment": Lady Ottoline, *Memoirs*, 154. . . . the happiest of men: Darroch, *Ottoline*, 90. ". . . quite enough nerve cases": *ibid.*, 34q. Asquith . . . would rush up the stairs: *ibid.*, 39. "poetry, religion and . . .": Gadd, *Loving Friends*, 65q. "I'm glad I'm not . . .": Darroch, *Ottoline*, 46q. Augustus John was late: *ibid.*, 63ff. the color of marmalade: Russell, *Autobiography*, 316. "a crimson tea-cozy . . .": Darroch, *Ottoline*, 80n. ". . . version of Disraeli": *ibid.*, 74. "a rather oversize Infanta . . .": Holroyd, *Strachey*, 447q. "Spanish Armada . . ." Gadd, *Loving Friends*, 73q. was exactly how John: Holroyd, *John*, 277–278. "You will not continue . . .": Darroch, *Ottoline*, 68q. Dorelia, Lady Ott and Henry Lamb: *ibid.*, 75ff; see also Lady Ottoline, *Memoirs*, 159–160. "a vision of Blake": *ibid.*, 160. "I burn to embrace you": Darroch, *Ottoline*, 82q. . . . in the Dog Inn: Lady Ottoline, *Memoirs*, 181. Would he come to Peppard . . . : Darroch, *Ottoline*, 80; see also Lady Ottoline, *Memoirs*, 181–182, and Holroyd, *Strachey*, 450ff. "wearing his hair . . . ": Lady Ottoline, *Memoirs*, 198–199. . . . of old dowager duchesses: Holroyd, *Strachey*, 454. "Our Lady of Bedford Square": *ibid.*, 536. locked in a violent embrace: *ibid.*, 453. make Lytton bisexual: Darroch, *Ottoline*, 112. all Lady Ottoline's roosters: *ibid.*, 104ff. ". . . & received me": *ibid.*, 105q. . . . returned from Paris to claim her: Russell, *Autobiography*, 315–316. "infuriatingly broadminded": Darroch, *Ottoline*, 52q. ". . . like a horse": Russell, *Autobiography*, 316. ". . . lack of physical attraction": Darroch, *Ottoline*, 102. "with all the passion . . .": *ibid.*, 91q. "What a pity . . .": *ibid.*, 201q.

Pp. 68–69. ". . . in a hornets' nest": Bell, *Woolf*, I, 171q. Brooke's, for example: Holroyd, *Strachey*, 469ff; see also Christopher Hassall, *Rupert Brooke: A Biography* (New York, 1964), 270ff, 296ff, 322–323, 353–354. ". . . a green field of clover": Noel Annan, "Patriot," *New York Review of Books*, September 24, 1981, 20q. "the subtle degradation . . .": Hassall, *Brooke*, 354q. a little deranged: *ibid.*, 354. Bloomsbury affected young Lawrence . . . : Garnett, *Great Friends*, 88ff; Woolf, *Sowing*, 154ff; Cornelia Nixon, "Lawrence in the Great War" (Ph.D. diss., University of California, Berkeley, 1981), 59ff. ". . . a knowledge passed into me": Garnett, *Great Friends*, 88–89q; see Zytaruk and Boulton, eds., *The Letters of D. H. Lawrence, II, June 1913–October 1916* (New York, 1981), 320–321 (hereafter Lawrence, *Letters, II, 1913–1916*). "I like men to be beasts . . .": *ibid.*, 331. ". . . love a woman": *ibid.*, 321; see also Garnett, *Great Friends*, 89q. "from the pugs . . .": Darroch, *Ottoline*, 173q. "All along the Bristol Channel . . .": *ibid.*, 187q. a young Cornish farmer: Moore, *Lawrence*, 354. "with a young coal miner": Jeffrey Meyers, "D. H. Lawrence and Homosexuality" in Stephen Spender, ed., *D. H. Lawrence: Novelist, Poet, Prophet* (New York, 1973), 139q.

Pp. 70–87. "The open sex war . . .": Philip Larkin, "Lover-Shadows in the

Flesh," *TLS*, September 28, 1984, 1075q. "twenty centuries . . .": Yeats, "The Second
Coming." "I like you better . . .": Humphrey Carpenter, "Incomparable Giggler,"
TLS, September 9–15, 1988, 980q. "a somewhat curious beginning . . .": Russell,
Autobiography, 86. Chesterton . . . the night of *his* wedding: Barker, *Chesterton*,
111. "O joy! . . .": Wordsworth, "Intimations Ode." Blatchford . . . disgusted:
Barker, *Chesterton*, 133. ". . . to study timetables": Hilary Spurling, "Advertisements
for Himself," *TLS*, August 15, 1986, 885. ". . . I shall wash myself": *ibid.* "Jolly
Journalist": Barker, *Chesterton*, 136. "Labour is blossoming . . .": Yeats, "Among
School Children." "a compulsive philanderer": Margot Peters, "As Lonely as God,"
in Holroyd, *Genius of Shaw*, 188. "flirtatious Moses": West, *Young Rebecca*, 24. had
loved . . . in his day: Peters, "As Lonely as God," 185ff; see also Peters, *Shaw*, 32ff.
to bed with . . . Jenny Patterson: Michael Holroyd, *Bernard Shaw, I 1856–1898*
(New York, 1988), 161ff. . . . with Florence Farr: *ibid.*, 247ff. Ejaculation he
came . . . : Peters, *Shaw*, 275; see also Holroyd, "Women and the Body Politic," in
Genius of Shaw, 170–171. "the syringeing of women . . .": Holroyd, *Shaw*, II, 256q;
see also Holroyd, "Women and the Body Politic," 170. The *ménage à trois* . . . :
Holroyd, *Shaw*, I, 28ff; see also John O'Donovan, "The First Twenty Years," in
Holroyd, *Genius of Shaw*, 14. . . . *l'ami de la maison*: Peters, "As Lonely as God,"
188; see also Peters, *Shaw*, 32ff. . . . the "Sunday husband": Holroyd, *Shaw*, I, 221.
. . . reduced men to slavery: Peters, *Shaw*, 305. all too licentious . . . : Shaw, *Letters*,
II, 560. in one room for eight hours: Peters, *Shaw*, 305–306. "a startling deterioration . . .": *ibid.*, 306q; see also 211. The last lines of *Candida* . . . : *ibid.*, 140; Holroyd, *Shaw*, I, 315ff. "Do you know anyone . . . ?": Peters, *Shaw*, 175q. . . .
Chesterton the real Peter Pan: Holroyd, *Shaw*, II, 215. "As I told you brutally . . .":
Edel, *Bloomsbury*, 184q. ". . . rather than the body": *ibid.*, 182q. "tiny tadpole
body . . . combined thinking": Pimlott, "Thinking in Combination," *TLS*, November 23, 1984, 1331q. "it is the head only . . .": Holroyd, *Shaw*, I, 264q. ". . . his soul
penetrated mine": Darroch, *Ottoline*, 114q. . . . in ecstatic relief: *ibid.*, 119. the
lives of Ruskin . . . : Lawrence, *Letters*, 477. ". . . same predicament": *ibid.*, 175.
"Sex, which breaks up . . .": Lawrence, "Tortoise Shout." ". . . but the lower kind":
Moser, "From Olive Garnett's Diary," *Texas Studies*, Fall 1974, 517q. ". . . sex shall
endure": Alun R. Jones, *The Life and Opinions of T. E. Hulme* (Boston, 1960),
121q. As for Norman Douglas . . . : Douglas, *South Wind*, 109–110. "a pleasant, affable sort . . .": Ford Madox Ford, *The Good Soldier* [1915] (New York, 1957), 35.
". . . frighten the horses": Ted Morgan, *Maugham* (New York, 1980), 78q. expel
from the court: Magnus, *King Edward*, 497. ". . . foulest possible language": Bell,
Woolf, I, 90q. "wives and mistresses . . .": *The Journal of Arnold Bennett* (New York,
1933), 641 (hereafter Bennett, *Journal*). . . . adjoining apartments: Morgan,
Maugham, 78. . . . "the Souls": Tuchman, *Proud Tower*, 49; Petrie, *Scenes*, 98–99.
"more pagan . . .": Mackenzie, *Wells*, 172q. ". . . cynical aristocrat": *ibid.*, 171. . . .
that knew its own father: Petrie, *Scenes*, 99. "an arch-vulgarian": James, *Letters*,
181. "first love": Edel, "Introduction," James, *Letters*, xvii. shaving the beard: *ibid.*,
139. ardent young men: *ibid.*, xviii. language of sensual affection: *ibid.*, 269, 453,
520. words like "penis" . . . : *ibid.*, xvii. . . . Shaw was astounded: *ibid.*, xix. "His
only words . . .": John Buchan, *Memory Hold-the-Door* (London, 1984), 152. "the
priapean . . .": James, *Letters*, xxv. "for her (not *them*)": R. W. B. Lewis, *Edith
Wharton: A Biography* (New York, 1977), 239q. "to dinner and for night": Edel,
James, 416q; see James, *Complete Notebooks*, 299ff (ed. note), and Lewis, *Wharton*,
262q. "I don't pretend . . .": James, *Letters*, 494–495. So Galsworthy . . . : Garnett,
Great Friends, 66. one Nellie Heath: *ibid.*, 69. he and Constance . . . : Lawrence,

Letters, 314. Archer . . . Robins: Stanley Weintraub, *The London Yankees: Portraits of American Writers and Artists in England, 1894–1914* (New York, 1979), 232–233. . . . as his "young cousin": Millgate, *Hardy*, 467; see also Gittings, *Thomas Hardy's Later Years*, ch. 10ff. "Look here, my dear . . .": Ian Watt, *Conrad in the Nineteenth Century* (Berkeley, 1981), 71q. "a lump of a wife": *ibid.*, 72q. "a good and reposeful . . .": *ibid.* "Waving from window . . .": W. H. Auden, "Something Is Bound to Happen." Bland, Hubert Bland . . . : Mackenzie, *Wells*, 174ff; West, *Wells*, 291ff; Dickson, *Wells*, 130ff. ". . . like the scream of an eagle": Shaw, *Letters*, II, 496. "a raffish Rossetti": Mackenzie, *Fabians*, 324; see also Mrs. Chesterton, *Chestertons*, 58. The romantic old house was filled . . . : H. G. Wells, *Experiment in Autobiography* (New York, 1934), 513ff; see also Dickson, *Wells*, 130–131. "Had they wished him . . .": Jepson, *Memoirs*, 20. ". . . perhaps three, at a time": *ibid.* "an arrangement . . .": *ibid.*, 21. Ellis and Carpenter: Hynes, "Science, Seers and Sex," ch. V in *Edwardian Turn of Mind.* sexual passion . . . simply there: *ibid.*, 153, 158–159. "Bigoted connubiality": Shaw, *Letters*, II, 561. "*Égoisme à deux*": Lawrence, *Women in Love*, 344. The monogamous marriage . . . : Havelock Ellis, *Psychology of Sex: A Manual for Students* (New York, 1966), 279ff. ". . . more than one person": *ibid.*, 282. . . . poor maiden aunts: Emile Delavenay, *D. H. Lawrence and Edward Carpenter: A Study in Edwardian Transition* (London, 1971), 45. "Why not . . .": *ibid.*, 91. "a sexual lunatic": Dickson, *Wells*, 89q. . . . as a social diversion: West, *Wells*, 94. . . . they called the "passade": Fromm, *Richardson*, 48. . . . conquests per annum: West, *Wells*, 94. Richardson . . . Hunt: Mackenzie, *Wells*, 229. "demanded to be my lover": Larkin, "Lover-Shadows," *TLS*, September 28, 1984, 1075q. "fucking": Garnett, *Great Friends*, 188–189. "limpid blue eyes": Mackenzie, *Wells*, 229. . . odor of violets: Brigid Brophy, "Sons and Lovers," *New York Review of Books*, December 6, 1984, 33. . . . smelled of honey: Somerset Maugham, "Some Novelists I Have Known," in *The Vagrant Mood* (London, 1952), 212. Bland was enraged: Dickson, *Wells*, 131; Mackenzie, *Wells*, 246–247; Stephen Winsten, *Jesting Apostle: The Private Life of Bernard Shaw* (New York, 1957), 134. seduce Amber Reeves: West, *Wells*, 6ff; Mackenzie, *Wells*, 250ff; Mackenzie, *Fabians*, 363, 370ff. "Give me a child!": Larkin, "Lover-Shadows," 1075q. "a ripping child": Shaw, *Letters*, II, 870. "Wells and his paramour . . .": West, *Wells*, 10. pistol beside him: Compton Mackenzie, *My Life and Times, 1907–1915* (London, 1965), 114. Enter, too, Shaw and . . . : Mackenzie, *Wells*, 254ff; West, *Wells*, 11ff. But Amber wasn't ready . . . : Mackenzie, *Wells*, 253. wasn't quite the folk hero: West, *Wells*, 8–9. "the Goethe-like libertine": Mackenzie, *Wells*, 251q. "I won't let you cut me, Mr. Wells": Garnett, *Great Friends*, 184q. "the dull home . . .": Holroyd, *John*, 195q. Would she, he asked Ida . . . : *ibid.*, 169. The *ménage à quatre*: *ibid.*, 265–266. *ménage à six*: Darroch, *Ottoline*, 79. "That Lamb family . . .": Holroyd, *John*, 265–266q. "Virgin's Prayer": Norman, *Pound*, 42q. "Lovely thou art . . .": *Personae: The Collected Shorter Poems of Ezra Pound* (New York, 1971), 177. On the mantel . . . : *The Autobiography of William Carlos Williams* (New York, 1951), 116; see also Stock, *Pound*, 122. "most charming woman in London": Louis Simpson, *Three on the Tower: The Lives and Works of Ezra Pound, T. S. Eliot and William Carlos Williams* (New York, 1975), 9q. ". . . never revealed to me": Williams, *Autobiography*, 116. "To build a dream . . .": Stock, *Pound*, 122q. "Ah me, the darn . . .": Ford, *Return*, 373q. In 1901 . . . the striking Miss Doolittle: Janice S. Robinson, *H.D.: The Life and Work of an American Poet* (Boston, 1982), 10ff. courting Miss Shakespear: *ibid.*, 24. make her his mistress: *ibid.*, 31, 58. ". . . a nomad!" *ibid.*, 15q. "You *ought* to go away . . .": Pound and Shakespear, *Letters*, 153q. . . . recite them his poems: Robinson, *H.D.*, 42–43. "Wife or mistress . . .": Timothy Materer, *Vortex: Pound, Eliot, and Lewis* (Ithaca, N.Y., 1979), 74q. T. E. Hulme must . . . : see Jones, *Hulme;* see also Patricia Hutchins, *Ezra Pound's Kensington: An Exploration* (London, 1965), 124ff. and so in the Tour Eiffel . . . : Jones, *Hulme,* 98. . . . throw him downstairs: Hutchins, *Pound's Kensington,* 125. a jovial giant: Epstein, *Autobiography,* 59–60. nagging nasal dialect: Hutchins, *Pound's Kensington,* 125; Jones, *Hulme,* 120. attending a fair: Garnett, *Golden Echo,* 237. for the weekend: Selver, *Orage,* 26. fond of sweets: Jones, *Hulme,* 98. "dangerous": Norman, *Pound,* 48q. "a big fellow . . .": Jones, *Hulme,* 20. broken shop windows . . . : *ibid.,* 119. "perpetual rows . . .": *ibid.,* 21. The knuckledusters . . . : *ibid.,* 124; Hutchins, *Pound's Kensington,* 125. ". . . a member of the middle classes?": Jones, *Hulme,* 119q. "I've a pressing engagement . . .": Garnett, *Golden Echo,* 237q. sexual satisfaction . . . : Jones, *Hulme,* 118; see also Petrie, *Scenes,* 100–101. It gave them great pleasure . . . : Jones, *Hulme,* 120. "the didactic amorist": Wyndham Lewis, *Blasting and Bombardiering* (London, 1937), 111. ". . . sexual prowess": Garnett, *Golden Echo,* 237. always prepared to discuss: Jones, *Hulme,* 120. "half the women . . .": *ibid.,* 118. ". . . I can only giggle!": Carpenter, "Incomparable Giggler," *TLS,* September 9–15, 1988, 980. ". . . For dreams—men": Tytell, *Pound,* 48q. a magical syringe: Philippa Pullar, *Frank Harris* (New York, 1976), 81. "I had got my fingers . . .": *ibid.,* 38–39q. "As I pushed back . . .": *ibid.,* 126q. . . . the air of a stallion: *ibid.,* 29. "I write of all these things . . .": John F. Gallagher, ed., *Frank Harris, My Life and Loves* (New York, 1963), 993 (hereafter Harris, *Life and Loves*). "We are developing . . .": *ibid.* . . . of a horse collar: Pullar, *Harris,* 120, 281n. ". . . all sorts of incongruities!": Shaw, *Letters,* II, 205. "a male Hedda Gabler": Pearsall, *Frank Harris,* 13q. ". . . vanity and greediness": Wells, *Autobiography,* 446. statues so erotic that even Roger Fry: Robert Speaight, *The Life of Eric Gill* (London, 1966), 53. . . . more alarmingly, "Fucking.": Fiona MacCarthy, "The Word Become Flesh," *TLS,* December 25, 1992, 14. establish at Ditchling: Speaight, *Gill,* 48–49. enormous nude statues: Malcolm Bull, "Prophet as Predator," *TLS,* February 17–23, 1989, 160. "precious cockney": Holroyd, *John,* 363n. "He is much impressed . . .": *ibid.* Not his wife, not his . . . : Bull, "Prophet as Predator," 160. As for Aleister Crowley . . . : Fiona MacCarthy, "For the Law of Thelema," *TLS,* January 5–11, 1990, 5. Florence Farr, for example . . . : Peters, *Shaw,* 66ff. "a pigsty": *ibid.,* 70. "set no bounds . . .": *ibid.,* 68. "Great minds have . . .": Pound, "Portrait d'Une Femme," in *Personae,* 61. ". . . a little shocked": Denis Donoghue, ed., W. B. Yeats, *Memoirs* (New York, 1973), 86. Mrs. Shakespear helping . . . : Tuohy, *Yeats,* 86. relieved of his troubled virginity: Weintraub, *London Yankees,* 261. "gave Bert sex": Moore, *Lawrence,* 149q. "Oh, darling . . .": H.D., *Bid Me to Live* (New York, 1960), 68. who reproached H. G. Wells . . . : Peter Gunn, *Vernon Lee* (London, 1964), 193ff. or Veronica Lee-Jones: Fromm, *Richardson,* 54–55. Like Katherine Mansfield . . . : Meyers, *Mansfield,* 44. ". . . hysterical ghoul": Carswell, *Lives and Letters,* 141q. "try and believe . . .": Claire Tomalin, letter to editor, *TLS,* April 5, 1991, 15q. battling the convention . . . : Eleanor Perenyi, "The Bloom Is Off," *New York Review of Books,* March 29, 1984, 36q.

Pp. 87–92. "Let yourself . . .": James, *Ambassadors,* 363. "a distinct variety . . .": Delavenay, *Lawrence and Carpenter,* 210q. . . . or color-blindness: Ellis, *Psychology of Sex,* 241. "the most romantic . . .": Delavenay, *Lawrence and Carpenter,* 207q. the Balonda and . . . : *ibid.* ". . . into the regions of love": *ibid.,* 78q. Assyrians and Egyptians: Ellis, *Psychology of Sex,* 219. "bestiality": *ibid.,* 179–180.

"... from true life": Delavenay, *Lawrence and Carpenter*, 56q. "allegory and expression": *ibid.*, 93q; see also 196–197. homosexual love ... superior: *ibid.*, 84, 209ff. "the interpreter ...": *ibid.*, 211q. "leveller ... class and caste": *ibid.*, 226q. "ungrown" "a child": *ibid.*, 100ff. "bond of personal affection ...": *ibid.*, 226q. "working-class bloke ...": Francis King, *E. M. Forster and His World* (New York, 1978), 57q. "Who with?": *ibid.* "... but I won't marry you": Morgan, *Maugham*, 179q. "pose of dandyism ...": *ibid.*, 164q. ... Ideal Companions: Rupert Hart-Davis, *Hugh Walpole* (New York, 1952), 84. Harold Cheevers, for one ...: Morgan, *Maugham*, 163. Hugh was ...: James, *Letters*, 574, 679, 585. "I can't ...": Edel, "Introduction," James, *Letters*, IV, xix–xx; but see also Edel, *James*, 407. "Have you seen Hugh ...?": Frank Swinnerton, *Background with Chorus: Changes · in English Literary Fashion, 1901–1917* (London, 1956), 122q. Young Lawrence may ...: Delavenay, *Lawrence and Carpenter*, 24–25. homosexual love had a place ...: Meyers, "Lawrence and Homosexuality," in Spender, ed., *Lawrence*, 140q. "the manly love ...": Delavenay, *Lawrence and Carpenter*, 228q. "... with the woman": Lawrence, *Women in Love*, 345. Lawrence's "Rananim" ...: Delavenay, *Lawrence and Carpenter*, 66. "fight clear ...": King, *Forster*, 60q. "his blood-stream ...": H. D., *Bid Me to Live*, 62. "... sex in everything": Mansfield, *Letters*, 261. "who talks to Hilda [Doolittle] ...": Mary Lago and P. N. Furbank, eds., *Selected Letters of E. M. Forster, I, 1879–1920* (London, 1983), 219 (hereafter Forster, *Letters*). "Oh do sit quiet": Furbank, *Forster*, 257q. "... above the buttocks": E. M. Forster, "Terminal Notes," *Maurice* [1914] (New York, 1981), 249–250; see also King, *Forster*, 57q. but Carpenter liked it ...: *ibid.*, 58. "But for Maurice ...": Forster, *Maurice*, 163. "... never their own souls": *ibid.*, 239. The buggers of Bloomsbury ...: King, *Forster*, 58. "yogified mysticism": Forster, "Terminal Notes," in *Maurice*, 249. "... little squeaks": *ibid.*, 252. enamored with Eric: Holloway, *Douglas*, 180, 183–185. "for being a suspected person ...": *ibid.*, 229ff. Conrad must have known: Ralph D. Lindeman, *Norman Douglas* (New York, 1965), 27. "His success with my sex ...": Jessie Conrad, *Conrad*, 97. "Even in 1915 ...": Garnett, *Great Friends*, 100. "that he was homosexual ...": Epstein, *Autobiography*, 45. Mrs. Webb was complaining: Skidelsky, "Fabian Ethic," in Holroyd, *Genius of Shaw*, 114q. In 1907 Florence Farr was proposing ...: Martin, *New Age*, 28. Doris Marsden was proposing ...: Jane Marcus, "Introduction," West, *Young Rebecca*, 8. Havelock Ellis was suggesting ...: Martin, *New Age*, 28. ... homosexual coupling a crime: Shaw, *Letters*, II, 890 (ed. note). "in an intellectual spring": Hunter, *Edwardian Fiction*, 5q. "a new society": Woolf, *Sowing*, 161. "a conscious revolt": *ibid.*, 160.

Pp. 93–95. "Who killed the King?": Tuchman, *Proud Tower*, 398q. For the old Victorian establishment ...: see Dangerfield, *Strange Death*, Part I, on the first phases of the struggle between Tories and Liberals; see also Tuchman, ch. 7, "Transfer of Power: England 1902–11." "Shall peers or people rule?": G. M. Trevelyan, *History of England*, III (New York, 1953), 269q. "A fully-equipped Duke ...": Magnus, *King Edward*, 527q. "And yet, when the Prime Minister and I ...": Dangerfield, *Strange Death*, 22–23q. ... contempt for their betters?: J. A. Spender, *Life of H. H. Asquith*, I (London, 1932), 256; see also Magnus, *King Edward*, 528q. It was not of course to be believed ...: Dangerfield, *Strange Death*, 24ff; Tuchman, *Proud Tower*, 385ff, 396ff. "a born cad": John Campbell, "In One Place or Another," *TLS*, March 8, 1985, 249q. strange new peers: Tuchman, *Proud Tower*, 393. "Zounds ...": Falstaff in *Henry IV, Part 1*. "You have killed the

King...": Spender, *Asquith*, I, 283. One day in July...: Dangerfield, *Strange Death*, 55ff; see also Tuchman, *Proud Tower*, 398ff. "white with anger": Tuchman, *ibid.*, 398q. "a disorderly assembly": *ibid.*, 399. the Lords met to decide...: *ibid.*, 399ff; Dangerfield, *Strange Death*, 43ff, 61ff. "... the last ditch": Tuchman, *Proud Tower*, 396. "to vulgarize our order": Campbell, "In One Place or Another," 249q. It was 131 to 114...: Dangerfield, *Strange Death*, 65; Spender, *Asquith*, 327.

Pp. 95–98. "force majeure": Dudley Barker, "Mrs. Emmeline Pankhurst," in *Prominent Edwardians*, 214. ... the lively suffragette business: see Dangerfield, *Strange Death*, Part II, ch. 3 ("The Women's Rebellion"), esp. 147ff. "The time comes...": Mackenzie, *Shoulder to Shoulder*, 73q. ... heckling *him*: Barker, *Prominent Edwardians*, 220. they would be pelting...: Mackenzie, *Shoulder to Shoulder*, 122ff. His face went white...: *ibid.*, 137. On his way home one night...: Blunt, *Diaries*, 335. ... must not walk on the greens: *ibid.*, 275. On Lord Mayor's Day...: Mackenzie, *Shoulder to Shoulder*, 137. like hardened criminals: *ibid.*, 124. a new and terrible tactic: Dangerfield, *Strange Death*, 176ff; Mackenzie, *Shoulder to Shoulder*, 110ff. forced feeding: *ibid.*, 122ff. ... case of Lady Constance: *ibid.*, 133ff, 146ff. Poor Miss Emily Davison: West, *Young Rebecca*, 95, 179. But the statesman...: Blunt, *Diaries*, 297. Nor was the king...: Magnus, *King Edward*, 479. "... should not be adopted": Mackenzie, *Shoulder to Shoulder*, 130q. there were rogues...: Barker, *Prominent Edwardians*, 216, 227. "the vicious rush...": Lawrence, *Letters*, 123. "a big splendid woman...": *ibid.*, 123–124. resumed their offensive: Dangerfield, *Strange Death*, 156ff; Mackenzie, *Shoulder to Shoulder*, 162ff; Barker, *Prominent Edwardians*, 226–227.

Pp. 98–101. little James Barrie sat...: Mackail, *Story of J.M.B.*, 380. and Hilaire Belloc...: Ward, *Chesterton*, 288. ... for Labour's Keir Hardie: Charlotte Shaw, *Diary*, January 4, 1910, entry, British Museum. "royal bastards... ancient kings": James Hepburn, ed., *Letters of Arnold Bennett*, I (London, 1966), 130n (hereafter Bennett, *Letters*). "some jolly Labour man": Brooke, *Letters*, 209. "... rid of the Lords": *ibid.*, 263. ... of his *Clayhanger*: Bennett, *Journal*, 358–359. ... end of the month 33,200: *ibid.*, 363. "... its damned Tory colors": *ibid.*, 360. On Saturday night...: *ibid.*, 361. "The fools won't...": *ibid.*, 362. Hewlett... traveled first class: Mrs. Belloc Lowndes, *The Merry Wives of Westminster* (London, 1946), 107. "RRRRomantik nuvls": Ezra Pound, in unpublished letter to Patricia Hutchins, Hutchins collection, British Museum. "a most proud...": Shaw, *Letters*, II, 840. declared himself a socialist: Mrs. Lowndes, *Merry Wives*, 107. and that January at Leicester...: Laurence Binyon, ed., *Letters of Maurice Hewlett* (London, 1926), 104 (hereafter Hewlett, *Letters*). "I have had such gifts...": *ibid.*, 105. "The Election fight...": Percy Lubbock, ed., *The Letters of Henry James*, II (New York, 1920), 155. "... a rabid socialist": Edel, *James*, 382–383. Buchan... Conservative candidate: Smith, *Buchan*, 56. friends on both sides: *ibid.*; see also Buchan, *Memory Hold-the-Door*, 144. "prevent a Liberal...": Birkenhead, *Kipling*, 256q. "howling syndicalism": Wilson, *Kipling*, 233q. "I am not so keen...": Wells, *New Machiavelli*, 383. "the class upon which...": *ibid.*, 388. didn't want power for the working class: Mackenzie, *Wells*, 185; West, *Wells*, 125–126. "children of the abyss": Dickson, *Wells*, 90q. "We must have an aristocracy": Wells, *New Machiavelli*, 334. "... a Tory Seat attached to it": Richard Ludwig, ed., *The Letters of Ford Madox Ford* (Princeton, 1965), 44. ... and the Roman Catholic Church: Ford, *Return*, 367. ... in the Divine Right of Kings: Hunt, *I Have This to Say*, 194q.

". . . must be a rebel": Furbank, *Forster,* 160. ". . . and the constitution!": Forster, *Letters,* 99. . . . for the governing classes: Holroyd, *Strachey,* 401n. Stick to writing . . . : *ibid.,* 520–521. . . . for the radical cause: Bell, *Woolf,* I, 161. and Keynes who was asking . . . : Harrod, *Keynes,* 153. all very male . . . : *ibid.,* 155. ". . . will seem very dull": *ibid.,* 154. It wasn't something Russell . . . : Russell, *Autobiography,* 311ff. "Do you think I'd vote . . .": *ibid.,* 313. booed at and stoned: Lady Ottoline, *Memoirs,* 167. ". . . over democratic disorder": *ibid.,* 168. "in an ecstasy of martyrdom": *ibid.,* 167. "in earnest about public life": Russell, *Autobiography,* 313. . . . had lost: Lady Ottoline, *Memoirs,* 168.

Pp. 102–104. Once at a dinner Vanessa . . . : Gadd, *Loving Friends,* 6. cheer for the great Liberal victory: Bell, *Woolf,* I, 161. "next Portuguese Jews . . .": Woolf, *Letters,* 441. One morning in February, the emperor of Abyssinia . . . : Bell, *Woolf,* I, 157ff; see also Adrian Stephen, "The *Dreadnought* Hoax," in S. P. Rosenbaum, ed., *The Bloomsbury Group* (Toronto, 1975), 32ff. confer with the First Lord himself: Woolf, *Letters,* 423.

Pp. 104–105. "Odors from the abyss": Forster, *Howards End,* 117. "They all knew him! . . .": Joseph Conrad, *The Nigger of the "Narcissus"* [1897] (New York, 1979), 6. "I'd batten them down . . .": Drabble, *Bennett,* 190q. "Labor will come out of it . . .": Birkinhead, *Kipling,* 255q. "The Government [was] proceeding . . .": James, *Letters,* 606. "he was never really . . .": Woolf, *Sowing,* 166; see also 107–108. "the poor [had] *suffered* . . .": Drabble, *Bennett,* 190. "Workmen on strike . . .": Bennett, *Hilda Lessways,* 291. "War on employers . . .": Bennett, *Old Wives' Tale,* 579. . . . with blacklegs and scabs: J. M. Cameron, "Innocent at Home," *TLS,* April 28, 1983, 25. "police shot down . . .": *ibid.* "the sanest, jolliest . . .": Barker, *Chesterton,* 183q. "the condescension with which . . .": West, *Young Rebecca,* 218. Nationalize . . . : Shaw, *Letters,* II, 718. "the old eastern plan . . .": *ibid.,* 946. Cunninghame Graham had early supported . . . : Karl, *Conrad,* 394. "It needed a volcano . . .": Watts and Davies, *Cunninghame Graham,* 232q. "I am not one of those . . .": *ibid.,* 271q. ". . . to feel aristocratic": *ibid.*

Pp. 106–110. ". . . gibbered with rage": Brooke, *Letters,* 247. a passionate hatred of Labor: Dangerfield, *Strange Death,* 169; Barker, *Prominent Edwardians,* 190. . . . expelled from the ranks: Dangerfield, *Strange Death,* 213, 369. to the utter dismay of Rebecca West . . . : West, *Young Rebecca,* 93. "Votes for Ladies": Ward, *Chesterton,* 302. ". . . to man, not to woman, them!": Hunt, *I Have This to Say,* 52q. "Write for . . . the *New Freewoman?*" Pound and Shakespear, *Letters,* 252. "I give it up": James, *Letters,* 606–607. "the most powerful argument . . .": Bennett, *Letters,* II, 271. ". . . they ought to": Woolf, *Wise Virgins,* 68. and Russell was suggesting . . . : Darroch, *Ottoline,* 119. "I believe the ladies . . .": Holroyd, *Strachey,* 339q. ". . . and be torn to pieces": *ibid.,* 434q. "very obtrusively feminine . . .": Hunt, *I Have This to Say,* 66. "had never voted once . . .": Edward Nehls, *D. H. Lawrence: A Composite Biography,* I (Madison, Wisc., 1957), 123q. that a distressed Lady Gregory . . . : Ford, *Return,* 411. "It will please them . . .": Karl, *Conrad,* 683n. "badgering cabinet ministers . . .": Wells, *Ann Veronica,* 154. "hurled herself . . .": James, *Letters,* 471. ". . . and very unpleasant": Forster, *Letters,* 128. "no reason why women . . .": Morgan, *Maugham,* 168q. a million more uninformed ballots: Weintraub, *London Yankees,* 281. . . . of their voting at all: Materer, *Vortex,* 72. ". . . the man's mistress will rule": Preface to *Misalliance,* in *Complete Plays,* IV, 66. "participation in public affairs . . .": Shaw, *Letters,* II, 491; see also Holroyd, "Women and the Body Politic," 177. "Unless Woman repudiates . . .": *ibid.,* 171q. ". . . they are given the vote": *ibid.,* 177q. "idiot-genius": Peters, *Shaw,* 313. votes for women were just as futile . . . : *ibid.,* 314. "What use is the vote? . . .": see Shaw, *Press Cuttings.* ". . . and Chastity for Men": Hynes, *Edwardian Turn of Mind,* 201. In her book *The Great Scourge . . . :* Dangerfield, *Strange Death,* 199. . . . of sexual perversion.: Hynes, *Edwardian Turn of Mind,* 206. "thought Sapphism disgusting": Bell, *Woolf,* II, 138q. Ethel Smyth the composer . . . : Hilary Spurling, "A Woman's March," *TLS,* July 3, 1987, 712. . . . was founding in 1911 the *Freewoman:* K. K. Ruthven, "Ezra's Appropriations," *TLS,* November 20–26, 1987, 1300ff. Rebecca West who at eighteen . . . : West, *Young Rebecca,* [ed. introduction], 4. "Shaw in skirts": *ibid.,* [ed. note], 24. a center for . . . : Harriet Monroe, *A Poet's Life* (New York, 1938), 222. "and her eloquent daughter Christabel": *ibid.* Violet Hunt had turned her house South Lodge . . . : Brigit Patmore, *My Friends When Young* (London, 1968), 53. . . . with other suffragette swells: Lawrence, *Letters,* 364. . . . not taking care of her children: Patmore, *My Friends,* 52. Katherine Mansfield was expelled . . . : Meyers, *Mansfield,* 75. "a dear old lady . . .": West, *Young Rebecca,* 162. Even Mrs. Webb . . . : Mackenzie, *Fabians,* 365; see *ibid.,* 335, and West, *Wells,* 305. "writing names like Cowgill . . .": Bell, *Woolf,* I, 161. ". . . just like a Wells novel": Woolf, *Letters,* 422. Dorothy Richardson was all . . . : Fromm, *Richardson,* 51. For sure Lady Ottoline . . . : Lady Ottoline, *Memoirs,* 158. . . . nothing whatever to do with them: Darroch, *Ottoline,* 119. When Christabel published . . . : West, *Young Rebecca,* 7, 206. she lamented the movement's . . . : *ibid.,* 93, 101ff. ". . . our women syndicalists?": *ibid.,* 104.

Pp. 111–113. Mrs. Webb . . . was beseeching the dramatists: Hynes, *Edwardian Turn of Mind,* 127–129; Mackenzie, *Fabians,* 367. "the condition of England": Hunter, *Edwardian Fiction,* ch. 15. It's even on record . . . : H. V. Marrot, *The Life and Letters of John Galsworthy* (New York, 1936), 255ff; Dudley Barker, *The Man of Principle: A View of John Galsworthy* (London, 1963), 150. ". . . the dark human problem": Lewis, *Wharton,* 242q. "it is a revelation": Marrot, *Galsworthy,* 257q. "We all cried . . .": *ibid.,* 258q. "great in its realistic form . . .": Hynes, *Edwardian Turn of Mind,* 129q. "I've always opposed . . .": Barker, *Galsworthy,* 150q. "His eyes were observed . . .": Marrot, *Galsworthy,* 261. But Winston Churchill . . . : *ibid.,* 283. ". . . into raptures!": *ibid.,* 267q. . . . would very much like to be classic: Edward Marsh, *A Number of People* (New York, 1939), 240.

Pp. 113–118. "had no use . . .": Hunt, *I Have This to Say,* 41. ". . . an ill-fed boy": *Howards End,* 45. "Give them money . . .": *ibid.,* 127. "the lilting step . . .": *ibid.,* 42. ". . . sort of way": *ibid.,* 48. "He put his hat on . . .": *ibid.,* 125. the failure of liberals . . . : see "Undecided Prophets," in Hynes, *Edwardian Turn of Mind.* . . . what bitter loathing: West, *Wells,* 272. "I hate low, uneducated people! . . .": Gissing, *Born in Exile* (London, 1893), 40. "that sallow, unhealthy . . .": Hugh Walpole, *Mr. Perrin and Mr. Traill* [1911] (London, 1925), 143–144. "beware of the man . . .": Edgar Lee Masters, "John Hancock Otis," in *Spoon River Anthology.* "troof" "togever": see, for example, Wells, *Kipps,* 295, 304. "The stupid little tragedies . . .": *ibid.,* 296. "a monster . . .": *ibid.,* 296–297. "They do very well . . .": *ibid.,* 319. Instead of living in the country . . . : E. Nesbit, *Five Children and It* [1902] (London, 1971), 20. "Of course there are the shops . . .": *ibid.* "But how badly . . .": E. Nesbit, *The Story of the Amulet* [1906] (London, 1980), 148–149.

"The servility that . . .": Bennett, *Hilda Lessways*, 195. "a dehumanized drudge": *ibid.*, 36. "the prone forms . . .": *ibid.*, 221. "the vein of greatness . . .": Bennett, *Old Wives' Tale*, 267. "the miraculous human power . . .": Bennett, *Hilda Lessways*, 316. The butler takes over . . . : *The Admirable Crichton,* in *The Plays of J. M. Barrie,* 210. ". . . born to wait at table": *ibid.*, 220. "the humble bearing . . ." and address-ing Lady Mary: *ibid.*, 230. ". . . something wrong with England": *ibid.*, 246. . . . how shocking it was: Andrew Birkin, *J. M. Barrie and the Lost Boys* (New York, 1979), 94. ". . . a word against England": *The Admirable Crichton,* 246. go accord-ing to precedence . . . : *ibid.*, 181. "Can't you see, Crichton . . .": *ibid.*, 178. In his novel *Fraternity* . . . : see Hunter, *Edwardian Fiction,* 225. "his duty in that state . . .": Wells, *Kipps,* 44. "the Argus eyes . . .": *ibid.*, 268. "Arthur Cuyps, frock-coated . . .": *ibid.*, 162. his wicked old mother: West, *Wells,* 168–169, 299.

Pp. 118–121. "But this is a woman's play. . . .": Peters, *Shaw,* 77q. Achurch, Farr, Robins: *ibid.*, 55, 73–74, 78–79. a new breed of actress . . . : *ibid.*, 123ff. "Don't you think . . .": *ibid.*, 125q. the wrath of the pit: Yeats, *Autobiography,* 186. Lena Ashwell received . . . : Peters, *Shaw,* 312. Gertrude Kingston would estab-lish . . . : G. B. Purdom, *Harley Granville Barker* (London, 1955), 122. She would rather have opened with . . . : Laurence Housman, *The Unexpected Years* (New York, 1936), 244ff. . . . also *by* the new woman: Peters, *Shaw,* 307. . . . the rebel-lious Elizabeth Robins: *ibid.*, 77ff. . . . started the New Century Theatre: *ibid.*, 237. *Votes for Women!*: *ibid.*, 307ff; see also Hynes, *Edwardian Turn of Mind,* 201ff. ". . . not to have a vote": Forster, *Howards End,* 77. "the woman who can't . . .": *ibid.*, 230. "now a little bundle . . .": *What Every Woman Knows,* in *Plays of J. M. Barrie,* 399. ". . . Every woman knows that": *ibid.*, 399. "a phase": Wells, *Ann Veronica,* 278. ". . . better stuff than herself": *ibid.*, 263. ". . . an attitude": Conrad, *Chance,* 124. . . . no scruples to stand in her way: *ibid.*, 50. "too sincerely hunger-struck": Rhoda Koenig, "A Genius for Revenge," *New York Review of Books,* Octo-ber 8, 1981, 34q. . . . to his lions and wolves: *ibid.* ". . . just like a man": Shaw, *Letters, 1911–1925,* III, 64. ". . . practically unsexed": Holroyd, "Women and the Body Politic," 170q. ". . . developed as a woman": Peters, *Shaw,* 299. ". . . fortified her courage": Holroyd, "Women and the Body Politic," 174q.

Pp. 121–124. "I had a sudden vision . . .": Bennett, *Journals,* 396. "I always do . . .": *The Voysey Inheritance* in Granville Barker, *Three Plays* (London, 1909), 116. "the faculty of men and women . . .": Bennett, *Hilda Lessways,* 293. ". . . to ex-perience": Wells, *Ann Veronica,* 4–5. "glorious young beast": Shaw, *Misalliance,* in *Complete Plays,* IV, 142. "Men like conventions . . .": *ibid.*, 165. "Oh home! home! . . .": *ibid.*, 143. "I want you. . . .": Wells, *Ann Veronica,* 322. "Come, hand-some young man . . .": Shaw, *Misalliance,* 163. "not accustomed . . .": *ibid.*, 154. "dolefully": *Admirable Crichton,* in *Plays of J. M. Barrie,* 235. emerald-green stock-ings: Lawrence, *Women in Love,* 2. "My heart aches . . .": Keats, *Ode to a Nightin-gale.* "like a girl's": *Svengali, George du Maurier's Trilby* [1894] (London, 1982), 103; see also 70, 75. ". . . as if they were men.": Barker, *Madras House* (London, 1977), 68. ". . . no such thing as a woman": Shaw, *Letters, 1911–1925,* III, 64. "I am a woman . . .": Holroyd, "Women and the Body Politic," 170q. "I believe . . .": Mackenzie, *Wells,* 283q. "with different shades . . .": Fromm, *Richardson,* 48q. "The mind reels . . .": West, *Young Rebecca,* 68. . . . "sunlit" Ann: Wells, *Kipps,* 201. "warm and welcoming": *ibid.*, 193. ". . . little girl woman": *ibid.*, 267. ". . . gladness in her eyes": *ibid.*, 195. "Sundayfied . . .": *ibid.*, 193. "glancing up . . .": Wells, *Tono-*

Bungay, 199. "my glad and pretty...": *ibid.,* 200. "Typical of...": Wells, *New Machiavelli,* 427. "jolly march...": *ibid.,* 457. "small and beautiful": Tom Paulin, "A Weight of Balls," *TLS,* July 6–12, 1990, 733q. "I could roll...": Wells, *Ann Veronica,* 351. "A woman is not...": Conrad, *Chance,* 45. "...who are really women": *ibid.,* 240.

Pp. 125–129. "To speke of wo...": Chaucer, "Wife of Bath's Tale," 1. 3. "To establish cruelty...": Wells, *Tono-Bungay,* 195–196. "your gratuitously...": Shaw, *Letters,* II, 429. "the present odious law...": Delavenay, *Lawrence and Carpenter,* 108q. Bennett's *Whom God Hath Joined...*: see Hynes, *Edwardian Turn of Mind,* 192ff. "Imagine being married to...": Shaw, Preface to *Getting Married,* in *Complete Plays,* IV, 368. The only sane grounds...: *ibid.,* 370. "knocked her flat down...": Shaw, *Getting Married,* 407. poor Reggie has had to arrange...: *ibid.,* 411. In 1903 the Society...: Hynes, *Edwardian Turn of Mind,* 192. "No moral cause...": Hewlett, *Letters,* 112. "which cannot be discussed...": Magnus, *King Edward,* 542q. "You can make...": Shaw, *Getting Married,* 455. No, said Wells...: Dickson, *Wells,* 158ff. "...why get married?": Barker, *Voysey Inheritance,* in *Three Plays,* 118. "...to get married": Bennett, *Hilda Lessways,* 54. "Surely, surely...": William York Tindall, *Forces in Modern British Literature* (New York, 1956), 32q. "I am strong...": *Misalliance,* 201. "...kissed her": Woolf, *Wise Virgins,* 247. "unfortunate amoor": Wells, *Mr. Polly,* 106. "Wiltou lover...": *ibid.,* 111. "...*you can change it*": *ibid.,* 172. "They say you can't...": Wells, *Kipps,* 79. "...in a world of lovers": Wells, *In the Days of the Comet* (New York, 1906), 377. "I have never concealed...": Shaw, *Letters,* II, 650. "Oh how silly...": Shaw, *Getting Married,* 414. "Married people should...": *ibid.,* 398. "as much Nature's way...": Barker, *Madras House,* 195. "with the rabbit-warren aspect...": Hynes, *Edwardian Turn of Mind,* 129q. "to see G.B.S....": *ibid.,* 195q. "Do you see this face...": Shaw, *Getting Married,* 462. "attack on marriage...": Shaw, *Letters,* II, 560. "The thing one wants...": *Getting Married,* 491. "...by the communion of saints": *ibid.,* 454. "My kingdom was not...": John Stewart Collis, "Religion and Philosophy," in Holroyd, *Genius of Shaw,* 93q. Erica Cotterill...: G. G. L. DuCann, *The Loves of G. B. Shaw* (New York, 1963), 233ff; Shaw, *Letters,* II, 562–563 (ed. note). mad for the beauteous actress...: Peters, *Shaw,* 330–350. "...rag-and-bone shop of the heart": Yeats, "The Circus Animal's Desertion."

Pp. 130–134. "...no moe marriages": *Hamlet.* "...pencilled eyebrows": Joseph Conrad, *Victory* [1915] (New York, 1921), 92. "...inside somewhere": *ibid.,* 106. "...problem of illicit love": Mrs. Lowndes, *Merry Wives,* 151. make sex the primary fact...: West, *Wells,* 236. Not enough for H.G....: *ibid.,* 14ff. "...not only in novels but in real life": Wells, *Autobiography,* 396. "the ferment of sex...": Wells, *Tono-Bungay,* 113. "Dame Nature driving [him]...": *ibid.,* 166. "...the fate of the nation": *ibid.,* 162. "the stupendous...": *ibid.,* 167. appetite... "roused and whetted": *ibid.,* 188. "trails about...": *ibid.,* 174–175. "The beauty which...": Wells, *New Machiavelli,* 438. "We lay side by side...": *ibid.,* 479. "...the blazing sunset sky behind us": *ibid.,* 483. "If I am to be a mother...": Shaw, *Getting Married,* 403. "Good Lord! Why hasn't she had a child?...": Woolf, *Wise Virgins,* 179. "...procure a baby at once": Diana Farr, *Gilbert Cannan: A Georgian Prodigy* (London, 1978), 133q. "the old maid's right...": Shaw, Preface, *Getting Married,* 346. "...their right to maternity?": *ibid.,* 347. "...every unmated member of her sex": Max Beerbohm, *Zuleika Dob-*

son [1911] (London, 1947), 15. ". . . it must have been the umbrella": King, *Forster,* 47–49q. "I am now going to read . . .": The Hon. Evans Charteris, *The Life and Letters of Sir Edmund Gosse* (London, 1931), 324. "our pretty little house . . .": Peters, "As Lonely as God," 187q. "There are larger loves . . .": Shaw, *Major Barbara,* in *Complete Plays with Prefaces,* I (New York, 1962), 408. "Eternal union . . .": Forster, *The Longest Journey* [1907] (New York, 1922), 292. "*the* problem . . .": Moore, *Lawrence,* 231q. "You've got to take down . . .": Lawrence, *Women in Love,* 345. neither "marriage nor giving in marriage": H.D., *Bid Me to Live,* 62. "sisters of Artemis . . .": Lawrence, *Women in Love,* 2. Not "the world all in couples . . .": *ibid.,* 344. "as sacred . . .": Meyers, "Lawrence and Homosexuality," 137q. ". . . additional to marriage": Lawrence, *Women in Love,* 345. "her hands full on his thighs . . .": *ibid.,* 305–306; see Meyers on the subject, "Lawrence and Homosexuality," 145–146. "I don't believe . . .": Douglas, *South Wind,* 111.

Pp. 134–135. "Where do we go . . .": T. S. Eliot, "Ezra Pound," in Walter Sutton, ed., *Ezra Pound: A Collection of Critical Essays* (New York, 1963), 17. "Now Swinburne is dead . . .": Woolf, *Letters,* 390. "About 1908 Letters . . .": Jepson, *Memoirs,* 131. ". . . the place for poesy": D. D. Paige, ed., *The Letters of Ezra Pound, 1907–1941* (New York, 1950), 7 (hereafter Pound, *Letters*). "a doughy mess of . . .": Hugh Kenner, *The Pound Era* (Berkeley, 1971), 80q. and at Cambridge the young undergraduates . . . : Woolf, *Sowing,* 167–168. "the great yard of the Museum . . .": Ford, *Return,* 51. "Good Heavens! Poetry!": Ada Leverson, *The Little Ottleys* [1908, 1912, 1916] (New York, 1982), 10. ". . . erotic verses": Robinson, *H.D.,* 64q. ". . . before I did": Pound, *Letters,* 17. One day in the British Museum . . . : Robinson, *H.D.,* 28.

Pp. 136–140. The city's West End . . . : Morgan, *Maugham,* 99. The actor, Gerald du Maurier . . . : Petrie, *Scenes,* 33. theatrical societies: Martin, *New Age,* 72ff. Poor Bernard Shaw: Shaw, *Letters,* II, 300, 389 (ed. notes); see also Shaw letter to Archer, 362ff, and Stanley Weintraub, *Shaw: An Autobiography, 1898–1950,* II (New York, 1970), 31 (hereafter Shaw, *Autobiography,* II). . . . the Royal Court Theatre: Holroyd, *Shaw, 1898–1918,* II, 97ff; Shaw, *Letters,* II, 389ff (ed. note); Mackenzie, *Fabians,* 305ff; Purdom, *Barker,* 26ff. a congenial place . . . : Purdom, *Barker,* 27. Opening in October with . . . : Shaw, *Letters,* II, 389 (ed. note). In the nearly three years . . . : Purdom, *Barker,* 64. . . . prevailingly Shavian: Shaw, *Letters,* II, 390 (ed. note); Shaw, *Autobiography,* II, 44. who commanded a performance: Mackenzie, *Fabians,* 307. . . . the chair he sat in collapsed: Barnet, Berman, and Burto, eds., *The Genius of the Irish Theater* (New York, 1960), 12. . . . spoil the performance: Collis, "Religion and Philosophy," in Holroyd, *Genius of Shaw,* 91. and Eliza Doolittle's "not bloody likely": Peters, *Shaw,* 362. Only Shaw's plays . . . : Shaw, *Letters,* II, 550. So London's established poets and novelists . . . : Purdom, *Barker,* 66. ". . . and Wessex torments me": Shaw, *Letters,* II, 757. . . . Masefield and Hewlett and Wells: Shaw, *Autobiography,* II, 34. He sent Chesterton . . . : Ward, *Chesterton,* 234. "I shall repeat . . .": Shaw, *Letters,* II, 759. ". . . Shaw's and not his": Shaw, *Autobiography,* II, 34. Nor in the end would it have to seek Barker out: Holroyd, *Shaw,* II, 93. Even Conrad . . . : Karl, *Conrad,* 561–562. . . . requesting a play: *ibid.,* 590. So a play at the Court . . . : Purdom, *Barker,* 28, 35, 38. Shaw himself . . . : Shaw, *Letters, 1911–1925,* III, 46. The great Mrs. Campbell . . . : Purdom, *Barker,* 50, 61; see also Peters, *Shaw,* 300. "£25 and 'find her own gowns' . . .": Shaw, *Letters,* II, 421. She turned down the offer: Peters, *Shaw,* 260.

... the exhausting rehearsals: Mackenzie, *Fabians*, 307–308; Shaw, *Autobiography*, II, 35. the players were drilled ... : Swinnerton, *Background*, 101. Shaw himself ... : Shaw, *Letters*, II, 271. "as Debussy's ...": Shaw, *Autobiography*, II, 35. "... Mozartian joyousness": Shaw, *Letters*, II, 216. "... stagey on the stage": *ibid.*, 391. "When I was a little girl ...": Shaw, *Autobiography*, II, 32q. "... in *Venice Preserved*": *ibid.*, 33. ... and even the staging: Shaw, *Letters*, II, 390–391, 580 (ed. notes). "We were members of ...": Mackenzie, *Fabians*, 307q. "... and not the actors the plays": Shaw, *Letters, 1911–1925*, III, 46. in 1904 no Janet Achurch ...: *ibid.*, 46. Or would Lawrence ... : Lawrence, *Letters*, 298. Ezra Pound would translate ...: Stock, *Pound*, 120. and Rupert Brooke ... : Brooke, *Letters*, 325. Henry James had been jeered ... : Maugham, *Vagrant Mood*, 198. But now it was 1909 ... : Compton Mackenzie, *My Life and Times, 1907–1915*, 57, 58; Edel, *James*, 368ff. "a London of 'Barker at the Court' ...": Ford, *Provence* (New York, 1979), 193–194.

Pp. 140–143. in chromatic titles like ... : Gordon N. Ray, "Introduction," Wells, *Mr. Polly*, viii. The fields of fiction were fallow ... : Hunter, *Edwardian Fiction*, 66. "they didn't seem ...": Wells, *Wheels of Chance*, 170. "When the Rudyards ...": Harris, *Life and Loves*, 951. Open it up to new facts ... : Hunter, *Edwardian Fiction*, 61ff. "We are not concerned ...": Forster, *Howards End*, 45. "Samuel had a mild ...": Bennett, *Old Wives' Tale*, 214. "your little house": Bennett, *Buried Alive*, 98. "Eggs! Toast! ...": *ibid.*, 110. "the ideal companion ...": *ibid.*, 111. "It seemed to breathe of romance ...": *ibid.*, 99. "nothing on earth ...": Wells, *Kipps*, 309. "Really, old Sid ...": *ibid.*, 217. "I seem to see it ...": *ibid.*, 262. It was this passion ... : Petrie, *Scenes*, 34. Was there anything at all Wells ... : Hunter, *Edwardian Fiction*, 61–62. ... and building of houses?: *ibid.*, 68. "the very romance of manufacture ...": *ibid.* "... of a great railway system": *ibid.* "the moral consciousness ...": James, *Partial Portraits* (London, 1919), 403. "Far from being adventurous ...": *Conrad's Prefaces to His Works* (London, 1937), 153. "the romance of yard-arm ...": Conrad, *Notes on Life and Letters* (London, 1949), 14. "golden hair ...": James, Albert Mordell, ed., *Literary Reviews and Essays* (New Haven, 1957), 213. "... fanciful invention": Conrad, *Last Essays* (London, 1955), 126. "those artistic perversions ...": James, *Partial Portraits*, 104. "the romance of the real": Leon Edel, ed., *Selected Letters of Henry James* (New York, 1960), 162. "a special imaginative freedom": *Conrad's Prefaces*, 153. "... no matter where they live": *ibid.*, 38. "J'ai vécu ...": Gerard Jean-Aubry, *Joseph Conrad, Life and Letters*, II (New York, 1927), 182q.

Pp. 144–150. "A little mad ...": Tytell, *Pound*, 49q. "break it up ...": Forster, *Aspects of the Novel* (New York, 1927), 152. "loose baggy monsters": James, *The Art of the Novel: Critical Prefaces* (New York, 1934), 84. Conrad and Hueffer descanted ... : Goldring, *Life Interests* (London, 1948), 192. "The finest French novel ...": Ford, "Dedicatory Letter," *The Good Soldier*, xx. "nuvvle": Swinnerton, *Background*, 117q. "my masters ...": Ford, "Dedicatory Letter", xx. "the highest form ...": see Ray, "Introduction," *Mr. Polly*, xiq. "... one great and simple effect": *ibid.*, xivq. "the bearing of ...": *ibid.*, ixq. "every sentence ...": *ibid.*, xivq. "that he cannot ...": *ibid.*, xiiq. "... I *will* write novels": *ibid.*, xxq. "Big, purblind ...": Swinnerton, *Background*, 115. ... bulging with manuscripts: *ibid.* Despairing of seeing it in print ... : Garnett, *Great Friends*, 30. that the Bosinney ... : *ibid.*, 108. "I simply *can't* ...": Karl, *Conrad*, 404. Young Lawrence was at a loss: Arthur

Mizener, *The Saddest Story: A Biography of Ford Madox Ford* (New York, 1971), 173; see also Swinnerton, *Background,* 115. "like a good angel": Mizener, *Ford,* 173q. *Sons and Lovers* would have . . . : Heilbrun, *Garnett Family,* 143. "jolly well": *ibid.,* 152. arrange for the collaboration . . . : Garnett, *Great Friends,* 14. Get published . . . : see *ibid.,* 61, and Heilbrun, *Garnett Family,* 106, 133. interested in the work of young writers: *ibid.,* 140. praised Frost, *Howards End, Old Wives' Tale: ibid.,* 136–137, 139; see also Drabble, *Bennett,* 157. "the true knight-errant . . .": Watt, *Conrad in the Nineteenth Century,* 68q. "the only man . . .": Heilbrun, *Garnett Family,* 140q. . . . let go by his Conrad and Lawrence: Karl, *Conrad,* 629; Swinnerton, *Background,* 115–116. "grey, jowl-like cheeks": *ibid.,* 116q. "with a very superior sourness . . .": Jepson, *Memoirs,* 143. "Oh Mr. Garnett . . .": Garnett, *Golden Echo,* 183q. "Huefferisms": Moser, "From Olive Garnett's Diary," 516. "poor H was dead in earnest . . .": Karl, *Conrad,* 483q. "the most serious . . .": Swinnerton, *Background,* 117q. "The novel is not . . .": Edward Garnett, *Letters from W. H. Hudson,* 162. "I don't care for . . .": Garnett, *Great Friends,* 30. plotting a new monthly journal: Mizener, *Ford,* 154ff. "copious carelessness . . .": Wells, *Autobiography,* 525. to serialize *Tono-Bungay:* Ford, *Letters,* 31. To serialize Conrad's . . . : Ford, *Return,* 191. To print poet Hardy's . . . : *ibid.,* 370. it was the *Fortnightly:* Millgate, *Hardy,* 452. "imaginative literature . . .": Ford, *Letters,* 40. ". . . might see the light": *ibid.,* 43. Wells was excited: Mizener, *Ford,* 154–155. "It's It this year!" Hunt, *I Have This to Say,* 10q. "If this Review . . .": Dickson, *Wells,* 167n. "The *ER* may have . . .": Mizener, *Ford,* 166q. He'd invite the editor down to Someries . . . : Goldring, *South Lodge,* 23–24; Mizener, *Ford,* 166. . . . in lamp oil and candles: Jessie Conrad, *Conrad,* 131. "a socialistic undertaking": Ford, *Letters,* 28. a guinea a page: Mizener, *Ford,* 159. . . . at 48 Holland Park Avenue.: Hunt, *I Have This to Say,* 11ff. ". . . smell of chickens": *ibid.,* 11–12. . . . carcases of rabbits: Goldring, *Life Interests,* 192. . . . to Dante Gabriel Rossetti: cf. Hunt, *I Have This to Say,* 12; Goldring, *Trained for Genius,* 52; Mizener, *Ford,* 16. His editorial procedures . . . : *ibid.,* 166ff. in the stalls of the Empire Theatre: Goldring, *Life Interests,* 193. . . . manner of making decisions: MacShane, *Ford,* 78. I'll take it, he said: Hunt, *I Have This to Say,* 13. worked editorial wonders: Mizener, *Ford,* 167ff. review of Anatole France's . . . : Goldring, *South Lodge,* 30. A young woman of Nottingham . . . : Philip Callow, *Son and Lover* (London, 1975), 140–141. Fresh from Paris . . . : Mizener, *Ford,* 168; see also Wyndham Lewis, *Rude Assignment* (London, n.d.), 121. Fresh from Venice . . . : Simpson, *Three on the Tower,* 12. "as near to the ideal . . .": Martin, *New Age,* 89q. Hueffer . . . in heaven: Ford, *Return,* 347ff; Mizener, *Ford,* 171ff. "looking like . . .": Hunt, *I Have This to Say,* 59. A party for Anatole France . . . : Patmore, *My Friends,* 54. A supper party . . . : Rhys, *Everyman Remembers,* 243ff. "genial warmth": Nehls, *Lawrence,* I, 125q. "the kindest man . . .": Lawrence, *Letters,* 138. "a much better fellow . . .": Karl, *Conrad,* 590q. Every morning at eleven . . . : Ford, *Return,* 347–348. "the great good place": Ford, *Provence,* 143.

Pp. 150–155. "London knew little . . .": Spalding, *Vanessa,* 92q. ". . . by pictures and painting": Woolf, *Sowing,* 128n. . . . the gift of a Degas: Morgan, *Maugham,* 78. In 1903 Camille Mauclair's . . . : Spalding, *Vanessa,* 37. exhibit of the classic impressionists: Hynes, *Edwardian Turn of Mind,* 324. ". . . license of artistic tradition": John, *Chiaroscuro,* 136. In 1907 he'd assemble . . . : Wendy Baron, *Sickert* (New York, 1973), 104ff. started her Friday Club: Spalding, *Vanessa,* 56; Bell, *Woolf,* I, 105. launching the Contemporary Art Society: Darroch, *Otto-*

line, 73. One early morning in January 1910 . . . : Spalding, *Vanessa*, 84ff; Bell, *Woolf*, I, 167ff; Edel, *Bloomsbury*, 158ff. ". . . and rather an ass": Jepson, *Memoirs*, 43. "une voix . . .": Desmond MacCarthy, *Memories* (New York, 1953), 177. ". . . for their own sakes": Woolf, *Fry*, 149q. Clive had journeyed to Paris: Edel, *Blooms-bury*, 101ff. Would he not?: Clive Bell, *Old Friends* (London, 1956), 80. "Wonder-ful! wonderful!": MacCarthy, *Memories*, 180q. By the time the show opened . . . : Edel, *Bloomsbury*, 163. "Oh, let's just call them . . .": *ibid.*; see also MacCarthy, *Memories*, 181. "a huge campaign . . .": Fry, *Letters*, 337. "a good rocking horse . . .": Woolf, *Fry*, 153q. Before the portrait of Cézanne's wife . . . : Mac-Carthy, *Memories*, 183. ". . . artistic insanities": Martin, *New Age*, 133q. . . . was splenetic: Blunt, *Diaries*, 343–344. "Whenever he spoke . . .": Jepson, *Memoirs*, 146. "a bloody show": Holroyd, *John*, 361ff, 356ff. Though he hated Matisse . . . : *ibid.*, 351. "a splendid fellow . . .": *ibid.*, 362. . . . as Roger himself: *ibid.*, 360–361. "rapid sketching . . .": Easton and Holroyd, *Art of Augustus John*, 17q. "uncanny notes . . .": *ibid.*, 19q. . . . the terrible Frenchmen themselves: *ibid.*, 18–19. When he called the show . . . : Holroyd, *John*, 361. "post impressed": *ibid.* "How insular . . .": Shone, *Bloomsbury Portraits*, 64q. In a letter to the *Nation* . . . : Drab-ble, *Bennett*, 180q. As for Orage and . . . : Martin, *New Age*, 132q. . . . five hun-dred pounds: MacCarthy, *Memories*, 183. The young artists of London . . . : Woolf, *Fry*, 159. . . . he was all postimpressionist: Shone, *Bloomsbury Portraits*, 57. Sick-ert's young rebels . . . : *ibid.*, 64ff; Baron, *Sickert*, 119–120. but the John . . . : Spalding, *Vanessa*, 109. as for the Lamb . . . : Shone, *Bloomsbury Portraits*, 87–89. Why, Roger inquired . . . : Woolf, *Fry*, 164. "I have come to connect . . .": Bennett, *Books and Persons* (New York, 1917), 283. ". . . have to begin again": *ibid.*, 284. "They taught me . . .": Carswell, *Lives and Letters*, 61q. Volumes with titles . . . : Martin, *New Age*, 135. and the imagist poets . . . : *ibid.* a Gauguin *Crucifixion*: Simpson, *Three on the Tower*, 107. ". . . as a painter takes painting?" Pound, *Letters*, 15. ". . . what Chekhov was about": Ashley Dukes, *The Scene Is Changed* (London, 1942), 36. . . . dead as mutton: Pound, *Letters*, 24. In 1910 Clive Bell . . . : Materer, *Vortex*, 198; see also Bell, *Old Friends*, 80. "changes as great . . .": Materer, *Vortex*, 30q.

Pp. 156–162. "By George, I believe . . .": Maugham, *Of Human Bondage*, 193. "Très-cher Maître": James, *Letters*, 520. "simply worshiped . . .": Hart-Davis, *Wal-pole*, 69–70q. "Mon cher maître": Ford, *Return*, 31. "I want to thank you . . .": Karl, *Conrad*, 382q. "so there is something . . .": Elsa Nettels, *James and Conrad* (Athens, Ga., 1977), 4q. ". . . cringing respect": Hunt, *I Have This to Say*, 32. "When Conrad is . . .": Bennett, *Books and Persons*, 231. ". . . gestures of a Con-rad": Wells, *Boon*, 145. . . . but in stodgy old London?: Maugham, *Vagrant Mood*, 206. "Dear Master": Morgan, *Maugham*, 159. "The world divided itself . . .": Michael Killigrew, ed., *Ford: Your Mirror to My Times* (New York, 1971), xii. "as if she and Murry . . .": Meyers, *Mansfield*, 76q. . . . *not* invited to come: Mrs. Lown-des, *Merry Wives*, 139. "I, & folk like me . . .": Patrick O'Connor, "Strange Re-ward," *TLS*, December 12, 1986, 1394q. "He gets angry . . .": Patmore, *My Friends*, 69q. "I know, my dear fellow . . .": Desmond MacCarthy, *Portraits*, London, 1931), 150. "Now then, Goldring . . .": Goldring, *South Lodge*, 34q. ". . . forgot his great-ness": Goldring, *ibid.* "chained . . .": *ibid.*, 30. Frank Harris . . . self-effacing . . . : S. N. Behrman, *Portrait of Max: An Intimate Memoir of Sir Max Beerbohm* (New York, 1960), 123. "the dignity of letters": Rothenstein, *Men and Memories*, 158q. "as a man of letters": Yeats, *Memoirs*, 247. ". . . like a man of letters": Yeats, *Autobi-*

ography, 111–112. "He breathed Letters . . .": Wyndham Lewis, "Early London Environment," in Hugh Kenner, ed., *T. S. Eliot: A Collection of Critical Essays* (New York, 1962), 34. ". . . a third order of the priesthood!": Yeats, *Autobiography,* 203q. "He affected . . .": Jones, *Hulme,* 96q. "Like Picasso she emanated . . .": Clive Bell, *Old Friends,* 94. ". . . his obvious genius": Rothenstein, *Men and Memories,* 157. "Everyone felt . . .": Holroyd, *John,* 342q. ". . . 'for my genius' ": MacCarthy, *Portraits,* 155. Conrad with his Englishman's bowler . . . : Goldring, *South Lodge,* 30. "romantically disordered": *ibid.,* 40. Strachey ridiculed . . . : Holroyd, *Strachey,* 279. . . . and a black Carlyle hat: Lady Ottoline, *Memoirs,* 199. the one turquoise earring: Stock, *Pound,* 107. ". . . peach blossom tint": Lawrence, *Letters,* 165. "bright green shirts . . .": MacShane, *Ford,* 89. . . . green billiard-cloth trousers: Ford, *Return,* 357. "his whole operatic outfit": Goldring, *South Lodge,* 48. "A mountain of a man": Frank Harris, *Contemporary Portraits,* 3rd Series (New York, 1920), 64. "that Falstaffian figure . . .": Barker, *Chesterton,* 99; see also 132–133. ". . . and oily curls": Edel, *James,* 366q. "a talent divorced from life": Harris, *Contemporary Portraits,* 68. . . . (the reports were various): see Hunt, *I Have This to Say,* 89; Epstein, *Autobiography,* 88; Gerald Cumberland, *Set Down in Malice: A Book of Reminiscences* (New York, 1919), 142. "the *panache* . . .": Garnett, *Golden Echo,* 68. "a long whip in one hand . . .": Cumberland, *Set Down,* 142. with Colt revolvers . . . : Epstein, *Autobiography,* 88. "May you ride . . .": Norman Sherry, *Conrad and His World* (London, 1972), 76q. "a romantic adventurous . . .": Wells, *Autobiography,* 530. "What he really is . . .": *ibid.,* 526. . . . to enrich the Chesterton legend: Barker, *Chesterton,* 143–144. Conrad's life was . . . : for the revised life see Najder, *Conrad;* see also Frederick Crews's review, "Conrad by Daylight," *New York Review of Books,* March 1, 1984, 3ff. "I shall have been . . .": James, *Complete Notebooks,* 233. "No man has a right . . .": Najder, *Conrad,* 320q. ". . . a mere born gem": Karl, *Conrad,* 607q. ". . . the stuff of masterpiece": Lawrence, *Letters,* 178. "You have written . . .": Heilbrun, *Garnett Family,* 133q. ". . . the masterpiece of my time": Hugh Walpole, "Introduction," *Fortitude* [1913] (New York, 1930), vii. "the divine diabolical law": James, *Complete Notebooks,* 237. "under the patronage . . .": Karl, *Conrad,* 531q. "Pray for me . . .": Hunt, *I Have This to Say,* 33q.

Pp. 162–165. "I shall change the world . . .": Mark Schorer, *D. H. Lawrence* (New York, 1968), 3q. the "greatness" idea: Stephen Spender, "Forster's Shadow," *New York Review of Books,* May 10, 1984, 32. "now entirely extinct": Woolf, *Moments,* 136. "We need not always . . ." Woolf, *Letters,* 383. "as for 'genius' . . .": *ibid.,* 406. "I hated . . .": Nehls, *Lawrence,* I, 103q. "as a genius": Lawrence, *Letters,* 171. "Lawrence's genius, you see . . .": Heilbrun, *Garnett Family,* 145q. "I never starved . . .": Lawrence, *Assorted Articles* (London, 1930), 146. "He is a man of genius": Conrad, *Under Western Eyes* [1910] (New York, 1951), 154. "exclusive superiority . . .": Conrad, *Notes on Life and Letters,* 7. "a mountebank . . .": James, *Letters,* 341. "very big and fat . . .": *ibid.,* 500. ". . . mercantile interests": Tindall, *Forces in Modern British Literature,* 4q. ". . . a mania for posterity": Gross, *Rise and Fall,* 213q. "I am in a way . . .": Shaw, *Letters,* 426. "Only do, for Heavens sake . . .": Shaw, letter to James Elroy Flecker, dated March 6, 1911, Bernard Shaw, General Correspondence, VIII, 1907–1910, British Museum. "I am not . . .": Shaw, *Letters,* II, 416. "STUPENDOUS . . .": *ibid.,* 321. "a MAGNIFICENT play . . .": *ibid.,* 599. "you are just . . .": *ibid.,* 352. "I have never claimed . . .": "H.G. and G.B.S., Varied Reflections on Two Edwardian Polymaths," *TLS,* November 27, 1969, 1349q. "My theatrical activity . . .": Shaw, *Letters,* II, 511. By 1908 he had written . . . : *ibid.,* 791.

"... perfectly indifferent": Desmond MacCarthy, *Shaw's Plays in Review* (New York, 1951), 216; see also 213. "Little sense of contemporary...": Wells, *Boon*, 150. "and the less we hear about authors...": *ibid.*, 156. "... I *am* great": Dickson, *Wells*, 102q. "... of being 'literary men' ": Frank Swinnerton, *Autobiography* (New York, 1936), 199. "It's awfully good...": *ibid.*, 152. Wells in fact liked what he called ...: Wells, *Boon*, 157. "... as I would of pigs": Hutchins, *Pound's Kensington*, 126q. "... it's a congregation": Swinnerton, *Background*, 138q. "The theatre is...": Charles Osborne, "The Music Critic," in Holroyd, ed., *The Genius of Shaw*, 74q. "We can change it...": Shaw, *Letters*, II, 828. The trouble with Shakespeare ...: *ibid.*, 551. "People don't want...": *ibid.*, 828. the theatre wasn't, said Wells, the way: Wells, *Autobiography*, 456–457. "All you who...": Wells, *Boon*, 170. But Wells wasn't interested: Fromm, *Richardson*, 40. "I hate Bennett's resignation": Lawrence, *Letters*, 459. "I can't forgive Conrad...": *ibid.*, 465. "They all made me feel...": Najder, *Conrad*, 318. "... the face of the world": Joseph Conrad, *A Personal Record* (London, 1946), 108.

Pp. 166–174. "Don't know yah": Trabb's boy, Pip's tormentor in Dickens's *Great Expectations*. It pained them ...: Goldring, *South Lodge*, 19. "Fun, isn't it, for...": Maugham, *Vagrant Mood*, 220q. "... cased in British tar": Tindall, *Forces in Modern British Literature*, 59q. ... of the English country gentleman: Goldring, *South Lodge*, 30. "... write for money": Ford, *Portraits*, 39. "a 'baron' five times over": Goldring, *South Lodge*, 38. "had no need...": Ford, *Return*, 232. "Not sure that...": David Daiches, "The Man Behind the Plot," *New York Times Book Review*, December 19, 1965, 1q. "like a Spanish hidalgo": Goldring, *South Lodge*, 33. "... Hidalgo of Spain": Epstein, *Autobiography*, 88. "grey hidalgo's beard": Ford, *Return*, 34. "... like a Spanish grandee": Holroyd, *Shaw*, I, 176. "... of a Spanish hidalgo": Buchan, *Memory*, 105. "Oh how that glittering...": Richard Aldington, *D. H. Lawrence: Portrait of a Genius But...* (New York, 1961), 74; see also Nehls, *Lawrence*, I, 126. "He knows W B Yeats and...": Lawrence, *Letters*, 145. "That's not your usual...": Nehls, *Lawrence*, I, 83. "I'm not keen a bit...": Lawrence, *Letters*, 305. A letter from Jessie's mother ...: Emile Delavenay, *D. H. Lawrence, The Man and His Work: The Formative Years, 1885–1919* (Carbondale, Ill., 1972), 76. "a terrific snob": Nehls, *Lawrence*, I, 137q. "a shy and gawky...": Garnett, *Great Friends*, 79. "Aren't the folks...": Lawrence, *Letters*, 145. "I really do honor...": Darroch, *Ottoline*, 149q. It didn't take Forster: Furbank, *Forster*, 176–177, 185. married beneath her: Millgate, *Hardy*, 397; Timothy O'Sullivan, *Thomas Hardy: An Illustrated Biography* (New York, 1975), 145. "I never heard him say...": *ibid.*, 89q. Not three weeks dead ...: Mrs. Lowndes, *Merry Wives*, 148. never permitted to enter Max Gate: Millgate, *Hardy*, 491. "a beady eye peering...": O'Sullivan, *Hardy*, 145. "Such and so little...": Hazlitt, "Mr. Coleridge," in *The Spirit of the Age*. But then he met Millicent ... collecting duchesses: Mackail, *J.M.B.*, 384. "Dear Duchess...": Birkin, *Barrie*, 132q. "... of respectful servility": Augustus John, *Finishing Touches* (London, 1964), 119. "endless miracle...": Mansfield, *Letters*, 296. "a maid going out...": Meyers, *Mansfield*, 132q. "cowboy songster": Lewis, *Blasting and Bombardiering*, 280. at Alice Meynell's ...: see "Introduction," Agnes Tobin, *Letters, Translations, Poems* (San Francisco, 1958), ix. "... and bad taste": Stock, *Pound*, 107. or at Lady Glenconner's: Aldington, *Life*, 70. "an almost insane relish...": *ibid.*, 134. "poor Ezra not knowing...": Nehls, *Lawrence*, II, 268; see also Norman, *Pound*, 130q. "If gold ruste...": Chaucer, "General Prologue," *Canterbury Tales*, 1. 500. that once he had worked with . . . : Mrs. Lowndes, *Merry Wives*, 144. . . . in calling him "Orridge": Carswell, *Lives and Letters*, 16. . . . he wrote Barker's wife Lillah: Shaw, *Letters*, II, 624–625. of the shotgun variety . . . : Holroyd, *Shaw*, I, 10; John O'Donovan, "The First Twenty Years" in Holroyd, *Genius of Shaw*, 18. Vandeleur Lee . . . a fearful *Catholic*: Holroyd, *Shaw*, I, 30. . . . offspring of *Catholic* tradesmen: *ibid.*, 35–36; O'Donovan, "First Twenty Years," 22, 24; Shaw, *Sixteen Self Sketches* (London, 1949), 22–23. his mother's connection with the great Vandeleur: Holroyd, *Shaw*, I, 26ff, 49ff. "her man": O'Donovan, "First Twenty Years," 27. . . . not at all sexual: Stanley Weintraub, *Shaw: An Autobiography, 1856–1898*, I (New York, 1969), 188ff (hereafter Shaw, *Autobiography*, I); Holroyd, *Shaw*, I, 24ff; O'Donovan, "First Twenty Years," 14, 16, 27. . . . in no way the son of the Other Man: Holroyd, *Shaw*, I, 24–27; O'Donovan, "First Twenty Years," 21. . . . snobbery of "the Shaws": Shaw, *Sixteen Self Sketches*, 92. . . . from the pawnbroker shop: Holroyd, *Shaw*, I, 9. "I sing my own class . . .": Shaw, *Autobiography*, I, 12. Not so . . . Hubert Bland: West, *Wells*, 292. "My God, how workmen smell . . .": Perenyi, "The Bloom Is Off," 34q. "I must go to tea now . . .": Kenner, *A Sinking Island*, 162n. ". . . and ultimately nauseating": Leonard Woolf, ed., Virginia Woolf, *A Writer's Diary* (New York, 1953), 46. ". . . can't be a gentleman": Terence de Vere White, "An Irishman Abroad," in Holroyd, *The Genius of Shaw*, 39. "Poor queer man": Najder, *Conrad*, 284q. "But, dear lady . . .": *ibid.*, 387–388. Publish Arnold Bennett!: Mrs. Lowndes, *Merry Wives*, 127. "a managing clerk . . .": Maugham, *Vagrant Mood*, 223. ". . . has never gone back": Mrs. Lowndes, *Merry Wives*, 128q. "a fourth-rate clerk . . .": Reginald Pound, *Arnold Bennett* (New York, 1953), 7q. It was "Mopesun" . . .": *ibid.*, 181. ". . . and a grey bowler hat": *ibid.*, 195q. "gastric jewelry": *ibid.*, 8q. "His elaborate pleated . . .": Lady Ottoline, *Memoirs*, 203. He was "vulgar" . . . : *ibid.*, 204. "cocksure and bumptious . . .": Maugham, *Vagrant Mood*, 227. "his thumbs in . . .": Clive Bell, *Old Friends*, 153. "the boy from Staffordshire . . .": *ibid.*, 145. "One of the low . . . : T. S. Eliot, *The Waste Land*. "never what in England . . .": Maugham, *Vagrant Mood*, 230. boots . . . rice pudding: Pound, *Bennett*, 23. No wonder he and Wells . . . : Maugham, *Vagrant Mood*, 221. "provincial": Cameron, "Innocent at Home," 24. . . . the instincts of a gentleman: West, *Wells*, 351. "It takes gentlefolk . . .": Ford, *Return*, 43q. "rather unromantic . . .": Lewis, *Blasting and Bombardiering*, 282. "Whenever I see H.G. Wells . . . ": *ibid.*, 282q. "A slab of a man . . .": Anne Olivier Bell, ed., *The Diary of Virginia Woolf, 1915–1919*, I (New York, 1977), 157. "the cockney accent . . .": *ibid.* "like an old washerwoman . . .": Woolf, *Moments*, 188. ". . . where there is hot pork": Lawrence, *Letters*, 543. . . . only the son of a miner: Delavenay, *Lawrence*, 77. ". . . some slum in him": Aldington, *Lawrence*, 92q. "like a mongrel terrier . . .": Garnett, *Great Friends*, 76. His nose . . . his hair: Garnett, *Golden Echo*, 241–242. "the shadow of the underworld": Woolf, *Diary*, I, 159, 156n; see also Bell, *Woolf*, II, 50. ". . . taken to street walking": Meyers, *Mansfield*, 138q. "Seeing what England is . . .": Lewis, *Letters*, 441.

Pp. 174–179. "The parish of rich women": Auden, "In Memory of W. B. Yeats." "the lust of authorship": Hunt, *I Have This to Say*, 59. "taking a diamond . . .": Florence Emily Hardy, *The Life of Thomas Hardy, 1849–1928* (London, 1972)), 342. ". . . showed me great kindness": Wharton, *Backward Glance*, 220. Millicent, Duchess of Sutherland . . . : Drabble, *Bennett*, 159. "jolly enough": Ward, *Chesterton*, 170q. "not only the most splendid . . .": Rothenstein, *Men and Memories*, 71. James Barrie . . . her parties: Mackail, *J.M.B.*, 384–385. "an unabashed hunter": Woolf, *Moments*, 188n; see also James, *Letters*, 700n. and Lady

Low whose drawing-room . . . : Stock, *Pound,* 122; Pound and Shakespear, *Letters,* 349. . . . the Pharos Club: Mrs. Chesterton, *Chestertons,* 7; see also Jepson, *Memoirs,* 78–79. As for Lady St. Helier . . . : Wharton, *Backward Glance,* 213. . . . in her Portland Square mansion: Lewis, *Wharton,* 242. ". . . would she lend him £5?": Wharton, *Backward Glance,* 215q. Mrs. Olivia Shakespear, for one . . . : Pound and Shakespear, *Letters,* 4fn. Ada Leverson . . . : Yeats, *Memoirs,* 80. . . . when he left Reading Gaol: Behrman, *Portrait of Max,* 84. Mrs. George Steevens . . . : Morgan, *Maugham,* 102–103; see also Frederic Raphael, *W. Somerset Maugham and His World* (New York, n.d.), 29. the Sangers, Charles and Dora . . . : Lady Ottoline, *Memoirs,* 93–94. Miss Ethel Sands . . . *ibid.,* 121. "the shape of my head": *ibid.,* 139. "golden stuff": *ibid.,* 137. . . . the arms of the prime minister himself: Holroyd, *Strachey,* 561. "an aristocracy of letters . . .": Hassall, *Brooke,* 222. "very rubicund . . .": Woolf, *Moments,* 177. "very sinister . . .": *ibid.* "Conversation, talk . . .": Lady Ottoline, *Memoirs,* 118. "He tried hard . . .": Mackenzie, *Wells,* 171. For all his airs . . . : Morgan, *Maugham,* 79–80. "the most beautiful house . . .": Hart-Davis, *Walpole,* 71q. ". . . lawn tennis greatness": *ibid.* ". . . cynical set of English 'society' ": Peters, *Shaw,* 289q. "So will G. Bernard Shaw": Winsten, *Shaw,* 132q. a few plays by Barker and Shaw . . . : Shaw, Preface, *Heartbreak House,* in *Complete Plays,* I, 451. "They refused . . .": *ibid.,* 452. "of extraordinary grace . . .": Mackenzie, *Fabians,* 303q. the light belletristic essay: Gross, *Rise and Fall,* 119. but Augustine Birrell . . . : *ibid.,* 120; see also Blunt, *Diaries,* 349. Even Asquith . . . : Gross, *Rise and Fall,* 119. "crackling with epigrams": Woolf, *Moments,* 177. ". . . in poetic travail": John, *Chiaroscuro,* 136. "Expecting life & smartness . . .": Woolf, *Diaries,* 71. "When I die . . .": Woolf, *Moments,* 187q. Balfour went to see . . . : Mackenzie, *Fabians,* 307. "the horrible force . . .": Purdom, *Barker,* 49. ". . . a diamond scarf pin": Shaw, *Letters,* II, 392. Churchill presided over . . . : *ibid.,* 629 (ed. note). and Lord Esher . . . : *ibid.,* 842. "There's a real poet . . .": Harris, *Life and Loves,* 951–952. Masterman wasn't too proud . . . : Gross, *Rise and Fall,* 128. to call Chesterton . . . : Barker, *Chesterton,* 147. and have them to supper . . . : *ibid.,* 152. At the home of the Webbs . . . : Ward, *Chesterton,* 169. of Mrs. Grenfell . . . : Barker, *Chesterton,* 148. at the Buxtons' . . . : Ward, *Chesterton,* 171. at the Asquiths' . . . : Chesterton, *Autobiography* (London, 1969), 121. After golfing together . . . : Morgan, *Maugham,* 151–152. "a man of much . . .": Blunt, *Diaries,* 310. "jolly nice folk . . .": Moore, *Lawrence,* 238q. "false entry": *ibid.,* 239. "Far removed from . . .": *ibid.* "of distinguished eminence": Mackail, *J.M.B.,* 321q. "a refuge in winter": Weintraub, *London Yankees,* 219. ". . . perfectly wonderful": Hart-Davis, *Walpole,* 68q. "dear Henry James": Nettels, *James and Conrad,* 19. "funny French wife": Hart-Davis, *Walpole,* 76q. Bennett would walk . . . : Swinnerton, *Autobiography,* 149. Violet Hunt would have . . . : Patmore, *My Friends,* 51–52, and Stock, *Pound,* 114. ". . . a decent suit": Lawrence, *Letters,* 286. National Liberal Club . . . : Goldring, *Trained for Genius,* 131. "almost like gentlefolks . . .": Wells, *Kipps,* 62. "The literary life is . . .": Ray, "Introduction," Wells, *Mr. Polly,* xxxiii–xxxivq.

Pp. 180–185. "stood up to him . . .": Morgan, *Maugham,* 89q. "the most swindling . . .": *ibid.,* 65q. ". . . more sickly than lepers": Callow, *Son and Lover,* 176. Hueffer felt for his . . . : Ford, *Return,* 384. Wells was inclined to change publishers . . . : James Hepburn, *The Author's Empty Purse, Or the Rise of the Literary Agent* (London, 1968), 91. To William Blackwood . . . : Najder, *Conrad,* 290. the three hundred pounds . . . : *ibid.;* see also 271. . . . in the matter of *Lord Jim:* Watt,

Conrad, 263. "... a swindle on my part": Najder, *Conrad,* 232. the Society of Authors: Hepburn, *Author's Empty Purse,* 42ff; see also Jeremy Treglown, "R. L. Stevenson and the Authors-Publishers Debate," *TLS,* January 15–21, 1988, 58. Pioneered by one A. P. Watt ...: Hepburn, *Author's Empty Purse,* 52ff. Of course they were hurt ...: *ibid.,* 2–3. When Somerset Maugham ...: Morgan, *Maugham,* 86. "do you not think...": Bennett, *Letters,* II, 131n. As for Heinemann ...: Hepburn, *Author's Empty Purse,* 77ff; also Sutherland, "The Great and the Cheeseparing," 442. "a lively row": James, *Letters,* 130. "Once an author...": Frederic Whyte, *William Heinemann* (London, 1928), 124q. Andrew Lang ...: Hepburn, *Author's Empty Purse,* 79. "favorite resort of persons...": *ibid.,* 85q. Indeed, the Society of Authors ...: *ibid.,* 43, 83ff. Just the same ... May Sinclair: *ibid.,* 86. "While publishers...": Heilbrun, *Garnett Family,* 72q. "that every author...": Hepburn, *Author's Empty Purse,* 91q. Worldly, urbane ...: Dickson, *Wells,* 178. much of the pleasure Heinemann ...: Whyte, *Heinemann,* 128. Conrad may have ridiculed ...: Najder, *Conrad,* 202n. and the only guests ...: *ibid.,* 214. It was Elkin Matthews ...: Kenner, *A Sinking Island,* 88; Stock, *Pound,* 92, 94; Weintraub, *London Yankees,* 262. Blackwood was more ...: Najder, *Conrad,* 214, 258; Watt, *Conrad,* 131. ... all generosity to desperate young prospects: Stock, *Pound,* 92. "Ah, eh, ah...": Pound and Shakespear, *Letters,* 351. "in an academical discussion...": Whyte, *Heinemann,* 230. James and Conrad he ...: *ibid.,* 128. would gladly have published ...: *ibid.,* 133–134. When the circulating ...: *ibid.,* 284–285. "carried away..." *ibid.,* 229. So Pawling was happy ...: *ibid.,* 230. When Heinemann died ...: Hepburn, *Author's Empty Purse,* 97. "Jy Bee": Morgan, *Maugham,* 65. loved ... riding to hounds: Hunt, *I Have This to Say,* 11. A short, sturdy ...: Drabble, *Bennett,* 118. ... a force or a rectitude: Swinnerton, *Background,* 128. "a gloomy vista...": Ford, *Return,* 65–66. to pay Arnold Bennett ...: Drabble, *Bennett,* 117; Morgan, *Maugham,* 117. ... to a prosperous celebrity: Drabble, *Bennett,* 85. His relations with Conrad ...: Karl, *Conrad,* 487ff. to the tune of some £1,600: *ibid.,* 489. his banker and accountant: *ibid.,* 526. "Were you as rich as...": Najder, *Conrad,* 279q. One day at the end of January 1910 ...: *ibid.,* 354ff; Karl, *Conrad,* 680ff; Jessie Conrad, *Conrad,* 140ff. "incredible as it seemed...": *ibid.,* 141. "Have you a complete copy...": *ibid.* "that mighty pile": *ibid.* "Speak English...": *ibid.,* 142q. ... as "Dear Sir": Jocelyn Baines, *Joseph Conrad: A Critical Biography* (London, 1971), 447. "Those books...": Karl, *Conrad,* 785q. "Pinker of agents": Drabble, *Bennett,* 118q. "Our relation...": Karl, *Conrad,* 785q. "In case of my early death...": *ibid.,* 527q. ... his old friend the first one to know: Hunt, *I Have This to Say,* 22. "Agents are created...": Ford, *Return,* 384. "that little parvenu...": Morgan, *Maugham,* 65q.

   Pp. 185–189. "Fit audience . . .": Milton, *Paradise Lost,* book VII, 30."My books make...": MacCarthy, *Portraits,* 151q. ... an embarrassing $211: Kenner, *A Sinking Island,* 70. "My productions affect...": Watts and Davies, *Cunninghame Graham,* 262q. "tried to read out...": Forster, *Longest Journey,* 79. "dear last style...": John T. Frederick, *W. H. Hudson* (New York, 1972), 129q. even the good Arnold Bennett ...: Swinnerton, *Background,* 124. "bogged down in his books": Morgan, *Maugham,* 114q. "so famous that...": Walpole, *Fortitude,* 31. "one of the great pundits...": Rothenstein, *Men and Memories,* 173. So at her fine country house ...: Lady Ottoline, *Memoirs,* 137. "the very flower and...": Tuchman, *Proud Tower,* 49. "holding dear H. J....": Pound, Canto LXXIX, *The Cantos,* 488. "It was the thing to do...": C. Lewis Hind, *Authors and I* (New York, 1920), 162.

After removing his beard . . . : Weintraub, *London Yankees,* 220; see also Millicent Bell, "Notes of a Friend and Brother," *New York Review of Books,* July 19, 1984, 40, and F. W. Dupee, *Henry James: His Life and Writings* (New York, 1956), 183–184. It was a Frenchman . . . : *ibid.,* 184. "Priest—fine eyes . . .": Edel, *James,* 386q. "the air of a divine . . .": Ford, *Return,* 22. "indicted his manners . . .": *ibid.,* 30. ". . . on the point of his sword": Lady Ottoline, *Memoirs,* 137. "You don't suppose . . .": Ford, *Portraits,* 112q. "My dear Virginia . . .": Bell, *Woolf,* I, 122q. "watching through a . . .": MacCarthy, *Portraits,* 150. "The massive head . . .": Weintraub, *London Yankees,* 281q. "the gallant and . . .": Edel, *James,* 398q. "by far the greatest . . .": *ibid.,* 399q. "has influenced me . . .": Boll, *May Sinclair,* 109q. "the first completely . . .": Fromm, *Richardson,* 66q. "writing and talking . . .": Woolf, *Sowing,* 107. "I long . . .": Edel, *James,* 389q; Holroyd, *Strachey,* 397q. Lamb House . . . stuffy and precious: Furbank, *Forster,* 164–165. "in the presence of a Lord": Forster, *Letters,* 92. James was a Master indeed . . . : Furbank, *Forster,* 163. "O poet . . .": Auden, "At the Grave of Henry James." . . . a weekend in Cambridge?: Edel, *James,* 394ff. "in an enormous letter . . .": Harrod, *Keynes,* 148q. So for forty-eight hours . . . : *ibid.,* 149. "I *liked* it . . .": Edel, *James,* 395q. "Well, I must say . . .": MacCarthy, *Memories,* 203. ". . . and white flannel trousers": Edel, *James,* 396; for a less cheerful account of the weekend, see Harrod, *Keynes,* 149. "You see, you can't . . .": Wells, *Boon,* 98. "Henry's *Anschauung* . . .": Pound, letter to Patricia Hutchins, British Museum. "marmoreal darling of the Few": Gross, *Rise and Fall,* 162q.

Pp. 189–193. Sir Walter Besant was . . . : Hunter, *Edwardian Fiction,* 51. "Never before . . .": *ibid.,* 51q. "the dilettante spirit . . .": Gross, *Rise and Fall,* 218q. "just to show . . .": Morgan, *Maugham,* 144q. Galsworthy's amounted to . . . : these figures are taken from J. H. Retinger, *Conrad and His Contemporaries* (London, 1941), 99. In 1904 . . . Shaw was reporting . . . : Shaw, *Letters,* II, 455. "I am sitting . . .": Watt, *Conrad,* 75q. . . . no more than 600: Najder, *Conrad,* 369. Even so, Shaw . . . : Shaw, *Letters,* II, 792. As for Wells . . . : see Ray, "Introduction," *Mr. Polly,* xvii, and West, *Wells,* 54. and when Davies's wooden leg . . . : Stonesifer, *Davies,* 73. and when . . . Arthur Symons: White, "The Critic, the Mirror and the Vamp," 1240q. As for . . . the Murrys and Mansfields: Meyers, *Mansfield,* 108; Carswell, *Lives and Letters,* 271. and Katherine . . . : *ibid.,* 101. "Yes, I *am* tired . . .": Mansfield, *Letters,* 138. a poet like Yeats . . . : Stonesifer, *Davies,* 82. "They expected me . . .": *ibid.,* 91q. Gaudier . . . Arch 25: Kenner, *Pound Era,* 251. like solid John Buchan: Smith, *Buchan,* 46. . . . like Middleton Murry: Carswell, *Lives and Letters,* 156. This new man of letters . . . : see Gross, *Rise and Fall,* 200q, or Karl, *Conrad,* 338q. . . . to fourteen thousand: Gross, *Rise and Fall,* 199. Would the folk not . . . : Moore, *Lawrence,* 101. "head gardener to . . .": Wells, *Autobiography,* 34. Bennett writing books of instruction . . . : Gross, *Rise and Fall,* 205. "the voice of . . .": Ray, "Introduction," *Mr. Polly,* xii. They were stars . . . : Goldring, *Life Interests,* 181; Mackenzie, *Wells,* 287; Swinnerton, *Background,* 119–120. "delivered himself . . .": *ibid.,* 120. As for Wells . . . : *ibid.* a butcher selling meat . . . : Shaw, *Letters,* II, 765; West, *Wells,* 139. He had a bad stammer . . . : Swinnerton, *Background,* 119–120. . . . in the dailies and weeklies: Pound, *Bennett,* 8. "My God! Is it you?": Drabble, *Bennett,* 172q.

Pp. 193–201. "to exhibit enthusiasm . . .": Hunt, *I Have This to Say,* 28. . . . the work of their enemies: Goldring, *Life Interests,* 197. "After all, my dear

Goldring...": *ibid.* "From first to last...": Pound, *Bennett*, 197q. "one of the greatest...": Drabble, *Bennett*, 183. Frank Harris... was impressed: Harris, *Life and Loves*, 769–770. "descended from...": Karl, *Conrad*, 373. Because he was Polish...: *ibid.*, 723q. "the *passionate*...": *ibid.*, 723fn. "indeed a rare happiness...": *ibid.* "the book, my dear fellow...": *ibid.*, 607q. "the book has...": James, *Letters*, 379. "the co-existence of...": Mackenzie, *Wells*, 282q. "more brimming with...": *ibid.* "a sewing-machine...": White, "An Irishman Abroad," in Holroyd, *The Genius of Shaw*, 36. Notwithstanding, the two great men...: Shaw, *Letters*, II, 274 (ed. note). "...and intellectual geniality": Chesterton, *Autobiography*, 227. "Occasionally you...": Mackenzie, *Wells*, 254q. "You are a great...": Shaw, *Letters*, II, 356–357q (ed. note). "I have never wavered...": Peters, *Shaw*, 398q. "that when he went...": *ibid.* Wells would bicycle...: Hunt, *I Have This to Say*, 51. Hueffer... would drop by: see, for example, Najder, *Conrad*, 278, 287–288. the great James himself...: Moser, "From Olive Garnett's Diary," 525. "Conrad haunts...": Edel and Ray, eds., *Henry James and H. G. Wells: A Record of Their Friendship* (Urbana, Ill., 1958), 77. "Mon cher confrère...": Ford, *Return*, 31. ... it was always "dear Jack": Curle, *Caravansary and Conversation*, 157. "could you conceive..." Watt, *Conrad*, 126q. "dear old fellow": Najder, *Conrad*, 228q. "That will be delightful...": Heilbrun, *Garnett Family*, 119. "I am proud...": *ibid.*, 130. "It is your heart...": *ibid.* "and something moved me...": *ibid.*, 132q. "Loves apart...": Clive Bell, *Old Friends*, 118q. In the meantime what jolly fun...: Barker, *Chesterton*, 152–153. "O born in days...": Arnold, "The Scholar Gypsy." For Auberon Quin...: Barker, *Chesterton*, 141. for her St. John Hirst...: Lyndall Gordon, *Virginia Woolf: A Writer's Life* (New York, 1984), 124–125. for Beatrice Normandy...: Hunt, *I Have This to Say*, 54. For his Bosinney...: Garnett, *Great Friends*, 108. and for the literary critic...: *ibid.*, 42. and was Hueffer himself...: Ford, *Portraits*, 10. It was Morton Fullerton: Edel, *James*, 122. Violet Hunt appearing...: Thomas Moser, *Life in the Fiction of Ford Madox Ford* (Princeton, 1980), 104, 112. ... have been Ezra Pound: *ibid.*, 112. "duty to posterity": Pound, *Letters*, 25. "a mark of respect...": Birkin, *J. M. Barrie*, 181q. Two magisterial figures...: Dickson, *Wells*, 80–81. would find him a cottage...: Stonesifer, *Davies*, 72. There was the generous Galsworthy...: Najder, *Conrad*, 202, 234, 246, 271, 471, etc. There was Wells...: *ibid.*, 279. Miss Agnes Tobin...: Karl, *Conrad*, 701. There was... Rothenstein: Najder, *Conrad*, 310. and James and Gosse...: *ibid.*, 283. there was Hueffer...: *ibid.*, 238ff; Karl, *Conrad*, 433ff; also Ford, *Return*, 186ff. "his cook, slut...": *ibid.*, 32. The collaboration...: Garnett, *Great Friends*, 14. when the gout-ridden genius...: Najder, *Conrad*, 298–300; Karl, *Conrad*, 544, 548, 558fn; MacShane, *Ford*, 57–58; Mizener, *Ford*, 114. He helped him convert...: Najder, *Conrad*, 296, 314–315; Karl, *Conrad*, 559n; Mizener, *Ford*, 108–109. it was to Fordie and Winchelsea...: Najder, *Conrad*, 284–285; Karl, *Conrad*, 536–538. From the publisher Blackwood...: *ibid.*, 438, 506, 421. He certainly helped Norman Douglas...: Holloway, *Douglas*, 173–175, 187. Wells would read...: Karl, *Conrad*, 525–526. and Galsworthy...: Najder, *Conrad*, 323–324. and Conrad not only...: *ibid.*, 269, 325. at the Master's request...: Karl, *Conrad*, 408. "a kind place...": Ford, *Portraits*, 86. They sought him out: Barker, *Chesterton*, 129ff. "where the jealous...": Ward, *Chesterton*, 111. made much of *les jeunes*...: Tytell, *Pound*, 91. "...a city of solitude": Goldring, *Trained for Genius*, 165. "put him over": Nehls, *Lawrence*, I, 553q. sending him to Heinemann: *ibid.*, 103. "I cannot say...": *ibid.*, 118q. "disturbing": Callow, *Son and Lover*, 176q. from the "folks"...: Lawrence, *Letters*, 145. From the good Thomas

Hardy . . . : Hart-Davis, *Walpole*, 79q. From Mrs. Lowndes . . . : Mrs. Lowndes, *Merry Wives*, 138. From Bennett and Wells . . . : Hart-Davis, *Walpole*, 76. "It isn't written . . .": *ibid.*, 77q. "like a fairy-tale": *ibid.*, 73q. fatherly interest in him": *ibid.*, 76q. persuaded Lord Stanmore . . . : Furbank, *Forster*, 186fn. "a hopeless book . . .": Walpole, Preface, *Fortitude*, ix. "Here is Hugh Walpole . . .": *ibid.*, x.

Pp. 202–203. It was Gosse . . . : Gross, *Rise and Fall*, 158ff. "the official British . . .": Wells, *Boon*, 76. there wasn't a mogul of letters . . . : Janet Malcolm, "The Unreliable Genius," *New York Review of Books*, March 14, 1985, 8. He had traveled . . . : Gross, *Rise and Fall*, 161–162. He had an instinct . . . : Tindall, *Modern British Literature*, 263–264. in volumes of poems . . . collections of essays: Gross, *Rise and Fall*, 158. "the pewking Gosse": Rhys, *Letters from Limbo*, 230q. When George Gissing died . . . : West, *Wells*, 263. "the difference of . . .": Malcolm, "Unreliable Genius," 7q. "little dapper grocer": *ibid.* "a Mr. Tulkinghorn . . .": Gross, *Rise and Fall*, 163q. "looked askance . . .": Mrs. Lowndes, *Merry Wives*, 160. "coarse in morals": Furbank, *Forster*, 189q. "that preposterous . . . : Gross, *Rise and Fall*, 161q. "I have not been invited . . .": *ibid.*, 158q. gold-rimmed spectacles: *ibid.*, 161. "the most lurid thing . . .": James, *Letters*, 34.

Pp. 203–206. "quasi-paternal": Nettels, *James and Conrad*, 8q. . . . like Housman and Masefield: Shaw, *Letters*, II, 792. "Neanderthal Shaw": Stanley Weintraub, "In the Picture Galleries," in Holroyd, *Genius of Shaw*, 58q. "Poor Aunt Augusta . . .": Einstein, *Autobiography*, 43q. Hulme and Pound would . . . : Garnett, *Golden Echo*, 238. As for Orage . . . : Carswell, *Lives and Letters*, 36. . . . the "No Wage": Selver, *Orage*, 16. for needy young talent: Martin, *New Age*, 57. "He did more to feed . . .": *ibid.*, 1q. Not from him came the heartless . . . : *ibid.*, 48–50. his warm hazel eyes . . . : Carswell, *Lives and Letters*, 272. "How sensible I am . . .": Meyers, *Mansfield*, 55–56q. Even Augustus John . . . : Holroyd, *John*, 282. "lust and life . . .": *ibid.*, 312q. "walked and walked . . .": *ibid.*, 314q. two months to live . . . : *ibid.*; see also B. L. Reid, *The Man from New York: John Quinn and His Friends* (New York, 1968), 71–72. John was all generosity: Holroyd, *John*, 315. "I cannot sin . . .": Symons, "Satiety." "all hell, damnation . . .": Holroyd, *John*, 315q. "Drawn blinds . . .": Symons, "In Bohemia." "As I lay on . . .": Symons, quoted in Bax, *Some I Knew Well*, 74. One wonderful evening . . . : Holroyd, *John*, 316; see Reid, *John Quinn*, 77. "I will arise . . .": Symons, "The Prodigal Son." It was the first place . . . : Rhys, *Wales England Wed*, 208. she'd gaily introduce him . . . : Boll, *May Sinclair*, 84. "Boaz Bobb . . .": Pound and Shakespear, *Letters*, 46n. "the new Montana . . .": Stock, *Pound*, 102. "Ezra Pound has more vitality . . .": Aldington, *Life*, 110q. But would he . . . : Donald Davie, *Ezra Pound* (New York, 1975), 17. "a somewhat Dakota Dante": H.D., *Bid Me to Live*, 41. "the great, easy-going . . .": Ford, *Return*, 401. . . . the literary "discovery": Jepson, *Memoirs*, 139ff. "But you *discovered* him": Nehls, *Lawrence*, I, 124q. "Fordie's discovered . . .": Moore, *Lawrence*, 141q. "To be a really . . .": Jepson, *Memoirs*, 133. but when Edward Thomas . . . : *ibid.*, 140–141. "terribly snappy": Goldring, *Trained for Genius*, 133q. "*physical* antipathy": *ibid.*, 64. "too blond for him": *ibid.*, 133q. ". . . upset our talks": *ibid.*, 132q.

Pp. 207–208. When a meeting of minds . . . : Curle, *Caravansary and Conversation*, 300. "I nearly bit him": Mackenzie, *Wells*, 177q. "oracular vanity": Rhys, *Everyman Remembers*, 299. "What do you think . . .": MacCarthy, *Shaw's Plays in*

Review, 217q. "You know, my dear fellow...": Wells, *Autobiography,* 530q. "Why not take...": Holroyd, *John,* 341–342; Pullar, *Harris,* 272. After one of Violet Hunt's...: Stock, *Pound,* 114; Lawrence, *Letters,* 144–145. "jolly nice...": *ibid.,* 145. "David Copperfield curls...": *ibid.,* 165. "... of jongleur": *ibid.* "There is no English poet...": Stock, *Pound,* 191q. "Detestable person": Pound, *Letters,* 17. One night at the Rhyses...: Rhys, *Everyman Remembers,* 243ff. Florence Farr's psaltery: Tuohy, *Yeats,* 115; Peters, *Shaw,* 292.

Pp. 208–213. Maugham would complain...: Maugham, *Vagrant Mood,* 196. The Adelphi Club...: Williams, *Autobiography,* 115. the Chelsea Arts Club...: Bennett, *Journal,* 365. The Writers' Club...: Morgan, *Maugham,* 130; Lawrence, *Letters,* 228. the Authors' Club...: Bennett, *Journal,* 408; see also Boll, *May Sinclair,* 93. "an appalling orgy...": Bennett, *Journal,* 410. "the Mecca...": Mrs. Lowndes, *Merry Wives,* 64. poor shrinking Hardy...: O'Sullivan, *Hardy,* 134. and where Wells...: Garnett, *Great Friends,* 182. Garrick Club which "damned him...": Raphael, *Maugham,* 35q. ... Barrie was also a member: Mackail, *J.M.B.,* 260. "what a fine place...": Wells, *Kipps,* 318. The Albemarle Club...: James, *Letters,* 619–620. for ladies who wrote...: Gittings, *Hardy's Later Years,* 139. like Lady Russell...: Hart-Davis, *Walpole,* 47. the first Mrs. Hardy...: Gittings, *Hardy's Later Years,* 139; see also Millgate, *Hardy,* 446. The Dramatists' Club...: Shaw, *Letters,* II, 799 (ed. note). "a clique of old stagers": *ibid.,* 848 (ed. note). The Square Club...: Goldring, *South Lodge,* 50; Jepson, *Memoirs,* 134ff. "old fogies": Goldring, *South Lodge,* 50. "... of childlike pleasure": Jepson, *Memoirs,* 135. "... of placid self-content": *ibid.,* 137. by Pound who...: *ibid.,* 142. "the literary friends...": *ibid.,* 138. "the literary club...": *ibid.,* 134. "a very smelly...": Goldring, *South Lodge,* 51. "its utter emptiness": Goldring, *Trained for Genius,* 132. ... Hulme's little poets' club: Jones, *Hulme,* 30ff; Hutchins, *Pound's Kensington,* 126ff. ... shattered a chair: *ibid.,* 127. "after dinner...": *ibid.,* 126q. "a few congenial spirits": Norman, *Pound,* 46–47. declaimed his "Sestina Altaforte"...: *ibid.,* 47; Jones, *Hulme,* 32. On Thursday evenings in Bloomsbury...: Edel, *Bloomsbury,* 148; Gadd, *Loving Friends,* 65. But on Sunday at four Edmund Gosse...: Morgan, *Maugham,* 80. the host apprehensive...: Marjorie Lilly, *Sickert: The Painter and His Circle* (London, 1971), 149. Mrs. Alice Meynell...: Agnes Tobin, *Letters, Translations, Poems.* "a preposterous opinion": Harriet Monroe, *A Poet's Life,* 223. Yeats was "at home"...: Stock, *Pound,* 101. "one grew a little weary...": Aldington, *Life,* 107. On Tuesday afternoon, Violet Hunt...: Patmore, *My Friends,* 52. and on Tuesday evening at eight...: Selver, *Orage,* 33ff; see also Stock, *Pound,* 167, and Tytell, *Pound,* 83. old Hudson and Emily...: Rothenstein, *Men and Memories,* 161. Sickert was "at home"...: Robert Emmons, *Life and Opinions of Walter R. Sickert* (London, 1941), 133–134. "Through all the ages...": Norman, *Pound,* 46q. So, on Tuesday evenings...: Jones, *Hulme,* 91ff. "unspeakably gregarious": Lewis, "Early London Environment," in Kenner, ed., *Eliot,* 31q. "incorrigibly hospitable": Goldring, *South Lodge,* 33. "lavish crumpets...": Mizener, *Ford,* 238q. and not indestructible chairs: *ibid.,* 238, 239n. Violet's senile old mother...: Moore, *Lawrence,* 152. the St. George...: Stonesifer, *Davies,* 75. the wine-shop, El Vino...: Mrs. Chesterton, *Chestertons,* 45. the Vienna Café where...: Hutchins, *Pound's Kensington,* 92; see also Lewis, *Blasting and Bombardiering,* 281. Across from the *New Age* office...: Martin, *New Age,* 42–43; Selver, *Orage,* 48–49; Jones, *Hulme,* 28–29. such heady talk that nowhere in London...: Martin, *New Age,* 44. "with its gilded...": John, *Chiaroscuro*, 77. "the *rendezvous* of...": Retinger, *Conrad*, 74. "...to be French": Frances Spalding, "Tavern Talk," *TLS*, October 21–27, 1988, 1166q. whose "natural majesty"...: Jones, *Hulme*, 98. Harold Monro's Poetry Bookshop...: Weintraub, *London Yankees*, 299–300; Norman, *Pound*, 81; Stonesifer, *Davies*, 104. Hulme found a roost: Jones, *Hulme*, 35. that Hueffer's Goldring...: Goldring, *South Lodge*, 64. "quantities of people": Aldington, *Life*, 106. and there too that Pound...: Pound and Shakespear, *Letters*, 316, 318n. "Those who cannot remember...": Ford, *Return*, 410. "O God, give me fame": Anne Chisholm, "Romantic Aspirations," *TLS*, December 26, 1986, 1442q.

Pp. 213–216. "I knew I shouldn't...": Furbank, *Forster*, 191q. "...like a fertile hen": *ibid.*, 186q. "No other age...": *ibid.* "a particularly hateful...": Lawrence, *Letters*, 162. "before the ambition...": Carswell, *Lives and Letters*, 130q. "If *we* believe in you...": *ibid.*, 137q. "I bang the door...": *ibid.* ...his own best archivist: *ibid.*, 275. "My letters shall be admired...": Kay Dreyfus, ed., *The Farthest North of Humanness: Letters of Percy Grainger, 1901–1914* (South Melbourne, Australia, 1985), 187. "Do not destroy them...": *ibid.*, 487–488. "these letters will one day...": Carswell, *Lives and Letters*, 161q. One rival the less?: Woolf, *Beginning Again*, 205q. With Derwent Wood...: Stock, *Pound*, 120–121. the happy American was running the show...: Goldring, *South Lodge*, 48–49. "I told you that being interrupted...": Tuohy, *Yeats*, 147–148q. "the wonders of our dusky...": Stock, *Pound*, 121q. hear Yeats deliver a lecture...: Williams, *Autobiography*, 115. "It would have killed...": *ibid.*, 117. Bennett who detested...: Bennett, *Books and Persons*, 229. "the long-haired literati...": Birkinhead, *Kipling*, 129q. "...of the 'littery' world": James, *Letters*, 332. "rarely found a man of letters...": Buchan, *Memory*, 150. "The greengrocers and...": Shaw, *Letters*, II, 298.

Pp. 216–223. "Shall we not seek...": Mrs. Chesterton, *Chestertons*, 60q. an English Academy: Charteris, *Gosse*, 319–320. "from the journalists...": Pound and Shakespear, *Letters*, 66n. Mrs. Humphry Ward challenged...: Shaw, *Letters*, II, 937 (ed. note). "a collection of...": *ibid.*, 936. In 1913 Pound's *imagiste*...: Pound and Shakespear, *Letters*, 280–282. Founded in 1853, the Society of Authors...: Hepburn, *Author's Empty Purse*, 42ff. "unbridled greed": *ibid.*, 79. As for the censorship...: Shaw, *Letters*, II, 799, 848 (ed. note); for its history see Hynes, *Edwardian Turn of Mind*, ch. 7–8. He had already denied it to...: Purdom, *Barker*, 90–91. and now he'd deny it to...: Hynes, *Edwardian Turn of Mind*, 220, 222, 232. The novelists, to be sure...: Hynes, *ibid.*, 254ff (ch. 8); Hunter, *Edwardian Fiction*, 63–64. wouldn't let Maugham...: Morgan, *Maugham*, 63. or Joyce the word...: *ibid.*, 63. or Lawrence the word...: Moore, *Lawrence*, 166. Violet Hunt wanted...: Whyte, *Heinemann*, 232. ...three months in prison: Hynes, *Edwardian Turn of Mind*, 260. and when Garnett's *The Breaking Point*...: *ibid.*, 220ff; Heilbrun, *Garnett Family*, 84ff. "that dreary, dreary...": Karl, *Conrad*, 631–632n. But it wasn't until...: Purdom, *Barker*, 73ff, 90ff; Hynes, *Edwardian Turn of Mind*, 222ff; Shaw, *Letters*, II, 747–750 (ed. note); Shaw, *Autobiography*, II, ch. 4. so that the Court Theatre movement...: Purdom, *Barker*, 73–75. confirming the Shavian suspicion...: Shaw, *Letters*, II, 748 (ed. note). It had heard Shaw declare...: Purdom, *Barker*, 91ff. "to ignoble dependences...": James, *Letters*, 533. and by 1910 would be uniting...: Hynes, *Edwardian Turn of Mind*, 279ff. "the great primal facts...": Epstein, *Autobiography*, 23. But when, the next year, Wells...: Hynes, *Edwardian Turn of Mind*, 293ff; West,

Wells, 14ff; Mackenzie, *Wells,* 256ff. . . . the good Canon Lambert: Woolf, *Contemporary Writers* (New York, 1965), 62q. "Such things have no . . .": Hynes, *Edwardian Turn of Mind,* 294q. no longer advertise . . . : Dickson, *Wells,* 176. At a meeting of . . . : Hynes, *Edwardian Turn of Mind,* 291ff, 296ff; Martin, *New Age,* 87ff. In the twelve lending libraries . . . : *ibid.,* 88. New books like Hall Caine's . . . : Hynes, *Edwardian Turn of Mind,* 304. "improper book": Martin, *New Age,* 89q. One dark day in December . . . : Hynes, *Edwardian Turn of Mind,* 274ff; Bennett, *Letters,* II, 270–271n. "If Germany . . .": Hynes, *Edwardian Turn of Mind,* 276q. After the scandal . . . : Mackenzie, *Wells,* 267ff; Dickson, *Wells,* 180ff. some of the libraries . . . : Bennett, *Books and Persons,* 294. and the city councils . . . : Dickson, *Wells,* 202. "all the offensive . . .": Lawrence, *Letters,* 158. he asked that . . . : *ibid.,* 276, 339. "I don't want . . .": *ibid.* "for the tradesmen . . .": Hynes, *Edwardian Turn of Mind,* 299q. Was it "for the reading class . . .": *ibid.* In June 1911 Frank Harris's . . . : Pullar, *Harris,* 276ff; Pearsall, *Harris,* 97ff. "the deep-breasted Mother": *ibid.,* 97q. "no liking for . . .": *ibid.* "the more natural in women . . .": Pullar, *Harris,* 276q. "recipe to make . . .": Pearsall, *Harris,* 97q. "see garbage being . . .": Pullar, *Harris,* 277q. "Strachery": *ibid.,* 278. "There is a pit fouler . . .": *ibid.,* 279q. ". . . erections and excrement": Forster, *Letters,* 135. "But Wells and Shaw . . .": Vincent Brome, *Frank Harris* (London, 1959), 140q. the Reverend James Marchant . . . : Tytell, *Pound,* 65. the Anti-Puritan League: Mrs. Chesterton, *Chestertons,* 60ff. As for Chesterton the Elder . . . : Cameron, "Innocent at Home," *New York Review of Books,* April 28, 1983, 25. In a bar across . . . : Barker, *Chesterton,* 135. the Reverend Stewart Headlam . . . : Mrs. Chesterton, *Chestertons,* 60. . . . could not have resisted: West, *Young Rebecca,* 130ff. ". . . for more riotous living": *ibid.,* 134.

Pp. 223–229. "on the whole the most possible . . .": James, *Complete Notebooks,* 218. Shaw was so bound . . . : White, "An Irishman Abroad," 31; see also Shaw, *Letters,* II, 395. London was after all . . . : Tuohy, *Yeats,* 10. "the stuff for new stories . . .": Harris, *Life and Loves,* 941. "You may call it dreary . . .": James, *Complete Notebooks,* 218. "Mud! London was . . .": Walpole, *Fortitude,* 175. ". . . the Strand roar": Woolf, *Diary,* 29–30. "the dusky streets . . .": *ibid.,* 9. "It's all rather dismal . . .": Hunt, *I Have This to Say,* 91q. "Come down! . . .": Dupee, *James,* 180q. "poor frowsy . . .": James, *Letters,* 445. "for the blessed . . .": *ibid.,* 128. "the electric . . .": *ibid.,* 175. "But I am sick of London . . .": Wilson, *Kipling,* 146q. ". . . within sound of Bow Bells": Ford, *Return,* 221. "I want a nice garden . . .": Drabble, *Bennett,* 64q. and Conrad's Someries house . . . : Karl, *Conrad,* 623. and Yeats's Stone Cottage . . . : James Longenbach, "The Odd Couple—Pound and Yeats Together," *New York Times Book Review,* January 10, 1988, 26q. "on a certain main-line . . .": Drabble, *Bennett,* 89q. "Can you suggest . . .": Shaw, *Letters,* II, 236. even Davies . . . : Stonesifer, *Davies,* 105–106. "the blackest most poisonous . . .": James, *Letters to A. C. Benson and Auguste Monod* (London, 1930), 71. His nephew Harry . . . : Edel, *James,* 440. ". . . Rye hibernations": James, *Letters,* 588. "beastly solitudinous life": Edel, *James,* 439q. "The remedy of London . . .": James, *Letters,* 597. "Yes, dear brave old London . . .": Lubbock, ed., James, *Letters,* II, 206. Dorothy Richardson was . . . : Fromm, *Richardson,* 29. Eric Gill, the libidinous one . . . : Speaight, *Gill,* 33. By the Royal Academy . . . : Lawrence, *Letters,* 113. By the secondhand . . . : Callow, *Son and Lover,* 136. "Damn, Wagner . . .": Lawrence, *Letters,* 247. They had taken the clever . . . : Carswell, *Lives and Letters,* 16–17. But the promising boy . . . : *ibid.,* 19. ". . . out of an egg": *ibid.,* 119q. "It's fang-de-seeyacle...": quoted by Dennis Farr in *English Art, 1870–1940*, 45. "where their social standing...": Lawrence, *Women in Love*, 10. "Class-barriers...": *ibid.*, 86. "Wales England wed...": Bax, *Some I Knew Well*, 70q. "To have the freedom": Fromm, *Richardson*, 23 (epigraph). It lifted one...: Ray, "Introduction," Wells, *Mr. Polly*, xxxiv. "the high majesty...": Henley, *London Voluntaries*, III. "the dreary rain...": Yeats, *Autobiography*, 204q. "avoid the drawing-room...": Baron, *Sickert*, 109q. "All great art...": Pound, *Letters*, 25. "Take, as it were...": Martin, *New Age*, 162q. "For some unknown reason...": Goldring, *Life Interests*, 64. Chesterton wrote...: Ward, *Chesterton*, 151. "Life in London": Bennett, *Journal*, 412. Hueffer's first popular work...: MacShane, *Ford*, 59. and James contracted...: James, *Letters*, 278, 278n. "as though it were...": Hunter, *Edwardian Fiction*, 66–67q. "the London novel": Ford, *Provence*, 138. "the assault...": James, *The Art of the Novel*, 59. "Satanic": Forster, *Howards End*, 84. "my little romance of London": Chesterton, *Autobiography*, 114. "The suburbs are commonly...": Ward, *Chesterton*, 151q. "about London": Drabble, *Bennett*, 75q. "a city so incredibly...": Bennett, *Buried Alive*, 115. "always filled him with...": *ibid.*, 177–178. Eliot's "stockings...": *The Waste Land*, 1. 227. "Illuminated calendars...": Bennett, *Buried Alive*, 117. "It seemed to me...": Wells, *New Machiavelli*, 524–525. "To speak against London...": Forster, *Howards End*, 108.

Pp. 233–238. "Pity spareth so many an evil thing": Pound, Canto XXX, *The Cantos*, 147. It had come into power...: Tuchman, *Proud Tower*, 383. Liberals...in a bind: *ibid.*, 368. "It will end...": *ibid.*, 367q. "its invariable alliance...": Ward, *Chesterton*, 296q. "before the next great measure...": *ibid.*, 298q. "I am relieved to be quit...": Barker, *Chesterton*, 210q. When their friend Charlie Masterman...: Hynes, *Edwardian Turn of Mind*, 57ff. "a young Moses...": Buchan, *Memory*, 170. "when London seemed...": letter from Lucy Masterman to Patricia Hutchins, February 9, 1965, Hutchins Collection, British Museum. "...a head full of feathers": Buchan, *Memory*, 170. His old idealism...: *ibid.* "luxuriant gloom...": Chesterton, *Autobiography*, 124. ...a note of discouragement: Tuchman, *Proud Tower*, 382. a "feeling...of helplessness": Gross, *Rise and Fall*, 130. these Liberal reformers...: See Hynes, "Undecided Prophets," ch. 3 in *Edwardian Turn of Mind*; on Galsworthy as Liberal: *ibid.*, 72ff; also Hunter, *Edwardian Fiction*, 222ff. It doesn't occur to him...: *ibid.*, 240, 225. Life, rotten life...: Maugham, *Of Human Bondage*, 561. "the natural order of things": *ibid.*, 568. "chaos of clear ideas": Collis, "Religion and Philosophy," in Holroyd, *Genius of Shaw*, 91. "There is something about...": Hynes, *Edwardian Turn of Mind*, 74–75q. "If the saviors of the poor...": *ibid.*, 77q. Its force was divided...: Mackenzie, *Fabians*, 377ff. The Webbs were doing...: *ibid.*, 367, 370. Old Bland was disgusted: *ibid.*, 377–378. There were resignations...: *ibid.*, 378. ...for younger and livelier wits: Shaw, *Collected Letters, 1911–1925*, III, 12. No doubt his marriage...: Peters, *Shaw*, 221, 253. "green-eyed millionairess": Peters, "As Lonely as God," 193q. Where were those millions...: Peters, *Shaw*, 220. "hygienic aridities": Speaight, *Gill*, 43. "...the Fabians so flat": Lawrence, *Letters*, 176. "Oh, the Fabians...": Mackenzie, *Fabians*, 370q. Strachey couldn't help noting...: Holroyd, *Strachey*, 559. As for the Fabian doctrine...: Mackenzie, *Fabians*, 379ff. "stuffed bishops": West, *Young Rebecca*, 303. ...a "distributivist": Mackenzie, *Fabians*, 379–380; Barker, *Chesterton*, 194; Cameron, "Innocent at Home," 25. and Eric Gill...: *ibid.* "to deprive Fabianism...": Mackenzie, *Fabians*, 343–344q. ...the romance of guild socialism: *ibid.*, 380; Carswell, *Lives and Letters*, 83. By 1908 he'd remove . . . : *ibid.*, 39. . . . to "leaders of thought": *ibid.* By 1909 he'd re-cruit . . . : Martin, *New Age*, 62. They tell us, he said . . . : *ibid.*, 41. . . . and Mr. Beatrice Webb: Cumberland, *Set Down in Malice*, 174. but new angry young men . . . : Carswell, *Lives and Letters*, 91. "dreaming of systems . . .": Eliot, "Cho-ruses from 'The Rock,' " VI, *Collected Poems, 1909–1935* (New York, 1936), 197. . . . the type-heading of the *New Age:* Speaight, *Gill*, 33. "the right answer to . . .": *ibid.*, 61q. "casting off socialism . . .": Dukes, *Scene Is Changed*, 40. "heroic values": *ibid.*, 42. Orage himself . . . : Carswell, *Lives and Letters*, 186ff. "that I dare show to God": *ibid.*, 181n. Shaw was despondent . . . : Mackenzie, *Fabians*, 394. quarrel with . . . the Webbs: Shaw, *Collected Letters, 1911–1925*, III, 176 (ed. note). . . . nearly four thousand members: Hynes, *Edwardian Turn of Mind*, 91. But they weren't attractive . . . : Cumberland, *Set Down in Malice*, 173–174; see also Wells, *Ann Veronica*, 138–154. Hubert Bland died . . . : Mackenzie, *Fabians*, 392. . . . that Fabianism had failed: *ibid.*, 409. So, more or less, did they all: *ibid.*, 394, 409.

Pp. 239–243. the Court Theatre movement went . . . : Purdom, *Barker*, 69ff; Shaw, *Letters*, II, 391–392 (ed. note); Mackenzie, *Fabians*, 349. . . . they'd attempt a revival: Purdom, *Barker*, 98ff. "plays by anybody . . .": Martin, *New Age*, 75q. Mr. Frohman's bold spirits . . . : *ibid.*, 75–76; Purdom, *Barker*, 104ff. Scarred and em-bittered . . . : *ibid.*, 121. "threw off . .": *ibid.*, viii. Even the old Court imperium . .": Holroyd, *Shaw*, II, 395–401; Shaw, *Autobiography*, II, 46ff. . . . as his natural successor: Holroyd, *Shaw*, II, 93–94. "The interpretation of life . . .": Dukes, *Scene Is Changed*, 34. "Mr. Galsworthy's views! . . ." : Gerald Cumberland, *Written in Friendship* (New York, 1923), 266. "The characters aren't . . .": Behrman, *Max*, 191q. "For a soul . . .": Wallace Martin, ed., *Orage as Critic* (Lon-don, 1974), 101q. "He nationalizes his . . .": Martin, *New Age*, 76q. At 67 Frith Street . . . : Dukes, *Scene Is Changed*, 42. "to see the beginning . . .": Brooke, *Letters*, 200. "kept us on the rack . . .": Woolf, *Letters*, 423. "We seem . . .": Brooke, *Letters*, 300. "I am getting too old": Mackenzie, *Fabians*, 361q. "my bolt as a . . .": Shaw, *Letters*, II, 871. "proud overbearing gaiety . . .": Shaw, *Collected Letters, 1911–1925*, III, 212. "a good sign . . .": Lewis, *Letters*, 44. "harmless bit . . .": Blunt, *Diaries*, 262. . . . the better plays of their time: Martin, *New Age*, 73. "the gaunt ill-dressed . . .": Dukes, *Scene Is Changed*, 39. what a treat were the Abbey . . . : Rothenstein, *Men and Memories*, 204. They scarcely moved at all . . . : Tuohy, *Yeats*, 122q. "We learned Irish . . .": Swinnerton, *Background*, 138q. From the second act on . . . : *ibid.*, 143. But the young cognoscenti . . . : Dukes, *Scene Is Changed*, 35. "one of the most savage . . .": Hynes, *Edwardian Turn of Mind*, 338q. It was art, he said . . . : Dukes, *Scene Is Changed*, 36. Rupert Brooke would . . . : Brooke, *Letters*, 267. and Ezra Pound . . . : Stock, *Pound*, 153. "Quand vous dansez . . .": Lady Otto-line, *Memoirs*, 151. ". . . like a hooked fish": Holroyd, *Strachey*, 561q. "a great bas-ket of . .": *ibid.*, 544. Leonard Woolf, just back . . . : Woolf, *Beginning Again*, 49. Even Alexandra . . . : Hynes, *Edwardian Turn of Mind*, 336. "it was possible . . .": Dukes, *Scene Is Changed*, 37. ". . . who are 'the old lot' ": Shaw, *Collected Letters, 1911–1925*, III, 46.

Pp. 243–245. *"read, Tono-Bungay . . .":* Lawrence, *Letters*, 127. "adiposity" . . . and "What! . . .": Martin, *Orage as Critic*, 120. "Who demanded . . .": *ibid.* "Mr. Wells knows no more . . .": *ibid.* By 1911 he was no longer . . . : Martin, *New Age*, 117. "the unspeakable vulgo . . .": Pound, *Letters*, 21. "giving a shove . . .": Ford, *Portraits*, 218. "he seemed like an infant . . .": MacShane, *Ford*, 80q. . . . lost control of his wondrous *Review:* Mizener, *Ford,* 157ff. Wells who had agreed . . . : Ford, *Letters,* 31; see also Mizener, 160ff, and Mackenzie, *Wells,* 241. "The early E. R. is . . .": Jean-Aubry, *Conrad, Life and Letters,* II, 323. "I have been in no sense . . ." *ibid.,* 99; apropos his involvement in the E. R., see Karl, *Conrad,* 638, 639, 641. He wrote long rambling letters . . . : see, for example, letters to Scott-James and Jepson in Ludwig, ed., Ford, *Letters,* 39–40, 44; also letters to Wells, 31ff. "The man's an ass": Mizener, *Ford,* 164q. "a fly blown . . .": Forster, *Letters,* 211. "he daubs his . . .": Lawrence, *Letters,* 227. "What is the sense of . . .": Ford, *Return,* 400q. Verisimilitude? Vicarious experience? . . . : Ford, *Portraits,* 219q. ". . . never heard of the feller": *ibid.,* 218. "grunted with . . .": *ibid.* "Henrietta Maria": *ibid.* "too monumental and . . .": Bell, *Woolf,* I, 122q. ". . . a block of smooth amber": *ibid.* "For an hour . . .": Brooke, *Letters,* 226.

Pp. 245–249. "And what rough beast . . .": Yeats, "The Second Coming." six volumes of Dostoevsky . . . : Martin, *New Age,* 143n; Heilbrun, *Garnett Family,* 189–190. a volume of Chekhov's . . . : Martin, *New Age,* 92; Heilbrun, *Garnett Family,* 190. There Augustus John had read . . . : John, *Finishing Touches,* 117. who together discussed . . . : Holroyd, *John,* 265. at James Strachey's table . . . : *ibid.,* 302; Holroyd, *Strachey,* 455n. "Colossal! Colossal! . . .": *ibid.,* 457q. "The Agamemnon is childish . . .": *ibid.,* 488n. . . . copy of *Le Crime et le Châtiment:* Spalding, *Vanessa,* 118. "spiritually a Russian . . .": Lewis, *Rude Assignment,* 148. Maurice Baring . . . : Paul Horgan, ed., *Maurice Baring Restored: Selections from his Work* (London, 1970), 244ff. "we have no writer . . .": Martin, *New Age,* 92q. The *New Age* would soon be . . . : *ibid.;* Drabble, *Bennett,* 165. In 1909 Baring's . . . : Swinnerton, *Background,* 141. It was, she replied, his masterpiece: Heilbrun, *Garnett Family,* 181. "one of the supreme marvels . . .": Hynes, *Edwardian Turn of Mind,* 337q. "now, Mr. Heinemann . . .": Martin, *New Age,* 93q. ". . . Garnett to do it?": *ibid.,* 94q. "I am still of opinion . . .": *ibid.,* 93–94q. ". . . the greatest thing ever written": *ibid.,* 94. "the wreckage of my life": Moore, *Lawrence,* 226q. . . . and loudly comparing: King, *Forster,* 51. Murry would have sat down . . . : Carswell, *Lives and Letters,* 115. and Koteliansky . . . : Meyers, *Mansfield,* 109–110. Katherine Mansfield's host . . . : *ibid.,* 66. as for "Yekaterina" . . . : *ibid.,* 134, 108, 66. "Dear Madam . . .": Heilbrun, *Garnett Family,* 166q. Lewis's all too . . . : Martin, *New Age,* 143. "to beat Dostoevsky . . .": West, *Wells,* 91. "depressed me about my own work": Bennett, *Journal,* 381. hence *Hilda Lessways* . . . : Martin, *New Age,* 95n. "It seems sketchy . . .": Forster, *Letters,* 105–106. "a tract, a treatise, a pamphlet": Moore, *Collected Letters of D. H. Lawrence,* I, 54. In an outburst . . . : *ibid.,* 488. "I hear that there are . . .": Shaw, *Letters,* II, 569. ". . . was this Russian incoherence": Maugham, *Vagrant Mood,* 200. "fluid pudding": James, *Letters,* 618–619; see also attack on Tolstoy, *ibid.,* 680–681. "Does he mean by it . . .": Jean-Aubry, *Life and Letters,* II, 289q. "the convulsed, terror-haunted . . .": Conrad, *Notes on Life and Letters,* 48. ". . . from prehistoric ages": Edward Garnett, ed., *Letters from Joseph Conrad, 1895–1924* (New York, 1928), 240. "damned souls . . .": Conrad, *Life and Letters,* 47. . . . his friendship with Garnett: Karl, *Conrad,* 703ff. . . . with poor Mrs. Garnett: Garnett, *Great Friends,* 17. "Russian Dickens": Swinnerton, *Background,* 117q.

Pp. 250–257. ". . . that Shakespeherian Rag": Eliot, "The Waste Land," l. 128. One day in July 1909 . . . : Janet Dunbar, *J. M. Barrie: The Man Behind the Image* (Boston, 1970), 220ff; Birkin, *Barrie,* 175ff; Farr, *Cannan,* 51ff. like Julien Sorel:

ibid., 44. She would have a divorce: Dunbar, *Barrie,* 221. It wasn't just that . . . : *ibid.,* 231; Farr, *Cannan,* 35–36. It was above all . . . the Davies family: Dunbar, *Barrie,* 135ff; Birkin, *Barrie,* 45ff. As for Gillie . . . : Farr, *Cannan,* 52. *"impossibly"*: Birkin, *Barrie,* 177q. "Sillies you are! . . .": Dunbar, *Barrie,* 230q. Slender and tall . . . : Farr, *Cannan,* 25, 36, 120. "Oh! Heaven . . .": *ibid.,* 26q. "deliberately portentous manner": *ibid.,* 120, 90. ". . . vacant Sir Galahad": *ibid.,* 95q. "an empty bucket . . .": *ibid.,* 65q. . . . but unseeing eye: *ibid.,* 181. "towering above her . . .": *ibid.,* 95q. There was the woman . . . : *ibid.,* 65, 132–133. . . . like Murry and Katherine: *ibid.,* 89. Would she, he asked her . . . : *ibid.,* 150. . . . his barrister's wig: *ibid.,* 197. When Lady Dilke . . . : Mizener, *Ford,* 176ff; MacShane, *Ford,* 88ff; Hunt, *I Have This to Say,* 63ff. Will you marry me . . . : *ibid.,* 68. . . . an English Colette: Goldring, *South Lodge,* 42. "sparrow-brown hair . . .": Patmore, *My Friends,* 50. "A thin viperish-looking . . .": Garnett, *Golden Echo,* 183. "a handsome witch": Derek Patmore, "Introduction" to Patmore, *My Friends,* 9. "Violet prefers . . .": *ibid.,* 52q. and the presence of unexplained spots . . . : Mizener, *Ford,* 149. with all the anguish . . . : Goldring, *Life Interests,* 177. of the "bloody Mary" . . . : Goldring, *South Lodge,* 22. "Tall, high-breasted . . .": Garnett, *Golden Echo,* 36. She summoned . . . : Jessie Conrad, *Conrad,* 139–140. "pale lemon moustache": Lewis, *Rude Assignment,* 122. "the color of raw veal": Garnett, *Golden Echo,* 129. his speech so muffled . . .": Patmore, *My Friends,* 53. "a lemonish pink giant . . .": Lewis, *Rude Assignment,* 148. One night at the Shepherd's . . . : Mizener, *Ford,* 175; Hunt, *I Have This to Say,* 60. She called him "Papa": Mizener, *Ford,* 175. . . . with his wife's younger sister: *ibid.,* 62. In October, 1909 . . . : Hunt, *I Have This to Say,* 84–85. "I can't breathe . . .": Karl, *Conrad,* 665q. "the lamentable position . . .": Hunt, *I Have This to Say,* 95q. . . . his Purple Patch: Patmore, *My Friends,* 69; Edel, *James,* 422. A few months later . . . : Hunt, *I Have This to Say,* 100ff. The baronial Hueffer . . . : *ibid.,* 102ff. "all veils and . . .": Garnett, *Golden Echo,* 183–184. would settle in Germany . . . : Mizener, *Ford,* 201ff. Until her death in 1942 . . . : Goldring, *South Lodge,* 114. When she became pregnant . . . : Robinson, *H.D.,* 95. and when the marriage collapsed . . . : *ibid.,* 122. and when, the year after that, . . . : *ibid.,* 152. "my only real criticism . . .": *ibid.* "the web of sophisticated . . .": H.D., *Bid Me to Live,* 68. "Funny, in the old days . . .": *ibid.,* 69. . . . the case of Katherine Mansfield: Meyers, *Mansfield,* 36ff; Carswell, *Lives and Letters,* 52ff. but Mr. George Bowden . . . : Meyers, *Mansfield,* 47. "we made love to each other . . .": *ibid.,* 58q. ". . . make me your mistress": *ibid.,* 67q; Maugham, *Points of View* (London, 1958), 179q. at Lady Ottoline's Garsington: Carswell, *Lives and Letters,* 132. But by this time Bertie . . . : T. S. Matthews, *Great Tom: Notes Towards the Definition of T. S. Eliot* (New York, 1973), 46. "Priapus in the shrubbery . . .": Eliot, "Mr. Apollinax." "I am sure you have . . .": Matthews, *Great Tom,* 47q. Anthony West, the son of H.G. . . . : West, *Wells,* 56; Brigid Brophy, "Sons and Lovers," 32. Ezra Pound's son . . . : Katha Pollitt, "She Was Neither Dryad Nor Victim," *New York Times Book Review,* March 11, 1984, 7. They called her "Perdita": Pollitt, *ibid.* Angelica Bell, the daughter . . . : Angelica Garnett, *Deceived with Kindness,* 134. "appropriately enough . . .": *ibid.,* 147. he'd marry their child: *ibid.* "precarious paradise": *ibid.,* 176.

Pp. 257–262. "telegrams and anger": Forster, *Howards End,* 103. And indeed it would come to an end . . . : Dangerfield, *Strange Death,* Parts II and III. the old British code of respect: *ibid.,* 198, 215, 217. "a steady rotting . . .": Wells, *Boon,* 225. At the turn of the century . . . : Watts and Davies, *Cunninghame Graham,*

221. Bitter and mutinous . . . : Dangerfield, *Strange Death*, 214ff; Tuchman, *Proud Tower*, 393–394. a new militant breed . . . : Dangerfield, *Strange Death*, 230ff, 308. The seamen and firemen . . . : *ibid.*, 248. and the railway men of Liverpool . . . : *ibid.*, 265. . . . the transport workers of London: *ibid.*, 256. and casks of butter . . . : *ibid.*, 260. "and famine-threatening strikes . . .": Lubbock, *Letters of Henry James*, II, 191. In 1912 a million workers . . . : Dangerfield, *Strange Death*, 281ff. and in 1913 the transport workers . . . : *ibid.*, 314ff. The year after that . . . : *ibid.*, 328, 389ff. Convention be damned . . . : *ibid.*, 215ff, 394–395. pretensions of the poor: *ibid.*, 226. "Then your blood . . .": *ibid.*, 268q. . . . and two hundred wounded: Tuchman, *Proud Tower*, 394. "The argument of the . . .": Dangerfield, *Strange Death*, 170q. Taking a taxi to . . . : *ibid.*, 171; Barker, *Prominent Edwardians*, 229. take hammers out of . . . : Mackenzie, *Shoulder to Shoulder*, 186. Three days later . . . : *ibid.*, 188; Dangerfield, *Strange Death*, 172. Christabel . . . a decision: *ibid.*, 180ff; Mackenzie, *Shoulder to Shoulder*, 200ff, 216ff; Barker, *Prominent Edwardians*, 233ff. . . . even churches: Mackenzie, *Shoulder to Shoulder*, 205. In 1913 alone . . . : Dangerfield, *Strange Death*, 206. in the first seven months of 1914: *ibid.*, 368. Mr. Lloyd George's country house . . . : *ibid.*, 310. A tea house at . . . : West, *Young Rebecca*, 159. Cricket pavilions . . . : Tuchman, *Proud Tower*, 382. The delicate greens . . . : Dangerfield, *Strange Death*, 182. "I naturally feel . . .": James, *Letters*, 712–713n. At the Epsom Derby . . . : Mackenzie, *Shoulder to Shoulder*, 240ff; Dangerfield, *Strange Death*, 200. Royalty itself . . . : Dangerfield, *Strange Death*, 376, 377, 382. It was not very womanly . . . : *ibid.*, 370–371. "alarming girls": Smith, *Buchan*, 47q. But then even their betters . . . : Dangerfield, *Strange Death*, 74ff, 333ff. . . . prepared to commit treason: *ibid.*, 96. Bonar Law, their new . . . : *ibid.*, 334, 336, 352. In 1912 Sir Edward . . . : *ibid.*, 111–112. "falling short of violence . . .": Wilson, *Kipling*, 257q. Committing what amounted to . . . : Dangerfield, *Strange Death*, 343ff. When in the nineties . . . : Tuchman, *Proud Tower*, 19. would later beg Balfour . . . : José Harris, "Women in the World of Men," *TLS*, April 10, 1987, 376. . . . smiling and laughing: Dangerfield, *Strange Death*, 37. "the best club in London": Price Collier, *England and the English* (New York, 1909), 408. "a drawing-room game . . .": Buchan, *Memory*, 153. Tories like the Earl of Balcarres . . . : Campbell, "In One Place or Another," *TLS*, March 8, 1985, 249q. At the Carlton Club . . . : Dangerfield, *Strange Death*, 65. "boiling with rage": *ibid.* "their friends [would] disown them . . .": Spender, *Asquith*, 327q. Lady Londonderry . . . unforgiving: Dangerfield, *Strange Death*, 362. "would be impolitic . . .": *ibid.*, 362–363q.

Pp. 262–273. "Now the leaves . . .": Auden, "Now the Leaves Are Falling Fast." ". . . all *Rot, clear Rot*": Margery Ross, ed., *Friend of Friends: Letters to Robert Ross* (London, 1952), 197. "exactly his right place": *ibid.*, 188. But what of the art critic Robert Ross . . . : Hynes, *Edwardian Turn of Mind*, 330. Picasso "a *faux fauve*": Shone, *Bloomsbury Portraits*, 62. "the worst art-school tricks": *ibid.* "John Bull and his lady . . .": Emmons, *Sickert*, 149q. "blasé, 'known-them-all . . .' ": Farr, *English Art, 1870–1940*, 201q. ". . . kind of old scarecrow": Yeats, "Among School Children." He began to discredit . . . : Emmons, *Sickert*, 147–148; see also Denys Sutton, *Walter Sickert* (London, 1976), 168ff. "a curious and pathetic . . .": Shone, *Bloomsbury Portraits*, 62q. Would Will Rothenstein . . . : Rothenstein, *Men and Memories*, 212ff. "The poor things . . .": Fry, *Letters*, 363. "It is killing me": Kenner, *A Sinking Island*, 128q. He circulated caricatures . . . : *ibid.*; see also Woolf, *Fry*, 156. ". . . too much for me": Morgan, *Maugham*, 161q. "I don't think . . .": Reid,

John Quinn, 96q. "Now that Clive . . .": Woolf, *Letters,* 440. "A modest sample . . .": *ibid.* Lytton didn't think much . . . : Holroyd, *Strachey,* 512. ". . . distressing oddments": Edel, *Bloomsbury,* 219q. As for the English contingent . . . : Holroyd, *Strachey,* 512. "a most shifty . . .": Edel, *Bloomsbury,* 219q. "I had to disown him": Holroyd, *Strachey,* 514q. Flushed with his failures . . . : Mizener, *Ford,* 157ff; Mac-Shane, *Ford,* 82ff; Mackenzie, *Wells,* 241ff. In the character of Pett . . . : Daniel Chaucer (Hueffer's pseudonym), *The New Humpty Dumpty* (London, 1912), 312, 313. "Mr. Parmont, the London critic": Daniel Chaucer, *The Simple Life Limited* (London, 1911), 55. the novelist Simon Bransdon: *ibid.,* 73. "wastes of desolation": James, *Letters,* 703. *Chance* was *done* . . . : Karl, *Conrad,* 744ff. ". . . affected me painfully": *ibid.,* 746q. "He's a megalomaniac . . .": Mizener, *Ford,* 185q. "You are so russianized . . .": Baines, *Conrad,* 453q. "contain his convictions . . .": Ray, "Introduction," *Mr. Polly,* xlvii. "the difference between us . . .": Mackenzie, *Wells,* 241q. a shop for fruitarians . . . : Wells, *Ann Veronica,* 144. ". . . vegetarianism and teetotalism": *ibid.,* 148. "prigs at play": Wells, *New Machiavelli,* 299. "of all the damned things . . .": *ibid.,* 301. Not for him the Academic Committee . . . : West, *Wells,* 42ff; Dickson, *Wells,* 212ff. "I would rather . . .": Edel and Ray, eds., *Henry James and H. G. Wells,* 160. on Gosse . . . : Wells, *Boon,* 90. on Conrad . . . : *ibid.,* 145. ". . . or a boulevard": "H.G. & G.B.S.," *TLS,* November 27, 1969, 1349q. "He doesn't find things out . . .": Wells, *Boon,* 102. "It is a magnificent but . . .": *ibid.,* 108. "Ought there to be . . .": *ibid.,* 101. "impossible cheek": Dickson, *Wells,* 88q. . . . left in the porter's box: West, *Wells,* 47. "an expression of blazing defiance . . .": Rosenbaum, *Bloomsbury Group,* 68q. "merciless chaff": George Spater and Ian Parsons, *A Marriage of True Minds: An Intimate Portrait of Leonard and Virginia Woolf* (New York, 1977), 151q. "Of course, you Miss Cole . . .": Rosenbaum, *Bloomsbury Group,* 2–3q. "bawling voice": Gadd, *Loving Friends,* 110q. "fat little mind": Edel, *Bloomsbury,* 219q. "fat little hand": *ibid.* "one of those men . . .": Woolf, *Wise Virgins,* 86–87. "Clive presents a fearful study . . .": Holroyd, *Strachey,* 468q. "He is limp and damp . . .": Woolf, *Letters, III, 1923–1928* (London, 1977), 266. "He's a mediocre man . . .": Holroyd, *Strachey,* 557q. ". . . a decayed and amorous spider": *ibid.,* 287q. "safety-bicycle with genitals": Noel Annan, "Portrait of a Genius as a Young Man," 37q; see also Holroyd, *Strachey,* 380ff. "the most offensive . . .": Woolf, *Sowing,* 158q. "loathing for him . . .": Darroch, *Ottoline,* 128q. "genial brutality": Quentin Bell, *Bloomsbury* (London, 1974), 32. Will Rothenstein . . . : Rothenstein, *Men and Memories,* 179. Katherine Mansfield . . . : Meyers, *Mansfield,* 138q. "They profess to live by feeling . . .": *ibid.,* 137q. "Lady Omega Muddle": Gadd, *Loving Friends,* 74q. "infinitely antique . . .": *ibid.* "it's beastly of them . . .": *ibid.* "To be devastatingly witty . . .": MacShane, *Ford,* 85q. ". . . as he was alive": Martin, *Orage as Critic,* 133. "You have really wiped . . .": Carswell, *Lives and Letters,* 160q. "Feel this teapot. . . .": Meyers, *Mansfield,* 139q. "Mediocrity is not . . .": Carswell, *Lives and Letters,* 74q. In one of his numbers . . . : Meyers, *Mansfield,* 71; Pullar, *Harris,* 284–285. Katherine and Beatrice had . . . : Carswell, *Lives and Letters,* 74. Gaudier once rushed . . . : Meyers, *Mansfield,* 73. "explosive-mouthed gang . . .": Ford, *Portraits,* 218. ". . . a *volcanic* island": Lewis, *Letters,* 64. Rebel Art Center: Goldring, *South Lodge,* 65. but also with Gauguin . . . : Geoffrey Wagner, *Wyndham Lewis* (New Haven, 1957), 118. "accelerated impressionism": Pound, *Gaudier-Brzeska* (New York, 1970), 90. "this family party . . .": Lewis, *Letters,* 49. "puce-colored monster": Robert Edward Murray, "Blasting Out of the Studio," *TLS,* April 10, 1987, 381q. Lewis promised the editor . . . : Ford, *Return,* 388. . . . break his Borrovian head: Holroyd, *John,* 141n.

"very muscular and forcible": Simpson, *Three on the Tower*, 41q. "a born revolutionary": Lewis, *Blasting and Bombardiering*, 285q. ". . . he became delirious": *ibid*. "nobody else will have *any*": Monroe, *Poet's Life*, 262q. "Nearly as bad as Milton": Selver, *Orage*, 37–38q. "at the cat-like angle . . .": Materer, *Vortex*, 54q. "the arthritic milieu": Tytell, *Pound*, 68q. "My one present consolation . . .": Pound and Shakespear, *Letters*, 147. ". . . all through the theatre": *ibid.*, 167. "I cannot imagine . . .": Ford, *Return*, 357. . . . to Lascelles Abercrombie: Weintraub, *London Yankees*, 289. Unhappy Hueffer, so fond and. . . : Ford, "Dedicatory Letter," *Good Soldier*, xviii–xix. "Poor fat Ford": Pound and Shakespear, *Letters*, 316. "How fat you are!": Ford, *Return*, 401q. "*Tu sais, tu es foûtu . . .*": *ibid.*, 400q. "eye-gouging": Materer, *Vortex*, 36q. Lewis . . . the 'Enemy': *ibid*. "At no time . . .": *ibid*. The hysterical Gaudier . . . : Lewis, *Blasting and Bombardiering*, 39. "Shut up . . .": Epstein, *Autobiography*, 56q. Percy wasn't happy with Hulme: Jones, *Hulme*, 122–123. As for Hulme, he wasn't happy with Pound: *ibid.*, 94. how long would he tolerate . . .": Epstein, *Autobiography*, 60. "the only health-giver . . .": Wagner, *Lewis*, 127q. There was Kipling: Wilson, *Kipling*, 151. . . . argued in *The Great Analysis* of 1911: Arthur Marwick, *The Deluge: British Society and the First World War* (New York, 1970), 27. ". . . for a chastening war": Wells, *New Machiavelli*, 355. ". . . A GREAT REMEDY": Materer, *Vortex*, 31q. "shatter the visible world . . .": *ibid*. He bravely condemned the war . . . : Peters, *Shaw*, 364. "the huge performing frivolity . . .": James, *Letters*, 733. "Splendid Rupert's": *ibid.*, 745–746. ". . . they mostly are": *ibid.*, 735. "a mind so fine . . .": Kenner, *Pound Era*, 18q.

Pp. 274–276. ". . . Hindhead's turn will come": Shaw, *Misalliance*, in *Complete Plays with Prefaces*, IV, 175. "Doesn't one feel lonely . . .": Najder, *Conrad*, 241q. For Arthur Symons . . . : Christophe Campos, *The View of France* (London, 1965), 163q. For Clive Bell . . . : Edel, *Bloomsbury*, 39; Shone, *Bloomsbury Portraits*, 24. For Arnold Bennett . . . : Drabble, *Bennett*, 122. for what could be said . . . : Bennett, *Books and Persons*, 281, 298. Augustus John had gone there . . . : Nigel Gosling, *The Adventurous World of Paris, 1900–1914* (New York, 1978), 99. "I shall be . . .": *ibid.*, 109q. and Somerset Maugham . . . : Morgan, *Maugham*, 107ff. "a Paris without effervescence": Ford, *Provence*, 139. Clive and Vanessa were thinking . . . : Bell, *Woolf*, I, 154. "no aesthetic intention": Spalding, *Vanessa*, 83q. "To go from London to Paris . . .": Woolf, *Wise Virgins*, 46. "I think I should burst . . .": Campos, *View of France*, 210q. Aldington would go there . . . : Norman, *Pound*, 90. Murry had gone there . . . : Carswell, *Lives and Letters*, 69. bring back to the boglands of London . . . : *ibid.*, 67. On June 28, 1914, Hueffer . . . : Ford, *Return*, 399. "our London . . .": Pound, Canto LXXX, *The Cantos*, 516.

Index

Individual works are indexed under their authors.

A NOTE ON THE AUTHOR

John Paterson is Emeritus Professor of English at the University of California, Berkeley. Born in Bathgate, Scotland, he grew up in Montreal and studied at McGill University, the University of British Columbia, and the University of Michigan. After teaching at Princeton University he went to Berkeley where for many years he taught British literature. He has reviewed books on public television in San Francisco and is the author of a number of articles and two other books, *The Novel as Faith* and *The Making of 'The Return of the Native.'*